DICTIONARY OF

HISTORICAL ALLUSIONS & EPONYMS

DICTIONARY OF HISTORICAL ALLUSIONS & EPONYMS

Dorothy Auchter

Santa Barbara, California
Denver, Colorado
Oxford, England

Library of Congress Cataloging-in-Publication Data

Auchter, Dorothy.
Dictionary of historical allusions and eponyms / Dorothy Auchter.
p. cm.
Includes bibliographical references and index.
ISBN 0-87436-950-9 (hc) 1-57607-099-9 (pbk) (alk. paper)
1. Allusions—Dictionaries. 2. Eponyms—Dictionaries.
3. History—Dictionaries. I. Title.
PN43.A83 1998
031.02—dc21 98-19641

03 02 01 00 99 98 10 9 8 7 6 5 4 3 2 1

ABC-CLIO, Inc.
130 Cremona Drive, P.O. Box 1911
Santa Barbara, California 93116-1911

This book is printed on acid-free paper ♾.
Manufactured in the United States of America

CONTENTS

PREFACE

It is doubtful if many of the people who use the expression *Draconian justice* as a reference to harsh repercussions have any idea who Draco was. Nevertheless, most people can immediately grasp the gist of what is being said and such expressions add zest and shading to our language. Draco is an example of an eponym, a person whose name has evolved into a common noun, verb, or adjective. Long after the details of this ancient Greek philosopher's life have become a blurred memory, his name can still evoke an immediate and visceral reaction. Draco's reputation for meting out onerous punishment derived from the fact that he was the first judge to codify the Greek legal system, rather than relying on whim, tradition, or impulse in rendering justice. The old Greek system often gave unfair advantages to the privileged few, and Draco insisted that justice was to be dispensed on the same basis for the aristocracy and the lower classes. His sense of fair play won the respect and admiration of most of his contemporaries, and it is ironic that his name came to be associated with mean-spirited punitive measures. He is one of many eponymous people who have been unfairly remembered by history.

Our language is peppered with eponyms, some of which are familiar (Victorian, pasteurize, Jezebel) and others that derive from people who are long forgotten (mesmerize, boycott, chauvinist). One of the purposes of this book is to bring the stories of these people back to life. Franz Anton Mesmer (mesmerize) was a flamboyant, eighteenth-century self-proclaimed wizard, who convinced hundreds of devoted followers that he could use magnets to manipulate and control fluids in the heavenly bodies, the earth, and the human body, thus curing a wide range of ailments. His antics became so outrageous that Benjamin Franklin and a group of other legitimate scientists sought to drive the charlatan out of practice. Captain Charles Boycott was a British overseer who was so hated by his Irish tenants that they simply refused to have any contact with him. Learning the stories behind the origins of these words helps us to appreciate the richness of both our language and our history.

In addition to eponyms, this book addresses a figure of speech known as an allusion. Historical allusions are indirect references to previous events which are cited to draw a comparison to a contemporary situation. The origin for many allusions is apparent. Although not aware of all the supporting details, most culturally literate people know that *crossing the Rubicon* is a reference to an irreversible decision made by Julius Caesar. This allusion, in which both the origin and the contemporary connotation are both clear is atypical. Most allusions have become completely disassociated from their original context. Although most will understand the meaning of the reference, how many people realize that the expression *mad as a hatter* refers to the dementia suffered by Victorian hat makers who were gradually poisoned by the mercury used in their craft? Or that the childhood rhyme "Ring around the Roses" dates back to the Renaissance and is actually a reference to the bubonic plague?

Preface

This book provides a concise definition of the current meaning for almost six hundred allusions and eponyms from all eras of history, including the twentieth century. The majority of each entry is devoted to providing insight into the historical events that gave rise to the expression. Historically verifiable people and events from the Bible, ancient history, and folklore are included. Allusions which originated in mythology or fictional works (such as the Midas touch or a scarlet letter) will be excluded, as there are already several excellent reference books which cover these topics.

The purpose of the *Dictionary of Historical Allusions and Eponyms* is to provide greater insight and historical background for these figures of speech than is currently available in reference literature. It is hoped that language and literature students, historians and word sleuths will all find something useful here. Aside from its academic utility, I hope that it will be a fun book to browse through, for what is more fascinating than to suddenly discover a piece of history encapsulated in a single word?

ACKNOWLEDGMENTS

There are too many people who have helped me with this book for me to adequately express my gratitude in this short space. I would like to give special mention to the library staff at Wright State University and Ohio State University, who provided me with the support, time, and resources to complete this project. It was a blessing to have such supportive colleagues who were willing to share their insights and perspectives. Beth Anderson, Kathryn Reynolds, Ray Glenn, and Karen Kimber all deserve special mention for their various roles in helping me see this project through to completion. Most of all I would like to thank Jane and John Auchter, the two people who read every word of the manuscript and offered both well-deserved criticism and unstinting encouragement. Both were needed and appreciated.

A-1. ***The best of its kind; a first-class rating.*** The expression *A-1* derives from the insurance association, Lloyd's of London. Lloyd's dates to 1688, when Edward Lloyd began a coffeehouse on Tower Street in London. It developed into an informal meeting place for well-to-do shippers and the mercantile community, including underwriters, who provided insurance for ships and companies. The coffeehouse became so well known as a place for concluding shipping agreements that in 1696 Edward Lloyd began publishing *Lloyd's News.* The paper was issued three times a week and contained news of shipping movements and other items of interest to merchants. Posted in the front rooms of the coffeehouse were lists that tracked the arrival and departure of ships, wrecks, salvage, and vessels missing at sea.

Over time the underwriters who frequented Lloyd's created a formal association for their business, named in honor of their favorite coffeehouse. Lloyd's did not actually issue insurance but was (and still is) simply an umbrella organization for individual underwriters or groups who supply insurance at their own risk. Marine insurance was a high-risk business, and the loss of a single ship could bankrupt an underwriter. Consequently, ships had to be carefully appraised for seaworthiness, and pertinent information was recorded in the *Lloyd's Registry,* which listed the name of the ship, captain, origin, destination, builder, and year of construction. The condition of the ship's hull was assigned a code, so that a hull in excellent condition earned an A, with B and C ratings given to ships whose structure was not so sound. Numeric rankings—1, 2, 3, and so on—assessed the quality of the onboard equipment, such as the cables and sails. Thus an *A-1* ranking was the highest a ship could receive and was probably a good bet for the underwriter.

Sources

Hodgson, Godfrey. *Lloyd's of London.* New York: Viking, 1984.

McHenry, Robert, ed. *The New Encyclopedia Britannica.* 15th ed. Chicago: Encyclopedia Britannica, 1992.

Worsley, Frank Arthur. *The Romance of Lloyd's: From Coffee-House to Palace.* New York: Hillman-Curl, 1937.

Wright, Charles. *History of Lloyd's from the Founding of Lloyd's Coffee House to the Present Day.* London: Macmillan, 1928.

According to Hoyle.
See Hoyle.

Albatross. ***A ceaseless, worrisome burden.*** The albatross is a large, white seafaring bird, which seamen have traditionally viewed with considerable awe—for good reason. The bird can soar for hours without ever flapping its wings, and some are capable of migrating across the Atlantic Ocean. The Great Wandering Albatross, the largest of the world's flying seabirds, has been known to migrate from the United States to Australia on a yearly basis. Although they usually feed on fish and squid, albatrosses will sometimes circle above ships in order to feed on garbage. Sailors believed that albatrosses embodied the souls of dead seamen and that an albatross would circle a ship to warn of impending bad weather. For these reasons it was considered extremely bad luck to kill an albatross, a belief that was reflected in the famous poem by Samuel Taylor Coleridge, "The Rime of the Ancient Mariner." A sailor wantonly kills an albatross, after which his ship is blown off course and a series of disasters overtakes the crew, leaving him the only survivor. The ancient mariner believes that he was left alive to suffer and, as a penance, must teach others to love all things, both great and small.

Suspicions about the albatross still linger among sailors in the twentieth century. In 1959 a British ship, the *Calpean Star,* had among its cargo an albatross bound for a German zoo. A series of technical problems plagued the ship, and it had to dock in Liverpool until engine problems could be rectified. The day after pulling into harbor the albatross was found dead in its cage, and about 50 of the crew members refused to continue the unlucky voyage.

Sources

Carver, Craig M. *A History of English in Its Own Words.* New York: HarperCollins, 1991.
Opie, Iona, and Moira Tatem, eds. *A Dictionary of Superstitions.* New York: Oxford University Press, 1989.
Radford, Edwin. *Encyclopedia of Superstitions.* New York: Rider, 1948.
Scott, Peter Markham, ed. *The World Atlas of Birds.* New York: Random House, 1974.

All-American. ***Clean-cut, all-around excellence.***

In 1889 Caspar W. Whitney, a part owner of the magazine *This Week's Sport,* conceived the idea of creating a list of the most outstanding college football players in each position. Selection was considered an honor and placed the athlete in an elite group of the country's finest. To develop the list, Whitney closely collaborated with Walter Camp (1859–1925), a sports authority and a major figure in the development of American football as a game distinct from British rugby. Over time Camp's name became more closely associated with the lists, and he is often inaccurately given credit for originating the idea. The concept of All-American teams became very popular, and before long *Harper's Weekly, Collier's,* and *Outing* all started choosing their own All-American football teams. Other sports, such as baseball and basketball, soon followed suit. Lists of All-American athletes are published today by the United Press International, the Associated Press, and *Sporting News.*

Individuals selected for this honor embody the clean-cut, hard-working athleticism admired by American society and often associated with the small-town athlete. Exceptional ability alone is not sufficient to be considered All-American, since substance abuse and unsportsmanlike behavior automatically disqualify many superior athletes. In the second half of the twentieth century, the term has often been broadened to refer to any person who is wholesome and hard-working.

Sources

Considine, Tim. *The Language of Sport.* New York: Facts on File, 1982.
Hickok, Ralph. *The Encyclopedia of North American Sports History.* New York: Facts on File, 1992.
Powell, Harford W. *Walter Camp: Father of American Football.* Boston: Little, Brown and Company, 1926.

Alpha and omega. ***Beginning and end; also, the entirety of something.***

The Greek alphabet, developed around 1000 B.C., is the ancestor of all modern European alphabets. The Greek alphabet had 26 letters, though they were arranged in a different order from today's English alphabet. The first Greek letter was the alpha and the last was the omega. The modern English equivalent for this expression is *a to z.*

The Book of Revelation, which was originally written in Greek, includes the following verse: "'I am the Alpha and the Omega,' says the Lord God, 'who is and who was and who is to come, the Almighty'" (Revelation 1:8). This powerful image translated into English as an expression of totality.

Sources
Bromiley, Geoffrey, ed. *The International Standard Bible Encyclopedia.* Grand Rapids, MI: W. B. Eerdmans, 1979.
Coulmas, Florian. *The Blackwell Encyclopedia of Writing Systems.* Cambridge, MA: Blackwell Publishers, 1996.
McHenry, Robert, ed. *The New Encyclopedia Britannica.* 15th ed. Chicago: Encyclopedia Britannica, 1992.
Simpson, J. A., and E. S. C. Weiner, eds. *The Oxford English Dictionary.* 2d ed. Oxford: Clarendon Press, 1989.
Stimpson, George. *A Book about the Bible.* New York: Harper and Brothers, 1945.

Amazon. ***A large, aggressive, strong-willed woman.***
Greek legend tells of a race of warrior women who lived in Asia Minor. They were tall and strong and so warlike that they reportedly cut off their right breast to prevent interference with their ability to draw a bow. To account for reproduction in a tribe consisting solely of women, some proposed that Amazons mated with men from neighboring tribes and kept only the female children. Others suggested that men did live among the Amazons, but they were used only for menial, domestic labor and the siring of children.

The sixteenth-century explorer Francisco de Orellana renamed the Maranon River in South America the Amazon River, after he claimed to have seen large, fierce women in the area.

Sources
McHenry, Robert, ed. *The New Encyclopedia Britannica.* 15th ed. Chicago: Encyclopedia Britannica, 1992.
Mercatante, Anthony S. *The Facts on File Encyclopedia of World Mythology and Legend.* New York: Facts on File, 1988.

America.
For several years after Christopher Columbus's landing in the New World, Europeans operated under the assumption that his discovery had placed him in the Orient—a supposition that underlay the misnomers "Indians" and "West Indies." Because of this misapprehension, the new continent eventually became associated with the name of Amerigo Vespucci (1454–1512), a Florentine navigator. Vespucci had reached the mouth of the river that is known today as the Amazon and had sailed along the coast of South America. One of the first navigators to recognize that South America was a separate continent, his writings deeply impressed the German geographer and mapmaker Martin Waldseemüller. In his pamphlet *Cosmographiae Introductio,* Waldseemüller proposed that this new land be named after Vespucci, although at first *America* signified only the South American continent. As later mapmakers began to sketch the outline of the entire continent, the name extended to northern landmasses as well.

Future scholars would often belittle the contributions of Vespucci, noting that most major discoveries had been made by other explorers and questioning the extent of his voyages. Yet during his lifetime he was well respected, and after he retired from the sea he was appointed chief navigator for the famous Commercial House for the West Indies, a position that demanded a thorough understanding of nautical science. After his death, his widow, Maria Cerezo, was granted a pension by the Spanish crown in recognition of the contributions of Vespucci.

Sources
Delpar, Helen, ed. *The Discoverers: An Encyclopedia of Explorers and Exploration.* New York: McGraw-Hill, 1980.
Hendrickson, Robert. *Dictionary of Eponyms: Names That Became Words.* New York: Stein and Day, 1985.
McHenry, Robert, ed. *The New Encyclopedia Britannica.* 15th ed. Chicago: Encyclopedia Britannica, 1992.
Stimpson, George. *A Book about American History.* Greenwich, CT: Fawcett Publications, 1960.

Amy Darden's horse. ***A symbol of legal procrastination.***
Amy Darden was a widow who lived in Mecklenburg County, Virginia, during the American Revolution. At some point, American soldiers requisitioned one of her horses,

yet the horse was never returned. Following the war, Darden petitioned Congress for restitution, but the representatives were apparently unwilling to devote time to such a trivial issue. She relentlessly petitioned every Congress between 1796 and 1815 with her claim, until she was finally awarded compensation for the horse she had lost over 30 years earlier. Thus Amy Darden and her horse became an example of dogged determinism in the face of legal procrastination.

Sources

Greene, Jack, and J. R. Pole. *The Blackwell Encyclopedia of the American Revolution.* Cambridge, MA: Blackwell Reference, 1991.

Mathews, Mitford M. *A Dictionary of Americanisms on Historical Principles.* Chicago: University of Chicago Press, 1951.

Ananias Club. ***A group of liars.***

In the years immediately following the death of Jesus of Nazareth, the early Christians lived in a state of constant expectation. They believed that the Second Coming was imminent, and they focused on preparing themselves for the day of judgment. To emulate the humility and love of their Savior, most of the converts abandoned their old lifestyle. As described in the Acts of the Apostles (Acts 5:1–12), those who had possessions sold them and used the money to help support the poor members of the Christian community. There was no private ownership of property, and everything was held in common for the good of the entire group.

A wealthy man named Ananias declared his wish to join the community, and he sold his property and pretended to lay all the proceeds at the feet of the apostle Peter. Peter saw deception in the face of Ananias and accused the man of withholding the income from the sale. Ananias, trapped in a lie, fell dead. A few hours later Ananias's wife Sapphira, unaware of the fate of her husband, approached the group. Peter questioned her about the property Ananias had sold, and when Sapphira repeated her husband's lie, she too fell down dead.

Although Ananias has long been an eponym for a liar, the expression *Ananias Club* was popularized by Theodore Roosevelt, who used it to refer to his political enemies, including journalists who published information they had agreed to keep confidential. Roosevelt also derogated journalists as *muckrakers,* a term he coined.

Sources

Bromiley, Geoffrey, ed. *The International Standard Bible Encyclopedia.* Grand Rapids, MI: W. B. Eerdmans, 1979.

McDonald, William J., ed. *New Catholic Encyclopedia.* New York: McGraw-Hill, 1967.

Stimpson, George. *A Book about American Politics.* New York: Harper, 1952.

Annie Oakley. ***A free pass or ticket of admission.***

Annie Oakley (1860–1926) was born Phoebe Ann Moses, the fifth of eight children. As a young girl she discovered her remarkable talent with an old cap-and-ball rifle that had belonged to her father. She spent much of her youth hunting for game in the Ohio woods where she grew up, and, according to legend, she earned enough to pay off the mortgage on her family's farm. At the age of fifteen she won a local shooting match, beating the professional marksman Frank Butler. The two were married in 1876 and traveled the vaudeville circuits as "Butler and Oakley." (She probably took the name "Oakley" from a Cincinnati suburb.) By 1885 she had caught the attention of Buffalo Bill and spent the next sixteen years touring the country with his Wild West Show. One of her acts was to toss a playing card into the air and pierce it with bullet holes before it hit the ground. These cards resembled show tickets, and since tickets had to be punched before gaining admittance to the show, the expression *Annie Oakley* was soon transferred to complimentary passes for the theater and railroad.

Sources

Hendrickson, Robert. *Dictionary of Eponyms: Names That Became Words.* New York: Stein and Day, 1985.

James, Edward T., ed. *Notable American Women, 1607–1950: A Biographical Dictionary.* Cambridge, MA: Belknap Press, 1971.

Riley, Glenda. *The Life and Legacy of Annie Oakley.* Norman: University of Oklahoma Press, 1994.

"Any color so long as it's black." *Being given no choice.*

Henry Ford (1863–1947) was very proud of his revolutionary design for the Model T and was determined to price the car so that any working American could afford one. The first Model Ts rolled off the production line in 1908 for $850, but Ford continued to streamline production. By eliminating optional features he was able to reduce production time of the car from 12 hours to 1 hour and 33 minutes. The price eventually dipped as low as $290 in 1924. The downside was that consumers could not choose any options or special colors, and all of the later Model Ts were produced solely in black. As Ford reportedly said, "People can have it in any color—so long as it's black."

By 1926 the Model T was facing stiff competition from other automobiles that were almost as inexpensive but were more in tune with public taste. Americans in the Roaring Twenties wanted more comfort and style in their cars, and the economical Model T was beginning to look hopelessly old-fashioned. Ford was stunned by this change in public preference, but in 1927 he took the Model T out of production and introduced the Model A. The new Fords made their debut in such vibrant colors as Niagara Blue, Arabian Sand, Dawn Gray, Gunmetal Blue, Balsam Green, Copper Drab, and Rose Beige. Within a year Ford had back orders for 800,000 Model As. However, the stock market collapse in 1929 ended the boom for the Ford Motor Company, and sales of the Model A plummeted, forcing it out of production in 1931.

Sources

Derdak, Thomas. *International Directory of Company Histories.* Chicago: St. James Press, 1988.

Ford Motor Company Historical Library (1997), from the Ford Motor Company Homepage [Online]. Available http://www.ford.com/archive [July 1997].

Fucini, Joseph, and Suzy Fucini. *Entrepreneurs: The Men and Women behind Famous Brand Names and How They Made It.* Boston: G. K. Hall, 1985.

Arcadia. *A region or setting of simple, pastoral beauty.*

Arcadia is a region of Greece in the central Peloponnesus known for its rustic simplicity and tranquillity. Although the area is mountainous, the fertile valleys abound with grapes, grains, and livestock. Cut off from the rest of the country by a mountain range, Arcadia's pastoral society was sheltered from the internecine conflicts that periodically ravaged the rest of Greece. Poets of ancient Greece and Rome often used Arcadia as a bucolic, paradisiacal backdrop. During the Renaissance this image of Arcadia was revived in the works of Jacopo Sannazzaro and Sir Philip Sidney. The word is now used to describe any setting characterized by rural simplicity and contentment.

Sources

Evans, Ivor H., ed. *Brewer's Dictionary of Phrase and Fable.* 14th ed. New York: Harper and Row, 1989.

Grant, Michael. *A Guide to the Ancient World: A Dictionary of Classical Place Names.* New York: H. W. Wilson, 1986.

Hornblower, Simon, and Antony Spawforth, eds. *The Oxford Classical Dictionary.* 3d ed. Oxford: Oxford University Press, 1996.

McHenry, Robert, ed. *The New Encyclopedia Britannica.* 15th ed. Chicago: Encyclopedia Britannica, 1992.

Armageddon. *A decisive and cataclysmic conflict.*

The term *Armageddon* is Hebrew for "hill of Megiddo" and is derived from the ancient Palestinian city of Megiddo, which dates back approximately 6,000 years. The city was strategically located on the historic route between Mount Carmel and the seacoast and had enviable access to a reliable water supply and fertile fields. Such a prize location invited the attention of conquerors.

Megiddo was captured by the Egyptian king Thutmose III in a bloody campaign in 1468 B.C. and was taken by Joshua when the Hebrews reclaimed the land for the Israelites around 200 years later.

Armageddon is cited in the Book of Revelation as the place of the final battle between good and evil on the day of reckoning. In the late twentieth century, it has become associated with the cataclysmic potential of nuclear warfare.

Sources

Blaiklock, Edward M., and R. K. Harrison, eds. *The New International Dictionary of Biblical Archaeology.* Grand Rapids, MI: Zondervan Publishing House, 1983.

Meyers, Eric M. *The Oxford Encyclopedia of Archaeology in the Near East.* New York: Oxford University Press, 1997.

Safire, William. *Safire's Political Dictionary.* New York: Random House, 1978.

Stimpson, George. *A Book about the Bible.* New York: Harper and Brothers, 1945.

Assassin. ***The murderer of a public official or of any prominent individual.***

The word *assassin* has its origins in an eleventh-century Islamic cult. Although the most famous schism within Islam was the rift between Sunni and Shi'ite, there were other factions that emerged throughout the Middle Ages, one of which was the Hashshashin. Led by Hasan-e Sabbah, better known as "the old man in the mountain," the group captured the hill fortress of Alamut in 1094 and then overwhelmed other strategic centers throughout Iran, Iraq, and Syria. Their practice of murdering political enemies was considered a religious duty, since striking down apostates was the ultimate proof of faith and devotion. Because the sect members were reputed to smoke hashish before their killings in order to induce ecstatic visions, they were called *Hashshashin,* which in Arabic means "hashish-smoker." However, subsequent research has not been able to verify the use of hashish.

As the Crusaders returned from the Holy Land, they brought with them tales of the *Assassins,* who were depicted as savage disciples of a strange cult and as relishing any opportunity to kill their enemies in a drug-induced haze of fanaticism. The stories were out of proportion to the danger actually presented by this small sect, but their reputation continued to terrify both Christians and mainstream Muslims. The account of a medieval archbishop illustrated the prevailing image of the Assassins:

> There is, in the province of Tyre, otherwise called Phoenicia, a people who possess ten strong castles. The bond of submission and obedience that binds this people to their Chief is so strong, that there is no task so arduous, difficult or dangerous that any one of them would not undertake to perform it with the greatest zeal, as soon as the Chief had commanded it. If, for example, there be a prince who is hated or mistrusted by this people, the Chief gives a dagger to one or more of his followers. At once whoever receives this command sets out on his mission, without considering the consequences of the deed or the possibility of escape. Zealous to complete his task, he toils and labors as long as may be needful, until chance gives him the opportunity to carry out his chief's orders. Both our people and the Saracens call them the Assassins.

Assassin power came to an end when Mongol invaders of the thirteenth century conquered their territory.

Sources

Burman, Edward. *The Assassins.* Wellingborough: Crucible, 1987.

Eliade, Mircea. *The Encyclopedia of Religion.* New York: Macmillan, 1986.

Lewis, Bernard. *The Assassins: A Radical Sect in Islam.* New York: Oxford University Press, 1987.

Mish, Frederick C. *The Merriam-Webster New Book of Word Histories.* Springfield, IL: Merriam-Webster, 1991.

Aubry's dog. ***Possessing unflagging loyalty.***

The Frenchman Aubry of Montdidier was murdered in 1371, but there was no trace of the murderer and no one was charged with the crime. It appeared that the murder would go unsolved until it was noticed that Aubry's faithful dog, Dragon, became ferocious whenever Richard of Macaire was near. This aroused suspicions, because the dog had displayed no strong aversion to any other individual. In medieval jurisprudence, combat could decide the guilt or innocence of an accused party, under the belief that the hand of God would intervene on the side of justice. Thus the authorities demanded that Richard of Macaire and Dragon meet in judicial combat. At the scheduled time, the canine champion promptly went for Macaire's throat and won the battle. With his dying breath Macaire confessed to killing Aubry and asked forgiveness. Since then, the expression *Aubry's dog* has evoked the qualities of extraordinary faithfulness and devotion.

Sources

Hendrickson, Robert. *Facts on File Encyclopedia of Word and Phrase Origins.* New York: Facts on File, 1987.

Mercatante, Anthony S. *Facts on File Encyclopedia of World Mythology and Legend.* New York: Facts on File, 1988.

Augustan Age. ***An idyllic period when a nation's culture and prosperity appear to be at their zenith.***

Augustus Caesar (63 B.C.–A.D. 14), born Gaius Octavius, was the first emperor of Rome, and his reign, which followed long years of strife and civil war, was renowned for its high prosperity, literary and artistic achievements, and internal peace. Surviving sculptures of Augustus Caesar portray him as a handsome man, and writers extolled his integrity, courage, and wisdom, depicting him as the personification of Roman ideals. Immensely popular with his subjects, Augustus undertook to rebuild Rome. Aqueducts and roads were constructed, as were the Pantheon and the great Forum of Augustus, and 82 temples were restored. To fill the new buildings, Augustus commissioned sculpture and other artwork, which primarily hailed the virtues of pastoral simplicity and traditional piety. The great literary masterpieces of Horace, Ovid, and Virgil were produced during this period. The emperor also promoted his rule as the period of *Pax Romana,* although wars of conquest continued. The *Augustan Age* became associated with an image of Rome at its finest and consequently has been used in connection with other nation-states seemingly at their zenith.

Sources

Bunson, Matthew. *Encyclopedia of the Roman Empire.* New York: Facts on File, 1994.

Hornblower, Simon, and Antony Spawforth, eds. *The Oxford Classical Dictionary.* 3d ed. Oxford: Oxford University Press, 1996.

Reinhold, Meyer, and Paul T. Alessi. *The Golden Age of Augustus.* Toronto: S. Stevens, 1978.

Turner, Jane, ed. *The Dictionary of Art.* New York: Grove Dictionaries, 1996.

Austrian lip. ***A strongly protruding jaw and chin, with extremely full lips.***

The Habsburg family was one of the great royal dynasties of Europe during the seventeenth century. In control of the thrones of Austria and Spain, the two branches of the family began a practice of almost exclusive intermarriage that continued for 200 years. Marriages between first cousins brought the Habsburgs wealth, solid political alliances, and the ability to preserve a royal bloodline. However, over time, some genetic quirks emerged, not least of which was a tendency toward insanity. On a more superficial level, intermarriage also ensured that the Habsburgs' rather unfortunate physical traits were passed down to posterity. The unattractive Habsburg profile, revealed in portraiture as an abnormally long chin, protruding jaw, and thick, fleshy lips, became more severe in each generation and gave rise to the expression *Austrian lip.* It was so pronounced in Carlos II of Spain that his jaws did not meet and he was unable to chew food.

By 1700 rampant infertility within the Habsburg family forced them to end the tradition of intermarriage. With the infusion of new blood, the Habsburgs of the next century were less prone to the infamous Austrian lip.

Sources

Evans, Ivor H., ed. *Brewer's Dictionary of Phrase and Fable.* 14th ed. New York: Harper and Row, 1989.

Langdon-Davies, John. *Carlos: The King Who Would Not Die.* Englewood Cliffs, NJ: Prentice-Hall, 1963.

McHenry, Robert, ed. *The New Encyclopedia Britannica.* 15th ed. Chicago: Encyclopedia Britannica, 1992.

Auto-de-fé. ***Biased proceedings in which an individual is publicly ruined.***

The practice of the *auto-de-fé* (act of faith) dates back to fifteenth-century Spain and was the sentencing phase of an Inquisition trial conducted by the Catholic church against suspected heretics. The trials themselves were lengthy and complex and were not intended for public consumption. By contrast, the elaborately planned autos-de-fé were designed to instruct the populace about the dangers of straying from orthodoxy. Staged in the city plaza, the harsh show trials came complete with a procession of the penitents, sermons, confessions of guilt, and reading of sentences. Short proceedings lasted a few hours, while others could fill an entire day and involve the sentencing of hundreds of heretics.

Life imprisonment was the most extreme punishment available to an inquisitor, since only civil authorities could hand down death penalties. However, the distinction was sometimes a formality, and the church might turn over an accused for another trial and sentence of death after the auto-de-fé was concluded. The last auto-de-fé was held in Mexico in 1850.

Inherent in the autos-de-fé was the proscription and public humiliation of nonconformists. In the twentieth century the term was adopted as a protest against the blackballing of politicians who strayed from the party line.

Sources

Lea, Henry C. *A History of the Inquisition.* New York: Macmillan, 1992.

McDonald, William J., ed. *New Catholic Encyclopedia.* New York: McGraw-Hill, 1967.

McHenry, Robert, ed. *The New Encyclopedia Britannica.* 15th ed. Chicago: Encyclopedia Britannica, 1992.

Metford, J. C. J. *The Dictionary of Christian Lore and Legend.* London: Thames and Hudson, 1983.

B

Baedeker. ***A detailed travel guide.***

The travel books produced by German bookseller Karl Baedeker (1801–1859) were so exceptionally good that his name has become synonymous with exhaustive guidebooks. Baedeker hoped to provide detailed, practical information that would allow the traveler to dispense with paid guides. In the nineteenth century, the newly prosperous bourgeoisie began to enjoy recreational travel, which had once been a privilege restricted to the wealthy elite. For middle-class travelers, the *Baedekers* were indispensable tools in planning affordable travel arrangements.

The early books were written by Baedeker himself, who traveled incognito to evaluate restaurant cuisines, theater ticket prices, hygiene in hotels, and tourist sights. Baedeker's guides were among the first to use "stars" to indicate items of exceptional interest. The compact, red manuals were eventually produced for most European cities and were considered essential for any traveler venturing onto the Continent. Later releases covered the United States, Canada, Russia, Egypt, and India. During both world wars, invading forces relied upon the guides, and it was reported that Adolph Hitler ordered "Baedeker raids" that would target areas of historical interest.

Sources

Mish, Frederick C. *The Merriam-Webster New Book of Word Histories.* Springfield, IL: Merriam-Webster, 1991.

Morris, Jan. "The World according to Baedeker." *Travel-Holiday* 179, 1 (1996): 54–59.

Baker's dozen. ***Thirteen.***

In the Middle Ages heavy fines were levied on merchants who sold items under a standard weight. Since potatoes, rice, and other starches had yet to be imported into Europe, bread was vital to the medieval diet and was regarded as the "staff of human life." In England the manufacture and sale of this valuable commodity was closely regulated to ensure that bakers did not exploit the hunger of the masses for their own profit. From the reign of King John until Edward I, there were strict laws on the allowable profit per loaf, the location of baker's shops, and who could qualify to sell bread. In 1266 the English Parliament passed a law that regulated the price of bread by weight. Accurately determining weight was a tricky business, and bakers customarily added an extra loaf to an order to protect themselves against selling short. Bakers usually sold their loaves to shopkeepers by the dozen, and the thirteenth loaf was called the vantage loaf, giving rise to the expression *baker's dozen.*

Sources

Chambers, Robert. *The Book of Days.* London: W. and R. Chambers, 1914.

Hendrickson, Robert. *Facts on File Encyclopedia of Word and Phrase Origins.* New York: Facts on File, 1987.

Simpson, J. A., and E. S. C. Weiner, eds. *The Oxford English Dictionary.* 2d ed. Oxford: Clarendon Press, 1989.

Wagner, Leopold. *Manners, Customs, and Their Observances: Their Origin and Signification.* London: William Heinemann, 1894.

Balkanization. ***The division of a territory or organization into smaller, weaker, and often hostile units.***

The Balkan peninsula in southeastern Europe is remarkable for the high degree of ethnic diversity contained within a relatively small region. The word *balkan* is Turkish for mountain, and in fact the area's mountainous terrain played a large part in segregating its ethnic communities. From the fifteenth century through the nineteenth century, the region was dominated and isolated by the Ottoman Empire, which fostered the development of feudal-like societies throughout the peninsula. As the Ottoman Empire began to decline in the nineteenth century, the European powers encouraged nationalistic movements in the Balkans in an attempt to further weaken the imperial controls.

As the Turks rolled back from the peninsula in the late nineteenth century, new nation-states began to emerge, including Bulgaria, Romania, Albania, Serbia, and Bosnia-Hercegovina. Many of these fledgling states contained a multitude of ethnic enclaves, which were forged into uneasy alliances. Throughout the twentieth century, the pressures of foreign wars, economic depression, and political instability have caused ethnic hostilities to turn violent and erupt into bloodshed.

The fracturing of the Balkan peninsula into small power blocs resulted in inefficiencies and rivalries that weakened the development of the entire region. Consequently, the term *balkanization* is often applied to businesses, local governments, and other organizations that suffer from fragmentation.

Sources

McHenry, Robert, ed. *The New Encyclopedia Britannica.* 15th ed. Chicago: Encyclopedia Britannica, 1992.

Newman, Bernard. *Balkan Background.* New York: Macmillan, 1945.

Simpson, J. A., and E. S. C. Weiner, eds. *The Oxford English Dictionary.* 2d ed. Oxford: Clarendon Press, 1989.

Banned in Boston. ***Something that is risqué to the easily offended.***

"Watch the Ward," a society for the suppression of vice, was founded in Boston during the 1870s. Its primary objective was to stamp out lewd publications, pornography, and prostitution. Initially, these objectives were not controversial, as morality was considered a public affair during the Victorian era. However, by the early twentieth century, the general population of Boston was moving on, while Watch the Ward members were still entrenched in Victorian morality. Similar societies in other cities were voluntarily disbanding, but the Boston group was gaining national attention as its censorship activities became ever more aggressive. When Watch the Ward decided that a book, newspaper, or magazine was unacceptable, booksellers were notified, and anyone caught selling the banned item with two days of notification was subject to prosecution. Throughout the twenties, a host of literary celebrities such as Ernest Hemingway, H. L. Mencken, and Sinclair Lewis were drawn into the fray as their writings came under attack. By the end of the decade, public sympathy was overwhelmingly in support of the banned authors and persecuted booksellers, and the law was liberalized in 1930.

The phrase *banned in Boston* launched a number of books to bestseller status, and it is still used in connection with music, writings, and films that are just shy of respectable.

Sources

Anderson, Charles B., ed. *Bookselling in the American World: Some Observations and Recollections in Celebration of the 75th Anniversary of the American Booksellers Association.* New York: Quadrangle/New York Times Book Company, 1975.

Boyer, Paul S. *Purity in Print: The Vice-Society Movement and Book Censorship in America.* New York: Scribner, 1968.

Green, Jonathan. *The Encyclopedia of Censorship.* New York: Facts on File, 1989.

Barbarian. ***A crude, uncivilized person.***

The ancient Greeks had good cause to be proud of their civilization. In the areas of science, architecture, sculpture, literature, and philosophy, the Greeks produced phenomenal achievements that are still deemed worthy of study and emulation over 2,000 years later. However, Greek pride was also expressed in the contempt in which non-Greeks were held, as revealed in the etymology of *barbarian*. The Germanic tongues of the peoples to the north of Greece contrasted starkly with the elegance of spoken Greek, and the Greeks ridiculed German speech as sounding like "bar-bar-bar." The word *barbaros* was coined to refer to anyone who did not speak Greek, but as it evolved, it began to encompass more than language. It has been used to brand entire civilizations as crude, ignorant, and lawless.

Sources

Katzner, Kenneth. *The Languages of the World.* London: Routledge, 1995.

Mish, Frederick C. *The Merriam-Webster New Book of Word Histories.* Springfield, IL: Merriam-Webster, 1991.

Simpson, J. A., and E. S. C. Weiner, eds. *The Oxford English Dictionary.* 2d ed. Oxford: Clarendon Press, 1989.

Barnum was right. ***A comment on the gullibility of the general public.***

Phineas Taylor Barnum (1810–1891) became enormously wealthy by profiting from the credulity of the American public. In 1835 he entered show business in association with a very old black woman named Joice Heth. Barnum claimed that Heth was 162 years old and had been George Washington's childhood nurse. For the price of admission, Heth, who had been coached on all the details of young George's life, relayed stories about Washington's early days, including the legend of the cherry tree (although Heth declared it had been a peach tree). When Heth died, an autopsy revealed that she was around 80 years of age.

Although Barnum's main attraction was dead and discredited, it was not long before he developed others, including such "freaks" of nature as dwarfs, Siamese twins, and bearded ladies. In 1842 he opened his famous American Museum. In addition to a mermaid from Fiji and woolly horses, there was a sign over a door directing visitors to the "Egress" beyond. Unfamiliar with the strange word, people eagerly went through the door, only to find that they had exited the museum—egress deriving from the Latin for *exit*.

One of Barnum's rivals, Joseph Bessimer, hoped to undermine Barnum's popularity by attributing to him the gibe "There's a sucker born every minute, but none of them ever die." Barnum never denied that the statement was his, and he thanked Bessimer for the free publicity. In fact, throughout his life Barnum commented openly on the feeblemindedness of the public and his willingness to exploit it.

Sources

Saxon, A. H. *P. T. Barnum: The Legend and the Man.* New York: Columbia University Press, 1989.

Stimpson, George. *A Book about a Thousand Things.* New York: Harper and Brothers, 1946.

Wallace, Irving. *The Fabulous Showman: The Life and Times of P. T. Barnum.* New York: Knopf, 1959.

Basket case. ***A person caught in a hopeless situation.***

During World War I, medical advances such as sterile surgical procedures and anesthesia were implemented for the first time on a large scale. Soldiers who previously would have perished from shock or infection were now able to survive the trauma of surgery and multiple amputations. The result was a significant number of triple and quadruple amputees, and the callous appellation *basket case* was coined in reference to such soldiers. The army was embarrassed by persistent rumors that these amputees were languishing in military hospitals. The situation became so serious that the surgeon general issued the following statement in March 1919:

> The Surgeon General of the Army, Major Gen. Merritte W. Ireland, denies emphatically that there is any foundation for the stories that have been circulated in all parts of the country of the existence of "basket cases" in our hospitals. A basket case is a soldier who has lost both legs and both arms and

therefore cannot be carried on a stretcher.

General Ireland says: "I have personally examined the records and am able to say that there is not a single basket case either on this side of the water or among the soldiers of the A.E.F. [American Expeditionary Force]. Further, I wish to emphasize that there has been no instance of an American soldier so wounded during the whole period of the war."

Sources

Dickson, Paul. *War Slang: Fighting Words and Phrases of Americans from the Civil War to the Gulf War.* New York: Pocket Books, 1994.

Evans, Ivor H., ed. *Brewer's Dictionary of Phrase and Fable.* 14th ed. New York: Harper and Row, 1989.

Ireland, Merritte W. *The Medical Department of the United States Army in the World War: Medical and Casualty Statistics.* Washington, DC: GPO, 1925.

Bayonet. ***A knife designed to fit into the muzzle end of a firearm and used in close combat.***

It is believed that the bayonet was invented by Maréchal de Puységur about 1640. It derives its name from Bayonne, the French city where Puységur lived, and was first used in battle when Puységur's troops took Ypres for Louis XIV in 1647. The original bayonet had significant drawbacks. Once it was inserted into the muzzle, the gun could not be fired. If it had been pushed in too tightly, it was difficult to remove. The advantage of the bayonet in combat was that it allowed a soldier to continue fighting after he had fired his weapon. Early guns could take over a minute to reload, slowing down the pace of a battle.

Musketeers were very vulnerable to attacks from cavalrymen, who could ride down an infantryman who had been rendered defenseless after firing his weapon. This danger was mitigated by the bayonet, which reached six feet in length after it had been attached to a musket and was long enough to reach a mounted soldier. Perhaps the greatest value of a bayonet was the terror it invoked among the enemy soldiers. Actual clashes between opposing infantry using bayonets were rare. Evidence indicates that one side usually lost their bravado and retreated in the face of an onslaught of bayonets.

The value of the bayonet was markedly decreased by the development of repeating firearms. Twentieth-century military rifles are often equipped with bayonets, but their primary purpose is to teach aggression, rather than for actual use in battle.

Sources

Lorimer, Lawrence T. *The Encyclopedia Americana.* Danbury, CT: Grolier, 1989.

Simpson, J. A., and E. S. C. Weiner, eds. *The Oxford English Dictionary.* 2d ed. Oxford: Clarendon Press, 1989.

Stimpson, George. *A Book about a Thousand Things.* New York: Harper and Brothers, 1946.

Beau Brummell. ***A fastidious dresser. A fashion setter.***

Beau Brummell's life could be the archetype of a meteoric rise to fame followed by a spectacular fall to penury and isolation. The grandson of a shopkeeper, Brummell (1778–1840) was allowed the unusual privilege of attending the exclusive boarding school Eton where he formed friendships with a number of young aristocrats. His flair for fashion and wit made him popular and led to an introduction to the Prince of Wales, with whom he became fast friends. He received a commission in the Tenth Hussars, the prince's regiment, and after reaching the rank of captain in 1798, Brummell retired at the ripe old age of twenty. When he inherited a fortune of £30,000, Brummell set himself up in a fashionable house. Moving in the highest social circles, he was renowned for his painstakingly elegant wardrobe. Friendship with the Prince of Wales, the Duke and Duchess of York, Lord Byron, and other trendsetters catapulted Brummell into the charmed inner circle of the royal court. He was acknowledged as the definitive connoisseur of fashion and manners, and his opinions could make or break a person's social ambitions.

Impeccable taste can be costly, and Brummell spent a staggering amount on tailors, bootmakers, jewelers, and hatmakers. Debts began to accumulate, and a serious quarrel with the Prince of Wales took some of the shine off Brummell's star. As his creditors closed in on him, Brummell fled to France, but he continued to live in high style, and in 1835 he landed in debtor's prison. A summer of confinement broke his spirit, and he began to show signs of mental illness after his release. Ironically, Brummell lost all interest in his appearance and became a dirty, disheveled man. Suffering from delusions, he held imaginary receptions for the elegant beauties and luminaries of his past. Brummell was finally placed in a charitable asylum for the insane, where he spent the last two years of his life.

Sources

Connely, Willard. *The Reign of Beau Brummell.* London: Cassell, 1940.

Franzero, Charles M. *The Life and Times of Beau Brummell.* London: A. Redman, 1958.

Stephen, Leslie, and Sidney Lee, eds. *The Dictionary of National Biography.* London: Oxford University Press, 1921.

Bedlam. ***A place of raucous noise and confusion.***

Bedlam is a contraction of Bethlehem and refers to the priory of Saint Mary of Bethlehem in England, which cared for insane patients during the fourteenth century. Although most religious institutions generally tended to the sick during the Middle Ages, Saint Mary of Bethlehem was unique in its willingness to look after the mentally ill. When Henry VIII confiscated the properties of the Catholic church, he donated the priory's hospital to the city of London for the care of the insane. Thereafter, *bedlam* became a synonym for lunatic asylum.

In later years, the hospital authorities decided to raise extra money by allowing sightseers to enter the facility for a fee of two pence. Thousands of visitors wandered freely throughout the hospital, ridiculing and provoking the patients. Records from the nineteenth century indicate that approximately 90,000 people per year paid to view the residents of Bedlam. No doubt the hospital's reputation as a place in which inmates were brutalized was confirmed by the stories these visitors related. The hospital was finally absorbed into the British National Health Service and renamed the Bethlehem Royal Hospital.

Sources

McHenry, Robert, ed. *The New Encyclopedia Britannica.* 15th ed. Chicago: Encyclopedia Britannica, 1992.

Strayer, Joseph R., ed. *Dictionary of the Middle Ages.* New York: Scribner, 1982.

Weinreb, Ben, and Christopher Hibbert. *The London Encyclopedia.* London: Macmillan, 1983.

Beecher's Bibles. ***A colloquialism for Sharp repeater rifles.***

Together with his sister Harriet Beecher Stowe, clergyman Henry Ward Beecher (1813–1887) was a fierce antislavery advocate, and his legendary skills as an orator were put to good use in the service of that cause. In 1854 the Kansas-Nebraska Act provided for the organization of those territories but left the question of slavery to be decided by popular vote. Beecher helped raise funds for a campaign to prevent the extension of slavery into the territories. He was convinced that the two items crucial to the struggle were Bibles and rifles. Both items were shipped to Kansas in boxes labeled "Bibles." For this reason, Sharp repeater rifles were often known as Beecher's Bibles, especially during the strife in Kansas.

Sources

Hendrickson, Robert. *Facts on File Encyclopedia of Word and Phrase Origins.* New York: Facts on File, 1987.

Hibben, Paxton. *Henry Ward Beecher: An American Portrait.* New York: The Press of the Reader's Club, 1942.

Johnson, Allen, and Dumas Malone, eds. *Dictionary of American Biography.* New York: Scribner's, 1964.

Bell, book, and candle. ***The shunning of an individual or organization.***

The phrase is a reference to the ritual of excommunication, as conducted by the Roman

Catholic Church. During the early centuries of Christianity, excommunication simply meant that an individual voluntarily severed himself from the fellowship of other Christians. By the Middle Ages, excommunication had evolved into a punishment imposed by church officials on those who were judged guilty of a grave sin. It was the penalty most feared, because the excommunicate was considered to be in a state of sin, and death while still under this sentence would mean automatic condemnation in the hereafter. There were also social sanctions that accompanied the ecclesiastical punishment. An excommunicate was denied all commerce with other Christians, which amounted to ostracism.

During an excommunication ritual, a bell was rung to call attention to the proceedings. The Bible, the book of life, was closed, and a candle was extinguished to symbolize the darkness to which the sinner was now consigned. The final lines spoken at the ceremony were "Cursed be they from the crown of the head to the sole of the foot. Out be they taken from the Book of Life, and as this candle is cast from the sight of men, so be their soul cast from the sight of God into the deepest pit of hell. Amen." Bell, book, and candle captured in a phrase the solemn act of exclusion.

If an excommunicate continued to rebel against the church, the secular authorities could exert pressure. In France, if the individual did not repent within one year, the state had the right to confiscate his property. In England, failure to repent within forty days could lead to arrest. The abuse of excommunication was one of the charges leveled against the Catholic church by Martin Luther. Excommunications declined sharply after the Reformation.

Sources

Evans, Ivor H., ed. *Brewer's Dictionary of Phrase and Fable.* 14th ed. New York: Harper and Row, 1989.

McDonald, William J., ed. *New Catholic Encyclopedia.* New York: McGraw-Hill, 1967.

Strayer, Joseph, ed. *Dictionary of the Middle Ages.* New York: Charles Scribner's Sons, 1984.

Vodola, Elizabeth. *Excommunication in the Middle Ages.* Berkeley: University of California Press, 1986.

Wagner, Leopold. *Manners, Customs, and Their Observances: Their Origin and Signification.* London: William Heinemann, 1894.

Bellwether. ***An indicator of future events; in politics, the name given to a precinct or state that has a record of voting for the winning ticket.***

Bellwethers are castrated male sheep that wear a bell and are used to lead a herd of sheep. The practice dates back at least as far as the Middle Ages, when it was recognized that sheep will docilely follow where they are led. Bellwethers were trained to obey a few simple commands, and through them, the shepherds controlled the flock. Bellwethers were usually left unshorn, making it easier to identify them, and the bell was loud enough for the entire herd to hear. Some shepherds distinguished between flocks by fastening bells with different pitches onto the various bellwethers.

By the early fifteenth century the word commonly referred to men who displayed leadership ability. The meaning has expanded in modern usage to include any reliable indicator of a trend.

Sources

Ryder, Michael L. *Sheep and Man.* London: Duckworth, 1983.

Safire, William. *Safire's Political Dictionary.* New York: Random House, 1978.

Webber, Elizabeth. *Grand Allusions.* Washington, DC: Farragut Press, 1990.

Benedict Arnold. ***A traitor.***

A pantheon of heroes emerged from the American Revolution, but only one diabolical traitor. Ironically, Benedict Arnold's early career in the American army was nothing short of heroic. Born into a prosperous New England family, Arnold (1741–1801) fought in the French and Indian War and, after the battles of Lexington and Concord in 1775, immediately volunteered for service in the Continental Army. Given the task of attacking Quebec by George Washington, Arnold led a band of 700 men through the wilderness of Maine. The assault failed, and Arnold was seriously wounded in the leg. After his recovery, he patched together a ragtag navy and fended off a vastly superior British fleet. Arnold was hailed as a hero, but the acclaim did not lead to the promotions he felt he deserved. Although he continued fighting for several years, his assorted battlefield injuries finally took him out of action.

In 1778 General Washington appointed Arnold commander of the Philadelphia area, where he socialized with a number of prominent loyalists and eventually married Margaret Shippen, who had strong loyalist sympathies. In May 1779, with his wife's approval, Arnold began to make overtures to the British. Although he had lost faith in the cause of American independence, it appears that he was motivated primarily by greed. He demanded £10,000 for his services and wanted double that figure if a key American post was surrendered with his assistance. In addition to other information, Arnold revealed the plans for an American invasion of Canada. When Arnold's British contact, Major John André, was captured, Arnold's treason was revealed. Arnold escaped on a British ship, leaving André to be hanged. He and his wife emigrated to England, where he was treated with disdain. Although Arnold received some payment for his collaboration, he struggled with his finances for the rest of his life and was badly in debt at his death.

Sources

Faragher, John M. *The Encyclopedia of Colonial and Revolutionary America.* New York: Facts on File, 1990.

Greene, Jack, and J. R. Pole. *The Blackwell Encyclopedia of the American Revolution.* Cambridge, MA: Blackwell Reference, 1991.

Johnson, Allen, and Dumas Malone, eds. *Dictionary of American Biography.* New York: Scribner's, 1964.

Kohn, George C. *The Encyclopedia of American Scandal: From Abscam to the Zenger Case.* New York: Facts on File, 1989.

Randall, Willard Stone. *Benedict Arnold: Patriot and Traitor.* New York: Morrow, 1990.

Benthamism. ***A utilitarian philosophy holding that promotion of the greatest happiness for the greatest number of people should be the guiding principle in public and private life.***

As the eighteenth century opened, most European nations had tax structures, exploitative working conditions, and hereditary laws that ensured the support of the upper classes while the vast majority of society lived in oppressive conditions. The aristocracy had long assumed that the advantages accruing from their privileged position were theirs to enjoy by birthright. Jeremy Bentham (1748–1832) believed that such a system was inherently wrong and needed to be redesigned to benefit the majority of society. Taking a radical position for his time, Bentham argued that achieving pleasure (or happiness) was the chief end of life. Therefore, people should have the freedom to organize their private life in a way that would maximize their ability to attain pleasure and avoid pain. The philosophy extended to public life, for Bentham advocated that government and laws should be structured so as to bring the greatest amount of good to the greatest number of people. *Benthamism* is still cited as a justification for government programs and policies designed to achieve social engineering.

Sources

Atkinson, Charles Milner. *Jeremy Bentham: His Life and Work.* New York: A. M. Kelley, 1969.

Edwards, Paul. *The Encyclopedia of Philosophy.* New York: Macmillan, 1967.

McHenry, Robert, ed. *The New Encyclopedia Britannica.* 15th ed. Chicago: Encyclopedia Britannica, 1992.

Stephen, Leslie, and Sidney Lee, eds. *The Dictionary of National Biography.* London: Oxford University Press, 1921.

Berserk. ***A violent, mindless, and destructive rage.***

When the Vikings raided the coasts of Europe in the eighth century, a reign of terror was launched. Because the pagan invaders initially targeted peaceful monastic communities, the raids were construed as an assault on Christianity—and thus on civilization itself. The first attack in 793 was on the tiny island of Lindisfarne, home of an exceptionally famous monastery. As the historian Simeon of Durham wrote, the Vikings "came to the church of Lindisfarne, laid everything waste with grievous plundering, trampled the holy places with polluted feet, dug up the altars and seized all the treasures of the holy church. They killed some of the brothers; some they took away with them in fetters; many they drove out, naked and loaded with insults; and some they drowned in the sea."

The Vikings were prompted to take up raiding because their Scandinavian land and resources could no longer meet the needs of their growing population. Norse culture glorified warriors, the fighting spirit, and victory in battle, but it was the frenzy of their attacks in particular that inspired a new word, *berserk*. Viking warriors were clad in bearskins, and in Norse, *bera* meant bear, and *serkr,* shirt. By extension, then, *berserkr* was the Norse word for "wild warrior or champion." Berserk passed into English as a description of the kind of ferocious behavior that was the Viking trademark.

Sources

Loyn, H. R. *The Vikings in Britain.* Cambridge, MA: Blackwell, 1995.

Magnusson, Magnus. *Vikings!* New York: Dutton, 1980.

Mish, Frederick C. *The Merriam-Webster New Book of Word Histories.* Springfield, IL: Merriam-Webster, 1991.

Beyond the pale. ***Unreasonable and unacceptable.***

In the Middle Ages the word "pale" referred to a crude fence of pointed stakes. As the English began to conquer territory in Scotland and Ireland, they built fortifications around their captured territory and named them pales. Within these pales the people were subject to English administration. In 1172 Henry II of England made substantial conquests in Ireland and established a pale in southeastern Ireland around Dublin, which was to be colonized by English settlers. Surrounded by Irish enemies, the settlers attempted to preserve English culture within their enclave. Citizenship and membership in trade guilds were restricted to those of English descent, the wearing of Irish dress was prohibited, intermarriage between Englishmen and Irish women was not permitted, and even friendly concourse was discouraged.

In 1317 the sense of isolation of those living in the Dublin Pale was sharpened when Scottish invaders attempted to take the city. The English settlers were thrown into such a panic they burned the bridges on the Liffey River. They tore down buildings and used the rubble to reinforce the town walls, and some of the suburbs that could not be adequately defended were deliberately burned down. The tactics worked, and English control of the pale was secure.

In 1494 an English pale was established in France, around the area of Calais. Within these zones English settlers were generally secure and able to live in the manner to which they were accustomed. *Beyond the pale* referred to the unsafe and hostile territory beyond control of the English. By the seventeenth century the phrase was often used in a figurative sense to denote wild, unacceptable situations.

Sources

Gardiner, Juliet, and Neil Wenborn, eds. *The Columbia Companion to British History.* New York: Columbia University Press, 1997.

Landon, Michael L. *Erin and Britannia: The Historical Background to a Modern Tragedy.* Chicago: Nelson-Hall, 1981.

McHenry, Robert, ed. *The New Encyclopedia Britannica.* 15th ed. Chicago: Encyclopedia Britannica, 1992.

Moody, T. W., ed. *A New History of Ireland: Early Modern Ireland, 1534–1691.* Oxford: Clarendon Press, 1976.

Strayer, Joseph R., ed. *Dictionary of the Middle Ages.* New York: Scribner, 1982.

Big Bertha. ***A fat woman. Also, a type of golf club with an oversized club face.***

There was never any doubt that Bertha Krupp (1886–1957) was a formidable woman. As owner of the Krupp armament empire, she ruled over the most powerful industrial concern of her time. Bertha's father had committed suicide in 1902, but it was unthinkable that a 16-year-old girl could run a company on which Germany's military might depended. The emperor Wilhelm II decided to choose a suitable husband for Bertha, and he settled on Gustov von Bohlen, who adopted the name of Krupp. Although he held the reins of the giant company and was an able administrator, Bertha often instructed her husband on what positions he should take. She was referred to as "Queen Bertha" by those who recognized her as the power behind the throne.

Founded in 1811, the Krupp factory initially produced steel, but it quickly expanded into the production of guns, cannons, and other armaments. In 1914 the Krupp factory produced its masterpiece, a 420-mm heavy howitzer. Each cannon required a crew of 1,000 men to move, clean, and prepare the weapon. Some sources claim that *die dicke Bertha,* or Fat Bertha, was named after the head of the Krupp family as a sign of respect. Others contend that the unflattering name was coined by French soldiers. Among English speakers, the enormous cannon was soon dubbed *Big Bertha.* When it was introduced, the cannon could fire shells over 7 miles, but continued modifications increased its range to the unprecedented distance of 76 miles.

Sources

McHenry, Robert, ed. *The New Encyclopedia Britannica.* 15th ed. Chicago: Encyclopedia Britannica, 1992.

Muhlen, Norbert. *The Incredible Krupps.* New York: Holt, 1959.

Pope, Stephen, and Elizabeth-Ann Wheal. *The Dictionary of the First World War.* New York: St. Martin's Press, 1995.

Bikini. ***A woman's two-piece bathing suit.***

A number of savvy marketing techniques accompanied the introduction of the bikini swimsuit in 1946. This was the year the United States began conducting a series of atomic bomb tests on the Bikini Atoll in the South Pacific. With good-natured audacity, French swimsuit designer Louis Reyard appropriated the name for his new creation, under the premise that it would have a similar bombshell effect. The original *bikinis,* consisting of a mere 30 inches of fabric, were sold in matchboxes. Although the bikini was an immediate sensation in Europe, it took the cultural revolution of the 1960s to encourage American women to wear the scanty swimsuit.

Sources

Martin, Richard, and Harold Koda. *Splash! A History of Swimwear.* New York: Rizzoli, 1990.

Simon, Scott. "The Bikini Turns 50 Years Old." National Public Radio, 30 March 1996.

Bill of health, a clean bill of health. ***An informal statement about the condition of a person, item, or organization.***

Before the twentieth century the shipping industry was a key culprit in the spread of infectious diseases. In the sixteenth century Mediterranean ports instituted a system whereby any ship wishing to dock had to produce a certificate from the previous port which declared that the town was free of infectious diseases. If a ship did not have this *clean bill of health,* all passengers and crew would be quarantined for 40 days. Presumably, contagious diseases would be purged by then. However, this strategy was only partially effective in halting the transmission of disease. Seasoned sailors often developed immunities to a whole range of contagions but still remained carriers, spreading diseases from port to port without ever displaying any symptoms.

Sources

Evans, Ivor H., ed. *Brewer's Dictionary of Phrase and Fable.* 14th ed. New York: Harper and Row, 1989.

Jeans, Peter D. *Ship to Shore: A Dictionary of Everyday Words and Phrases Derived from the Sea.* Santa Barbara, CA: ABC-CLIO, 1993.

McNeill, William. *Plagues and Peoples.* Garden City, NJ: Anchor Press, 1976.

Billingsgate. ***Coarse, abusive language.***

Since medieval times, London has been known for local markets that sell particular goods. At Covent Garden, for example, fruit and vegetables were sold, while Queenhithe was known for grain, Smithfield for meat, and Leadenhall for hardware and leather goods. Billingsgate, located at the north end of London Bridge, was the city's most famous fish market. Between four and seven o'clock in the morning the streets leading to Billingsgate were crammed with the carts of fishmongers transporting their goods from the docks. Aggressive haggling commenced as soon as the fish were unloaded into the stalls. Hucksters, fishwives, and sellers tried to shout one another down as they competed for the attention of the customers. The fish market was a smelly, slimy place, and these unpleasant conditions did little to improve the mood of the fishmongers. Billingsgate was so notorious for its shrill, vituperative clamor that it became a byword for coarse language. No doubt reflecting the prominent contribution of the fishwives to the Billingsgate clamor, one eighteenth-century commentator said that the word *billingsgate* was synonymous for a scolding, impudent slut. Its evolution continued in the United States. When objecting to the decline of civility displayed in government, Thomas Jefferson wrote, "We disapprove the constant billingsgate poured on them officially."

Like so many of the local markets in London, the Billingsgate fish market fell victim to the twentieth-century supermarket, and it officially closed in 1982.

Sources

Hibbert, Christopher. *London: A Biography of a City.* New York: Morrow, 1970.

McHenry, Robert, ed. *The New Encyclopedia Britannica.* 15th ed. Chicago: Encyclopedia Britannica, 1992.

Mish, Frederick C. *The Merriam-Webster New Book of Word Histories.* Springfield, IL: Merriam-Webster, 1991.

Bite the bullet. ***To brace oneself in preparation for an unpleasant task.***

The most common explanation for the origin of this term is that, before the introduction of anesthesia, wounded soldiers were given a bullet to clench between their teeth as a brace against pain during surgery. This is almost certainly untrue. Contemporary medical texts do not mention such a practice, although there are references to giving a patient a wooden spoon or piece of cloth to bite on. In fact, a bullet between the teeth could be quite dangerous if a patient began to convulse. Another argument against this origin for the expression is that medical practitioners were aware of effective ways to alleviate pain. Opium had been used for thousands of years in the Far East, and there is strong evidence to suggest that the drug had made its way into Europe by A.D. 200. In the sixteenth century, German physician Hans von Gersdorff regularly employed opium in the treatment of gunshot wounds and amputations. In cases of emergency surgery when physicians were unavailable, strong doses of rum were used. Anesthesia was widely available to military surgeons by the mid-nineteenth century.

Some authorities suggest that *bite the bullet* derives from the process of firing early rifles. A rifleman had to bite off the end of a cartridge in order to expose the powder to the spark. Reloading in the heat of a battle was a nerve-wracking procedure, and the rifleman had to have steady hands to get the job done. *Biting the bullet* implied the need to steel oneself for a difficult and stressful task.

Sources

Ammer, Christine. *Fighting Words: From War, Rebellion, and Other Combative Capers.* New York: Paragon House, 1989.

Haeger, Knut. *The Illustrated History of Surgery.* New York: Bell Publishing Company, 1988.

Hendrickson, Robert. *The Facts on File Encyclopedia of Word and Phrase Origins.* New York: Facts on File, 1987.

Leonardo, Richard A. *History of Surgery.* New York: Froben Press, 1943.

Black Hole of Calcutta. ***An extremely cramped and stifling space.***

In 1756 the British presence in Bengal, a region of eastern India, was strained to the breaking point by the arrogant actions of the colonial commanders and the Indian mistrust of the East India Company. Determined to expel the British, the nawab Siraj-ud-Dawlah launched an attack on Fort William in the port city of Calcutta. On June 20 the fort surrendered, and the British survivors were forced to spend the night in the company's lockup, a room only 18 feet by 14 feet that was commonly known as the Black Hole by the soldiers. The room had been designed to hold four or five prisoners, but according to the British commander, 146 people were crammed into the cell. It was a stiflingly hot night, and there were only two small ventilation windows. Many people died of suffocation. Others resorted to drinking their own urine or sucking perspiration from their clothing. The prisoners spent ten hours in the cell, and by morning, only 22 men and 1 woman were left alive. Although later historians have claimed that the number of those forced into the cell was exaggerated, witnesses and the survivors testified to the truth of the original count. In retaliation for this incident, the British army returned the following year and defeated the nawab's army, making the British the uncontested rulers of Bengal.

Sources

Barber, Noel. *The Black Hole of Calcutta: A Reconstruction.* Boston: Houghton Mifflin, 1966.

Macfarlane, Iris. *The Black Hole: The Makings of a Legend.* London: G. Allen and Unwin, 1975.

McHenry, Robert, ed. *The New Encyclopedia Britannica.* 15th ed. Chicago: Encyclopedia Britannica, 1992.

Stimpson, George. *A Book about a Thousand Things.* New York: Harper and Brothers, 1946.

Black Maria. *A police van.*

Maria Lee was a near-legend in Boston during the early 1800s. A free black woman of enormous size and strength, she occasionally worked as a teamster, driving heavy wagons and controlling a large team of horses. In 1798, Secretary of State Alexander Hamilton sought to arm American vessels in response to French depredations on American shipping. At his request, Lee undertook to deliver a shipment of guns to the American cutter *Scammel.* She succeeded despite terrible weather and an ambush attempt by smugglers.

Lee owned a boardinghouse in Boston, and it had a reputation as the most orderly spot on the waterfront, because Lee's boarders were afraid of her formidable strength. She once rescued a police officer trapped by criminals, and thereafter the police often called on her to help bring rowdy men into line or to escort criminals to prisons in her wagon. When British police vans or patrol wagons were introduced in the 1830s, it is said that they were named *Black Marias* in honor of this impressive woman. Some scholars doubt the accuracy of this attribution, questioning whether her fame would have spread with such force to England. However, a better explanation for the curious term has yet to surface.

Sources

Hendrickson, Robert. *Facts on File Encyclopedia of Word and Phrase Origins.* New York: Facts on File, 1987.

Safakis, Carl. *The Encyclopedia of American Crime.* New York: Facts on File, 1982.

Black sheep. *A member of a family who is considered less respectable than the others; an oddball.*

Black sheep are genetic rarities, and before the nineteenth century, it was difficult to sell their wool because there was never enough of it to be marketable. With no practical method to dye it another color, the wool of a black sheep was not nearly as valuable as that of a standard white sheep. The birth of a black sheep was considered bad luck, and superstitious farmers believed that the devil was somehow at work in this oddity.

The expression *black sheep* in reference to family members has been in common use since the eighteenth century.

Sources

Evans, Ivor H., ed. *Brewer's Dictionary of Phrase and Fable.* 14th ed. New York: Harper and Row, 1989.

Ryder, Michael L. *Sheep and Man.* London: Duckworth, 1983.

Blackball. *To exclude a person from a group or organization.*

This expression comes from the clubs of eighteenth-century England, which were the refuge of the elite. Men who shared similar literary, artistic, scientific, or recreational interests formed societies where they could gather for coffee, cards, and relaxation. Membership was strictly controlled, and admittance to an exclusive club was an indication of social prominence. No one was allowed into a club without the approval of the majority of members, and voting was kept anonymous by the use of colored balls instead of ballots. White or red balls indicated approval, black balls meant a negative vote.

One famous London club was the Athenæum, a handsome Greco-Roman building where the city's most influential people relaxed in graceful surroundings. Many eager to improve their social status clamored to join its exclusive ranks. As John Timbs commented, "All the little crawlers and parasites, and gentility-hunters, from all corners of London, set out upon the creep; and they crept in at the windows, and they crept down the area steps, and they crept in unseen at the doors. . . . The consequence has been, that ninety-nine hundredths of this Club are people who rather seek to obtain a sort of standing by belonging to the Athenæum." The Athenæum subsequently made heavier use of blackballing in an attempt to maintain its elite reputation.

Sources

Carver, Craig M. *A History of English in Its Own Words.* New York: HarperCollins, 1991.

Simpson, J. A., and E. S. C. Weiner, eds. *The Oxford English Dictionary.* 2d ed. Oxford: Clarendon Press, 1989.

Timbs, John. *Clubs and Club Life in London: With Anecdotes of Its Famous Coffee Houses, Hostelries, and Taverns, from the Seventeenth Century to the Present Time.* London: Chatto and Windus, 1908.

Blacklist. ***A list of people singled out for mistreatment or boycotts.***

The term *blacklist* was used in England as early as 1619, but it was popularized during the Restoration as part of the attempt to identify and punish the men responsible for the execution of Charles I. After the king was beheaded in 1649, the royal family had fled the country, but his son Charles II made a triumphant return to the throne in 1660. The new king quickly passed the Act of Indemnity and Oblivion, granting a general pardon to all those who had wronged him and his father. The only people excluded from the pardon were the regicides—the men who had actually participated in the trial and execution of Charles I.

A blacklist identified 67 individuals guilty of this capital crime, but Charles II, eager to heal the wounds of civil war and unrest, was reluctant to execute such a large number of influential people. The list was whittled down to the major culprits, while the others were to stand trial for lesser offenses and given sentences short of the death penalty. Many on the list fled the country, but eventually 13 of the so-called regicides were tried and executed. Many of the men most despised by the Restoration government, such as Oliver Cromwell and Henry Ireton, had already died of natural causes. Their bodies were exhumed, hanged, dismembered, and thrown into a common pit.

In the twentieth century, the most famous example of blacklisting occurred in Hollywood during the 1950s, when screenwriters, actors, and directors were targeted for their suspected communist sympathies and banned from working in the movie industry. Unsubstantiated rumors and innuendo fueled the accusations, and since this episode, the blacklist has frequently been associated with witch-hunt tactics.

Sources

Fritze, Ronald H. *Historical Dictionary of Stuart England, 1603–1689.* Westport, CT: Greenwood Press, 1996.

Hendrickson, Robert. *The Facts on File Encyclopedia of Word and Phrase Origins.* New York: Facts on File, 1987.

Hutton, Ronald. *The Restoration: A Political and Religious History of England and Wales, 1658–1667.* Oxford: Clarendon Press, 1985.

Blackmail. ***To extort something valuable from an individual in exchange for leaving the person's reputation or person unharmed.***

Although the word *blackmail* has become associated with disreputable activities, it was originally a legitimate way of paying rent in the Scottish Highlands of the sixteenth century. Among the Scots, *mail* was an ancient word for tribute. Landlords assessed rent in silver, commonly known as white mail. Because farmers were rarely able to accumulate large amounts of silver coins, payment in goods, services, or produce was often accepted in lieu of silver. Such in-kind payment was known as *black mail.* There was a risk involved in black mail; while the value of a coin was set, greedy landlords could alter the value of goods by proclaiming that a cow was unhealthy, or that there was a surplus of barley that year, or that the quality of wool was not very good. The wildly fluctuating value of black mail, in which the farmer almost always came out the loser, gave the term an exploitative connotation. Later, when the borders of Scotland were under pressure from English invaders, Highland chiefs demanded black mail as "protection" money, although whether the farmer was being protected from the English or Scottish freebooters was certainly up for debate.

By the nineteenth century, blackmail had become one word, and it referred exclusively to payments extorted by pressure and intimidation.

Sources

Hendrickson, Robert. *The Facts on File Encyclopedia of Word and Phrase Origins.* New York: Facts on File, 1987.

Mish, Frederick C. *The Merriam-Webster New Book of Word Histories.* Springfield, IL: Merriam-Webster, 1991.

Simpson, J. A., and E. S. C. Weiner, eds. *The Oxford English Dictionary.* 2d ed. Oxford: Clarendon Press, 1989.

Blarney stone, kissing the. ***Possessing the skill to pass off fibs, flatteries, and exaggerations with a straight face.***

Blarney Castle, in County Cork, Ireland, was in possession of the McCarthy family for centuries. In the sixteenth century the lord of this castle was Cormac MacDermott MacCarthy, the baron of Blarney. Elizabeth I of England, attempting to extend her royal prerogatives in Ireland, decreed that the lords of Ireland would henceforth take their tenure directly from the English Crown rather than from the clan. MacCarthy agreed to comply with the queen's order, but he managed to avoid actually doing so. Elizabeth's advisors repeated the demand several times, but each time the baron sent elegantly worded replies that sidestepped the queen's request.

After yet another gracious but evasive message from the baron, the exasperated queen responded, "This is all Blarney; what he says he never means." Since then, *blarney* has referred to flattering speech that is deceptive in nature or purpose.

A legend later developed around a stone in a tower of the ruins of the castle. Set in the top of a window about 100 feet off the ground, it bears the inscription: *Cormach MacCarthy fortis me fierie fecit* A.D. *1446* ("Cormac MacCarthy made me become strong, A.D. 1446"). The origin of this legend derives from a folktale about Cormac MacCarthy. It was said that when Cormac was worried about losing his property in a lawsuit, a spirit came to him in a dream. The spirit instructed Cormac to "Kiss the stone you come face to face with in the morning, and the right words will pour out of you." Cormac kissed the first stone he saw upon waking, and won his lawsuit. In fear that anyone in Ireland would come to his estate to kiss his charmed stone, Cormac hid the Blarney stone in the parapet of a tower, where it rests to this day. Kissing this stone is said to endow the individual with the gift of glib, flattering speech.

Sources

Leach, Maria, ed. *Funk & Wagnalls Standard Dictionary of Folklore, Mythology and Legend.* New York: Funk & Wagnalls, 1972.

Lurie, Charles. *Everyday Sayings.* Detroit, MI: Gale Research, 1968.

McHenry, Robert, ed. *The New Encyclopedia Britannica.* 15th ed. Chicago: Encyclopedia Britannica, 1992.

Mish, Frederick C. *The Merriam-Webster New Book of Word Histories.* Springfield, IL: Merriam-Webster, 1991.

Bligh, Captain. ***Strict, tyrannical leadership and inept use of authority.***

When historical events are translated into novels or movies, personalities and events are often distorted in favor of creating an exciting tale. In the case of the mutiny on the *Bounty,* the most famous naval mutiny in history, Captain Bligh's character was slanted to make him an unambiguous villain.

William Bligh (1754–1817) was an accomplished navigator, having sailed around the world with Captain Cook and producing several important surveys for the Royal Navy. It was on a 1789 voyage to the South Pacific to transport breadfruit that the notorious mutiny occurred. Although the exact causes may never be known, it is likely that Bligh's ferocious temper played a large role in it. Bligh was a strict and exacting captain, but he made far less use of corporal punishment than many other captains of his day, and living conditions on his ship were good. However, in the end, his verbal abuse severely demoralized his crew. Some members of the crew mutinied, and Bligh and 18 loyal crewmen were cast adrift in a tiny lifeboat that was only 23 feet long. They had few provisions on board and no chart. In a phenomenal display of seamanship, Bligh navigated the boat over 3,600 miles to safety to a small island off the coast of Java. The voyage lasted three months, and six of the men perished. Bligh was hailed as a hero in Britain, but he was subjected to two more mutinies before he retired. One of these involved the entire fleet, and Bligh was only one of many officers placed ashore. The last occurred while Bligh was serving as governor of New South Wales in Australia.

The 1932 novel *Mutiny on the Bounty* by Charles Nordhoff and James Norman Hall contained a damning portrait of Bligh, but it was the movies that would fix his lasting public image. Sinister portrayals by the brilliant actors Charles Laughton in 1934 and Anthony Hopkins in 1994 turned Bligh into an eponym for harsh, sadistic leadership.

Sources

Comfort, N. A. *Brewer's Politics: A Phrase and Fable Dictionary.* London: Cassel, 1993.

Dening, Greg. *Mr. Bligh's Bad Language: Passion, Power, and the Theatre on the Bounty.* Cambridge: Cambridge University Press, 1992.

McHenry, Robert, ed. *The New Encyclopedia Britannica.* 15th ed. Chicago: Encyclopedia Britannica, 1992.

Stephen, Leslie, and Sidney Lee, eds. *The Dictionary of National Biography.* London: Oxford University Press, 1921.

Blind eye, to turn a blind eye. ***To deliberately ignore.***

This phrase dates to the battle of Copenhagen in 1801, which was fought between the British and Danish navies in the Napoleonic wars. On the British side, Admiral Horatio Nelson (1758–1805) was serving as second in command to the aging Admiral Hyde Parker. Nelson's ships were bearing the brunt of intense cannon fire, while Parker was four miles away at the opposite end of the harbor, with his field of view almost totally obscured by the thick smoke of cannon fire. After three hours of combat Parker signaled Nelson to discontinue the action. From Nelson's vantage point, almost every Danish ship was so badly crippled that victory was close. Nelson fought on, and when a fellow officer hesitantly called Nelson's attention to the signal he was obviously ignoring, the admiral reportedly replied, "I have only one eye and have a right to be blind sometimes." Raising his telescope to his blind eye, he looked directly at Parker's ship and said, "I really do not see the signal."

The battle was won an hour later by the British. Parker was aware of Nelson's insubordination, but he realized that a court-martial proceeding against Nelson for a heroic victory would have been embarrassing, so he chose to ignore the matter.

Sources

Simpson, J. A., and E. S. C. Weiner, eds. *The Oxford English Dictionary.* 2d ed. Oxford: Clarendon Press, 1989.

Walder, David. *Nelson, A Biography.* New York: Dial Press, 1978.

Whipple, Addison B. *Fighting Sail.* Alexandria, VA: Time-Life Books, 1978.

Blitz, blitzkrieg. ***A fast, furious assault that overwhelms its object.***

In German *blitz* means lightning, and in the late 1930s writer Eugen Hadamovsky described the Nazi attack on Poland as a *blitzkrieg,* meaning a lightninglike strike. The strategy behind the blitzkrieg was to launch a massive tank attack in conjunction with strong air cover. Rather than overwhelming the enemy with superior numbers, a fast, surprise attack of concentrated firepower would paralyze the opponent's ability to respond. The tactic was first tested by the Germans in the Spanish Civil War (1936–1939) and again in the 1939 invasion of Poland. During World War II, Belgium, France, and the Netherlands would all experience the terror of a blitzkrieg. The shorter term *blitz* was widely used to refer to the Nazi air attacks on Britain.

The term caught on in popular idiom, and by the end of the war it was used figuratively in reference to developments in business, sports, and even romance.

Sources

Ammer, Christine. *Fighting Words: From War, Rebellion, and Other Combative Capers.* New York: Paragon House, 1989.

McHenry, Robert, ed. *The New Encyclopedia Britannica.* 15th ed. Chicago: Encyclopedia Britannica, 1992.

Zentner, Christian, and Friedemann Budurftig, eds. *Encyclopedia of the Third Reich.* New York: Macmillan, 1991.

Blockbuster. ***A tremendous success, usually in reference to the release of a book or movie.*** During World War II, *blockbuster* referred to 4,000-pound bombs, which were capable of leveling an entire city block. The Royal Air Force dropped the first such bomb on Berlin in 1941. Packed with nearly two tons of high explosives, the bomb released a shock wave that could be felt by aircraft crews flying 14,000 feet above. The bomb's capacity was later increased to hold up to 8,000 pounds of explosives. This model was known as a "factory buster," as it was said that no building could withstand a direct hit.

By the 1960s the word *blockbuster* had been adopted by the entertainment industry in reference to the extravagant expenditures that were lavished on particular motion pictures. By loading a film with star-power and special effects, movie executives were hoping to create a product that would put all competition in its shadow.

Sources

Crane, Conrad C. *Bombs, Cities, and Civilians: American Airpower Strategy in World War II.* Lawrence: University Press of Kansas, 1993.

Parrish, Thomas, and S. L. A. Marshall. *Simon and Schuster Encyclopedia of World War II.* New York: Simon and Schuster, 1978.

Quick, John. *Dictionary of Weapons and Military Terms.* New York: McGraw-Hill, 1973.

Radford, Edwin. *Unusual Words and How They Came About.* New York: Philosophical Library, 1946.

Blood and iron. ***A policy that requires war or the threat of war for its implementation.*** Coined by Otto von Bismarck (1815–1898) in 1862, the expression reflects his authoritarian approach to government. Bismarck's goal was to implement a series of liberal reforms such as national unification, improved education, pensions, and a loosening of the control of the church over social institutions. In his view, these changes could only be successful if German society was united behind them, and such cohesion could only be achieved if there was an external enemy. As Bismarck stated, "It is not by means of speeches and majority resolutions that the great issues of the day will be decided—that was the mistake of 1848 and 1849—but by blood and iron." Despite the authoritarian means by which Bismarck achieved his aims, the Prussian standard of living was the envy of the world for decades.

Bismarck, meanwhile, always claimed that *blood and iron* was misinterpreted by those eager to believe he had tyrannical designs on Germany and the rest of Europe. In his view, he was creating a strong militaristic state whose population shared a sense of community. Without that, the society would be a prison, "against whose wardens the captives would rise one day."

Sources
Crankshaw, Edward. *Bismarck.* Harmondsworth: Penguin, 1983.
Darmstaedter, F. *Bismarck and the Creation of the Second Reich.* New York: Russell and Russell, 1965.
Simpson, J. A., and E. S. C. Weiner, eds. *The Oxford English Dictionary.* 2d ed. Oxford: Clarendon Press, 1989.

Bloody Mary. *A cocktail of vodka and tomato juice.*

The Mary in question was Mary Tudor (1516–1558), whose primary objective upon taking the throne was to restore the Roman Catholic Church to England. Mary's father, Henry VIII, had broken with Rome in order to divorce Mary's mother. Henry established the Anglican Church, and adherence to Catholicism was discouraged in England. The brief reign of his son, Edward VI, committed the kingdom more firmly to Protestant worship. Mary had remained a devout Catholic, and soon after she became queen in 1553, she married the Catholic Philip of Spain. This alliance, together with Mary's desire to reinstate the Roman church among her subjects, threatened the English Protestants. Riots broke out, and the executions began. Some 300 men and women were martyred during Mary's reign.

The sobriquet "bloody Mary" is generally considered to be unfair, since her reign was no more bloody than others of that age. In Germany and France entire villages had been wiped out during the religious and political strife of the sixteenth century. The difference was that Mary was extremely unpopular after she took the throne, and her victims included several high-profile Protestants. Mary's successor, Queen Elizabeth, refused to allow religion to divide the country, and her determination to steer a middle course in religious affairs contrasted starkly with her half-sister's stridency—which served to blacken further the memory of Mary's reign.

Sources
Erickson, Carolly. *Bloody Mary.* Garden City, NJ: Doubleday, 1978.
Stephen, Leslie, and Sidney Lee, eds. *The Dictionary of National Biography.* London: Oxford University Press, 1921.
Weir, Alison. *The Children of Henry VIII.* New York: Ballantine Books, 1996.
Williamson, David. *Brewer's British Royalty.* London: Cassell, 1996.

Bloody shirt, waving the. *To inflame public opinion by calling attention to someone's sacrifice.*

In the United States, the phrase *wave the bloody shirt* usually alluded to the Civil War. As federal elections resumed after the war, northern Republicans felt they were entitled to rule the Union uncontested, since the Democrats were blamed for starting the war. Throughout the 1870s and 1880s, a favorite political tactic to whip up animosity against the South and the tainted Democrats was to remind voters of the sacrifices of their slain brothers, husbands, and sons. *Waving the bloody shirt* helped the Republicans hold the White House for twenty years after the Civil War. The tactic was employed whenever the South fell under indictment. During Reconstruction, Benjamin Franklin Butler held up before a crowd a blood-stained shirt that he claimed had belonged to an Ohio carpetbagger who had been assaulted for trying to win justice for black men in Mississippi.

Displaying blood-stained garments is an age-old device to incite revenge. Marcus Antonius displayed Julius Caesar's bloody robes to the populace after his assassination. In the eighteenth century, young Virginia lawyer Patrick Henry displayed to the jury the blood-stained clothes of a murdered man. In lieu of bloody clothes, prosecutors are often eager to bring to court grisly autopsy photos, which produce the same effect.

Sources
Hendrickson, Robert. *Facts on File Encyclopedia of Word and Phrase Origins.* New York: Facts on File, 1987.
Safire, William. *Safire's Political Dictionary.* New York: Random House, 1978.
Stimpson, George. *A Book about American Politics.* New York: Harper, 1952.
Trefousse, Hans Louis. *Historical Dictionary of Reconstruction.* New York: Greenwood Press, 1991.

Bloomers. ***Loose pants worn by women at the end of the nineteenth century.***

Amelia Jenks Bloomer (1818–1894) was a social reformer and advocate for women's rights. In 1849 she founded the feminist newspaper *The Lily* (1849–1855), which is believed to be the first newspaper in the United States edited entirely by a woman. Using *The Lily* as a medium of publicity, Bloomer advocated pants for women as a more practical and liberated alternative to the dress, with its restrictive corset and petticoats. She defended the actress Fanny Kemble for wearing "pantalettes," and soon Bloomer herself began appearing in this new fashion, which quickly became known as the "Bloomer Costume." For several years she shunned dresses altogether in favor of these loose pants, claiming that long skirts and petticoats collected dirt and were therefore unsanitary. When ministers denounced the concept of women dressing as men, Bloomer observed that both Adam and Eve wore the same type of fig leaves. Eventually she decided that the controversy surrounding her attire was drawing attention away from her other work in the feminist movement, so she reverted to wearing dresses.

The next group of women who began wearing bloomers in large numbers were female athletes. Women of the early 1900s who participated in track and field events were often ridiculed for the shortened bloomers and sleeveless tops they wore. As sports such as cycling, tennis, and skating became popular recreational pastimes among women, the sight of a woman in bloomers became less shocking, if not altogether respectable.

Wearing pants became acceptable for women when large numbers entered the factories during World War II, a place where skirts were impractical. At the same time, actress Katherine Hepburn made wearing slacks glamorous and fashionable, rather than merely functional.

Sources

Gattey, Charles Neilson. *The Bloomer Girls.* New York: Coward-McCann, 1968.

James, Edward T, ed. *Notable American Women, 1607–1950: A Biographical Dictionary.* Cambridge, MA: Belknap Press, 1971.

Weatherford, Doris. *American Women's History.* New York: Prentice-Hall, 1994.

Whitman, Alden. *American Reformers.* New York: H. W. Wilson, 1985.

Blue blood. ***Of noble or aristocratic lineage.***

This expression comes from Spain during the Moorish occupation. Beginning in the seventh century, the Moors began to cross the Strait of Gibraltar and take control of the peninsula. They met with little resistance from the disorganized local population, who were often permitted to keep their land in exchange for tribute. The Moors controlled three-quarters of Spain for over 700 years. The influx of the Moors meant that medieval Spain had three distinct cultural and racial groups: Europeans, Arabs, and Jews. Attempting to guard their lineage, the Spanish aristocracy limited its circle to those with no taint of Moorish ancestry and called themselves *blue bloods,* possibly derived from the visible veins of fair-complexioned Europeans. In a figurative sense, *blue blood* has become synonymous with good breeding and family background.

Sources

Davis, Paul K. *Encyclopedia of Invasions and Conquests from Ancient Times to the Present.* Santa Barbara, CA: ABC-CLIO, 1996.

Simpson, J. A., and E. S. C. Weiner, eds. *The Oxford English Dictionary.* 2d ed. Oxford: Clarendon Press, 1989.

Blue hen's chickens. ***Someone from the state of Delaware.***

During the American Revolution, a regiment of Scots-Irish immigrants from the colony of Delaware was especially noted for its bravery in battle. The regiment was led by Captain Jonathan Caldwell, a man who took great pleasure in raising gamecocks. Several of the fighting birds traveled with the regiment to keep the troops amused during the long hours of inactivity. At the Battle of Camden in 1780, the Delaware regiment was confronted by a superior force but fought valiantly despite terrible odds. At the end of the day, their numbers were reduced from 500 to 175. The surviving soldiers were formed into a company and incorporated into a Maryland regiment. There the Delaware soldiers' reputation for bravery and fierce fighting skills continued, and they were dubbed the *blue hen's chickens* because of their blue gamecocks, a breed renowned for vicious fighting skills. The company took great pride in its name, and the expression was later applied to anyone from the state of Delaware.

Sources

Evans, Ivor H., ed. *Brewer's Dictionary of Phrase and Fable.* 14th ed. New York: Harper and Row, 1989.
Stimpson, George. *A Book about a Thousand Things.* New York: Harper and Brothers, 1946.

Blue laws. ***Laws regulating work or commerce on Sundays.***

There are two possible derivations for this term. It may originate from Samuel A. Peter's *General History of Connecticut* (1781), which details at great length the stiff and uncompromising regulations enacted by the Puritan settlers in New England. The book was printed on blue paper, and it is possible that *blue law* was a reference to this work. A more likely source dates back to the colonial connotation of *blue,* which was used in reference to rigid piety. Maryland's law of 1692, for example, was specific in its regulation of Sunday activities: "No person or persons whatsoever within this Province, shall work or do any bodily labor or occupation upon the Lord's Day, commonly called Sunday . . . (the works of absolute necessity and mercy always excepted) . . . nor shall abuse or profane the Lord's Day by drunkenness, swearing. . . . And if any person or persons shall offend in any or all of these premises, he shall forfeit and pay for every offense the sum of one hundred pounds of tobacco."

Blue laws persisted into the twentieth century, with various states prohibiting such Sunday activities as the sale of liquor, engaging in dancing, card playing, public sports, smoking, or even digging for clams. Since the 1960s blue laws have steadily been repealed, although the prohibition on the sale of alcohol on Sunday continues in many states.

Sources

Chase, Harold W., ed. *The Guide to American Law: Everyone's Legal Encyclopedia.* St. Paul: West Publishing Co., 1983.
Faragher, John M. *The Encyclopedia of Colonial and Revolutionary America.* New York: Facts on File, 1990.
Laband, David N., and Deborah H. Heinbuch. *Blue Laws: The History, Economics, and Politics of Sunday-closing Laws.* Lexington, MA: Lexington Books, 1987.

Bluestocking. ***A woman with intellectual or literary interests.***

In eighteenth-century England, card playing and tea parties were the primary social diversions of upper-class women. The formation of literary societies, open to both sexes, was an attempt to inject some intellectual activity into women's lives. In Bath, Mrs. Elizabeth Montagu began one such group. Because one of their most prominent members, Benjamin Stillingfleet, habitually wore blue stockings, the literary society decided to draw from historical precedent to call attention to their membership. In fifteenth-century Venice, a well-known intellectual society, the *della calza,* had worn distinctive stockings as a sign of their membership; the Bath group informally adopted the name bluestocking. When the movement for women's rights began to gather momentum in the nineteenth century, *bluestocking* assumed a derogatory connotation, implying that women with a passion for learning or intellectual pursuits necessarily lacked feminine graces. As the philosopher Jean-Jacques Rousseau claimed, "A bluestocking is a woman who will remain a spinster as long as there are sensible men on earth."

Sources

McHenry, Robert, ed. *The New Encyclopedia Britannica.* 15th ed. Chicago: Encyclopedia Britannica, 1992.
Myers, Sylvia Harcstark. *The Bluestocking Circle: Women, Friendship, and the Life of the Mind in Eighteenth-century England.* Oxford: Clarendon Press, 1990.

Stephen, Leslie and Sidney Lee, eds. *The Dictionary of National Biography.* London: Oxford University Press, 1921.

Blurb. ***A brief descriptive sentence or paragraph used to promote books or other publications.***

For most of the nineteenth century, book covers were generally plain, and any decoration was limited to some scroll designs stamped into the binding and perhaps the author's name and the book title in fancy lettering on the front. In the late 1890s, book jackets were introduced by American publishers, and advertisers were called in to provide advice on how the jacket should be designed. For the first time, there was a convenient way to put an interesting illustration on a cover, descriptive text on the flaps, and brief promotional statements from celebrities and writers testifying to the value of the book.

The text on the book jacket was initially referred to as "flap copy," and the cover illustrations often featured attractive young women who were either sweet, languishing, heroic, or in distress. In 1907 humorist Gelett Burgess selected for the cover of his book *Are You a Bromide?* a drawing of a fetching young lady in a pose that exaggerated her exceptionally lush figure. He named the lass "Miss Belinda Blurb," and soon all the promotional material that appeared on the jackets of books became known as *blurb* material.

Sources

Holt, Alfred H. *Phrase and Word Origins.* New York: Dover Publications, 1961.

McHenry, Robert, ed. *The New Encyclopedia Britannica.* 15th ed. Chicago: Encyclopedia Britannica, 1992.

Mish, Frederick C. *The Merriam-Webster New Book of Word Histories.* Springfield, IL: Merriam-Webster, 1991.

Schreuders, Piet. *Paperbacks U.S.A.: A Graphic History, 1939–1959.* San Diego: Blue Dolphin Enterprises, 1981.

Bob's your uncle. ***Indicates everything will be all right or has been taken care of.***

Although Arthur James Balfour (1848–1930) was a wise, intelligent man who made a number of important contributions to international statesmanship, his achievements were initially overlooked by the British people because of his close association with his uncle, Robert Arthur Talbot Gascoyne-Cecil, the powerful marquess of Salisbury. Salisbury was the leader of the Conservative party in the House of Lords and became prime minister of Britain in 1885. When young James entered Parliament, he was immediately placed in a number of key positions. When Salisbury retired from politics in 1902, his nephew became prime minister. People could not help but wonder how much of Balfour's meteoric rise to power was due to pure nepotism, and the phrase *Bob's your uncle* was coined to refer to situations in which one's path had been smoothed by powerful connections.

Sources

McHenry, Robert, ed. *The New Encyclopedia Britannica.* 15th ed. Chicago: Encyclopedia Britannica, 1992.

Simpson, J. A., and E. S. C. Weiner, eds. *The Oxford English Dictionary.* 2d ed. Oxford: Clarendon Press, 1989.

Stephen, Leslie, and Sidney Lee, eds. *The Dictionary of National Biography.* London: Oxford University Press, 1921.

Bogart. ***To refuse to share a cigarette or marijuana joint.***

Images from the golden era of Hollywood in the 1930s and 1940s frequently featured glamorous movie stars smoking cigarettes. Sirens of the silver screen dangled thin cigarettes from their perfectly manicured hands while trails of smoke wafted upward to frame their faces. Tough guys always seemed to brood more effectively when they took a nice long pull on a cigarette. No movie star was tougher than Humphrey Bogart (1899–1957), and he was a master at using a cigarette as an acting device. Bogart took long, slow pulls for every move, from pondering a dilemma to seducing a woman. He was so closely associated with smoking that his name became a verb: to *bogart* became slang for hogging a cigarette.

Humphrey Bogart died at the age of 58

from throat cancer, which was no doubt exacerbated by smoking.

Sources

Coe, Jonathan. *Humphrey Bogart: Take It and Like It.* London: Bloomsbury, 1991.
Lighter, J. E., ed. *Random House Dictionary of American Slang.* New York: Random House, 1994.

Bolivia. ***A nation in western South America.***

Simon Bolivar (1783–1830) is one of the few men in history to have a nation named for him during his lifetime. Born into an aristocratic Venezuelan family, he benefited from wealth, education, and family connections. Bolivar traveled to Spain to complete his education in 1799 and imbibed the ideas of the European Enlightenment, especially regarding constitutional principles of governance. As Napoleon was hammering out the French imperial system, young Bolivar returned to Venezuela, where he joined the underground Latin American independence movement. When Napoleon's invasion of Spain in 1808 undermined Spanish authority in the New World, Bolivar was ready. The next fifteen years of his life were spent in the diplomatic, military, and political struggle to achieve liberation for South America.

Despite some major defeats, Bolivar was regarded as a hero, and in 1819 he was appointed president of Grand Colombia, which comprised what is now Colombia, Ecuador, Panama, and Venezuela. In 1824 he organized the government of the newly founded Peru and repeated his efforts for Bolivia in 1825. Toward the end of his life, his dominance over South American affairs stirred resentment and suspicion, and he was distinctly unpopular when he died of tuberculosis in 1830. However, later historians idealized Bolivar's unflagging efforts to win independence for the people of South America and played down his dictatorial tendencies.

Sources

Eggenberger, David I., ed. *The McGraw-Hill Encyclopedia of World Biography.* New York: McGraw-Hill, 1973.
Madariaga, Salvador de. *Bolivar.* Coral Gables: University of Miami Press, 1967.
McHenry, Robert, ed. *The New Encyclopedia Britannica.* 15th ed. Chicago: Encyclopedia Britannica, 1992.

Book burner. ***Used disparagingly for someone who attempts to restrict access to works he or she condemns.***

Censorship in the form of huge bonfires dates back to ancient times. The Chinese emperor Tsin Chi Hwangti, better known for building the Great Wall of China, was convinced that men who become too wise would become worthless, so in 213 B.C., he ordered the burning of all books that did not deal specifically with agriculture, science, or medicine. To press his point, any "worthless" authors who could be found were executed. Oxford University held a book burning in 1683. An assassination attempt on the life of Charles II prompted the university professors to destroy books that contained "damnable doctrines, destructive to the sacred person of princes, their State and Government, and of all Human Society." Perhaps the strangest episode occurred in colonial North America. Books that had been deemed objectionable were considered criminal in themselves and could be publicly whipped before burning.

A particularly notorious example of book burning is also the most recent. Four months after Adolph Hitler became chancellor of Germany, a procession of students marched to a public square opposite the University of Berlin and burned an estimated 20,000 books. The criteria were dictated by Joseph Goebbels and included any books that "act subversively on our future or strike at the root of German thought, the German home, and the driving force of our people." The nightmarish image of Nazi bonfires has helped to make *book burner* a derogatory term for advocates of certain types of censorship.

Sources

Green, Jonathan. *The Encyclopedia of Censorship.* New York: Facts on File, 1989.
Zentner, Christian, and Friedemann Budurftig, eds. *Encyclopedia of the Third Reich.* New York: Macmillan, 1991.

Boondocks. ***Rural, backwoods area.***

U.S. Marines stationed in the Philippines during World War II coined *boondocks* from the Tagalog word *bundok,* which meant "mountain." In the soldiers' usage, the term encompassed any wild, dense territory that was difficult to penetrate. Stateside, the word was applied to the wilderness areas surrounding the training camps where recruits practiced field maneuvers. Because it was associated with roughing it in an isolated area, boondocks seeped into the mainstream as an unflattering description of rural areas.

Sources

Dickson, Paul. *War Slang: Fighting Words and Phrases of Americans from the Civil War to the Gulf War.* New York: Pocket Books, 1994.

Hendrickson, Robert. *Facts on File Encyclopedia of Word and Phrase Origins.* New York: Facts on File, 1987.

Simpson, J. A., and E. S. C. Weiner, eds. *The Oxford English Dictionary.* 2d ed. Oxford: Clarendon Press, 1989.

Boondoggle. ***Useless busy work, especially that funded by the government.***

The word *boondoggle* had no negative connotation when it was coined in the 1920s. Boy Scouts referred to the decorative, braided leather lanyards they wore on their uniforms as boondoggles, and it was also slang for simple handmade crafts. During the Great Depression, the term assumed a new character. Given the massive unemployment, Roosevelt's New Deal created a wide variety of jobs in areas in which many people felt federal government intervention was inappropriate. Agencies commissioned people to create artwork, write plays, and clear trails in parks. One supervisor, Robert C. Marshall, testified that his people were employed making "leather crafts, three-ply carvings, and boondoggles." Reporters latched onto the boondoggles as an example of busywork and as the government's waste of taxpayers' money. In a speech to relief workers, President Roosevelt tried to turn the table on his critics: "If we can boondoggle ourselves out of the depression," he declared, "that word is going to be enshrined in the hearts of the American people for years to come." Subsequent decades have not vindicated his prediction.

Sources

Hendrickson, Robert. *Facts on File Encyclopedia of Word and Phrase Origins.* New York: Facts on File, 1987.

Mish, Frederick C. *The Merriam-Webster New Book of Word Histories.* Springfield, IL: Merriam-Webster, 1991.

Simpson, J. A., and E. S. C. Weiner, eds. *The Oxford English Dictionary.* 2d ed. Oxford: Clarendon Press, 1989.

Stimpson, George. *A Book about American Politics.* New York: Harper, 1952.

Bootlegger. ***Someone who makes or sells liquor illegally.***

With the exception of a few tribes, alcohol was unknown to Native Americans before the arrival of Europeans. Having had no contact with it, the Indians had not developed a set of social norms to govern alcohol consumption. Moreover, some tribes added it to religious rites that employed psychoactive drugs to induce visions. As a result, a large number of Indians slipped into alcoholism. In 1834, the Indian Trade and Intercourse Act was signed to prohibit the sale of alcohol to Indians. To circumvent this law, traders would slip flasks of alcohol into their boots. According to one estimate, offering alcohol in trade instead of other European goods could bring five times as many animal skins.

During Prohibition (1920–1933), traffic in illegal liquor skyrocketed, and *bootlegging* became much more elaborate than merely hiding an extra flask on one's person. Boats, trucks, and trains were used in the transport of liquor, and entire crime syndicates rose and fell based on their success in the bootleg business. During Prohibition, Americans probably consumed more than 100 million gallons of illegal liquor per year. Even after its repeal, the bootleg industry continued to thrive. The quest to avoid paying taxes on alcohol likely means there will always be bootleggers.

Sources

Jaffe, Jerome H., ed. *Encyclopedia of Drugs and Alcohol.* New York: Macmillan Library Reference USA, 1995.

Kellner, Esther. *Moonshine: Its History and Folklore.* Indianapolis: Bobbs-Merrill, 1971.
Sifakis, Carl. *The Encyclopedia of American Crime.* New York: Facts on File, 1982.

Bork. ***To destroy a candidate for a position by demonizing and distorting his or her views.***
Judge Robert Bork (1927–) was not the first qualified candidate for an important position to be defeated for political reasons, but his experience was such a textbook case of vilification that his name became an eponym. Pluralistic societies are reluctant to acknowledge that people of exceptional ability can be denied public office merely because of their political philosophy. It is easier to defeat a nomination by dredging up damaging material from the candidate's past, gleefully dangling it before the eyes of the public in order to prove that the candidate is not suitable for the appointment. If there is no scandal to be found, the person's ideology must be attacked and presented in a manner that will arouse opposition.

In 1987 Justice Lewis Powell announced that he would resign from the United States Supreme Court. Because the remaining bench was evenly split between liberals and conservatives, whoever filled the vacant seat would be the swing vote. Pending cases involved abortion, affirmative action, and other controversies that promised to affect broad segments of society. When President Ronald Reagan nominated Judge Bork, a man with a long record of handing down conservative decisions, liberal forces joined ranks to defeat the nomination. Uncovering a scandal in the candidate's personal life has been the tried-and-true method of demonstrating an individual's unsuitability, but when Bork proved to be scandal-free, opponents attacked and disparaged his intellectual philosophy.

A campaign of advertisements and grassroots activism was mounted to block the nomination. On the day of the nomination, Senator Edward Kennedy launched the first salvo when he described Robert Bork's vision for American society as one in which "women would be forced into back-alley abortions, blacks would sit at segregated lunch counters, rogue police could break down citizens' doors in midnight raids, school children could not be taught about evolution, writers and artists could be censored at the whim of the government, and the doors of the federal courts would be shut on the fingers of millions of citizens." Other gross distortions of Bork's judicial rulings continued over the course of the next four months, and his confirmation was ultimately denied by the Senate.

The *Wall Street Journal* was the first to coin the expression *borked,* in reference to the systematic destruction of a nominee's reputation.

Sources

Bronner, Ethan. *Battle for Justice: How the Bork Nomination Shook America.* New York: W. W. Norton, 1989.
Gitenstein, Mark. *Matters of Principle: An Insider's Account of America's Rejection of Robert Bork's Nomination to the Supreme Court.* New York: Simon and Schuster, 1992.
Goode, Stephen. "Robert Hernon Bork: Judge, Lawyer, Legal Scholar, Educator." *Insight on the News* 13, no. 27 (1997): 16–18.
Nocera, Joseph. "Getting Borked." *Gentlemen's Quarterly* 65, no. 9 (1995): 246–253.

Borscht belt. ***Resort hotels in the Catskill Mountains that are owned by and cater to Jewish people.***
Borscht is a soup made from beef stock containing red beets, potatoes, and sour cream. It has always been a very popular dish with the Jews of Eastern Europe, who emigrated in large numbers to the United States in the nineteenth and early twentieth centuries. Throughout this period Jews were often excluded from the social clubs in the Northeast, where many in the upper classes tacitly subscribed to anti-Semitism. Jewish entrepreneurs began to build their own resorts in the Catskill Mountains of New York. In addition to sports and recreation, the resorts offered a wide variety of entertainment, including singers, comedians, and dancers. The performers, often Jewish themselves, called work in these resorts the *borscht*

circuit, from the dish that was so popular with the clientele. The expression now refers to the entire region in which these resorts are located.

Sources

Adams, Joey. *The Borscht Belt.* New York: Bobbs-Merrill, 1966.

Kanfer, Stefan. *A Summer World: The Attempt to Build a Jewish Eden in the Catskills from the Days of the Ghetto to the Rise and Decline of the Borscht Belt.* New York: Farrar, Straus and Giroux, 1989.

Boswell, to be one's Boswell. ***A biographer, or a person who promotes or immortalizes another.***

Samuel Johnson (1709–1784) was an extraordinarily talented essayist, conversationalist, critic, and lexicographer. His *Dictionary of the English Language* (1755) is regarded as the basis for all subsequent English-language dictionaries. His wicked sense of humor was woven into the normally dry prose of a dictionary, as evidenced by his definition of oats: "A grain, which in England is generally given to horses, but in Scotland supports the people." In spite of all of his accomplishments, it was the writings of James Boswell that made Samuel Johnson a legendary figure.

James Boswell (1740–1795) was an ardent admirer of Dr. Johnson, and he sought out and cultivated an abiding friendship with the object of his hero-worship. Throughout the course of their 20-year association, Boswell kept detailed notes of their conversations. Compiling these and other observations, Boswell published the two-volume *Life of Samuel Johnson* in 1791. Frequently cited as the greatest biography in the English language, the work magnifies Johnson. Boswell had created a brilliant forum for Johnson's sparkling wit, keen intelligence, and biting social analysis. In immortalizing Johnson, he himself became an eponym for someone who sings the praises of another.

Sources

Boswell, James. *Boswell's Life of Johnson.* Oxford: Clarendon Press, 1934.

McHenry, Robert, ed. *The New Encyclopedia Britannica.* 15th ed. Chicago: Encyclopedia Britannica, 1992.

Stephen, Leslie, and Sidney Lee, eds. *The Dictionary of National Biography.* London: Oxford University Press, 1921.

Bowdlerize. ***To expurgate material from a work that may be considered offensive.***

Three generations of the Bowdler family were actively involved in a variety of efforts to improve the moral character of the English people. The most famous Bowdler was Thomas (1754–1825), a physician and philanthropist. Although he spent much of his adult life in the admirable but thankless task of reforming English prisons, his name became synonymous with self-righteous prudery because of his efforts to purge literature of obscenity. Claiming that many of the world's great works were flawed by the inclusion of shocking and indecent language, Bowdler believed that "if any word or expression is of such a nature that the first impression it excites is an impression of obscenity, that word ought not to be spoken nor written or printed; and, if printed, it ought to be erased."

In an effort to make great literature "safe" for the entire family, Bowdler began purging the works of Shakespeare. He released *The Family Shakespeare* in 1818, writing in the preface that "Many words and expressions occur which are of so indecent a nature as to render it highly desirable that they should be erased." Despite howls of outrage from critics and defenders of England's most revered playwright, *The Family Shakespeare* sold very well. Bowdler later turned his attention to another English classic, Edward Gibbon's *Decline and Fall of the Roman Empire.* Although he died before the work was finished, his nephew completed the job and had the six-volume, expurgated version published in 1826. Bowdler's nephew noted with pride that because of his family's efforts, such works would no longer "raise a blush on the cheek of modest innocence nor plant a pang in the heart of the devout Christian."

Bowdler's editions were generally ridiculed, and by 1838 the word *bowdlerize* was used in connection with priggish censorship.

Sources

Green, Jonathan. *The Encyclopedia of Censorship.* New York: Facts on File, 1989.

Mish, Frederick C. *The Merriam-Webster New Book of Word Histories.* Springfield, IL: Merriam-Webster, 1991.

Perrin, Noel. *Dr. Bowdler's Legacy: A History of Expurgated Books in England and America.* New York: Atheneum, 1969.

Stephen, Leslie, and Sidney Lee, eds. *The Dictionary of National Biography.* London: Oxford University Press, 1921.

Bowie knife. ***A large fighting knife, about 15 inches long, with a guard piece on the hilt.***

The Bowie knife has become enshrined in the folklore of the Wild West. Tradition has associated the knife with James Bowie (c.1796–1836), the legendary frontiersman and hero of the Alamo. Although his older brother Rezin Pleasant Bowie may have actually designed the weapon, it won its fame through the adventures of Jim. As the story goes, after a fight with an Indian, one of the Bowie brothers commissioned a blacksmith to create a knife with a substantial guard at the base of the hilt to prevent injuries. Designed for hand-to-hand fighting, the knife was more than a foot long and had a thick steel blade capable of cutting through bone.

In 1830 James Bowie was traveling to Texas when he was ambushed by three hired assassins. Using the lethal knife, Bowie killed all three men, decapitating one and splitting another's skull. Stories of the fight made the knife popular throughout the West, and blacksmiths were deluged with requests to produce a knife like Jim Bowie's. Other famous fights using Bowie knives fueled its reputation. In 1837 the speaker of the Arkansas House of Representatives, John Wilson, became enraged when a fellow representative poked fun at him. He buried his 9-inch blade into the chest of his colleague. Expelled from the House, he was later acquitted of murder. Demand for the Bowie knife dropped off after the Civil War, indicating the society's increasing reliance on the court system for the enforcement of justice.

Sources

Beeching, Cyril Leslie. *Dictionary of Eponyms.* London: Clive Bingley, 1979.

Johnson, Allen, and Dumas Malone, eds. *Dictionary of American Biography.* New York: Scribner's, 1964.

Keener, William G. *Bowie Knives.* Columbus: Ohio Historical Society, 1962.

Thorp, Raymond W. *Bowie Knife.* Albuquerque: University of New Mexico Press, 1948.

Boycott. ***To refuse to buy from, associate with, or cooperate with someone or some group, usually as a protest.***

The majority of farming land in nineteenth-century Ireland was held by absentee landowners. One such owner, the earl of Erne, hired Charles Cunningham Boycott (1832–1897) to oversee his estates in County Mayo. Boycott was a retired British army captain and was determined to run an efficient and profitable estate for Lord Erne. Shortly after he became estate manager, a series of bad harvests prompted the Irish tenant farmers to form the Land League, an agrarian organization committed to protecting the living conditions of farmers. In 1880 the Land League requested a reduction in rent because of the poor harvests. Boycott refused, and the league advocated that the community retaliate by refusing to have any commerce or communication with Boycott.

Socially and economically isolated, Boycott was without farmhands and mail delivery and was excluded from local shops. Blacksmiths refused to repair his farm tools, and his servants quit. Boycott appealed to the London press for sympathy, depicting himself as the target of hostile Irish rebels. Pictures of the female members of Boycott's family being forced to toil in the garden and perform other manual labor appeared in British newspapers. Although Boycott had the sympathy of the English, the Irish were steadfast in their insistence that he ease the burden of taxation before they would relent. To harvest his potato crop, he had to import laborers from Ulster, who were guarded by British soldiers as they worked. Boycott finally capitulated and resigned his position the same year. He eventually became an estate agent in Suffolk, England.

Sources

Davitt, Michael. *The Fall of Feudalism in Ireland: Or, The Story of the Land League Revolution.* London: Harper and Brothers, 1904.

Hendrickson, Robert. *Dictionary of Eponyms: Names That Became Words.* New York: Stein and Day, 1985.

Marlow, Joyce. *Captain Boycott and the Irish.* London: Deutsch, 1973.

McHenry, Robert, ed. *The New Encyclopedia Britannica.* 15th ed. Chicago: Encyclopedia Britannica, 1992.

Brahmin, Boston. ***A member of the socially exclusive New England establishment characterized by cultural and aristocratic pretensions.***

Brahman is the highest caste in India—the pinnacle of a system of rigidly defined social ranking based on descent, marriage, and occupation. Brahmans are generally very well educated and enjoy an exclusive position in society as the heirs to thousands of years of aristocratic privilege.

Boston society of the nineteenth century had a class of extremely well-educated, wealthy, and powerful elites. *Boston brahmin* was originally a humorous reference to such distinguished Bostonians as Oliver Wendell Holmes, Henry Wadsworth Longfellow, and Henry Adams. Irish- and Italian-American politicians used the term to rouse popular feeling against the small clique that wielded such control over Boston's industry and finances. Over the years, the association with Boston has diminished, and the expression has broadened to include any group of eastern elites who sit in positions of power, especially in law and banking and at the exclusive universities.

Sources

McHenry, Robert, ed. *The New Encyclopedia Britannica.* 15th ed. Chicago: Encyclopedia Britannica, 1992.

Rice, Stanley. *Hindu Customs and Their Origins.* London: G. Allen and Unwin, Ltd., 1937.

Stutley, Margaret, and James Stutley. *Harper's Dictionary of Hinduism: Its Mythology, Folklore, Philosophy, Literature, and History.* New York: Harper and Row, 1977.

Webber, Elizabeth. *Grand Allusions.* Washington, DC: Farragut Press, 1990.

Braille. ***A system of reading and writing for the blind based on raised dots.***

Louis Braille (1809–1852) was blinded at the age of three in an accident while he was playing in his father's harness shop. For his education, he joined sighted children at the village school, and at the age of 16 he began attending the National Institute for Blind Children in Paris, where he eventually became a teacher. Braille was convinced that the ability to read was essential for the blind, as he doubted that anyone could excel without access to the knowledge stored in books. At the institute the only books at the students' disposal were bulky volumes with raised and embossed letters, which could be discerned by touch. This method was slow and difficult for blind students to follow, and Braille began to seek an alternative method. Braille discovered that a French army officer was developing a language of raised dots and dashes that could be used for transmitting messages on a battlefield at night. Braille modified this system by eliminating the dashes and reducing the size of the characters. Although sighted educators for the blind were initially skeptical of his approach, the enthusiastic response of the blind students indicated that the Braille system was a vast improvement over the use of standard raised letters.

Louis Braille died at the age of 43 from tuberculosis. He is buried in the Pantheon in Paris.

Sources

Hendrickson, Robert. *Dictionary of Eponyms: Names That Became Words.* New York: Stein and Day, 1985.

McHenry, Robert, ed. *The New Encyclopedia Britannica.* 15th ed. Chicago: Encyclopedia Britannica, 1992.

Travers, Bridget, and Jeffrey Muhr, eds. *World of Invention.* Detroit, MI: Gale Research, 1994.

Bread and circuses. ***Free food and entertainment to keep the masses pacified and distracted from more important issues.***

Speculation on the decline of the Roman Empire has kept historians busy for centuries. Contemporary writers at the height of the empire were the first to murmur about the depravity and excesses of the day. The satirist Juvenal (d. A.D. 127) was one of Rome's keenest social critics, and his caustic poetry exposed the corruption of Roman society and the brutalities of humanity in general. Perhaps his most famous epigram was: "People long eagerly for two things . . . bread and circuses." Throughout the first century, the emperor and the senate had been sponsoring free circuses for the Roman people that promised ever-increasing barbarity and innovations in the macabre (see *Roman Holiday*). The entertainment was successful in diverting people's attention from their social and economic problems. Circuses and subsidies continued for centuries, until the empire finally succumbed to internal decay.

Sources

Plass, Paul. *The Game of Death in Ancient Rome: Arena Sport and Political Suicide.* Madison: University of Wisconsin Press, 1995.

Poliakoff, Michael. *Combat Sports in the Ancient World: Competition, Violence, and Culture.* New Haven, CT: Yale University Press, 1987.

Wiedemann, Thomas E. *Emperors and Gladiators.* New York: Routledge, 1995.

Brick. *A good-natured, solid individual.*

This rather curious usage, usually associated with the British expression of approval, "he/she is a brick," is said to derive from a story recorded by Plutarch in the *Life of Lycurgus.* Around 800 B.C. an ambassador from the Greek city Epirus was visiting Sparta. At that time Sparta was ruled by the great lawgiver and king Lycurgus, who believed that walls were unnecessary for a city that had trained its soldiers well. The ambassador commented that it must be very unsafe for Sparta to have no protecting walls, to which Lycurgus replied, "But we have walls, and if you will come with me I will show them to you." The king led the ambassador to a field where the Spartan army was at drill. "There are the walls of Sparta, and every man is a brick."

Etymologists doubt that Plutarch's histories were familiar enough to the British people to account for the expression. Furthermore, *brick* did not refer to a likable, dependable person until the nineteenth century. However, no better attribution has appeared.

Sources

Stimpson, George. *A Book about a Thousand Things.* New York: Harper and Brothers, 1946.

Trench, Richard Chenevix, ed. *Origin of Things Familiar: Sketches on the Origin of Common Things.* Cincinnati, Ohio: United Book Corporation, 1934.

Broadcast. *To transmit a radio or television program.*

One of the earliest forms of planting involved the scattering of seeds by hand and then lightly covering them with soil. Small seeds, such as barley and millet, could be planted in this manner, which was known as *broadcasting.* The Englishman Jethro Tull (1674–1741) later developed a seed drill in order to put seeds into small holes, and after that broadcasting would never be as popular. However, the concept of indiscriminately spreading something around was adapted in the early twentieth century to mean the imparting of information to a general audience. Early radio operators also picked up on the term. Private radio signals can be targeted to a specific receiver, or they can be sent out to any receiver tuned to the correct wavelength. *Broadcasting* was appropriated for the latter type of signal.

A new variation on this word has emerged with the recent explosion of cable television channels and Internet sites. *Narrowcasting* refers to tailoring a channel or site to a specialized segment of the population, such as women over 40 or science fiction buffs.

Sources

Ernle, Rowland E. *English Farming, Past and Present.* Chicago: Quadrangle Books, 1962.

McHenry, Robert, ed. *The New Encyclopedia Britannica.* 15th ed. Chicago: Encyclopedia Britannica, 1992.

Simpson, J. A., and E. S. C. Weiner, eds. *The Oxford English Dictionary.* 2d ed. Oxford: Clarendon Press, 1989.

Broom, jumping the. ***To get married.***
In the antebellum South, jumping over a broomstick was often featured in many weddings between slaves. Slave marriages had to be solemnized by innovative means since slaves could not enter into legal contracts. Moreover, a traditional Christian wedding ceremony, culminating with the words "till death do us part," seemed to challenge the property rights of slaveowners.

Jumping the broomstick symbolized sweeping away the old and welcoming in the new. If it was included in the ceremony, it occurred at the very end. A broomstick was held about a foot off the ground, and the couple would jump over the stick together. There was a superstition that if the pair did not jump at the same moment, the wedding was jinxed and the courting process had to begin again. Also, if one of the partners brushed against or stumbled over the broom, he or she was doomed to be subservient in the marriage.

The tradition probably derived from African rituals. Brides of the Kgatla people of southern Africa, for instance, joined other village women in sweeping the courtyard clean on the morning after the wedding. Performing this chore sealed their admittance into the village community. Another source for jumping the broom may have been the West African tradition of placing sticks on the ground to symbolize the couple's eventual home. In recognition of their heritage, modern African American weddings sometimes incorporate the broomstick ritual into their ceremonies.

Sources

Cole, Harriette. *Jumping the Broom: The African-American Wedding Planner.* New York: Henry Holt, 1995.

Genovese, Eugene D. *Roll, Jordan, Roll: The World the Slaves Made.* New York: Pantheon Books, 1974.

Hudson, Larry E. *To Have and To Hold: Slave Work and Family Life in Antebellum South Carolina.* Athens: University of Georgia Press, 1997.

Brother Jonathan. ***A national nickname for the United States, similar to Uncle Sam.***
The spirit of a nation is often embodied in some character. The British, for example, have John Bull, the bluff, prosperous country squire. The wiry and dapper Uncle Sam, who first appeared in the early nineteenth century, is the best-known personification of the United States. Before Uncle Sam, the most common characterization of the country was Brother Jonathan.

The most plausible theory for the origin of Brother Jonathan is Jonathan Trumbull, governor of Connecticut from 1769 to 1784. Trumbull was one of the few colonial governors who was sympathetic to the American rebels. As the story goes, shortly after being appointed commander of the Continental Army, Washington was traveling through New England organizing and arranging supplies for the newly assembled troops. None of the local officers knew how to remedy the lack of ammunition and provisions, and Washington's response was, "We must consult Brother Jonathan on this." Governor Trumbull furnished invaluable assistance with food, clothing, and munitions, and Washington later said that Trumbull's services "justly entitled him to the first place among patriots." During the war, the American army was always short of supplies, and the expression "someone must consult Brother Jonathan" became a wry catchphrase. After the war the term *Brother Jonathan* became a nickname for Americans in general, although it soon faded in popularity after the creation of Uncle Sam in the nineteenth century. The characterization, though obsolete in the United States, is still occasionally heard in Britain.

Sources

Mish, Frederick C. *The Merriam-Webster New Book of Word Histories.* Springfield, IL: Merriam-Webster, 1991.

Safire, William. *Safire's Political Dictionary.* New York: Random House, 1978.

Stimpson, George. *A Book about a Thousand Things.* New York: Harper and Brothers, 1946.

Bruce and the spider. ***An allegorical tale about Robert the Bruce, advising perseverance and persistence.***
Robert the Bruce (1274–1329) was born into a noble Scottish family in a time when

the Scots were organizing rebellions against English rule. In his youth Bruce supported the rebellion of William Wallace, although he apparently withdrew his support when it became obvious that Wallace would not succeed. Little else is known of Bruce until 1306, when he seized the throne of Scotland. This triggered fierce English retaliation, and Bruce's armies endured a series of disastrous encounters with the English. By the end of the year he was forced to flee for his life to the remote island of Rathlin.

The legend of the spider emerged from this period of isolation. Knowing that he faced overwhelming odds and that many of his supporters, including three of his brothers, had been beheaded, Bruce was doubtful of his ability to keep the throne. Despondent, he watched a spider trying to repair its web. As the creature failed six times, Bruce was struck with the realization that he too had failed six times in battles against the English. When the spider succeeded on its seventh try, Bruce resolved to lead another attack. He left the island in 1307, and his fortunes began to change. Winning several battles, Bruce was able to unite many of the Scottish clans in support of his claim. Although his troops were outnumbered three to one, in 1314 Bruce routed the English in a decisive battle at Bannockburn. This victory established Scottish independence, and Bruce was thereafter known as Robert I, king of Scotland.

A nineteenth-century poem by Eliza Cook immortalized the tale of Bruce and the spider:

> Whenever you find your heart despair
> Of doing some goodly thing
> Cover this strain, try bravely again,
> And remember the Spider and the King!

Sources

Mercatante, Anthony S. *Facts on File Encyclopedia of World Mythology and Legend.* New York: Facts on File, 1988.

Scott, Ronald McNair. *Robert the Bruce: King of Scots.* New York: P. Bedrick Books, 1982.

Stimpson, George. *A Book about a Thousand Things.* New York: Harper and Brothers, 1946.

Bunkum. ***Insincere or hypocritical remarks; often shortened to bunk.***

American politicians are notorious for indulging in tedious speeches, and North Carolina congressman Felix Walker (1753–1828), whose district include the county of Buncombe, was known to be particularly long-winded. On 25 February 1820, the debate in the House on the Missouri Compromise was nearly exhausted when Walker insisted on having another go at the speaker's podium. As was typical of Walker's speeches, it was a rambling and annoying discourse that seemed endless. Other members were ready to call the question and repeatedly begged him to desist. As reported in the *Annals of Congress,* the clamor became so rowdy that Walker had to pause several times while the House was called to order. Walker persevered, declaring, "You're not hurting my feelings, gentlemen. I am not speaking for your ears. I am only talking for Buncombe."

Speaking for Buncombe soon became a jest among members of Congress, used to describe bombastic and excessive political speeches. When the expression spread beyond the Capitol walls, the spelling was changed to *bunkum.* Further abridged, its most common form in the late twentieth century is *bunk.*

Sources

Mish, Frederick C. *The Merriam-Webster New Book of Word Histories.* Springfield, IL: Merriam-Webster, 1991.

Safire, William. *Safire's Political Dictionary.* New York: Random House, 1978.

Simpson, J. A., and E. S. C. Weiner, eds. *The Oxford English Dictionary.* 2d ed. Oxford: Clarendon Press, 1989.

Stimpson, George. *A Book about a Thousand Things.* New York: Harper and Brothers, 1946.

Burke, to be in Burke. ***To be from an aristocratic or socially prominent family.***

John Burke (1787–1848), a genealogist by profession, initially published *Burke's Genealogical and Heraldic History of the Peerage, Baronetage, and Knightage* in 1826. Known simply as *Burke's Peerage,* it was the first book to provide an alphabetical listing of the aristocracy of Great Britain. Keeping track of the profusion of titles, lineages, and heraldry was difficult for even the most ardent royal watcher, and Burke's catalogue of all pertinent information about the aristocracy was an instant bestseller with the socially conscious class. *To be in Burke* meant that an individual was a member of the upper crust.

The success of his book on the peerage inspired Burke to write other histories of the well-to-do. In 1833 *The Portrait Gallery of Distinguished Females, including Beauties of the Courts of George IV and William IV* was published, followed by works that traced the principal families in various British colonies. He tried to launch a periodical entitled *The Patrician,* but it was not nearly as successful as his books. *Burke's Peerage* was revised and issued at irregular intervals until 1847, after which it came out annually. Long after his death Burke's name continued to be attached to other projects that focused on the socially prominent, such as *Burke's Guide to Country Houses, Burke's Presidential Families of the United States of America,* and *Burke's Royal Families of the World.*

Sources

Evans, Ivor H., ed. *Brewer's Dictionary of Phrase and Fable.* 14th ed. New York: Harper and Row, 1989.

Stephen, Leslie, and Sidney Lee, eds. *The Dictionary of National Biography.* London: Oxford University Press, 1921.

C

Cadet. ***A student at a military school.***
Cadet is borrowed from the French word for "younger brother." As in most European countries, aristocratic French families followed the practice of primogeniture, which dictated how land and money was transferred from one generation to another. Instead of dividing wealth equally among the children, the eldest son inherited the title, lands, and most of the money. Since land generated the revenue, younger sons had no source of steady income. It was unthinkable for an aristocrat to engage in manual labor or enter a profession, so military service and the church were the only respectable options. So many of the younger sons of French aristocrats chose the former alternative that *cadet* became synonymous with military service.

While some saw the military as simply the least objectionable of the available choices, others welcomed it as an opportunity to achieve power and wealth. For example, Arthur Wellesley was the fifth son of an earl, but he made a career of the army, and his triumphs against Napoleon earned him a fortune and a title—the Duke of Wellington.

Sources

Mish, Frederick C. *The Merriam-Webster New Book of Word Histories.* Springfield, IL: Merriam-Webster, 1991.

Pool, Daniel. *What Jane Austen Ate and Charles Dickens Knew: From Fox Hunting to Whist—The Facts of Daily Life in Nineteenth Century England.* New York: Simon and Schuster, 1993.

Caesar. ***The title of the Roman emperors.***
Caesar was the family name of Julius Caesar, whose skills as a warrior, diplomat, and statesman have become legendary. After Caesar's assassination, his adopted son and heir, the 18-year-old Gaius Octavius, took his name to obtain leverage and stature among the Roman senators. Octavius emerged from the Roman civil wars victorious, was granted the honorary title *Augustus,* and was henceforth known as Augustus Caesar. His reign as emperor of Rome lasted over forty years (see *Augustan Age*). Although Nero (d. A.D. 68) was the last Roman emperor who could trace his succession to Julius Caesar, all subsequent rulers appended Caesar to their names to associate themselves with the great Julius and Augustus.

Caesar eventually became synonymous with any imperial leader, rather than with the Caesarean family. One variation, *kaiser,* was used by the Holy Roman Empire between 962 and 1806 and also by the German monarchy between 1871 and 1918. The term was adopted by the Russian monarchy in 1547 in the form of *czar,* and in Arabic the word evolved into *qaysar.*

Sources

Bradford, Ernle D. *Julius Caesar: The Pursuit of Power.* New York: Morrow, 1984.

Fuller, J. F. C. *Julius Caesar: Man, Soldier, and Tyrant.* New Brunswick, NJ: Rutgers University Press, 1965.

McHenry, Robert, ed. *The New Encyclopedia Britannica.* 15th ed. Chicago: Encyclopedia Britannica, 1992.

Simpson, J. A., and E. S. C. Weiner, eds. *The Oxford English Dictionary.* 2d ed. Oxford: Clarendon Press, 1989.

Caesar's wife must be above suspicion. ***Maintaining the appearance of virtue is as important as possessing virtue.***
In 67 B.C. Pompeia became the second wife of Julius Caesar. He divorced her six years later after a bizarre incident in which she was accused of adultery. Pompeia was celebrating the sacred ritual of Bona Dea, a goddess who was so chaste she allowed no man but her husband to see her after her marriage. To honor her delicate sensibilities, even sculptures and paintings of men had to be veiled during her ceremonies. Only women celebrated her festivals, and only under the cover of darkness. On this occasion, the patrician Clodius Pulcher supposedly dressed in women's clothing and gained entrance to the rituals in an attempt to seduce Pompeia. He was quickly discovered and driven out. According to the Roman historian Suetonius, the ensuing scandal prompted Caesar to divorce Pompeia, not because he believed that his wife had encouraged any indecent overtures but because he could not "allow members of my house to be accused or under suspicion."

Sources

Bunson, Matthew. *Encyclopedia of the Roman Empire.* New York: Facts on File, 1994.
Dunan, Renee. *The Love Life of Julius Caesar.* New York: E. P. Dutton and Co., 1931.
Lurie, Charles. *Everyday Sayings.* Detroit, MI: Gale Research, 1968.

Camelot. ***The Kennedy administration.***
This idealization of the Kennedy administration is due partly to the youth and glamour of the First Family and partly to the brevity of Kennedy's time in office. Jacqueline Kennedy set the tone immediately following the assassination of her husband on 22 November 1963. In an interview with *Life* magazine reporter Theodore H. White, Mrs. Kennedy said that her husband was always able to draw on classical quotations at the appropriate moment but that all she was able to think of to sum up her feelings was a line from the musical *Camelot,* which was very popular at the time: "Don't let it be forgot, that once there was a spot, for one brief shining moment that was known as Camelot."

"There will be great Presidents again," Mrs. Kennedy added, "but there'll never be another Camelot again." The analogy struck a chord, and the Kennedy administration was crystallized in the American memory as one of hopeful idealism that was cut tragically short.

Sources

Pickering, David, ed. *Brewer's Dictionary of Twentieth Century Phrase and Fable.* Boston: Houghton Mifflin Company, 1992.
Safire, William. *Safire's Political Dictionary.* New York: Random House, 1978.
White, Theodore. "For President Kennedy: An Epilogue." *Life* 55, no. 12 (1963): 158–159.

Cannae. ***To suffer a crippling defeat after a record of success.***
During the Second Punic War, the Battle of Cannae (216 B.C.) represented a numbing defeat for the Roman army at the hands of the great Carthaginian general Hannibal. In the First Punic War, Rome had triumphed over Carthage and demanded heavy tribute from the conquered African kingdom. Hannibal was only a child then, but his father had made him swear eternal hatred for Rome. When Carthaginian forces succeeded in gaining a foothold in Spain, it was decided that a renewed war with Rome might bring victory this time. Hannibal assembled a large group of allies from Africa, Spain, and Gaul and launched his campaign from Spain. Crossing the Alps with an army of over 20,000 men, he invaded Italy.

Cannae was a small village in southeastern Italy where Hannibal's forces met a Roman army of approximately 80,000 soldiers. The Roman legions were under the command of Lucius Aemilius Paulus and Gaius Terentius Varro, two well-respected leaders. As Hannibal's army stretched out in a huge crescent shape before them, the Roman consuls made the disastrous decision to deploy most of their manpower in an attack on the center, attempting to break through the line. Hannibal responded by encircling the Romans and cutting them to pieces. About 14,000 Romans escaped, another 10,000 were captured, and the rest were killed. The Carthaginians lost about 6,000 men. Paulus and Varro never regained their reputations after this terrible rout, and the word *Cannae* became synonymous with a staggering defeat.

Sources

Ammer, Christine. *Fighting Words: From War, Rebellion, and Other Combative Capers.* New York: Paragon House, 1989.

Evans, Ivor H., ed. *Brewer's Dictionary of Phrase and Fable.* 14th ed. New York: Harper and Row, 1989.

Hornblower, Simon, and Antony Spawforth. *The Oxford Classical Dictionary.* Oxford: Oxford University Press, 1996.

Canossa, to go to Canossa. ***To submit; to be humiliated.***

Canossa, a now-ruined castle in northern Italy, was the site of the eleventh-century showdown between Henry IV of Germany and Pope Gregory VII. Beginning in 1046 a succession of popes had attempted to address corruption within the church. Simony (the selling of church offices) was particularly troubling to the papacy, which feared that officials would be indebted to kings in exchange for their appointments. Pope Gregory was able to regain control over clerical offices in Germany because Henry IV was only six years old when he ascended to the throne. Two archbishops acted as regents for the young king, which further smoothed the way for the pope's ambitions.

In 1065 Henry attained his majority and attempted to regain the imperial rights lost during his regency. Several years of hostility boiled over into a crisis in 1076–1077. Henry insisted on appointing his own candidate to the archbishopric of Milan, and the pope retaliated by excommunicating the king. This was the most powerful weapon in Gregory's arsenal, for if a ruler was declared to be outside the faith, his subjects were released from their oaths of fealty. Henry's barons revolted against him in 1076. Without the backing of the church, the king knew he was in very real danger of being deposed. He reluctantly traveled to Canossa, an Italian castle at which the pope was in residence, to seek Gregory's forgiveness. Barefoot and wearing the humble garb of a penitent pilgrim, Henry begged for admission into the castle but was forced to wait for three days outside the gates. After this display of humility, the pope agreed to revoke his excommunication, and the German rebellion was quelled. However, within a few years Gregory and Henry renewed their struggle, which ended only when the pope died in 1085.

Eight hundred years later the German chancellor Otto von Bismarck declared, "We are not going to Canossa," in reference to his desire to purge Germany of Roman Catholic influences. More generally, *Canossa* has been associated with any submission to a stronger power.

Sources

Evans, Ivor H., ed. *Brewer's Dictionary of Phrase and Fable.* 14th ed. New York: Harper and Row, 1989.

McHenry, Robert, ed. *The New Encyclopedia Britannica.* 15th ed. Chicago: Encyclopedia Britannica, 1992.

Strayer, Joseph R., ed. *Dictionary of the Middle Ages.* New York: Scribner's, 1982.

Captain Bligh.

See Bligh, Captain.

Cardinal. ***A species of crested finch, native to the Americas, in which the male bird is almost completely red.***

When European explorers landed in the New World, they encountered a huge variety of plant and animal life that was unknown in Europe. Among the specimens of flora and fauna brought back to the royal courts, colorful birds were especially prized. One species of finch was noted for the striking red plumage of its males. Although the females were a dull olive brown, the vibrant feathers of the males were reminiscent of the scarlet robes worn by the cardinals, top church officials who rank just below the pope and are often papal envoys. The ecclesiastical robes of cardinals have traditionally been red, to symbolize their zeal in the faith, dignity, and priestly power. In the rush to name the multitude of new species encountered in the New World, naming the splendid red bird after the cardinals seemed a natural choice.

Sources

McDonald, William J., ed. *New Catholic Encyclopedia.* New York: McGraw-Hill, 1967.

Mish, Frederick C. *The Merriam-Webster New Book of Word Histories.* Springfield, IL: Merriam-Webster, 1991.

Carpetbagger. ***An opportunist who seeks position or success in a new locality by preying on the weakness of the inhabitants.***

With their land, businesses, and farms devastated by four years of civil war, Southerners were forced to accept Northern businessmen and politicians who streamed into the South to take advantage of the confusion. These newcomers were dubbed *carpetbaggers* because they often arrived with all their belongings hastily stuffed into hand-carried satchels. Carpetbags such as these were far less expensive than leather suitcases or trunks, which only the well-to-do could afford. Although many of the arriving Northerners were legitimate businessmen who hoped to invest their talents, energy, and resources into rebuilding the region, it was difficult for Southerners to shake the suspicion that these men were exploiting the vulnerability of the South after it had been destroyed and pillaged by Northern armies.

Two years after the war, the Reconstruction acts enabled many transplanted Northerners to win election to important government offices. Since their success had depended on the support of the newly enfranchised blacks, white Southerners saw the carpetbaggers as a double threat. They were not only gaining economic and political control over the region, but they were undermining the racial status quo that was based on a hierarchy of white over black.

Although the caricature of the greedy, evil carpetbaggers was often an exaggeration, there were enough who were worthy of the derogation to make the image stick. Soaring inflation and the collection of back taxes left many Southerners at the mercy of businessmen who were only too glad to foreclose rather than extend credit. The manipulation of elections was another frequent tactic of the carpetbaggers, since a corrupt government was a sure way to obtain legislation favorable to their goals.

Sources

Faust, Patricia L. *Historical Times Illustrated Encyclopedia of the Civil War.* New York: Harper and Row, 1986.

Richter, William L. *The ABC-CLIO Companion to Reconstruction, 1862–1877.* Santa Barbara, CA: ABC-CLIO, 1996.

Trefousse, Hans Louis. *Historical Dictionary of Reconstruction.* New York: Greenwood Press, 1991.

Trowbridge, J. T. *The Desolate South, 1865–1866.* New York: Duell, Sloan, and Pearce, 1956.

Carthaginian peace. ***A settlement in which the losing party is devastated.***

Rome and Carthage were two of the greatest powers of the ancient world, and their close proximity to each other provoked terrible power struggles. A series of three wars, collectively referred to as the Punic Wars, was fought between these two city-states. At the start of hostilities, Rome held most of Italy, while Carthage dominated northwest Africa and the trading islands of the Mediterranean. It was control of these islands that sparked the First Punic War in 264 B.C. The Carthaginians lost the first two wars with Rome and were forced to surrender some colonies, but they were able to maintain sovereignty in Africa. However, the Third Punic War (149–146 B.C.) brought the final devastation of Carthage. The Roman forces surrounded Carthage and began a two-year siege. Weakened from the previous wars and paying heavy tribute, Carthage was still able to rally its defenses in a valiant attempt to save the city. Famine and disease took their toll, and the Romans were eventually able to breach the city walls. Carthage was razed and set on fire; it took seventeen days for the flames to subside. Observing the destruction of the once-mighty city, the Roman general Scipio grimly feared for Rome: "For her too I dread the vicissitude of human affairs, and in her turn she may exhibit another flaming Carthage."

The city remained leveled for thirty years, after which colonists from Rome began to repopulate the region.

Sources

Davis, Paul K. *Encyclopedia of Invasions and Conquests from Ancient Times to the Present.* Santa Barbara, CA: ABC-CLIO, 1996.

McHenry, Robert, ed. *The New Encyclopedia Britannica.* 15th ed. Chicago: Encyclopedia Britannica, 1992.

Simpson, J. A., and E. S. C. Weiner, eds. *The Oxford English Dictionary.* 2d ed. Oxford: Clarendon Press, 1989.

Carthusian silence. ***Absolute, total silence.***
The Carthusian monastic order is purely contemplative and is known for the severity of the members' lifestyle. Founded in 1084 by Saint Bruno, the first Carthusian monastery was established in a remote area of the French Alps, an austere and isolated setting that influenced the development of the order. Monks lived like hermits in cells where they ate, slept, studied, and prayed in absolute silence. Although they met for communal service, minimal talking was permitted. The monks practiced austerity in their diet and clothing as well. The Carthusian order was very popular throughout the Renaissance, and nearly two hundred Carthusian monasteries sprang up throughout Europe. Their popularity has sharply declined in the modern era, and today there are fewer than a dozen Carthusian monasteries in Europe and only one in the United States.

The absolute silence practiced by these monks is thought to be necessary for profound recollection and prayer. Silence is not merely refraining from speech but involves calming inner thought and turmoil. The Carthusians hold that it is in this state of internal tranquillity that the soul is most likely to be receptive to inspiration.

Sources

Evans, Ivor H., ed. *Brewer's Dictionary of Phrase and Fable.* 14th ed. New York: Harper and Row, 1989.

Hyamson, Albert. *A Dictionary of English Phrases.* Detroit, MI: Gale Research, 1970.

McDonald, William J., ed. *New Catholic Encyclopedia.* New York: McGraw-Hill, 1967.

Casanova. ***A man who is gallantly attentive to women; a philanderer.***
Giovanni Giacomo Casanova (1725–1798) was an Italian adventurer whose accomplishments as a writer, soldier, librarian, musician, spy, and diplomat have been overshadowed by his reputation as a monumental libertine. Casanova began his professional life in a seminary, but he was expelled for bad conduct shortly after taking minor orders. In the 1750s he traveled through France, Italy, Germany, and Austria, all the while depending on his charm and on gambling to support himself. Casanova adored women, and they returned the compliment. Indulging in liaisons with all classes of women—countesses, nuns, and serving girls, experienced and virginal, married and single—Casanova cut a swath through Europe and the Mediterranean. He claimed that he had enjoyed the favors of 122 women, whose identities he protected by giving them pseudonyms in his autobiography. None of his dalliances were long-lived, since, as he explained, once a man has slept with a woman, "nothing is surer than that he will no longer desire her, for one does not desire what one possesses."

Casanova recorded his many adventures in his twelve-volume autobiography, entitled *The History of My Life.* The work, which became world-famous, was a chronicle of eighteenth-century Europe, with compelling portrayals of its extravagance and decline, bawdy indulgence and puritanical rigidity, superstition and cool rationality. Although best known as a free-wheeling sensualist, Casanova has been acknowledged as one of the most gifted and authoritative social historians of his age. He spent his last years in the Bohemian castle of Dux as a librarian for his friend Count von Waldstein and eventually died there of syphilis.

Sources

Casanova, Giacomo. *The History of My Life.* New York: Harcourt, Brace and World edition, 1966.

Eggenberger, David I., ed. *The McGraw-Hill Encyclopedia of World Biography.* New York: McGraw-Hill, 1973.

Hendrickson, Robert. *Dictionary of Eponyms: Names That Became Words.* New York: Stein and Day, 1985.

McHenry, Robert, ed. *The New Encyclopedia Britannica.* 15th ed. Chicago: Encyclopedia Britannica, 1992.

Cat, no room to swing a cat. ***An area that is cramped or confined.***

The *cat* in this phrase refers to the cat-o'-nine tails, a whip used to discipline seamen. These whips had a rope handle attached to nine lengths of cord, each around 18 inches long. Each lash had between one and three knots tied into the cord, which served to deliver an extra sting. Punishments were generally carried out on deck, since flogging required some room to wield the whip. Hence, any spot too cramped to swing a cat must have been rather small.

Sailors generally endorsed the use of the cat, recognizing the need for strict discipline to maintain order on board a ship in the middle of the ocean. Nevertheless, the profound physical damage that a cat-o'-nine tails could inflict led to its abolition as a means of punishment in 1879.

Sources

Jeans, Peter D. *Ship to Shore: A Dictionary of Everyday Words and Phrases Derived from the Sea.* Santa Barbara, CA: ABC-CLIO, 1993.

Morris, William, and Mary Morris. *Morris Dictionary of Word and Phrase Origins.* New York: Harper and Row, 1977.

Catherine wheel. ***A type of fireworks that revolves on a pin, sending out sparks or colored flames.***

The name of this amusement was derived from the torture device unsuccessfully used on Saint Catherine of Alexandria (d. circa 310). According to legend, Catherine was born into a wealthy pagan family in Alexandria and was converted to Christianity by a vision. She was seized and tried for her faith, but during her trial she succeeded in converting 50 pagan philosophers with her passionate eloquence. The emperor Maxentius had all 50 executed, and he ordered that Catherine be imprisoned until she renounced Christianity. When she proceeded to convert her jailers, the emperor ordered her execution. She was condemned to be tortured to death on a spiked wheel, but the wheel miraculously broke. She was subsequently beheaded. Although Catherine of Alexandria was one of the most venerated saints throughout the Middle Ages, her feast was dropped in 1969 from the Catholic liturgical calendar because of doubts about the factual details of her life.

Sources

McDonald, William J., ed. *New Catholic Encyclopedia.* New York: McGraw-Hill, 1967.

Metford, J. C. J. *Dictionary of Christian Lore and Legend.* London: Thames and Hudson, 1983.

Walsh, Michael, ed. *Butler's Lives of the Saints.* San Francisco: Harper and Row, 1985.

Cesarean section. ***The delivery of an infant by surgical removal from the uterus.***

Legend claims that Julius Caesar was delivered by this surgical technique. However, this is unlikely, since it would have been virtually impossible for Caesar's mother, Aurelia, to have survived a cesarean section in the first century B.C. Yet she did survive and lived to be a strong influence on him. More plausible is a derivation from the Latin phrase *lex caesarea,* meaning "law of incision." In 715 B.C. a Roman king proclaimed that it was unlawful to bury a dead pregnant woman without attempting to cut the child from her body. From ancient times through the Middle Ages, cesarean sections were performed but only on the dead. The first attempts to use the procedure on living women occurred in the sixteenth century. Before the twentieth century about 75 percent of the women who underwent a cesarean section died, almost certainly because unsanitary procedures led to massive infection.

Sources

Hendrickson, Robert. *Dictionary of Eponyms: Names That Became Words.* New York: Stein and Day, 1985.

McHenry, Robert, ed. *The New Encyclopedia Britannica.* 15th ed. Chicago: Encyclopedia Britannica, 1992.

Rothman, Barbara Katz. *Encyclopedia of Childbearing: Critical Perspectives.* Phoenix, AZ: Oryx Press, 1993.

Chair of Saint Peter. ***The papacy.***

Roman Catholics claim Saint Peter as their first pope, on the basis of Jesus' declaration: "You are Peter, and on this rock I will build my church, and the gates of Hades shall not prevail against it. I will give you the keys of the kingdom of Heaven, and whatever you bind on earth will be bound in heaven, and whatever you loose on earth will be loosed in heaven" (Matthew 16:18). No biblical passage indicates that Peter was ever a bishop or served as a local administrator, but he probably spent his last years in Rome. The Christian writer Ignatius of Antioch (d. 107) claimed that Peter wielded unique authority over the nascent Christian movement in Rome, and other early writers contended that Peter, in conjunction with the apostle Paul, founded the concept of a succession of bishops in Rome. It is widely believed that Peter was crucified in the city in either 64 or 67. Believing himself unworthy to be executed in the same manner as Jesus, Peter asked to be crucified upside-down. The authorities complied with his request, and Peter was buried on Vatican Hill, the site from which all future popes would rule.

Sources

Brusher, Joseph Stanislaus. *Popes through the Ages.* Princeton, NJ: Van Nostrand, 1964.

Gontard, Friedrich. *Chair of Peter.* New York: Holt, Rinehart and Winston, 1964.

Kelly, J. N. D. *The Oxford Dictionary of Popes.* Oxford: Oxford University Press, 1986.

Chappaquiddick. ***An event that leads to political ruin.***

A small island off Martha's Vineyard, Chappaquiddick gained national attention in July 1969, when Senator Edward Kennedy (1932–) drove his car off a bridge leading to the island. With him was 28-year-old Mary Jo Kopechne, who was drowned. Kennedy fled the scene, reemerging nine hours later to report the accident. There were rumors that Kennedy had been intoxicated, which, if true, could have led to serious charges, including involuntary manslaughter. Kennedy, who was married, was also forced to dodge questions about his relationship with Kopechne. Kennedy denied accusations of intoxication and adultery and pled guilty to a misdemeanor charge of leaving the scene of an accident. He received a two-month suspended sentence and lost his driver's license for one year. However, lingering suspicion about the events at Chappaquiddick marred Kennedy's presidential ambitions, and the issue has resurfaced each time he runs for reelection.

Chappaquiddick is used to refer to shady events that plague the careers of otherwise promising politicians. In public relations, *Chappaquiddick theory* describes the recommended method for handling damaging information. That is, the only appropriate time for a political figure to deliver bad news is immediately following the event; the longer the individual waits, the more sinister the information appears. The experiences of Richard Nixon in Watergate and Bill Clinton in Whitewater bear out the Chappaquiddick theory.

Sources

Goldberg, Philip. *The Babinski Reflex: And 70 Other Useful and Amusing Metaphors from Science, Psychology, Business, Sports, and Everyday Life.* Los Angeles: J. P. Tarcher, 1990.

Kohn, George C. *The Encyclopedia of American Scandal: From Abscam to the Zenger Case.* New York: Facts on File, 1989.

McGinniss, Joe. *The Last Brother.* New York: Simon and Schuster, 1993.

Moritz, Charles. *Current Biography Yearbook.* New York: H. W. Wilson, 1978.

Chauvinism. ***A belief in the absolute superiority of one's own group, gender, or nationality.***

Nicolas Chauvin was one of Napoleon's most ardent and courageous followers. He was reportedly wounded 17 times in the general's service and was so badly handicapped by his injuries that he had little to do but recount his days of glory and his admiration for Napoleon. Chauvin gained a reputation among his contemporaries as a weaver of bellicose tales and mindless patriotism. In 1831 a character in the play *La Cocarde Tricolore* was based on Chauvin, and soon other French playwrights (Charet's *Conscript Chauvin* and Bayard and Dumanoir's *Les Aides des Camp*) began to employ him as a type. By the late nineteenth century the word *chauvinism* had found its way into common circulation in the English language.

Sources

Hendrickson, Robert. *Dictionary of Eponyms: Names That Became Words.* New York: Stein and Day, 1985.

Lurie, Charles. *Everyday Sayings.* Detroit, MI: Gale Research, 1968.

Mish, Frederick C. *The Merriam-Webster New Book of Word Histories.* Springfield, IL: Merriam-Webster, 1991.

Checkers speech. ***A contrived, sentimental plea that distracts attention from the real issue.***

This 1952 televised speech by Senator Richard Nixon (1913–1994) successfully defused a damaging allegation that backers had set up an illegal $18,000 slush fund for his vice-presidential candidacy. Because of rumors of financial dishonesty, Dwight Eisenhower had been considering dropping Nixon from the ticket. Nixon had to make the American public see him as a sympathetic figure, and his opportunity was a live television broadcast following the Milton Berle show. Although some of his advisors counseled him to resign at the end of his speech, Nixon refused to reveal his intentions. That evening the senator did his best to portray himself as an ordinary American, coming from a middle-class background and even borrowing money from his parents to buy a house that he was still in the process of paying off. He could not afford to buy his wife a fur coat, he said, but she wore a "respectable Republican cloth coat." Although the majority of the 30-minute speech was a rather dry accounting of Nixon's income and debts, the last two minutes he devoted to the family dog, Checkers, which was the only gift Nixon would acknowledge:

> A little cocker spaniel in a crate that was sent all the way from Texas. Black and white spotted. And our little girl, Trish, the six-year-old one, named it Checkers. And you know, the kids love the dog, and I just want to say this right now, that regardless of what they say about it, we're going to keep it!

Public reaction to the speech was immediate and positive. Eisenhower declared that Nixon was not only "completely vindicated as a man of honor but, as far as I am concerned, he stands higher than ever before." Nixon remained on the ticket and was elected as vice-president later in the year. Despite the initial public approval of the Checkers speech, it was not long before journalists and opinion makers began to criticize its maudlin, self-pitying tone. One of Eisenhower's consultants said that the only thing Nixon left out of the speech was the part where "Checkers crawled on Dick's lap and licked the tears off his face."

Nixon may have gotten the idea for the Checkers ploy from an incident involving Franklin D. Roosevelt. In 1944 there were rumors that Roosevelt had inadvertently left his pet dog, a Scottish terrier named Fala, on an island in the Aleutians and had sent a destroyer to fetch the dog. Instead of denying the story, Roosevelt used it as an attack against the Republicans by implying they were now maligning a poor, harmless dog. "His Scotch soul was furious, he has not been the same dog since!"

Sources

Comfort, N. A. *Brewer's Politics: A Phrase and Fable Dictionary.* London: Cassell, 1993.

Halberstam, David. *The Fifties.* New York: Villard Books, 1993.

Lorimer, Lawrence T. *The Encyclopedia Americana.* Danbury, CT: Grolier, 1989.

Magill, Frank N., ed. *Great Events from History: North American Series.* Pasadena, CA: Salem Press, 1997.

Safire, William. *Safire's Political Dictionary.* New York: Random House, 1978.

Cincinnatus, American. ***George Washington.***
Cincinnatus (b. 519 B.C.) was a celebrated Roman statesman who gained fame for his devotion to the state and willingness to surrender power when a crisis was over. Legend claims that Cincinnatus was elected dictator by the senate when Rome was being attacked by the Volsci and Aequi. He reluctantly left his farm, rallied an army, and defeated the enemy. Sixteen days after this crisis had passed he laid down the reins of power and returned to his plow. In similar fashion, George Washington's retirement to his Virginia plantation after leading the American forces to victory in the Revolution earned him the nickname *American Cincinnatus.* He was called out of retirement six years later when he was asked to run unopposed for the presidency. He declined a third term in office and once again returned to his beloved plantation.

Sources

Johnson, Allen, and Dumas Malone, eds. *Dictionary of American Biography.* New York: Scribner's, 1964.
Lurie, Charles. *Everyday Sayings.* Detroit, MI: Gale Research, 1968.
McHenry, Robert, ed. *The New Encyclopedia Britannica.* 15th ed. Chicago: Encyclopedia Britannica, 1992.

Clean Bill of Health.
See Bill of Health.

Clear out for Guam. ***Embark on a journey with no particular destination in mind.***
In the nineteenth century there was a mass migration to Australia, where land was cheap, gold had been discovered, and settlers were eager for merchants' goods. Ships heading for the continent never had any problem filling their passenger and cargo holds. Not so when it was time to leave Australia. With little cargo and almost no passengers, ships set sail in hopes of finding a homebound cargo to fill their empty holds. Custom-house regulations in Melbourne required that, on clearing out of port, a destination be stated. If a captain did not know where he was headed, the standard practice was to list Guam, a small island in the middle of the Pacific Ocean. Few ships probably ended up in Guam, but its remote location made it a convenient hypothetical stop for captains who were not certain of their actual destination.

Sources

Evans, Ivor H., ed. *Brewer's Dictionary of Phrase and Fable.* 14th ed. New York: Harper and Row, 1989.
Lurie, Charles. *Everyday Sayings.* Detroit, MI: Gale Research, 1968.

Cleopatra's nose. ***A slight happenstance that has enormous consequences.***
This expression arose from the seventeenth-century French philosopher Blaise Pascal, who wrote, "If the nose of Cleopatra had been shorter, the whole face of the earth would have been changed." It alludes to the power wielded by the Egyptian queen, whose beauty and charm aided her in seducing both Julius Caesar and Marcus Antonius. Had she been a bit less captivating, she might not have won the assistance of either Caesar or Antonius, and she might have then lost the throne to her brother, a man much less receptive to Rome. As clever as Pascal's quip was, his estimation of Cleopatra gave her too much credit. Although she has been portrayed in films by very beautiful women, including Elizabeth Taylor, Vivian Leigh, and Claudette Colbert, coins with Cleopatra's profile reveal a rather plain, strong-boned woman. As for her influence on world history, that too has been exaggerated. Antonius and Cleopatra came close to gaining control over the Mediterranean world, but they ultimately failed, and their efforts had little long-term impact on subsequent events.

Sources

Holland, Barbara. "Cleopatra: What Kind of Woman Was She, Anyway?" *Smithsonian* 27, no. 11 (1997): 56–64.
Hughes-Hallett, Lucy. *Cleopatra: Histories, Dreams, and Distortions.* New York: Harper and Row, 1990.
Samson, Julia. *Nefertiti and Cleopatra: Queen Monarchs of Ancient Egypt.* London: Rubicon, 1990.

Clink. ***A prison.***

Many slang expressions for prisons, such as the lockup, the big house, or the slammer, are descriptive. At first glance one would think that *clink* also fit that category, given its association with the sound of rattling chains. In fact, the word has its historical roots in an actual prison, the Clink, that was located in the borough of Southwark in London. Established sometime in the fifteenth century, the Clink was unique because it housed both male and female prisoners with no segregation by sex. The Clink became associated with people imprisoned on religious grounds, including members of the clergy, because it was located very close to the residence of the bishop of Winchester, who wanted close supervision of suspected heretics.

When the Great Fire of London swept through the city in 1666, four-fifths of the city was destroyed. The Clink survived the conflagration, but most of the surrounding area was devastated. When the city was rebuilt, the character of the borough changed dramatically. Prosperous tradesmen and businessmen began building residences in the area, and the presence of a prison became an annoyance. Many of London's prisons had been destroyed in the fire, so closing the Clink was not an immediate possibility. As other prisons were built, the number of inmates at the Clink sharply declined until, by 1732, there were fewer than a dozen left. The remaining prisoners were transferred, and the structure was torn down. No trace now remains, except the name Clink Street.

Sources

Burford, E. J. *In the Clink.* London: New English Library, 1977.

Mish, Frederick C. *The Merriam-Webster New Book of Word Histories.* Springfield, IL: Merriam-Webster, 1991.

Weinreb, Ben, and Christopher Hibbert. *The London Encyclopedia.* London: Macmillan, 1983.

Cobalt. ***A silvery white metallic element used primarily in making alloys; also, a vivid blue color.***

During the Renaissance, German silver miners often found a whitish metal mixed in with their silver. Its presence annoyed the miners, since it had no practical purpose and interfered with their work. Moreover, handling it resulted in skin abnormalities, nausea, and impaired nerve functioning. The miners named the substance *kobalt,* after a type of goblin, since German folklore held that malicious spirits lived in the mines and enjoyed tormenting the workers.

The miners were not wrong to be suspicious of the metal. Modern research has revealed that the mineral cobalt is almost always found in conjunction with arsenic and sulfur. The combination of these harmful substances can cause serious digestive and nerve damage. Even so, cobalt has become indispensable to some twentieth-century industries. Cobalt alloys are very heat resistant, which makes them ideal for use in jet engines, gas turbines, and other machinery that operates at intensely high temperatures. Cobalt has long been associated with the color blue. When mixed with potassium carbonate, cobalt can be ground into an intense blue pigment that has been used for centuries in oil paints and ceramics.

Sources

Gettings, Fred. *Dictionary of Demons: A Guide to Demons and Demonologists in Occult Lore.* North Pomfret, VT: Trafalgar Square, 1988.

Turkington, Carol. *Poisons and Antidotes.* New York: Facts on File, 1994.

Coca-Cola. ***The best-selling carbonated soft drink in the world.***

It has long been rumored that Coca-Cola, or Coke, as it is better known, is so named because when the drink was invented it contained a healthy dose of cocaine. Unlike so many urban legends about big business, this particular rumor is true.

The beverage was invented by the Atlanta pharmacist Dr. John Styth Pemberton, whose goal was to create a drink that not only tasted good but had medicinal value. The best-selling beverage in Europe at that time was Vin Mariani, a Bordeaux wine made with a substantial infusion of the coca leaf, the plant from which cocaine is obtained. Pemberton wished to surpass the

French by combining wine, coca leaves, and the kola nut, which is a natural source of caffeine. Pemberton hoped that his French Wine Cola would be a delightful cure for a huge range of nervous disorders, as demonstrated by an advertisement in 1885:

> All who are suffering from nervous complaints we commend to use that wonderful and delightful remedy, French Wine Cola, infallible in curing all who are afflicted with nerve trouble, dyspepsia, mental and physical exhaustion, all chronic and wasting diseases, gastric irritability, constipation, sick headache, neuralgia, etc. It is a wonderful invigorate of the sexual organs and will cure seminal weakness, impotency, etc., when all other remedies fail.

The citizens of Atlanta were as excited about French Wine Cola as Pemberton was, and his sales throughout 1885 were very encouraging. However, national temperance campaigns were gaining momentum, and when Atlanta and Fulton County voted to experiment with prohibition for two years, Pemberton decided to remove the alcohol from his drink. After trying a variety of fruit and essential oil formulas, he realized that the simple combination of kola nuts and coca leaves in carbonated water had a pleasing flavor. Beyond the addition of a little sugar, he decided not to tamper with success, and he began searching for a name for his "temperance drink." *Coca-Cola* not only described the two principal ingredients but had the bonus of alliteration.

The original Coca-Cola had 8.45 milligrams of cocaine per serving; by way of comparison, the typical "dose" of cocaine for drug users is 20 to 30 milligrams. Recent studies have indicated that there is a symbiotic relationship between cocaine and caffeine, causing the effects of the cocaine to be intensified. Since a person might consume two or three Cokes in the space of a few hours, the early Coca-Colas must have provided quite a rush.

By 1891 people were questioning the possible addictive content of the beverage. The new owner of Coca-Cola, Asa Chandler, vigorously denied that there was any significant amount of cocaine in the drink, and he may have already modified the formula to reduce the quantity of that ingredient. Negative press, temperance crusaders, and zealous preachers continued to charge that consuming Coca-Cola was no better than "morphine-eating," and Chandler finally removed all cocaine from the drink in 1901.

Sources

Derdak, Thomas, ed. *International Directory of Company Histories.* Chicago: St. James Press, 1988.

Oliver, Thomas. *The Real Coke, the Real Story.* New York: Random House, 1986.

Pendergrast, Mark. *For God, Country, and Coca-Cola: The Unauthorized History of the Great American Soft Drink and the Company That Makes It.* New York: Scribner's, 1993.

Codfish aristocracy. ***People who have newly acquired wealth; nouveau riche.***

This expression originated in Massachusetts, where codfish was vital to the nineteenth-century economy. Salted cod and other fish were shipped in enormous quantities to other states as well as Europe and the West Indies. Some Boston merchants became millionaires and ostentatiously displayed their newfound wealth through ornate houses, jewelry, and lavish entertaining. Members of the landed aristocracy who had inherited their wealth tended to look down on those who dirtied their hands in trade, and they denigrated as particularly loathsome those who dealt in fish. *Codfish aristocracy* is a derogatory term, implying a lack of culture and taste despite wealth.

Sources

Hendrickson, Robert. *The Facts on File Encyclopedia of Word and Phrase Origins.* New York: Facts on File, 1987.

Lorimer, Lawrence T. *The Encyclopedia Americana.* Danbury, CT: Grolier, 1989.

Stimpson, George. *A Book about a Thousand Things.* New York: Harper and Brothers, 1946.

Comstockery. ***A prudish attempt to censor literature or other material deemed immoral.*** Anthony Comstock (1844–1915) was the foremost crusader against vice in the United States after the Civil War. His puritanical upbringing led him to be extremely critical of his own perceived moral failings. Once he had conquered his personal demons, he was ready to confront the moral failings of others. Proclaiming himself a "weeder in God's garden," Comstock founded the Society for the Suppression of Vice, which was primarily concerned with stamping out pornography. In 1873 his society successfully pushed the passage of the Comstock Law, which amended the 1865 Mail Act to prevent the transport of lewd or obscene material through the mail system. Comstock enthusiastically assisted in the enforcement of the law that bore his name. By his own estimate, over a period of forty years he took part in over 3,500 investigations and destroyed 160 tons of "obscene" material. He eventually expanded his crusade against pornography to include contraception, lotteries, and anything promoted by "long-haired men and short-haired women"—his term for those licentious liberals.

As the Victorian era gave way to the twentieth century, Comstock became an object of ridicule from well-known and respected writers, such as H. L. Mencken and Havelock Ellis. The word *comstockery* was coined by George Bernard Shaw in 1905.

Sources

Bates, Anna Louise. *Weeder in the Garden of the Lord: Anthony Comstock's Life and Career.* Lanham, MD: University Press of America, 1995.

Chase, Harold W., ed. *The Guide to American Law: Everyone's Legal Encyclopedia.* St. Paul, MN: West Publishing Co., 1983.

Green, Jonathan. *The Encyclopedia of Censorship.* New York: Facts on File, 1989.

Tompkins, Vincent, ed. *American Eras: 1878–1899.* Detroit, MI: Gales Research, 1997.

Connaught, to hell or Connaught. ***Consigned to one of two undesirable choices.*** When Oliver Cromwell became lord protector of England in 1653, his immediate problem was the legacy of debt from the bloody civil war. The outstanding amount of £300,000 did not include the salaries of the 35,000 soldiers in Cromwell's army. The intolerance for Catholicism and for the Irish was at an all-time high in Puritan England, so Cromwell sought to solve several problems at once by dispossessing wealthy Catholic landowners in Ireland and offering free land to his soldiers.

Cromwell declared that all Catholic landowners in eastern and central Ireland would be forced to relocate to Connaught, a sparsely settled region whose barren land was practically useless. Any who refused removal could be put to death. The phrase *to hell or Connaught* became common throughout Ireland in response to this draconian policy. Approximately 40,000 Catholic landowners and their families were dispossessed, and horror stories have come down through history about their forced winter migration to Connaught. With insufficient land to support the population, some of the emigrants were forced into brigandage, prostitution, or vagrancy.

Only about 12,000 soldiers in Cromwell's army chose to accept Irish land in exchange for back pay. The landless poor of Ireland, a Catholic peasantry comprising about three-quarters of the total population, now became the tenants of a Protestant aristocracy. The cruel policies of the Cromwell era laid the foundation for much of the strife that has plagued Ireland in subsequent centuries.

Sources

Ellis, Peter Berresford. *Hell or Connaught! The Cromwellian Colonisation of Ireland.* New York: St. Martin's Press, 1975.

Esson, Denis Main. *The Curse of Cromwell: A History of the Ironside Conquest of Ireland, 1649–53.* Totowa, NJ: Rowman and Littlefield, 1971.

Fritze, Ronald H., and William B. Robison. *Historical Dictionary of Stuart England, 1603–1689.* Westport, CT: Greenwood Press, 1996.

Hirst, Derek. *Authority and Conflict: England, 1603–1658.* Cambridge, MA: Harvard University Press, 1986.

Cook your goose. ***To deliver a comeuppance.***

The origin of this expression is uncertain, but one widely held theory gives the credit to Eric XIV of Sweden. According to legend, the king arrived at a town he intended to capture but with him were very few troops. The villagers began to jeer and taunt the would-be conquerors, and they hung a goose on the town walls and told the king that his troops could use it for target practice. However, when soldiers began a siege on the town, the residents realized that this was no joke and sent out envoys to parley with the king. When asked what he wanted from them, King Eric replied, "To cook your goose." He then proceeded to capture and burn the town.

As colorful as this story is, etymologists doubt its authenticity. This event would have taken place in the 1560s, while the expression *cook your goose* is not recorded until the mid-nineteenth century. However, no other credible source has emerged.

Sources

Hendrickson, Robert. *The Facts on File Encyclopedia of Word and Phrase Origins.* New York: Facts on File, 1987.

Lurie, Charles. *Everyday Sayings.* Detroit, MI: Gale Research, 1968.

Costa Rica. ***A nation in South America, located between Nicaragua and Panama.***

Christopher Columbus made a number of famous errors when he arrived in the New World—most notably, believing to his dying day that he had found a sea route to India. Another of his blunders occurred when he named the region now known as Costa Rica. In 1502, while on his fourth voyage to the New World, Columbus cast anchor in a harbor in order to repair his ships and provide his crew with some rest. He established friendly relations with the natives, who had had no previous contact with Europeans. Noticing the fine gold disks that some of the tribesmen were wearing, Columbus believed that he had stumbled on an area of great riches. He dubbed the region *Costa Rica,* meaning "the rich coast." As time would prove, Costa Rica has probably the least amount of mineral wealth of any country in Central America.

Sources

Guardia, R. F. *History of the Discovery and Conquest of Costa Rica.* New York: Thomas Crowell and Co., 1913.

McHenry, Robert, ed. *The New Encyclopedia Britannica.* 15th ed. Chicago: Encyclopedia Britannica, 1992.

Coventry, to be sent to Coventry. ***To shun a person.***

There are two related theories for the origin of this rather curious expression, which was once very common in Great Britain. Both date from the English Civil War. When the rift between king and Parliament turned into armed conflict in 1642, certain segments of the countryside remained loyal to Charles I. Parliamentary leaders feared that the king's men in the key town of Birmingham might somehow conspire to assist the royalist cause, so they were rounded up and sent to Coventry, a stronghold of parliamentary sentiment. Safely isolated, the king's supporters were also shunned by the local community for their loyalties.

A variation of this story is that, as tensions between king and Parliament escalated, soldiers of the king were so unpopular in Coventry that they were ostracized by the people. No soldier wanted to be sent to Coventry, where he knew he would be given the cold shoulder.

Sources

Lurie, Charles. *Everyday Sayings.* Detroit, MI: Gale Research, 1968.

Evans, Ivor H., ed. *Brewer's Dictionary of Phrase and Fable.* 14th ed. New York: Harper and Row, 1989.

Simpson, J. A., and E. S. C. Weiner, eds. *The Oxford English Dictionary.* 2d ed. Oxford: Clarendon Press, 1989.

Crapper. ***A toilet.***

According to urban legend, a British mechanical engineer named Thomas Crapper (1836–1910) invented the flush toilet. Crapper was a mechanical engineer who patented several inventions for various drain and manhole designs, but there is no evidence that he had any role in the development of the toilet. However, the myth has gained currency since a 1969 book by Wallace Reyburn. At first glance, *Flushed with Pride: The Story of Thomas Crapper* appears to be a serious biography, but the number of puns soon suggests otherwise. According to Reyburn, Crapper was born in the town of Throne and was descended from a French family named La Crappere. He had a good friend whom he called B.S., and his first working model of the "Crapper W. C. Cistern" was created "after many dry runs." Casting further suspicion on Reyburn's account is the fact that he also produced an eponymous biography of Otto Titzling, supposedly the inventor of the brassiere.

One of the earliest versions of the flush toilet was actually designed by British watchmaker Alexander Cumming in 1775. It included a water tank set above the main unit and a hand-operated valve that released this water and flushed out the toilet. Later, the patent for the "Valveless Water Waste Preventer," which improved the operation of the toilet, was held by Albert Giblin, a man who once worked for Crapper.

Sources

Panati, Charles. *Extraordinary Origins of Everyday Things.* New York: Perennial Library, 1987.

Reyburn, Wallace. *Flushed With Pride: The Story of Thomas Crapper.* Englewood Cliffs, NJ: Prentice-Hall, 1971.

"Thomas Crapper: Myth and Reality," *Plumbing and Mechanical Magazine* (1993). Available http://www.theplumber.com/crapper.html [August 1997].

Croesus, rich as Croesus. ***To be very wealthy.***

Croesus (d. 546 B.C.) was a king whose fabulous wealth inspired tales of ancient prosperity and splendor. He was the last ruler of Lydia, a kingdom in western Anatolia in Asia Minor. A commercial people, the Lydians were perhaps the first to establish retail shops and use metal coinage as an official medium of exchange. When Croesus became their king in 560 B.C., he proceeded to vanquish the entire mainland of Ionia. With the accumulated wealth, he made lavish offerings to the oracle of Delphi. By 550 B.C. a new power, Cyrus the Great, had emerged in Persia. Croesus formed an alliance with Babylon and Egypt in a futile effort to contain the encroaching Persian empire. The Lydian kingdom was absorbed by the Persians in 546 B.C., but Croesus may have survived the conquest to become an advisor to Cyrus.

Croesus's symbolic value as the personification of wealth was reinforced by the Greek historian Herodotus. He told of a meeting between the king and the famed Athenian lawgiver Solon, in which the wise man admonished Croesus that good fortune, rather than wealth, was the basis of happiness. The account is probably fictitious.

Sources

Hawatson, M. C., ed. *The Oxford Companion to Classical Literature.* New York: Oxford University Press, 1989.

Hornblower, Simon, and Antony Spawforth, eds. *The Oxford Classical Dictionary.* 3d ed. Oxford: Oxford University Press, 1996.

Sacks, David. *Encyclopedia of the Ancient Greek World.* New York: Facts on File, 1995.

Cross of gold. ***A negative reference to the gold standard.***

William Jennings Bryan (1860–1925) was a famed orator whose most renowned speech was delivered at the Democratic National Convention of 1896. Bryan had been a two-term congressman from Nebraska (1890–1894), and when his bid for the U.S. Senate failed, he threw his hat into the presidential race. Like many in the Populist movement, Bryan favored the unlimited coinage of silver, which would pump more currency into circulation. "Free silver" would especially benefit debtors, whose numbers had been steadily increasing in the depression of the 1890s. Opponents of free silver, who tended to be members of the urban middle class, supported the gold standard, which the United States had been following since the 1870s.

Lambasting the gold supporters for their disregard of the plight of farmers and laborers, Bryan declared, "You shall not press down upon the brow of labor this crown of thorns, you shall not crucify mankind upon a cross of gold." On the strength of this "Cross of Gold" speech, the 36-year-old Bryan won the Democratic nomination. However, in the election he lost decisively to William McKinley. The Democrats thereafter eschewed free silver as political suicide, and with increasing prosperity and the distraction of foreign affairs, the public began to lose interest in the issue.

Sources

Johnson, Allen, and Dumas Malone, eds. *Dictionary of American Biography.* New York: Scribner's, 1964.

Magill, Frank N., and John L. Loos, eds., *Great Events from History: North American Series.* Pasadena, CA: Salem Press, 1997.

Stimpson, George. *A Book about American Politics.* New York: Harper, 1954.

Cross the Rubicon.

See Rubicon.

Crossing the Delaware. *To take bold and decisive action.*

This is an allusion within an allusion. Although it refers to Julius Caesar's crossing of the Rubicon, its modification makes it especially appropriate for American politicians. It derives from the famous battle for Trenton in the first year of the Revolutionary War. The Continental Army under George Washington (1732–1799) had suffered a series of defeats and by December had been forced to retreat through New Jersey and across the Delaware River. The rebels were ill equipped, dispirited, and in desperate need of a victory. Trenton, New Jersey, was being held by the Hessian colonel Johann Rall, who had contempt for the "country clowns" who constituted the American army. Although the town was isolated from the British garrisons of Princeton and Bordentown, Rall did not bother to construct fortifications and trenches or send out scouting parties, believing that he was safe for the duration of the winter.

General Washington decided to take advantage of the Christmas holiday to launch a surprise attack on the Hessians. The Americans left camp at 2:00 P.M. on Christmas Day and began crossing the Delaware River at nightfall, intending to complete the operation by midnight. The bitter cold, sleet, and wind slowed their progress. Impeded by floating ice and the swift current, the last troops did not disembark until 3:00 A.M. The soldiers marched in darkness toward Trenton and reached the town at daybreak. Many of the Hessians, including Colonel Rall, were in an alcoholic stupor from the celebrations of the previous night. When the rebels began firing at 8:00 A.M., the Hessians were taken completely unawares, and the battle was over in less than two hours. One hundred and six Hessians were killed, and over 900 were captured. Four Americans were killed. Washington quickly followed up the victory at Trenton with another at Princeton. These battles were the first major successes of the war, and they breathed new life into the American cause.

The daring, midnight crossing of the Delaware River has been immortalized in the monumental painting by Emmanuel Gottlieb Leutze. The expression is often used in association with politicians or entrepreneurs embarking on a bold, challenging task.

Sources

Boatner, Mark Mayo. *Encyclopedia of the American Revolution.* New York: D. McKay Co., 1966.

Fast, Howard. *The Crossing of the Delaware.* New York: William Morrow, 1971.

Purcell, L. Edward, and David F. Burg, eds. *The World Almanac of the American Revolution.* New York: World Almanac, 1992.

Stryker, William S. *The Battles of Trenton and Princeton.* Boston: Houghton Mifflin, 1898.

Crow, to eat crow. *To accept or perform an undesirable task.*

The only explanation for this phrase is a story that, though unlikely, appears in a number of well-respected sources dating back to the nineteenth century. During the War of 1812, a New Englander was hunting along the banks of the Niagara River when he unwittingly strayed into an area controlled by the British. He landed a crow, but his shot attracted the attention of a British officer. Resolving to teach the Yankee a lesson, the officer approached the man, praised his marksmanship, and admired his excellent weapon. In a sociable gesture, the American handed over his gun for a closer inspection. The British officer then berated the man for trespassing and ordered him to take a bite of the crow. Despite his pleas for mercy, the New Englander was forced to do so. When the officer returned the gun, the American turned the tables and ordered his adversary to finish eating the crow.

Sources

Evans, Ivor H., ed. *Brewer's Dictionary of Phrase and Fable.* 14th ed. New York: Harper and Row, 1989.
Hendrickson, Robert. *Facts on File Encyclopedia of Word and Phrase Origins.* New York: Facts on File, 1987.

Crusade. *A vigorous movement characterized by moral fervor.*

The Crusades (1095–1270) were a series of military expeditions launched from Europe in an attempt to wrest control of the holy city of Jerusalem from the Muslims. The Middle Ages was a time of constant infighting among the European nations, and Pope Urban II sought a way to unite all of Christendom in a common cause. In 1095 he delivered an impassioned speech that decried the atrocities committed by the Muslims against Christian pilgrims to the Holy Land. The pope called for a demonstration of faith by righteous Christians, to be embodied in a reconquest of Jerusalem. The initial response was overwhelming. Thousands of nobles, soldiers, peasants, and pilgrims streamed toward the Holy Land, moved by a mixture of religious zeal, political ambition, greed, and the search for adventure. From 1099 to 1187 the Crusaders succeeded in their goal of retaking Jerusalem, but the Crusades themselves were ultimately considered a failure.

By the eighteenth century, the word was used in a general sense to refer to any impassioned movement against something perceived as detrimental. In 1786 Thomas Jefferson wrote, "Preach, my dear Sir, a crusade against ignorance." In his first inaugural speech, Franklin Roosevelt advocated a crusade against poverty and a restoration of the American way of life. General Dwight Eisenhower evoked the earlier military connotation of the word when he called for a crusade against the evils of the Nazi regime. The word is frequently used today in reference to social issues, such as a crusade against drugs, teenage pregnancy, or racism. *Crusade* comes from *crux,* the Latin word for cross, but its derivation is from the French *croiser,* meaning "to take the cross as a soldier."

Sources

Cowley, Robert, and Geoffrey Parker, eds. *The Reader's Companion to Military History.* Boston: Houghton Mifflin, 1996.
Mish, Frederick C. *The Merriam-Webster New Book of Word Histories.* Springfield, IL: Merriam-Webster, 1991.
Safire, William. *Safire's Political Dictionary.* New York: Random House, 1978.
Strayer, Joseph R., ed. *Dictionary of the Middle Ages.* New York: Scribner's, 1982.

Curfew. *A regulation requiring certain people to be off the streets during prescribed hours.*

In the Middle Ages, most houses were constructed of either wood, wattle and daub, or thatching. Fire posed an extreme danger and could spread rapidly. The possibility of an entire village being burned out was frighteningly real. In an effort to control the risk of nighttime fires, regulations were established in medieval Europe that required all fires to be extinguished at a certain hour. The word comes from Old French: *covrir,* to cover, and *feu,* fire.

One tradition states that the practice of curfews was introduced to England by William the Conqueror, who was appalled at the number of careless fires caused by allowing embers to burn late into the night for heat and illumination. The native Saxons were unused to extinguishing all fire at night and viewed the curfew as a form of political repression. This account has been popular since the Renaissance, but some historians doubt its validity.

Sources

Hazlitt, William Carew. *Faiths and Folklore of the British Isles.* New York: B. Blom, 1965.
Simpson, J. A., and E. S. C. Weiner, eds. *The Oxford English Dictionary.* 2d ed. Oxford: Clarendon Press, 1989.

Curse of Scotland. ***The nine of diamonds.***
James II was the last of the Stuart dynasty to rule England and Scotland (1685–1688), but his reign was cut short because of his Catholic sympathies. James stopped attending Anglican services in the 1670s and was probably baptized a Catholic during the decade. When he and his Catholic wife ascended to the throne in 1685, he issued a number of pro-Catholic measures, which further inflamed the Protestant court. The final straw came when the queen delivered a healthy son in 1688, threatening an uninterrupted succession of Catholic monarchs. The result was the Glorious Revolution, in which James was forced off the throne in favor of his Protestant son-in-law, William of Orange.

For the next 60 years there were sporadic attempts by James's supporters, known as Jacobites, to restore the Stuart monarchy. The most famous occurred in 1746, when James's grandson, Bonnie Prince Charlie, led his weak and starving Highlanders against a British force of 9,000 at a tract of moorland called Culloden. The battle lasted only 40 minutes; over 1,000 Scots were killed, compared with 50 on the British side. The slaughter obliterated once and for all the aspirations of Jacobites.

The nine of diamonds entered the story through the duke of Cumberland, who led the British forces. Cumberland was known to be fond of cards, and he always carried a pack on his person. When the Battle of Culloden was over, he took a card from his pack and sent a scrawled message to London reporting the victory. That card was the nine of diamonds, which has remained the *curse of Scotland* since then.

Sources

Evans, Ivor H., ed. *Brewer's Dictionary of Phrase and Fable.* 14th ed. New York: Harper and Row, 1989.
McHenry, Robert, ed. *The New Encyclopedia Britannica.* 15th ed. Chicago: Encyclopedia Britannica, 1992.

Custer's last stand. ***A foolish or hopeless situation.***
George Armstrong Custer (1839–1876) had been a golden boy of the United States Army. At the age of 23, he had become a brigadier general and had distinguished himself in the closing days of the Civil War by his relentless pursuit of General Robert E. Lee, which hastened Lee's surrender at Appomattox. After the war he went west, where he was involved in various minor disputes that offered little opportunity for advancement. Then gold was discovered in the Dakotas. The second Treaty of Fort Laramie (1868) had guaranteed the Sioux tribes possession of the Dakota Territory west of the Missouri River. Suddenly white miners began encroaching on Indian lands in search of gold, but the U.S. government was unwilling to enforce the Indians' rights to the land. After a few Indian raids on white settlements, the government considered itself released from the treaty and ordered all Indians to move to designated reservations by 31 January 1876. Even had they been willing, lack of adequate notification made compliance with such an order almost impossible for the nomadic tribes.

The U.S. Army planned a three-pronged punitive expedition against the Sioux that was to converge at the Little Bighorn River. Custer was in command of the Seventh Cavalry and was hoping to lead a surprise attack on an encampment of Indians. According to the plan, Captain Frederick Benteen, Major Marcus Reno, and Colonel Custer would use their three separate divisions to encircle the Indians and launch a simultaneous assault. The timing went awry, causing Benteen and Reno to retreat and leaving Custer to bear the brunt of the attack of over 2,000 Indian warriors. Custer and his 225 men were overwhelmed, and in a last-ditch effort he ordered his men to shoot their horses to form a protective wall. All of Custer's men were killed, and Custer himself was found shot through the temple, a possible suicide. The lone survivor of the battle on the U.S. side was a horse, Comanche, belonging to Captain Myles Keogh. For years the horse was used in military parades to represent the Seventh Cavalry and always appeared riderless.

The rout at Little Bighorn is often known as *Custer's last stand*. Although it was a high point for the Plains tribes in their struggle against white expansion, it so stunned and outraged the American public that government troops soon flooded the area and forced the tribes onto reservations.

Sources

Hatch, Thom. *Custer and the Battle of Little Bighorn: An Encyclopedia of People, Places, Events, Indian Culture and Customs, Information Sources, Art and Films.* Jefferson, NC: McFarland & Co., 1997.

Johnson, Allen, and Dumas Malone. *Dictionary of American Biography.* New York: Scribner's, 1964.

McHenry, Robert, ed. *The New Encyclopedia Britannica.* 15th ed. Chicago: Encyclopedia Britannica, 1992.

Panati, Charles. *Panati's Extraordinary Endings of Practically Everything and Everybody.* New York: Perennial Library, 1989.

Cyrillic alphabet. *The alphabet of Slavic languages.*

Saint Cyril (827–869) is best remembered for his creation of an alphabet for the Slavic people, although he and his brother Methodius made a number of other vital contributions. Ninth-century Europe was still feeling the power vacuum left by the fall of the Roman Empire. The Mediterranean world feared the great migrations of Germanic and Slavic tribes, and it was hoped that if these newcomers could be converted to Christianity, they could be more easily controlled by the ecclesiastical powers of Rome. A number of moderately successful evangelical missionaries began practicing in the Slavic speaking regions, but the Slavs had no written language or established church leadership. Without these two things, the newly Christianized people would quickly fall prey to "heathen" influences.

Cyril and his brother Methodius were selected to lead a mission to the region of the Danube basin and develop a written language for the Slavic people. The brothers had been raised in Greece and, from their contact with Slavic immigrants there, had already developed a fluency in the Slavic tongue. However, the Greek alphabet could not express some of the sounds in the Slavic language, so Cyril developed new letters that became known as the *Cyrillic alphabet*. When the brothers traveled to Moravia in 863, they began training the native clergy in the alphabet Cyril had devised, and they completed a translation of the Bible and other church texts. The new language met with fierce opposition from some of the Latinized clergy, and the brothers were forced to travel to Rome in 867 to seek papal approval of their work. Pope Adrian II, who agreed that the church would have more success appealing to these new peoples in their native tongues, ratified their efforts. A few months after reaching Rome, Cyril fell seriously ill and died at the age of 42. Methodius continued their work alone, but the alphabet was eventually named in honor of Cyril.

Over the coming centuries the alphabet was simplified from the original 42 letters to 32 letters in Russian, 33 letters in Ukrainian, and 30 letters in Serbian.

Sources

Coulmas, Florian. *The Blackwell Encyclopedia of Writing Systems.* Cambridge, MA: Blackwell Publishers, 1996.

McHenry, Robert, ed. *The New Encyclopedia Britannica.* 15th ed. Chicago: Encyclopedia Britannica, 1992.

Walsh, Michael, ed. *Butler's Lives of the Saints.* San Francisco: Harper and Row, 1985.

D

Daguerreotype. ***An old-fashioned photograph.***

In the early nineteenth century, there were a number of inventors who independently tried to produce photographic images by exposing chemical solutions to light. Most experiments used salts or bitumen, which became sensitized to light after long exposure. In the 1820s Joseph Nicephore Niepce developed the first permanent photographic process, but the image was poor and grainy and required eight hours of exposure time. In 1829 Niepce heard of a French painter, Louis Jacques Mandé Daguerre, who was also trying to develop photographs. The two inventors began a partnership that soon resulted in a vast improvement in photography.

Daguerre (1787–1851) used a sheet of silver-plated copper that had been polished to a mirrorlike sheen. It was made light-sensitive by spreading a layer of iodine vapors on its surface, and it was then exposed to an image for 20 to 30 minutes through a sharply focused lens. The plate was treated with mercury fumes to develop the image, and the picture was set by bathing it in sodium thiosulphate. (Daguerre's wife frequently complained about the malodorous vapors that permeated their house.) The resulting image was known as a *daguerreotype* (Niepce had died before the completion of the process). Daguerreotypes had a sharp, clear image with an excellent range of tones. The necessary exposure time was later reduced after Daguerre perfected his technique, and it was possible to create portraits with the new camera. The daguerreotype was a tremendous success, spreading throughout Europe, Russia, North Africa, and the United States in the space of a few years. Many artists abandoned their paint brushes in favor of the camera and began to earn a respectable income taking photographs. Daguerre himself became wealthy from his invention and was appointed an officer in the Legion of Honor, with an annuity of 6,000 francs.

There were drawbacks to the new invention. Only one image could be produced at a time, and since there was no negative, it was impossible to create additional copies of an image. The surface of the copper plates was prone to tarnish, and because the daguerreotype created a mirror image of the subject, the pictures always appeared in reverse. By the mid-1850s other photographic inventions solved these problems and eventually rendered the daguerreotype obsolete.

Sources

Gernsheim, Helmut. *L. J. M. Daguerre: The World's First Photographer.* Cleveland, Ohio: World Publishing Company, 1956.

McHenry, Robert, ed. *The New Encyclopedia Britannica.* 15th ed. Chicago: Encyclopedia Britannica, 1992.

Damascus, road to Damascus conversion. ***A sudden conversion to a radically different view.***

Saint Paul (Saul of Tarsus) was born into a Jewish family around the year A.D. 10. As a young man he was an ardent supporter of the Pharisees, a Jewish sect that advocated strict adherence to the law of Moses and so had opposed the teachings of Jesus of Nazareth. As Christianity began to attract converts in Jerusalem, Paul became a violent opponent and took part in the stoning of Saint Stephen. Eager to continue stamping out the new sect, Paul applied to the high priest for a commission to travel to Damascus and arrest all Jews who had proclaimed Jesus as savior. As he approached Damascus, he was struck blind by a light and heard a voice saying, "Saul, Saul, why dost thou persecute me?" When he asked who was speaking, the voice replied, "Jesus of Nazareth, whom thou persecutest. It is hard for thee to kick against the goad." At that moment Paul was converted to Christianity. He continued on to Damascus, where his sight was healed, he was baptized, much to the astonishment of his friends, and he began preaching about his conversion experience. He spent the rest of his life traveling throughout the Middle East, mostly on foot, to preach the gospel. Many scholars contend that without the exhaustive travels and letters of the apostle Paul, Christianity might not have developed into a world religion but might have remained a small sect within Judaism.

Sources

Metzger, Bruce M., and Michael D. Coogan. *The Oxford Companion to the Bible.* New York: Oxford University Press, 1993.

Segal, Alan F. *Paul the Convert: The Apostolate and Apostasy of Saul the Pharisee.* New Haven, CT: Yale University Press, 1990.

Walsh, Michael, ed. *Butler's Lives of the Saints.* San Francisco: Harper and Row, 1985.

Damon and Pythias. ***A devoted friendship.***
Pythias was a Greek philosopher in the fifth century B.C. Condemned to death for treason by the ruthless tyrant Dionysius, Pythias requested permission to return home to settle his domestic affairs. Dionysius agreed on the condition that he find another person willing to be executed in his place should he fail to return. Pythias's lifelong friend Damon volunteered.

A series of calamities delayed Pythias, and as the hour approached, it appeared that Damon would be executed. As his friend was being led out, Pythias returned in time to take his place. The notoriously callous Dionysius was so moved by this display of loyalty and devotion that he pardoned Pythias and entreated the two men to allow him to share in their friendship.

Sources

L'Empriere, John. *Classical Dictionary of Proper Names Mentioned in Ancient Authors, with a Chronological Table.* London: Routledge and Paul, 1949.

Sacks, David. *Encyclopedia of the Ancient Greek World.* New York: Facts on File, 1995.

Dark and bloody ground. ***Kentucky.***
This phrase originally described the region consisting of present-day Kentucky, West Virginia, and Ohio. The "dark" probably refers to the dense forest cover. This area was hunting ground to the Delawares, Hurons, Shawnees, and Miamis. As white settlers pushed westward in the eighteenth century, they met fierce resistance from these Eastern Woodland tribes. The ongoing struggle inflicted heavy losses on both sides, giving rise to the epithet *bloody ground.*

Sources

Evans, Ivor H., ed. *Brewer's Dictionary of Phrase and Fable.* 14th ed. New York: Harper and Row, 1989.

Kleber, John E., ed. *The Kentucky Encyclopedia.* Lexington: University of Kentucky Press, 1992.

Davy Jones's locker. ***The bottom of the sea, often used in connection with those who have died at sea.***
Several insubstantial theories have been offered about the origin of this term, which dates back to the mid-eighteenth century. One is based on the superstition that Davy Jones was an evil spirit who haunted ships, lurked among the rigging during foul weather, and lured sailors to their death. Another theory gives credit to a sixteenth-century pub owner in London named Jones, who rendered sailors unconscious with spiked ale. The victims were carted off in Jones's locker chest to be impressed into service on some ship (see *Shanghai*). A large percentage of impressed sailors were never

heard from again, and their fate became associated with disappearing into the sea.

Sources

Jeans, Peter D. *Ship to Shore: A Dictionary of Everyday Words and Phrases Derived from the Sea.* Santa Barbara, CA: ABC-CLIO, 1993.

Lurie, Charles. *Everyday Sayings.* Detroit, MI: Gale Research, 1968.

Dead as a dodo.

See Dodo.

Dead man's hand. ***In poker, a combination of aces and eights.***

James Butler Hickok (1837–1876), better known as Wild Bill Hickok, had recently moved to Deadwood in the Dakota Territory when he sat down to play his last hand of cards. Hickok was acquainted with Jack McCall (1851–1877), a man described as a "cross-eyed, broken-nosed, whiskey-besotted saddle tramp," and had played poker with him. On the afternoon of 2 August 1876, McCall walked into Carl Mann's Saloon Number 10 and shot Hickok in the back of the head. Wild Bill died immediately, still clutching his cards: two aces and two eights, known since then as a *dead man's hand.*

McCall was apprehended and tried before a miners' court the following day. He claimed that he was avenging the death of his brother whom Hickok had supposedly killed. The jury voted 11 to 1 to set McCall free, a verdict that was probably more indicative of Hickok's unpopularity than McCall's innocence. For months after the incident, McCall bragged to all listeners that he had killed Hickok in a duel, believing that the law had cleared him. However, a miners' court had no official standing, and territorial authorities finally arrested him and put him on trial. It was discovered that although McCall had three sisters, he never had a brother. Since his only defense for murdering Hickok had crumbled, he was found guilty and sentenced to hang. When asked why he had shot Hickok from behind rather than give the man a fair chance, McCall replied, "I didn't want to commit suicide."

Sources

Hendrickson, Robert. *Facts on File Encyclopedia of Word and Phrase Origins.* New York: Facts on File, 1987.

Rosa, Joseph G. *Wild Bill Hickok: The Man and the Myth.* Lawrence: University Press of Kansas, 1996.

Safakis, Carl. *The Encyclopedia of American Crime.* New York: Facts on File, 1982.

Stimpson, George. *A Book about a Thousand Things.* New York: Harper and Brothers, 1946.

Decimate. ***To destroy, critically damage, or annihilate.***

The term *decimate* comes from the Latin word *decimus,* meaning "tenth," and refers to the practice in the Roman army of executing every tenth soldier as a disciplinary measure. Among the military forces of the ancient world, Roman discipline was legendary, and punishment for infractions was swift and severe. If an entire unit was guilty of an act of cowardice on the field or an attempted mutiny, 10 percent of the men would be selected by lot to be beaten or stoned to death. Surviving members of the unit would receive reduced rations and would be segregated from the rest of the legion, thus singling them out for contempt.

The word is currently used to refer to something that kills large numbers of people, as in "AIDS continues to decimate the hemophiliac community." Etymologists regard as incorrect its figurative usage in a nonlethal context.

Sources

Cowley, Robert, and Geoffrey Parker, eds. *The Reader's Companion to Military History.* Boston: Houghton Mifflin, 1996.

Peck, Harry Thurston. *Harper's Dictionary of Classical Literature and Antiquities.* New York: Cooper Square Publishers, 1962.

Simpson, J. A., and E. S. C. Weiner, eds. *The Oxford English Dictionary.* 2d ed. Oxford: Clarendon Press, 1989.

Deep Throat. ***A person within an organization who covertly supplies information about the wrongdoings of colleagues to outside sources.***

The Watergate scandal began to unravel in 1972, and it was the *Washington Post* reporters Bob Woodward and Carl Bernstein who had first found and then continued to pull at its thread. Their 1974 book, *All the President's Men,* detailed their investigation and disclosed Woodward's claim that he had a major source within the executive branch who supplied vital information. Woodward named this source *Deep Throat,* after a celebrated pornographic movie.

Woodward stated that each morning he checked page 20 of the *New York Times,* which was delivered to his apartment before 7:00 A.M. When Deep Throat wanted to meet, he circled the page number and drew the hands of a clock to indicate the time the rendezvous was to take place—usually in the wee hours, in an underground parking garage. Deep Throat revealed to Woodward that the Nixon administration had used a campaign of dirty tricks, including bugged phones, false press leaks, canceling campaign rallies, and stealing documents, to undermine the Democratic race for the presidency. Nixon tried to cover up his involvement by attempting to manipulate officials in the Justice Department and the FBI.

In the years since the publication of *All the President's Men,* a number of commentators have speculated that there never was a Deep Throat, or that he was a composite of several individuals. Woodward continues to insist that the source did exist but that he will never identify him or his position.

Sources

Bernstein, Carl, and Bob Woodward. *All the President's Men.* New York: Simon and Schuster, 1974.

Magill, Frank M., ed. *Great Events from American History: North American Series.* Pasadena, CA: Salem Press, 1997.

Mann, James. "Deep Throat: An Institutional Analysis." *Atlantic* 269, no. 5 (1992): 106–112.

Delaware. *A mid-Atlantic state, bordered by Maryland and Pennsylvania.*

Thomas West De La Warr (1577–1618) was a member of the council of the Virginia Company and was appointed the first colonial governor of Virginia in 1610. He prepared a huge expedition to the New World, bringing 150 colonists and several shiploads of supplies. When he arrived at Jamestown, he found the settlement in deplorable condition. Starvation and disease had reduced their numbers to 60, and the despondent survivors were preparing to depart for England when De La Warr landed. Under his administration the colony was reorganized, industry and farming were revived, and better relations were established with the Indians. De La War sent Captain Samuel Argall on voyages to surrounding lands to gather livestock, grain, and other necessities for the colonists. During his travels, Captain Argall spotted a large bay and named it for his superior. Over time the bay and the land mass became known as Delaware. De La Warr's success was short-lived, since illness forced his return to England the following year. Relations between De La Warr and Argall were not always so cordial. After De La Warr returned to England, Argall began serving as Virginia's deputy governor until De La Warr could return. Rumors soon reached England that Argall was exercising tyrannical rule over the colonists, and De La Warr resolved to return to Virginia and set things right. He died en route and was buried at sea.

Sources

Johnson, Allen, and Dumas Malone, eds. *Dictionary of American Biography.* New York: Scribner's, 1964.

Spofford, Ainsworth R., ed. *The National Cyclopedia of American Biography.* Clifton, NJ: J. T. White, 1926.

Stimpson, George. *A Book about American History.* Greenwich, CT: Fawcett Publications, 1960.

Delphic. *Something that is ambiguous or obscure.*

The temple of the oracle at Delphi was located north of the Corinthian gulf in the region once known as Phocis, at a site the Greeks believed was the center of the world. Within the shrine was the *omphalos,* or "navel stone." Dedicated to the god Apollo, the priestess known as the Pythia would chew on laurel leaves and enter a trancelike state. As she muttered incoherent phrases that were supposedly messages from Apollo, an attending priest would translate the messages into hexameter verse.

The Greeks consulted the Delphic oracle for a variety of concerns, ranging from advice on marriage and family matters to military strategy and politics. Much as contemporary horoscopes render bland advice, the Delphic oracle offered generally vague predictions. Of the 75 Delphic messages that have been preserved in the ancient record, most are ambiguous or mere common sense. One cryptic Delphic prophecy read: "Thou shalt go thou shalt return never in battle shalt thou perish." Depending on the punctuation, the message could have drastically different meanings.

As the most prestigious of all the oracles, Delphi was a rich and influential organization. Its priestesses were personally acquainted with the most powerful rulers of Greece, and they made it their business to keep abreast of court intrigue. Forecasts could remain deliberately vague yet have the ring of truth in their familiarity with current happenings. However, during the Persian wars of the fifth century B.C., the oracle broke from tradition and began making highly partisan predictions. The Greeks were advised that resistance to the powerful Persians was useless and that they should seek to accommodate the invaders. When the Greeks triumphed over the Persians in 479 B.C., the oracle at Delphi was stigmatized, and the priestesses reverted back to their obscure messages.

The temple at Delphi was finally closed A.D. 390 by the order of the Christian emperor Theodosius. Its practice of ambiguous pronouncements survives in the word *delphic.*

Sources

Dempsey, T. *The Delphic Oracle: Its Early History, Influence, and Fall.* New York: B. Blom, 1972.

Evans, Ivor H., ed. *Brewer's Dictionary of Phrase and Fable.* 14th ed. New York: Harper and Row, 1989.

Mish, Frederick C. *The Merriam-Webster New Book of Word Histories.* Springfield, IL: Merriam-Webster, 1991.

Parke, H. W., and D. E. W. Wormell. *The Delphic Oracle.* Oxford: Basil Blackwell, 1956.

Sacks, David. *Encyclopedia of the Ancient Greek World.* New York: Facts on File, 1995

Demosthenic. ***Powerful and eloquent oratory.***

Demosthenes (384–322 B.C.) was considered to be the greatest of Greek orators. His vitriolic speeches denouncing Philip of Macedonia were so powerful that the word *philippic* was coined to describe that type of damning oratory (see *Philippics*).

In his youth, Demosthenes struggled with a profound speech defect: a feeble voice and a stammer that was accentuated by nervous twitching. When he argued his first case before the Greek assembly at the age of 17, he started well but his stammering and awkward gestures eventually drew the ridicule of his audience. Determined to improve himself, Demosthenes devised a number of exercises for himself. He learned to speak with pebbles in his mouth to improve his clarity, and he practiced reciting before the crashing waves of the ocean so as to develop a voice strong enough to carry over loud disruptions.

He diligently studied the two major styles of Greek oratory. Lysias was known for a mild, persuasive tone that appealed to logic and reason. Thucydides used a bold, exuberant style designed to persuade the listener by appealing to emotion. Demosthenes combined the best of both styles into his own, unique oratory. However, his renowned eloquence landed him in fatal trouble. His emphatic denunciation of Philip of Macedonia left him little room to maneuver when it became apparent that the Macedonians would conquer Greece. Demosthenes swallowed poison to avoid being captured.

Sources

Adams, Charles Darwin. *Demosthenes and His Influence.* New York: Cooper Square Publishers, 1963.

Hendrickson, Robert. *Facts on File Encyclopedia of Word and Phrase Origins.* New York: Facts on File, 1987.

Hornblower, Simon, and Antony Spawforth, eds. *The Oxford Classical Dictionary.* 3d ed. Oxford: Oxford University Press, 1996.

Sacks, David. *Encyclopedia of the Ancient Greek World.* New York: Facts on File, 1995.

Derby. ***A formal racing event, usually with horses but sometimes with dogs or cars.***
In eighteenth-century England, horse racing was a pastime of the idle rich, since only the very wealthy could afford to train thoroughbred horses for a leisure sport. These races were social events in which aristocrats, royalty, and other well-to-do people gathered from throughout England to witness the running of the horses. Weekend house parties in the country were usually planned around the races.

A great aficionado of the horse race was the twelfth Earl of Derby. In 1779, the earl organized a horse race called the Oakes to be run every year at Epsom Downs. The success of the event encouraged Derby and his friend Sir Charles Banbury to establish a second annual race at Epsom Downs, restricted to three-year-old horses running a two-mile course. The two men resorted to the toss of a coin to determine whose name would be given to the event. Derby won the toss. The Derby races became enormously popular, as indicated by the nineteenth-century tradition of adjourning Parliament for the race. The continued prestige of the derby is demonstrated by the adoption of the name for other events, most notably the Kentucky Derby.

Sources

Bagley, John J. *The Earls of Derby.* London: Sedgwick and Jackson, 1985.
Longrigg, Roger. *The History of Horseracing.* London: Macmillan, 1972.
Stimpson, George. *A Book about a Thousand Things.* New York: Harper and Brothers, 1946.

Derelict. ***A homeless or jobless person; also, an abandoned piece of property.***
Derelict is derived from the Latin word *derelictum,* meaning "wholly forsaken, abandoned." It was coined in the seventeenth century to refer to ships that had been abandoned at sea. The most common reason for deserting a ship was fire, since vessels were ill equipped to handle such a disaster. The only escape route was the lifeboats, but these were liable to catch fire too, unless they were cut free of the ship. For this reason, sailors were inclined to abandon the ship in favor of the lifeboats before the fire got out of hand. Damage to the hull of a ship from submerged coral reefs or icebergs could also force sailors to take to the lifeboats. Abandoned vessels were called *derelicts,* and the image of a listing, deserted ship, with tattered sails flapping in the wind, gave a dilapidated connotation to the word. It was soon applied as well to shabby people and unkempt property.

Sources

Jeans, Peter D. *Ship to Shore: A Dictionary of Everyday Words and Phrases Derived from the Sea.* Santa Barbara, CA: ABC-CLIO, 1993.
Maddocks, Melvin. *The Atlantic Crossing.* Alexandria, VA: Time-Life Books, 1981.
Simpson, J. A., and E. S. C. Weiner, eds. *The Oxford English Dictionary.* 2d ed. Oxford: Clarendon Press, 1989.

Derrick. ***A large crane for hoisting and transporting heavy objects; also, the tall framework over the opening of an oil well.***
Between 20 and 30 criminals were put to death each day in sixteenth-century England, and it was not uncommon for a condemned prisoner to be offered a pardon in exchange for performing the unsavory task of public executioner. According to folklore, Godfrey Derrick made such a bargain. Sentenced to death for rape, the former soldier was pardoned by the earl of Essex and assigned to the infamous Tyburn Prison just outside of London. Hanging was the most common form of execution, but hangmen might use a short rope for unpopular criminals, which meant death not from a broken neck but by slow strangulation. Hangmen could usually be bribed to ensure a quick end by using a long length of rope, but that required a larger gallows. As the story goes, Derrick helped to build a bigger and more substantial gallows at Tyburn, and the improved device was referred to as a *derrick.*

In a twist of fate, Derrick's savior, the earl of Essex, was sentenced to death for treason in 1601. According to a street ballad, the task of executing the earl fell to Derrick, who felt awkward but was nevertheless willing to carry out his orders. Members of the nobility were generally beheaded rather than hanged, but Derrick had little experience with decapitation and it took him three blows to sever the earl's head. Supporters of the popular earl were so outraged that they attacked Derrick, who had to be rescued by prison guards. The earl's last plea to his executioner was repeated in the ballad *Essex's Good Night:*

Derrick, thou knowes't at Calais I saved
Thy life lost for a rape there done
But now thou seest myself is come
By chance into thy hands I light;
Strike out thy blow, that I may know
Thou Essex loved at his good-night.

By the early seventeenth century, the tall rigging used for hanging a man was usually referred to as a derrick. The word later expanded to cover hoisting devices that bear a resemblance to the gallows.

Sources

Chambers, Robert. *The Book of Days.* Philadelphia: J. B. Lippincott Co., 1914.
McHenry, Robert, ed. *The New Encyclopedia Britannica.* 15th ed. Chicago: Encyclopedia Britannica, 1992.
Mish, Frederick C. *The Merriam-Webster New Book of Word Histories.* Springfield, IL: Merriam-Webster, 1991.

Derringer. *A short-barreled pistol.*

Henry Deringer (1786–1868) was a well-respected gunsmith from Philadelphia. Around 1835 he incorporated a unique design feature into his guns: an extremely short barrel. Although most guns of that era were long, heavy weapons, with barrels between eight and ten inches long, Deringer's gun barrel was only two inches. These small weapons could easily be tucked into a coat pocket or even down the bodice of a dress.

Deringer said that he made a pair of the guns for Major Armstrong, who was then a territorial governor. When Armstrong relocated to Washington, he showed them to some of the leading men in government. Demand for the stubby-looking pistols skyrocketed, and Deringer could not keep up. Soon over half a dozen other Philadelphia gunsmiths were producing replicas of the compact weapon. Since every gun maker stamped his name on his version of the gun, there was no fraud involved. However, some of Deringer's employees, led by the gun finisher Henry Schlotterbeck, quit and created their own company, named Slotter and Company. The guns they produced were very similar to the original deringers, and they stamped theirs with the name *derringer,* inserting an extra "r" in order to avoid charges of infringement. Henry Deringer had never filed for a patent on his gun, so he had little recourse for action. Soon a number of gunsmiths, both American and foreign, were producing derringers. These guns sold as well as the originals, and after Deringer's company closed in the late 1870s, the imitators dominated the market with their "double-r" derringers.

Derringer is now associated with any gun having a short barrel. When gun collectors refer to Henry Deringer's original weapon, it is called a deringer-derringer.

Sources

Chapel, Charles Edward. *Guns of the Old West.* New York: Coward-McCann, 1961.
Hendrickson, Robert. *The Dictionary of Eponyms: Names That Became Words.* New York: Stein and Day, 1985.
Parsons, J. E. *Henry Deringer's Pocket Pistol.* New York: Morrow, 1952.

Deutschland über alles. *A belief in the superiority of one's nation or group.*

Deutschland über alles was the first line of "Deutschlandlied," the German national anthem. Translated, the first stanza reads:

Germany, Germany above all
above all else in the world,
When it steadfastly holds together,
offensively and defensively,
with brotherhood.
From the Maas to the Memel,
from the Etsch to the Little Belt,
Germany, Germany above all,
above all else in the world.

This 1848 composition by the nationalist poet August Heinrich Hoffmann von Fallersleben was intended to help unite the loose confederation of German states into a single sovereign nation. His dream came true after the Franco-Prussian War of 1870–1871 when the German Empire was formally established. In 1922, the song was selected to become the national anthem of Germany, again to inspire allegiance to the German nation over regional loyalties. Outside German borders, the phrase *Deutschland über alles* smacked of bombastic German chauvinism, especially after the Nazi party adopted the song as their anthem in 1933 when they came to power. After World War II the victorious Allied powers imposed a ban on the song in Germany, but the Germans were reluctant to surrender their national anthem. In 1952 it was decided that the third verse of the poem would be used as the official song. With the unification of Germany in 1990, "Deutschlandlied" was adopted as the national anthem, minus the controversial first verse.

It is unlikely that the phrase will ever overcome its fascist association. Writers today employ the expression *über alles* when they wish to vilify a subject. For example, when the controversial book *The Bell Curve* was published, with its suggestion that intelligence is inherited along racial lines, one review was titled, "IQ über alles?"

Sources

McHenry, Robert, ed. *The New Encyclopedia Britannica.* 15th ed. Chicago: Encyclopedia Britannica, 1992.

Zentner, Christian, and Friedemann Budurftig, eds. *Encyclopedia of the Third Reich.* New York: Macmillan, 1991.

Devil's advocate. ***Someone who argues against an idea to test its validity.***

The Roman Catholic Church uses devil's advocates, properly known as "promoters of faith," in the process of examining a candidate for sainthood. In the early days of the church, the process of canonization lacked any sort of formal guidelines. As a result, a number of people were acknowledged as saints based on bizarre and sensational accounts that were usually accepted without question. By 973, systematic and rigorous procedures were in place and were first used in the canonization of Saint Udalricus.

The process is initiated by the bishop in whose diocese the candidate lived; he presents a case for sainthood to the papacy. The papacy then appoints a promoter of faith, or *devil's advocate,* whose job it is to examine critically the candidate's life and writings, searching for any evidence that the individual is not worthy of beatification. The task is similar to that of a prosecuting attorney, who always seeks to counter the evidence presented by the defense.

Sources

McDonald, William J., ed. *New Catholic Encyclopedia.* New York: McGraw-Hill, 1967.

McHenry, Robert, ed. *The New Encyclopedia Britannica.* 15th ed. Chicago: Encyclopedia Britannica, 1992.

Woodward, Kenneth L. *Making Saints: How the Catholic Church Determines Who Becomes a Saint, Who Doesn't, and Why.* New York: Simon and Schuster, 1990.

Dewey decimal system. ***A classification system for arranging the contents of a library.***

The Dewey decimal system was created by Melvil Dewey (1851–1931), a librarian and one of the founders of the American Library Association. Before the development of the system, there was no widely accepted method for the arrangement of books, and libraries were poorly organized and difficult to use. Dewey designed a very logical system for subdividing the world's knowledge into 100 general divisions, with room for specificity after a decimal point. For example, the ten numbers within the 940s are reserved for European history. French history is covered under 944, and the history of the French Revolution is under 944.04.

The simplicity of Dewey's system made it very popular, and it rapidly became the standard for organizing libraries in the English-speaking world. It is less useful for cataloging very large libraries, because there are simply not enough numbers to cover the entire collection. As a result, most major university libraries have adopted the Library of Congress classification system, while public libraries still generally prefer the Dewey decimal system.

Sources

Hendrickson, Robert. *Dictionary of Eponyms: Names That Became Words.* New York: Stein and Day, 1985.

Wiegand, Wayne A. *Irrepressible Reformer: A Biography of Melville Dewey.* Chicago: American Library Association, 1996.

Wynar, Bohdan S., ed. *Dictionary of American Library Biography.* Littleton, CO: Libraries Unlimited, 1978.

DeWitt. ***To lynch a person, particularly for political reasons.***

Considered "one of the greatest statesmen of his age," Jan De Witt (1625–1672) of Holland was an ardent supporter of republican rights as against the prerogatives of authoritarian kingship, and he eloquently advocated such principles from his position as a foremost political leader. Holland had been nearly bankrupted from a series of wars in the 1650s, but De Witt's brilliant economic policies restored the finances of the country and helped it achieve commercial ascendancy over the East Indies. However, by the 1670s De Witt's popularity had sharply declined in favor of William, Prince of Orange. When Holland was invaded in 1672 by Louis XIV of France, the people cried out for the leadership of William, and there were violent demonstrations against the prince's rivals, Jan and his brother Cornelius. Cornelius was arrested and charged with conspiring against William. When Jan came to visit him in prison, an angry crowd gathered and called for the blood of the two brothers. Evidently, guards allowed some of the mob to enter the prison, and the brothers were dragged into the street, where Cornelius was beaten to death and Jan was killed by gunshot. The crowd continued to pummel and fire shots into their bodies and finally strung the corpses up on a scaffold.

It did not take long for the word to make its way into the English language. When some of King William's advisors became too friendly with French spies, a political pamphlet (*A Modest Enquiry into the Causes of the Present Disasters in England*) of 1689 proclaimed, "It's a wonder the English nation have not in their fury De-Witted some of those men."

Sources

McHenry, Robert, ed. *The New Encyclopedia Britannica.* 15th ed. Chicago: Encyclopedia Britannica, 1992.

Rowen, Herbert H. *John de Witt: Grand Pensionary of Holland, 1625–1672.* Princeton, NJ: Princeton University Press, 1978.

Simpson, J. A., and E. S. C. Weiner, eds. *The Oxford English Dictionary.* 2d ed. Oxford: Clarendon Press, 1989.

Trahair, R. C. S. *From Aristotelian to Reaganomics: A Dictionary of Eponyms with Biographies in the Social Sciences.* Westport, CT: Greenwood Press, 1994.

Die is cast. ***An irrevocable decision.***

Upon crossing the Rubicon, Julius Caesar is reputed to have said, "The die is cast." (*See* Rubicon.)

Diehard. ***Someone who does not give up easily.***

This odd expression emerged during the Napoleonic Wars. In 1811 Colonel William Inglis (1764–1835) and his regiment, the British 57th Foot, were pinned down by the French at the small Spanish town of Albuera. It was vital that the regiment hold its position, but the odds were against them. The colonel had lost his mount in the siege and then was shot in the neck. Knowing he was unable to fight and seeing the French close in, Inglis shouted to his men, "Die hard, 57th! Die hard!" His men must have heard him. Of 579 soldiers, 438 were either killed or wounded. None fled their posts, and it was later remarked that all the wounded had been facing their attackers when they were shot. The British won the battle, and from that day on the 57th regiment has been known as the Diehards.

The word *diehard* now refers to political groups and to individuals who stick to their convictions no matter the odds against them.

Sources

Hendrickson, Robert. *Facts on File Encyclopedia of Word and Phrase Origins.* New York: Facts on File, 1987.

Safire, William. *Safire's Political Dictionary.* New York: Random House, 1978.

Stephen, Leslie, and Sidney Lee, eds. *The Dictionary of National Biography.* London: Oxford University Press, 1921.

Diesel engine. ***A highly efficient internal combustion engine that uses the heat of compressed air to spark ignition.***

The son of German parents, Rudolph Diesel (1858–1913) lived in France until the outbreak of the Franco-Prussian War in 1870. Forced to flee the country, the Diesels settled in a shabby apartment in London, where they had difficulty supporting themselves. Twelve-year-old Rudolph was sent to live with relatives in Bavaria and began attending a technical school. He displayed a natural aptitude for science, languages, and engineering, which earned him a four-year scholarship to college. Intrigued to learn that standard steam engines were only 6 to 10 percent effective in their consumption of fuel, Diesel spent the next several years tinkering with variations on combustion engines. In 1892 he received a patent on an engine in which the ignition starts from highly compressed air rather than an electric spark, as in the case of a gasoline engine. Diesel's new design tripled the efficiency of fuel use.

Diesel became rich as a result of his invention. He sold the rights to the North American patent for one million marks and drew substantial annual revenues from several European firms. As good as Diesel was at making money, he was better at spending it. He appreciated fine art and acquired expensive pieces for his mansion, which overlooked the Isar River in Munich. He also purchased expensive racing cars, hosted lavish dinner parties, and lived life in the same opulent manner as the European aristocracy with whom he now associated. Eventually, a series of poor investments and a devastating lawsuit nearly bankrupted Diesel. He mortgaged his splendid Munich estate and his automobiles and entered a sanitarium to be treated for nervous exhaustion. His life came to a mysterious end in 1913 when he disappeared off a steamship bound for England. After dinner with friends, he excused himself to take a stroll around the deck, and he was never seen again, though his coat and hat were found near the railing. There was some unfounded speculation that he had been murdered by rival businessmen, or by agents of the kaiser who feared Diesel was passing industrial secrets to the British. However, his huge debts (amounting to $400,000) and his history of nervous disorders pointed to a suicide. Diesel's own family believed that he had probably taken his own life.

Sources

Fucini, Joseph, and Suzy Fucini. *Entrepreneurs: The Men and Women behind Famous Brand Names and How They Made It.* Boston: G. K. Hall, 1985.

Hendrickson, Robert. *Dictionary of Eponyms: Names That Became Words.* New York: Stein and Day, 1985.

Nitske, W. Robert. *Rudolf Diesel: Pioneer in the Age of Power.* Norman: University of Oklahoma Press, 1965.

Dime novel. ***A paperback novel, characterized by a swift-moving and simple plot.***

Before the 1860s books were fairly expensive items, with a price ranging between $1 and $3 ($20 to $50 in 1995 terms). As a result, few people owned books beyond a family Bible and one or two practical household guides. After the Civil War, improvements in the printing industry and cheaper paper made the production of books less expensive. The dime novel was invented to create a market among readers who did not generally purchase books. Selling for 10 cents (about $2.00 in 1997 terms), the first dime novel was *Malaeska: The Indian Wife of the White Hunter,* by Mrs. Ann S. Stephens. Published by I. P. Beadle in 1860, this novel was a fast-paced adventure story and was the model for subsequent works in the genre. Books about the American Revolution, cowboys and Indians, and the Civil War were the most popular topics of the early dime novels.

In the twentieth century, *dime novel* refers not to the price but to the literary value. Capturing a huge segment of the paperback market, contemporary mysteries, romances, and thrillers that fit this description are usually action-packed and fairly predictable. Ironically, the original dime novel, *Malaeska,* is now a collector's item and sells for well over $500.

Sources

Haller, Margaret. *The Book Collector's Fact Book.* New York: Arco Publishing Company, 1976.

Schreuders, Piet. *Paperbacks U.S.A.: A Graphic History, 1939–1959.* San Diego: Blue Dolphin Enterprises, 1981.

Sullivan, Larry E., and Lydia Cushman Schurman, eds. *Pioneers, Passionate Ladies, and Private Eyes: Dime Novels, Series Books, and Paperbacks.* New York: Haworth Press, 1996.

Dine with Duke Humphrey. *To go without dinner.*

This expression may originate in the suspicion that Humphrey Plantagenet (1391–1447), duke of Gloucester, starved to death while in prison. Humphrey was the youngest brother of Henry V. After the king died suddenly in 1422, the duke was appointed Protector for the infant king Henry VI. This was a position fraught with danger during the Middle Ages. Although lacking the full authority of the throne, the Protector was still subject to the political rivalries that were rampant in aristocratic power circles.

As the young monarch came of age, he began to favor his half-brother, Bishop Henry Beaufort, who had long been a rival of Humphrey's. The duke's influence and power declined, and he became an easy target when national tensions increased. Arrested and imprisoned, he died five days later, though no formal charges were brought against him. When it was announced that the duke had expired from "pure melancholy," there were inevitable murmurings of foul play. Despite the association of the expression with lack of food, it is unlikely that the duke could have starved to death in five days, unless he had also been deprived of water. Some historians have speculated that the duke, who was 57, may have suffered a heart attack brought on by stress.

Another possible explanation for *dining with Duke Humphrey* is the mistaken belief that the duke was buried in Saint Paul's Cathedral. The aisle known as "Duke Humphrey's Walk" is frequented by tramps and beggars, and some etymologists propose that those unable to afford a meal jested about dining with the duke as they loitered in the cathedral.

Sources

Hendrickson, Robert. *Dictionary of Eponyms: Names That Became Words.* New York: Stein and Day, 1985.

Stephen, Leslie, and Sidney Lee, eds. *The Dictionary of National Biography.* London: Oxford University Press, 1921.

Stimpson, George. *A Book about a Thousand Things.* New York: Harper and Brothers, 1946.

Vizetelly, Frank H. *A Desk-Book of Idioms and Idiomatic Phrases.* New York: Funk and Wagnalls Co., 1923.

Dirge. *A doleful, melancholy song or poem.*

Medieval Catholic funerals were lengthy, formal affairs, which included a wake extending a half a day after death to insure that the individual had actually died. The body was then carried to the church, accompanied by the singing of psalms and alleluias. A Mass was celebrated, followed by a procession to the cemetery where additional psalms were sung. Traditionally, the first song at the funeral was based on the eighth verse of the fifth psalm: *Dirige, Domine, Deus meus, in conspectu tuo viam meam,* meaning "Direct, O Lord, my God, my way in thy sight."

Most of the people who attended the funerals could not understand Latin, but the *Dirige* was so well known that it was eventually shortened to *dirge* and was used in reference to any mournful, funereal song.

Sources

McDonald, William J., ed. *New Catholic Encyclopedia.* New York: McGraw-Hill, 1967.

Mish, Frederick C. *The Merriam-Webster New Book of Word Histories.* Springfield, IL: Merriam-Webster, 1991.
Sadie, Stanley, ed. *The New Grove Dictionary of Music and Musicians.* Washington, DC: Grove's Dictionaries of Music, 1980.
Simpson, J. A., and E. S. C. Weiner, eds. *The Oxford English Dictionary.* 2d ed. Oxford: Clarendon Press, 1989.

Dismal. ***Indicating gloom, depression, and lack of hope.***

Medieval calendars designated two days of each month to be *dies mali,* or "evil days." Regarded as inauspicious, these were the days that people should avoid bloodletting, travel, or important undertakings. The *dies mali* were January 1 and 25; February 4 and 26; March 1 and 28; April 10 and 20; May 3 and 25; June 10 and 16; July 13 and 22; August 1 and 30; September 3 and 21; October 3 and 22; November 5 and 28; and December 7 and 22.

The *dies mali* were also called "Egyptian days" because it was said that Egyptian astronomers computed them. Another claim was that these unlucky days were associated with the biblical plagues of ancient Egypt. Eventually the expression was generalized to refer to any unpropitious events or unfortunate people, and by the end of the sixteenth century, it was condensed into one word, *dismal.*

Sources

Mish, Frederick C. *The Merriam-Webster New Book of Word Histories.* Springfield, IL: Merriam-Webster, 1991.
Simpson, J. A., and E. S. C. Weiner, eds. *The Oxford English Dictionary.* 2d ed. Oxford: Clarendon Press, 1989.

Dixie. ***The southern states, usually referring to the Confederate states.***

"Dixie" was the title of a song written by Daniel Decatur Emmett in 1859 that extolled the South. Adopted by the Confederate army as a marching song, it was generally considered to be the Confederate anthem. Although this word is significant in American history, its origin is uncertain, and the guesses as to its derivation are unsatisfying.

One explanation cites the Citizens' Bank of New Orleans, which circulated ten-dollar bills known as *dix,* meaning "ten" in French. Hence, the *land of dixies* would refer to the southern area where these notes were accepted. The story most frequently cited is also the most bizarre. In 1885 the *Charleston Courier* claimed that the word dated to antebellum days. A New York slaveowner named Dixie was well liked by his slaves, as he treated them kindly. When the abolition sentiment in the state made slavery illegal, the slaves were sent south, but they recalled the "land of Dixie" as a place of happiness and ease. How this sentiment came to be identified with the Old South is not explained. Another account claims that *Dixie* is a reference to the Mason-Dixon line. Although this derivation seems most logical, etymologists have not been able to establish a solid connection.

Sources

Hendrickson, Robert. *The Facts on File Encyclopedia of Word and Phrase Origins.* New York: Facts on File, 1987.
Lurie, Charles. *Everyday Sayings.* Detroit, MI: Gale Research, 1968.
Panati, Charles. *Panati's Extraordinary Origins of Everyday Things.* New York: Perennial Library, 1989.
Wilson, Charles Reagan, and William Ferris, eds. *Encyclopedia of Southern Culture.* Chapel Hill: University of North Carolina Press, 1989.

Doctor Fell syndrome. ***The inexplicable unpopularity of a person, despite seemingly sterling qualities.***

Campaign consultants coined this phrase to describe an electorate's unaccountable dislike of a candidate. John Fell (1625–1686) was an Oxford professor and Anglican priest noted for the many useful reforms he introduced into the university. Fell was known as a man of extraordinary courage, who risked his entire career and personal fortune by holding traditional Church of England services during the Protectorate of Cromwell. Despite these credentials, he is best remembered for a curious poem penned by one of his students, Thomas Brown. Fell had threatened to expel Brown if the student could not translate a Latin couplet. Instead of submitting the translation, Brown wrote the following jingle:

I do not love thee, Dr. Fell,
The reason why I cannot tell;
But this alone I know full well,
I do not love thee, Dr. Fell.

Fell accepted the poem with good grace and did not expel Brown, who was apparently reflecting a common sentiment. Although Fell was acknowledged as a man of courage and vision, some people simply did not care for him but were hard-pressed to say precisely why.

A modern example of the *Doctor Fell syndrome* was Adlai Stevenson (1900–1965), who has been widely regarded as one of the most qualified, wise, and insightful men to run for the presidency in the twentieth century. Regardless, the voting public simply did not like Stevenson but rarely furnished a good reason for their aversion. Stevenson was thoroughly beaten by Dwight Eisenhower in both the 1952 and 1956 elections. Barry Goldwater, Robert Dole, and Michael Dukakis are other politicians who were respected by the voters for their credentials and positions, but suffered in the polls because they simply did not appeal to the voters.

Sources

Hendrickson, Robert. *Facts on File Encyclopedia of Word and Phrase Origins.* New York: Facts on File, 1987.

Safire, William. *Safire's Political Dictionary.* New York: Random House, 1978.

Stimpson, George. *A Book about a Thousand Things.* New York: Harper and Brothers, 1946.

Dodo, dead as a dodo. ***Completely lifeless; also, outdated and forgotten.***
Dodo birds were native to the Mascarene Islands, located between Australia and Madagascar. The islands, isolated by thousands of miles of ocean, were uninhabited and had no large animal predators. As such, dodo birds lacked an instinctive fear of human beings, which might have saved them when the islands were discovered by Dutch explorers in the sixteenth century. The friendly dodo birds resembled turkeys, with fat, clumsy bodies and tiny wings incapable of flight. Because the birds were completely docile, it was commonly assumed that they were also stupid. When settlers colonized the Mascarene Islands, they feasted on the plump birds, and the dodo population plunged. Since the birds laid only one egg a year, they were unable to repopulate fast enough to suit the hungry colonists. By the 1680s the dodo birds were extinct on the islands. Although specimens had been taken back to Europe as curiosities, none had been bred. Despite the sketches that circulated of the pot-bellied birds, within a hundred years people began to doubt that the species had ever existed, and the dodo was dubbed a mythological creature, like a unicorn or phoenix. Later, a nineteenth-century naturalist exploring the Mascarene Islands uncovered a mass of complete dodo skeletons, which proved the existence of the friendly, harmless bird.

Sources

Campell, Bruce, and Elizabeth Lack. *Dictionary of Birds.* Vermillion, SD: Buteo Books, 1985.

Panati, Charles. *Panati's Extraordinary Endings of Practically Everything and Everybody.* New York: Perennial Library, 1989.

Dog days. ***The hottest part of the summer.***
The ancient Roman belief in astrology underlies the expression *dog days.* In that epoch, the star Sirius rose with the sun from July 3 to August 11. Sirius was known as the dog star because it was at the head of the constellation Caius Major, or "greater dog." It was one of the closest and brightest stars in the night sky, and when it appeared in conjunction with the sun, the Romans believed that it produced hot, sultry weather. These days were referred to as *canicularis dies,* "the days of the dog," and they were regarded as unpropitious. During the hottest days of the year, people were listless, there was drought, and pestilence often occurred at the same time. All were blamed on the influence of the dog star.

Over the last two millennia, there have been gradual shifts in the patterns of the stars, which means that the dog star now rises several weeks later. However, the expression *dog days* will probably always be associated with the intense heat of July and August.

Sources

Chambers, Robert. *The Book of Days.* London: W. and R. Chambers, 1914.

Gettings, Fred. *Dictionary of Astrology.* London: Routledge, 1985.

Mish, Frederick C. *The Merriam-Webster New Book of Word Histories.* Springfield, IL: Merriam-Webster, 1991.

Donkey. ***The symbol of the Democratic party.***

Both the donkey and the elephant as symbols of the two major American political parties were invented by the cartoonist Thomas Nast (1840–1902), who was a lifelong Republican. The first cartoon that used the donkey to symbolize the Democratic party appeared in the *Harper's Weekly* issue of 15 January 1870. Nast's famous picture showed a lion being kicked over by a donkey. Edwin M. Stanton, who had died a few weeks before, was the lion. Stanton, a staunch Democrat, had been Lincoln's secretary of war throughout most of the Civil War, and his outspoken support of antislavery issues had endeared him to Nast. The donkey was labeled "Copperhead Papers," referring to the northern Democrats who had opposed the Civil War and were stigmatized as disloyal to the Union. The caption read, "A live Jackass kicking a dead lion. And such a lion! and such a Jackass!"

Nast later used the donkey on a regular basis to represent the Democratic party. The image was fostered by Ignatius Donnelly, a congressman from Minnesota, who stated that "the Democratic party is like a mule—without pride of ancestry or hope of posterity." As other cartoonists adopted the symbol, the Democrats became irreversibly associated with it and eventually embraced it. Clinton Rossiter, a modern historian, made the following observation about the appropriateness of the donkey and elephant images: "the slightly ridiculous but tough and long-lived Donkey—the perfect symbol of the rowdy Democrats; the majestic but ponderous Elephant—the perfect symbol of respectable Republicans. Can anyone imagine the Donkey as a Republican and the Elephant as a Democrat?"

Sources

Safire, William. *Safire's Political Dictionary.* New York: Random House, 1978.

Stimpson, George. *A Book about American Politics.* New York: Harper, 1954.

Donnybrook. ***A rowdy, disorderly gathering.***

In medieval Europe, fairs were vital for the distribution of livestock, textiles, grain, and other goods, but they also had an important social function. Athletic competitions were held, traveling bands of actors staged performances, and people indulged in food and drink. In 1204 King John of England issued a charter that established an eight-day fair in Donnybrook, a village just west of Dublin. Although the Donnybrook fair was not out of the ordinary in its early years, it later earned a reputation for raucous behavior and violence. In the seventeenth and eighteenth centuries, there were fierce rivalries between trade guilds, and these spilled over into brawls when the various guilds came in contact with one another at the fair. The event was also an opportunity to indulge in religious hostility, and Catholic and Protestant gangs were known to unleash their grievances during the general excitement of the carnival-like atmosphere.

By the nineteenth century, the Donnybrook fair had become a byword for unrestrained revelry and chaos. A movement to suppress the fair gained strength in the 1830s, on the grounds that it menaced public morality and family life and undercut temperance efforts. Physicians added that the fair was a danger to public health, given the transmission of disease facilitated by the crowds of attendees. In 1855 permission to hold the fair was withdrawn. For several years disappointed Dubliners attempted to continue the fair at another location, but pressure from the clergy and refusal of a liquor license doomed it to failure. The last attempt to hold the Donnybrook fair was in 1868 when police reported that 120 people "of the lowest class" gathered on a Sunday afternoon to be entertained by a handful of tumblers. After this demoralizing turnout, the fair passed into memory.

Sources

Lurie, Charles. *Everyday Sayings.* Detroit, MI: Gale Research, 1968.

O'Maitiu, Seamus. *The Humours of Donnybrook: Dublin's Famous Fair and Its Suppression.* Dublin: Irish Academic Press, 1995.

Simpson, J. A., and E. S. C. Weiner, eds. *The Oxford English Dictionary.* 2d ed. Oxford: Clarendon Press, 1989.

Doozy. ***An exceptional example of something, used in both a positive and negative sense.***

The son of German immigrants, Frederick Samuel Duesenberg (1877–1932) was fascinated by speed. In his youth he was an amateur bicycle racer and set world speed records for two- and three-mile races. Entering the automobile business, he began designing cars with his brother Augie, and their cars, named Duesenbergs, were some of the best of the era. The engines were so compact, powerful, and well crafted that the Duesenbergs were asked to adapt the design to boats and airplanes.

Duesenberg cars were very popular among the jet set, who admired their speed and elegance: Gary Cooper and Clark Gable, for example, had custom-made Duesenbergs. Although the company went out of business in 1937, the automobile's nickname, *doozy,* soon became synonymous with a remarkable example of something. Duesenbergs are now collector's items and sell for between $250,000 and $1 million.

Sources

Lighter, J. E. *Random House Historical Dictionary of American Slang.* New York: Random House, 1994.

Spofford, Ainsworth R., ed. *The National Cyclopedia of American Biography.* Clifton, NJ: J. T. White, 1926.

Yates, Brock. "Duesenberg." *American Heritage* 45, no. 4 (1994): 88–99.

Doubting Thomas. ***Someone who refuses to believe unless incontestable proof is offered.***

Saint Thomas the Apostle was one of Jesus' most devoted followers, but he is remembered primarily as the disciple who doubted that others had seen the resurrected Christ. In the Gospel of John, Thomas declares, "Unless I see the scars of the nails in his hands and put my finger on those scars and my hand in his side, I will not believe." A week later, when Jesus appeared to the twelve, Thomas was given visual proof to dispel his doubts. In an apocryphal variation, Thomas refused to believe that Mary, the mother of Jesus, had been bodily taken up into heaven. Mary let her mantle fall to earth, thus convincing the doubting Thomas.

Little is known of Thomas's life after the death of Jesus. Christian tradition states that he traveled to India, established the first Christian communities there, and then was martyred.

Sources

McDonald, William J., ed. *New Catholic Encyclopedia.* New York: McGraw-Hill, 1967.

Metford, J. C. J. *Dictionary of Christian Lore and Legend.* London: Thames and Hudson, 1983.

Stimpson, George. *A Book about the Bible.* New York: Harper and Brothers, 1945.

Walsh, Michael, ed. *Butler's Lives of the Saints.* San Francisco: Harper and Row, 1985.

Draconian justice. ***A form of justice that is swift, harsh, and merciless.***

Draco was an Athenian lawyer in the seventh century B.C. In the courts of ancient Greece, all laws were oral, which made the administration of justice arbitrary. Judges were often the same men who made the laws, and the system was heavily weighted in favor of aristocratic plaintiffs. By Draco's time, economic and political hostility between the middle and elite classes had created a tense political climate. With the spread of writing came a recognition of the need for an inscribed set of laws. Draco's contribution to the legal system was to compile the first written code of justice, accomplished in 621 B.C. The laws were inscribed on four wooden-faced blocks called *axones* and were available to the public, which meant they could no longer be easily ignored or manipulated to suit the whim of the judges. Almost nothing survives of Draco's code, but tradition endowed it with its harsh reputation. Apparently Draco relied on the death penalty for most offenses, including minor infractions such as idleness and petty theft. His legal code was overturned when the famed Athenian statesman Solon devised a new one in 594 B.C.

Although Draco's name has acquired a sinister and ominous connotation, during his lifetime he was admired by the Greek people. In fact, his popularity proved fatal. According to Plutarch, Draco made an appearance at an Athenian theater and, as was the custom, was showered by the crowd with garments and flowers in an expression of their adulation. Draco was smothered to death under the profusion of gifts.

Sources

Gagarin, Michael. *Drakon and Early Athenian Homicide Law.* New Haven, CT: Yale University Press, 1981.

Hornblower, Simon, and Antony Spawforth, eds. *The Oxford Classical Dictionary.* New York: Oxford University Press, 1996.

McHenry, Robert, ed. *The New Encyclopedia Britannica.* 15th ed. Chicago: Encyclopedia Britannica, 1992.

Sacks, David. *Encyclopedia of the Ancient Greek World.* New York: Facts on File, 1995.

Duke of Exeter's daughter. ***The rack.***
John Holland (1395–1447), better known as the duke of Exeter, was a close associate of Henry V and was well known for his bravery in battle. In 1420 the king gave Exeter a lifetime appointment as the constable of the Tower of London as a reward for his years of service. The duke introduced the rack as an instrument of torture of tower prisoners in the 1440s, and it was thereafter known as the *duke of Exeter's daughter.*

Before the thirteenth century, European courts had depended on the use of ordeals to determine guilt or innocence. Suspects were subjected to bodily harm, and their fate depended on the healing of their injury (see *Trial by fire*). When the Fourth Lateran Council abolished the use of ordeals in 1215, another method for determining facts was sought, and most countries, including England, turned to torture. Confessions and accusations obtained through the use of the iron maiden and the rack were legally valid. As one fifteenth-century English warrant stated, the rack was the "accustomed torture" in the Tower of London. It involved attaching the victim's feet and hands into manacles and stretching him until the desired information was obtained or until most of the victim's joints had become dislocated.

The judicial use of torture was banned in England in the 1640s, and the rest of Europe followed suit by the next century.

Sources

Langbein, John H. *Torture and the Law of Proof: England and Europe in the Ancien Regime.* Chicago: University of Chicago Press, 1977.

Stephen, Leslie, and Sidney Lee, eds. *The Dictionary of National Biography.* London: Oxford University Press, 1921.

Dun. ***To demand payment for a debt.***
According to *The Oxford English Dictionary,* one of the most effective bailiffs for the collection of debts was a doggedly persistent man named Joe Dun. He lived in London during the reign of Henry VII (1485–1509), a time when slipping into debt was dangerously easy. Shopkeepers regularly extended credit to their customers, and people whose income was at the mercy of the weather or seasonal work might find themselves unable to pay. Failure to settle a debt was a crime punishable by imprisonment. Creditors were not always willing to track down their debtors, so they simply sold the note to third parties, including professional debt collectors and court bailiffs. "Send Dun" was common advice to anyone having trouble

collecting amounts owed. By the early seventeenth century, the name of this particularly effective court bailiff had become an eponym.

Sources

Hendrickson, Robert. *The Dictionary of Eponyms: Names That Became Words.* New York: Stein and Day, 1985.

Simpson, J. A., and E. S. C. Weiner, eds. *The Oxford English Dictionary.* 2d ed. Oxford: Clarendon Press, 1989.

Dunce. *Someone who is reluctant to learn; a dullard.*

John Duns Scotus would have been horrified had he known the eponym associated with his name. Duns Scotus (1266–1308) was highly educated and a respected theologian. An ordained priest, he was instrumental in the development of the doctrine that Mary, the mother of Jesus, was conceived without sin. Duns Scotus advanced other controversial ideas as well, such as the beliefs that the will is superior to the intellect and that the Incarnation was not dependent on original sin.

The convictions of Duns Scotus were in direct contradiction to the teachings of Thomas Aquinas. Because Aquinas would ultimately gain greater acceptance within Catholicism, Duns Scotus came to be regarded as the defender of an outmoded form of belief. After his death a number of his passionate followers, dubbed Dunsmen, continued to champion his ideas. By the fifteenth century the views of Aquinas and the "new theology" were ascendant, and the Dunsmen were branded as resistant to change, eventually becoming the target of ridicule. The term *dunsmen* evolved into *dunce,* and today it refers to someone who is unable or unwilling to learn.

Sources

Beeching, Cyril Leslie. *A Dictionary of Eponyms.* London: Clive Bingley, 1979.

Harris, Charles Reginald. *Duns Scotus.* New York: Humanities Press, 1959.

McHenry, Robert, ed. *The New Encyclopedia Britannica.* 15th ed. Chicago: Encyclopedia Britannica, 1992.

Mish, Frederick C. *The Merriam-Webster New Book of Word Histories.* Springfield, IL: Merriam-Webster, 1991.

Dunkirk. *A desperate, last-ditch effort to stave off utter defeat.*

During May 1940, the Allied armies were almost encircled by German forces in northeastern France. The German capture of Abbeville and the loss of a number of channel ports made an Allied withdrawal essential, but by late May Dunkirk was the only viable evacuation point left. The operation lasted from May 26 to June 4 and utilized 41 destroyers and dozens of troopships, minesweepers, and patrol craft in the transport of hundreds of thousands of men across the English Channel. A brigade of civilian volunteers assisted in ferrying soldiers to safety in small craft that ranged from yachts to fishing boats. Withdrawal was facilitated by an error in judgment on the part of Luftwaffe commander Hermann Goering, who had assured Hitler that his aircraft would be sufficient to halt the evacuation. Instead, largely through the heroic defensive efforts of the Royal Air Force, a total of 340,000 men escaped to England. Because this represented a substantial portion of Great Britain's experienced soldiers, their rescue had a profound effect on future events.

The evacuation at Dunkirk can be called a victory only if that is defined as the avoidance of annihilation. Nevertheless, the word carries with it a connotation of heroism and courage in the face of seemingly insurmountable odds.

Sources

Jackson, Robert. *Dunkirk: The British Evacuation 1940.* New York: St. Martins Press, 1976.

McHenry, Robert, ed. *The New Encyclopedia Britannica.* 15th ed. Chicago: Encyclopedia Britannica, 1992.

Parrish, Thomas, and S. L. A. Marshall. *Simon and Schuster Encyclopedia of World War II.* New York: Simon and Schuster, 1978.

Young, Peter, ed. *The World Almanac of World War II: The Complete and Comprehensive Documentary of World War II.* New York: World Almanac, 1986.

E

Eat Crow.
See Crow.

Eichmann phenomenon. ***A psychological term to describe a willingness to perform a morally offensive act if directed to do so by an authority figure.***

Adolf Eichmann (1906–1962) has been referred to as a "desk criminal." Although he did not participate in the actual execution of prisoners during World War II, he arranged for the identification, collection, and transport of over three million Jews to death camps. Since Eichmann visited Auschwitz, it is certain that he was aware of the fate of the people he was "relocating." Briefly detained by American forces following the war, Eichmann escaped to Argentina where he lived under various aliases for the next 15 years. In 1961 Israeli secret agents tracked down the chief administrator of the "final solution" (see *Final solution*) and abducted him to Israel to face charges. The Nuremberg trials of 1945–1946 (see *Nuremberg defense*) had defined the concept of crimes against humanity as offenses that are so morally reprehensible that a person could not shift responsibility to a commanding officer. Regardless, at his trial Eichmann claimed that he was merely following orders. His plea failed, and he was hanged in 1962.

Psychologists continued to be intrigued by such unconscionable submission to authority figures. In 1966 Yale professor Stanley Milgram designed his now-famous "Eichmann experiment." Forty adult men were told that they were participating in a test to examine the effect of punishment on learning and memory. The test subjects were instructed to ask questions of fellow volunteers, who were actually trained actors. When the actor gave an incorrect response, the test subject was to administer increasingly painful electric shocks to the actor. As the actors feigned pain and asked that the experiment be stopped, stern-looking administrators in white coats insisted that the test proceed. One-half of the test subjects completed the experiment over the anguished cries from the actors, while the other half refused to continue. Milgram's highly controversial results stunned Americans, who believed that the horrendous crimes of the Nazis could never have happened in their country. Instead, Milgram revealed that many people with a deferential attitude toward authority figures could be manipulated into committing heinous acts. The volunteers who administered painful electric shocks to others simply because they were "following orders" were eerie reminders of the Nazi rank-and-file. This dangerously obedient character trait has been dubbed the *Eichmann phenomenon*.

Sources

Elms, Alan, and Stanley Milgram. "Personality Characteristics Associated with Obedience and Defiance toward Authoritative Command." *Journal of Experimental Research in Personality* 1, no. 4 (1966): 282–289.

Goldberg, Philip. *The Babinski Reflex: And 70 Other Useful and Amusing Metaphors from Science, Psychology, Business, Sports, and Everyday Life.* Los Angeles: J. P. Tarcher, 1990.

Zentner, Christian, and Friedemann Budurftig, eds. *Encyclopedia of the Third Reich.* New York: Macmillan, 1991.

Eighth wonder of the world. ***A magnificent achievement; also used sarcastically to refer to colossal failures.***

Efforts to define magnificent works of human achievement date back at least to the fifth century B.C., when the Greek historian Herodotus wrote about the extraordinary achievements of various civilizations that surrounded the Mediterranean. The chief librarian of the great library at Alexandria, Callimachus of Cyrene (305–240 B.C.), also compiled "A Collection of Wonders in Lands throughout the World," although his list was lost when the library burned. By the Middle Ages, a list of Seven Wonders of the Ancient World had been finalized from the opinions of various writers and intellectuals. They were

The Pyramids of Giza, the oldest of the wonders and the only one still in existence

Hanging Gardens of Babylon, a series of landscaped terraces

Statue of Zeus at Olympia, a 40-foot statue (the equivalent of a four-story building) made by Phidias of Athens in 430 B.C.

Temple of Artemis at Ephesus, an enormous temple liberally adorned with beautiful works of art

Mausoleum of Halicarnassus, a monumental tomb built by the widow of King Mausolus (see entry for *Mausoleum*)

Colossus of Rhodes, a 110-foot bronze statue of the sun god that stood at the harbor of Rhodes

Pharos of Alexandria, the most famous lighthouse of the ancient world, built on an island off the coast of Alexandria in 280 B.C.

The list of the seven ancient wonders has inspired imitation: seven natural wonders of the world, seven wonders of the modern world, seven architectural wonders, etc. The expression *eighth wonder* is often used for purposes of promotion—as when it was attached to the Houston Astrodome. However, more often than not, the phrase is employed sarcastically. For example, an 1831 letter by novelist Maria Edgeworth described "a spoiled child of 30 whose mother and father having not been able to conceal from him that they think him the eighth wonder of the world have at last brought him to acquiesce in their opinion."

Sources

Clayton, Pater A. *The Seven Wonders of the Ancient World.* London: Routledge, 1988.

McHenry, Robert, ed. *The New Encyclopedia Britannica.* 15th ed. Chicago: Encyclopedia Britannica, 1992.

Simpson, J. A., and E. S. C. Weiner, eds. *The Oxford English Dictionary.* 2d ed. Oxford: Clarendon Press, 1989.

Elephant. ***The symbol of the Republican party.***

A political cartoon drawn by Thomas Nast in 1874 popularized the elephant as the symbol of the Republican party. In the cartoon, a number of animals, representing various states, parties, and causes, are gathered in a forest and menaced by a donkey wearing a lion's skin labeled "Caesarism." The tag referred to charges made by the Democrats that President Grant was contemplating running for the presidency for a third term. A fearful elephant is running away from the donkey straight toward a number of pitfalls, labeled "Inflation, Reform, and Repudiation."

Republicans may have used the elephant as their symbol before Nast. Some of Abraham Lincoln's banners at the Republican National Convention of 1860 may have sported elephants, but the pachyderm did not become closely associated with the Republicans until Nast's popular cartoons began appearing in *Harper's Weekly.* As Nast was one of the most influential cartoonists of his day, his characterizations were quickly picked up by other satirists.

In the twentieth century, Democratic

presidential candidate Adlai Stevenson furnished a famous explanation for the selection of the elephant: "The elephant has a thick skin, a head full of ivory, and as everyone who has seen a circus parade knows, proceeds best by grasping the tail of its predecessor."

Sources

Safire, William. *Safire's Political Dictionary.* New York: Random House, 1978.
Stimpson, George. *A Book about American Politics.* New York: Harper, 1954.

Elginism. ***The acquisition of the art and artifacts of other countries by more powerful nations and by wealthy collectors; cultural piracy.***

Since 1816 the British Museum has been the proud possessor of a magnificent collection of Greek sculptures and architectural features known as the Elgin marbles. Thomas Bruce (1766–1841), the seventh Lord Elgin, was British ambassador to the Ottoman Empire at a time when the Mediterranean world was under threat from alternating waves of invading armies from France and Turkey. Elgin was a lover of antiquity and was concerned about the decay into which a number of fine Greek temples had fallen. Glorious monuments had been turned into ammunition dumps and storage facilities, pieces of statuary were sold at bargain rates, and marble was ground into powder for lime. To save the Parthenon from such a fate, Lord Elgin obtained permission from the proper Ottoman officials to dismantle the monument and ship major portions back to England at his own expense. His motive was not entirely unselfish, since he intended to adorn his estate in Scotland with the statues, columns, and carvings. However, he went bankrupt in the removal, transportation, and storage of the Elgin marbles, and he eventually sold the lot to the British government for £35,000. There was a storm of controversy over the acquisition of the Greek treasures, and Lord Byron angrily demanded, "By what right had Elgin acquired these glorious remnants . . . the last poor plunder from a bleeding land?" Byron's argument fell on deaf ears, and the Elgin marbles remain to this day in the British Museum.

In the late twentieth century, the word *Elginism* is used by nations who believe their cultural heritage has been and continues to be plundered by wealthy foreigners. A number of countries have passed laws to prohibit the export of items with cultural or historic significance, but the result has been a flourishing black market for illegally removed artifacts. According to the United Nations Educational, Scientific, and Cultural Organization, the illegal market in antiquities may amount to over a billion dollars a year. Even the ownership of legally obtained artwork, such as the Elgin marbles, has now been called into question. Greece, for instance, has persistently demanded the return of the collection, so far without success.

Sources

Hitchens, Christopher. *The Elgin Marbles: Should They Be Returned to Greece?* London: Chatto and Windus, 1987.
Jackson, Donald Dale. "How Lord Elgin First Won—and Lost—His Marbles." *Smithsonian* 23, no. 9 (1992): 135–146.
Stephen, Leslie, and Sidney Lee, eds. *The Dictionary of National Biography.* London: Oxford University Press, 1921.

Éminence grise.

See Gray eminence.

Epicure. ***A person with refined tastes, especially regarding food and wine.***

Epicurus (341–270 B.C.) was a Greek philosopher whose belief in the value of simple pleasure, relaxation, and friendship formed the basis of his teachings. He was considered something of an oddity among the Greeks of his day. He recommended abstaining from political activity and public life, and his school admitted women and slaves. Although Epicurus believed that the pursuit of pleasure should be the primary goal in life, he defined pleasure as the absence of pain, which could be achieved by lessening desire. At his school, meals were simple but adequate, bodily delights were secondary to the contentment of the soul, and sexuality, though not forbidden, was not to be pursued to excess. Epicurus's philosophy spread widely throughout the Mediterranean world, but most of his extensive writings have not survived, which has encouraged misinterpretation. Today Epicureanism has strayed far from its original meaning and implies hedonism and gratification of the senses rather than the pursuit of a simple and virtuous life.

Sources

Edwards, Paul, ed. *The Encyclopedia of Philosophy.* New York: Macmillan, 1967.

Hendrickson, Robert. *Dictionary of Eponyms: Names That Became Words.* New York: Stein and Day, 1985.

McHenry, Robert, ed. *The New Encyclopedia Britannica.* 15th ed. Chicago: Encyclopedia Britannica, 1992.

Sacks, David. *Encyclopedia of the Ancient Greek World.* New York: Facts on File, 1995.

Erastianism. ***The doctrine of state supremacy over ecclesiastical affairs.***

Thomas Erastus (1524–1583) was the Swiss physician and theologian who gave his name to this concept, although it was a doctrine he never preached. In 1568 he wrote the *Seventy-Five Theses,* one of which objected to excommunication, a punishment that deprives a person of the right to belong to a church. Erastus believed that the sacraments should be available to anyone who genuinely wished to receive them. He also wrote that if a government is headed by a Christian, that person is qualified to pass judgment and, in conjunction with the clergy, to correct the immoral conduct of his people. Erastus never argued that the Church was subordinate to the State, merely that a Christian ruler was competent to administer justice.

The contemporary meaning of *Erastian* originated with the Presbyterians in seventeenth-century England, who used it as a derogatory term for advocates of state supremacy over church affairs.

Sources

McDonald, William J., ed. *New Catholic Encyclopedia.* New York: McGraw-Hill, 1967.

McHenry, Robert, ed. *The New Encyclopedia Britannica.* 15th ed. Chicago: Encyclopedia Britannica, 1992.

Et tu? ***Used when questioning the loyalty of a trusted friend or subordinate.***

In the process of building his great empire, Julius Caesar overthrew the Roman Republic and set himself up as a dictator. He counted among his numerous enemies the people of conquered provinces, the senators whose powers he had usurped, and even comrades who envied his power. One such adversary was Marcus Junius Brutus (d. 42 B.C.). Brutus was raised in a staunchly republican family, but his ambitions got the better of him. When Caesar offered him the governorship of Cisalpine Gaul in 46 B.C., Brutus could not resist, and he fell in line behind the dictatorship. Two years later, Brutus, now dissatisfied, agreed to participate in an assassination plot in order to restore the Republic. Because of Brutus's stature, many other senators were persuaded to join, and eventually more than 60 conspirators, including Caesar's trusted friends, were allied with Brutus and Cassius, the mastermind of the plot.

The assassination was scheduled to occur on 15 March 43 B.C. Shortly after Caesar entered the Senate, he was surrounded and stabbed to death. The historian Suetonius reported that as Brutus delivered a blow to his thigh, Caesar looked at him and said, "Et tu, Brute?" ("You too, Brutus?") Caesar then fell dead from the twenty-three wounds in his body. The conspirators, however, had misjudged the sentiments of the Roman people, and instead of being hailed as heroes, they were soon in a fight for their lives. Within a few years, Brutus was forced to commit suicide and so passed into history as one of the great traitors of all time. In Dante's *Inferno,* the deepest circle of Hell is reserved for traitors, with places of particular torment for the three most infamous betrayers: Judas, Cassius, and Brutus.

Sources

Bradford, Ernle D. *Julius Caesar: The Pursuit of Power.* New York: Morrow, 1984.

Bunson, Matthew. *Encyclopedia of the Roman Empire.* New York: Facts on File, 1994.

Fuller, J. F. C. *Julius Caesar: Man, Soldier, and Tyrant.* New Brunswick, NJ: Rutgers University Press, 1965.

McHenry, Robert, ed. *The New Encyclopedia Britannica.* 15th ed. Chicago: Encyclopedia Britannica, 1992.

Eureka! ***An exclamation at a moment of insight.***

Archimedes (287–212 B.C.), a Sicilian mathematician, made this expression famous when he was commissioned by Heiron II of Syracuse to investigate a potential fraud. The king had ordered a solid gold crown of a specified weight. When it arrived, it weighed in correctly, but Heiron suspected that the artist had added alloys to the precious metal. There was no proof against the goldsmith, since a visual inspection was the only known method of evaluating the crown's composition. Archimedes arrived at the solution to the problem as he lay in his bath, and he reportedly cried out "heureka!" meaning "I have found it!"

Archimedes' insight arose from his understanding of volume. Because no metal has the exact density of gold, other metal objects that share the same weight as a specified amount of gold will not share the same volume. Volume can therefore be measured by immersing objects in water. Archimedes used a lump of gold weighing exactly what the king had specified for his crown and measured the amount of water displaced. If the king's crown was pure gold, it would displace the exact amount of water. If the metal in the crown was an alloy, it would displace a different amount of water. As it happened, the king had been cheated. The fate of the artist is unknown, but the event added to the fame of Archimedes.

Sources

Hornblower, Simon, and Antony Spawforth, eds. *The Oxford Classical Dictionary.* 3d ed. Oxford: Oxford University Press, 1996.

Marcone, Michael. *Eureka! What Archimedes Really Meant and 80 Other Key Ideas Explained.* New York: HarperCollins, 1994.

McHenry, Robert, ed. *The New Encyclopedia Britannica.* 15th ed. Chicago: Encyclopedia Britannica, 1992.

Eyeball-to-eyeball. ***A close and dangerous confrontation.***

In October 1962, the Cuban Missile Crisis was touched off by the claim of Senator Kenneth B. Keating of New York that offensive missile bases were being constructed in Cuba. The small island nation, located 90 miles from the Florida coast, had recently formed a strong alliance with the Soviet Union. Although Keating did not reveal the source of his information, U-2 reconnaissance planes confirmed his assertion and further determined that the bases were not yet operational. President John Kennedy ordered an immediate naval blockade of Cuba and issued demands to the Soviets that they dismantle the bases.

In public proclamations the Soviets refused to respect the U.S. quarantine of Cuba, but on October 24, Soviet supply ships sailing to Cuba stopped in their tracks. Four days later Moscow radio carried an announcement from Soviet Premier Khrushchev: "In order to eliminate as rapidly as possible the conflict which endangers the cause of peace . . . the Soviet Government . . . has given a new order to dismantle the arms which you have described as offensive, and to crate and return them to the Soviet Union." Secretary of State Dean Rusk told ABC correspondent John Scali: "Remember when you report this that, eyeball-to-eyeball, they blinked first." *The Saturday Evening Post* popularized the expression with its version: "We're eyeball to eyeball and the other fellow just blinked."

Sources

Detzer, David. *The Brink: Cuban Missile Crisis, 1962.* New York: Crowell, 1979.

Magill, Frank N., and John L. Loos. *Great Events from History: North American Series.* Pasadena, CA: Salem Press, 1997.

Safire, William. *Safire's Political Dictionary.* New York: Random House, 1978.

F

Fabian tactics. ***A cautious policy that avoids direct confrontation and seeks to delay action.***

Fabius (d. 203 B.C.) was consul in Rome during the early stages of the Second Punic War (218–201 B.C.). Hannibal of Carthage had invaded Italy and won successive battles in Cannae, Trebia, Ticinus, and Lake Trasimene. The momentum of the invaders appeared unstoppable as the Roman armies repeatedly met defeat at the hands of the advancing Carthaginians. In 217, Fabius implemented a strategy of attrition. Rather than confront the invaders in direct battles, Fabius cut off Hannibal's supply lines and harassed his army, thereby wearing down the Carthaginians. Although he was called a coward by those who preferred confrontation, it was Fabius's dilatory tactics that halted Hannibal's drive toward Rome. Fabius was given the surname Cunctator, meaning "delayer."

The Fabian Society of Britain drew its name from the Roman general. Founded in 1884, the Fabians advocated a gradual shift to democratic socialism. The society sought to avoid the violent revolutions that had threatened other nations and instead pinned their hopes on the tools of education and public advocacy. The most famous members of the Fabian Society were George Bernard Shaw and Sidney Webb.

Sources

Goldberg, Philip. *The Babinski Reflex: And 70 Other Useful and Amusing Metaphors from Science, Psychology, Business, Sports, and Everyday Life.* Los Angeles: J. P. Tarcher, 1990.

Hornblower, Simon, and Antony Spawforth, eds. *The Oxford Classical Dictionary.* 3d ed. Oxford: Oxford University Press, 1996.

McHenry, Robert, ed. *The New Encyclopedia Britannica.* 15th ed. Chicago: Encyclopedia Britannica, 1992.

Faction. ***A cohesive group separated from a larger majority.***

Roman chariot races were organized by teams, known as *factiones,* each of which raced under a particular color. The "Whites" and the "Reds" were the original teams but were later joined by the "Blues" and the "Greens." Similar to a modern sports franchise, factions constituted a full-fledged business enterprise, complete with financial backers, physicians, horse trainers, and craftsmen. Many of the major cities of the Roman Empire had their own local Blue, Green, Red, and White factions, vastly enlarging the scale of the sport.

The Romans were passionate about their chariot races, and on race day the majority of the city's population could be found in or milling outside the arena. The rivalry between the Blues and the Greens was fierce, and they eventually became the dominant two factions of the sport. The influence of the teams extended beyond the arena. Supporters of the Blues were usually from the aristocracy, while the Greens were the team of the common people. Because of this identification with certain classes, social tensions could rise or fall depending on the outcome of a chariot race. In 509, for example, the Blues and Greens played a major role in a Roman riot. In Byzantium in 532, a disturbance known as the Nika riot was fueled by conflict among the factions. The Blues were retaliating for the murders of some of their number, and the Greens became outraged when the emperor Justinian and his wife Theodora displayed no interest in restraining the Blues. During a chariot race, the crowd became restless. Justinian berated the Greens, and the faction's supporters left the arena in a deliberate insult to the emperor. Surprisingly, the Blues supported the Greens in their snub, but the ensuing riot eventually claimed 30,000 victims.

Sources

Bunson, Matthew. *Encyclopedia of the Roman Empire.* New York: Facts on File, 1994.

Cameron, Alan. *Circus Factions: Blues and Greens at Rome and Byzantium.* Oxford: Clarendon Press, 1976.

Fahrenheit. ***The scale mostly commonly used in the United States for measuring temperatures.***

The first method for accurately measuring temperature was developed by Daniel Gabriel Fahrenheit (1686–1736), a Dutch physicist. He choose two reliable and easily reproducible reference points and then defined a number of small intervals between the points to create a degree scale. The coldest temperature that Fahrenheit was able to produce in his laboratory was the point at which saltwater froze. This temperature represented zero degrees. The other reference point was the temperature of the human body, which he set at 100 degrees. (More precise measures would later establish that normal human body temperature is 98.6 degrees.) By dividing the intervening temperatures into 99 small intervals, Fahrenheit created the first reliable and reproducible temperature scale.

Fahrenheit's selection of the freezing point of saltwater and human body temperature as his reference points explains the odd measurements for water's freezing and boiling points, which are 32 and 212 degrees respectively.

Sources

Gillispie, Charles Coulston, ed. *The Dictionary of Scientific Biography.* New York: Scribner's, 1970.

Hazen, Robert M., and James Trefil. *Science Matters: Achieving Scientific Literacy.* New York: Doubleday, 1991.

McHenry, Robert, ed. *The New Encyclopedia Britannica.* 15th ed. Chicago: Encyclopedia Britannica, 1992.

Fallout. ***Side effects; the by-product of a disagreeable situation.***

The term *fallout* was coined in 1946 and referred to the radioactive debris that lingered after a nuclear explosion. The matter that is vaporized upon nuclear detonation is lifted into the air where it mixes with radioactive particles and forms a huge, traveling cloud of radioactive dust. It is estimated that a one-megaton nuclear bomb would be capable of spreading fallout over 1,000 square miles.

Immediately after the United States dropped the atomic bombs that brought about the Japanese surrender in August 1945, surveys indicated that 85 percent of Americans and Europeans approved of the action. Popular culture embraced the new bomb as a positive development, and the scientists who had created it were heroes. The mood changed when the Soviet Union detonated an atomic bomb in 1949. The Cold War began, and fallout shelters served as a constant reminder of the long-term effects of nuclear warfare.

The word has now been extended to other situations whose negative consequences continue to manifest themselves long after the event, as in "the White House is still dealing with the fallout from the Whitewater controversy."

Sources

Arms, Thomas S. *Encyclopedia of the Cold War.* New York: Facts on File, 1994.

Findling, John E., and Frank W. Thackeray. *Events That Changed America in the Twentieth Century.* Westport, CT: Greenwood Press, 1996.

McHenry, Robert, ed. *The New Encyclopedia Britannica.* 15th ed. Chicago: Encyclopedia Britannica, 1992.

False colors, to sail under false colors. ***To practice deliberate deception in order to gain an advantage.***
Before the advent of radio and Morse code, the only way ships at sea could communicate with one another was through the use of flags, later systematized in semaphore signals. Flying national flags was the most common means of identifying friendly ships, and by 1700 designs had been established for all the major trading nations.

When pirates stalked ships at sea, they carefully observed the vessel for several hours to evaluate the manpower, weapons, and likely cargo. If the decision was to attack, the pirate ship could draw near by flying the flag of a friendly nation and feigning amicable intentions. Lulling an unwary ship into a false sense of security was the height of deception, and that was the sense conveyed by the expression *sailing under false colors.* Once the pirates had sufficiently closed the gap, they raised the infamous "jolly roger," a red or black flag emblazoned with a skull or other menacing symbols, such as a bleeding heart, cutlasses, an hourglass, or a whole skeleton. By the 1730s the skull and crossbones edged out the other emblems and became the standard calling card of pirates.

It is uncertain why the skull and crossbones flag is known as a Jolly Roger, but three theories have emerged. One is that it is an anglicized version of the French *jolie rouge,* or red flag, as many of the early pirate flags were predominantly red rather than black. This is the least likely explanation, as the French were not particularly well known for piracy. Another theory gives credit to a notorious Tamil pirate, Ali Raja, who operated in the Indian Ocean. The most likely explanation is that it is derived from "Old Roger," a common eighteenth-century nickname for the devil.

Sources

Botting, Douglas. *The Pirates.* Alexandria, VA: Time-Life Books, 1978.

Cordingly, David. *Under the Black Flag: The Romance and Reality of Life among the Pirates.* New York: Random House, 1996.

Jeans, Peter D. *Ship to Shore: A Dictionary of Everyday Words and Phrases Derived from the Sea.* Santa Barbara, CA: ABC-CLIO, 1993.

Ferris wheel. ***An amusement park ride with a large, upright rotating wheel carrying cars with passengers.***
In 1893 Chicago hosted the World's Columbian Exposition, which celebrated the 400th anniversary of Columbus's voyage to the New World. Such international expositions were popular in the late nineteenth century. Philadelphia had hosted a centennial in 1876, and Paris had celebrated the 100th anniversary of the French Revolution in 1889 with an exposition whose highlight was the new Eiffel Tower. Organizers of the World's Columbian Exposition hoped to rival the success of the Eiffel Tower and issued a challenge to American civil engineers. George Washington Ferris (1859–1896) of Pittsburgh responded with his vision of a totally new kind of amusement ride. A large, mechanical wheel rose 250 feet and carried 36 cars. Since each car could hold 40 people, the original Ferris wheel had a capacity of 1,440 people. It weighed 1,200 tons and was designed to withstand the strong winds blowing off Lake Michigan. The Ferris wheel was a spectacular attraction and helped to make the Chicago fair the first international exposition in the United States that turned a profit. Other amusement parks soon began constructing modified versions of the ride, although none would rival the size of the original.

Sources

Johnson, Allen, and Dumas Malone, eds. *Dictionary of American Biography.* New York: Scribner's, 1964.

McHenry, Robert, ed. *The New Encyclopedia Britannica.* 15th ed. Chicago: Encyclopedia Britannica, 1992.

Tompkins, Vincent, ed. *American Eras: 1878–1899.* Detroit, MI: Gale Research, 1997.

Fiasco. ***A disaster; a complete failure.***
The English word *fiasco* is borrowed from the Italian word for "flask." The history of its meaning began with the glass makers of Venice, renowned for centuries for the

production of the highest quality glass. A combination of excellent natural resources, an intensive apprentice system, and a willingness to experiment with innovative techniques gave the Venetian glass-making industry its unparalleled reputation. The Venetians pioneered a number of beautiful glass styles, ranging from the delicate *cristallo* to glasses that incorporated swirled serpentine details. They were also skilled at pulling the molten glass into thin *latticinio* rods and weaving them into ribbons and "netted" glass. Despite their expertise, Venetian glass makers did occasionally make mistakes while they were producing their expensive masterpieces. Although selling an inferior product was unthinkable, they did not want to waste the materials. If a piece of glass was badly damaged or not up to par, it was blown into a simple flask, or *fiasco,* and sold cheaply. Among the glass makers, the word *fiasco* took on the connotation of a failure and a waste.

Sources

Lurie, Charles. *Everyday Sayings.* Detroit, MI: Gale Research, 1968.

Mish, Frederick C. *The Merriam-Webster New Book of Word Histories.* Springfield, IL: Merriam-Webster, 1991.

Turner, Jane, ed., *The Dictionary of Art.* New York: Grove Dictionaries, 1996.

Fiddle while Rome burns. ***To be distracted by petty issues in the midst of a crisis.*** Nero (37–68) was one of the most reviled of all the Roman emperors, and his name has been permanently blackened by his despotic reign. Nero's megalomania was evident in his driving ambition to build himself a great palace called the Golden House, complete with parks, artificial lakes, and monumental architecture. Had it been completed, it would have covered almost one-third of the city. In the year 64 a tremendous fire destroyed much of Rome, spreading quickly between the city's tightly packed buildings and timber roofs. At the time it was widely believed that Nero may have started the fire in order to raze the city and make way for his palace. Since the emperor was not in Rome when the conflagration began, it is unlikely that he was instrumental in setting the fire, but the Roman people were ready to blame him. His eagerness to begin laying the foundations for his house as soon as the flames were extinguished tended to confirm popular suspicion. Nero's callousness in the face of disaster inspired another rumor, that the emperor, who fancied himself a great musician, had played on his fiddle while the city burned.

Not even the self-absorbed Nero could fail to hear the murmurings of a hostile Roman populace eager to blame him for the fire. He and his advisors decided to find another scapegoat, and a new religious sect, the Christians, became a convenient target. This diversionary tactic worked briefly, but Nero was never able to repair his tattered reputation. Within four years his stature had sunk so low that his overthrow was almost inevitable. Nero fled the city and committed suicide before he could be assassinated.

Sources

Bunson, Matthew. *Encyclopedia of the Roman Empire.* New York: Facts on File, 1994.

Grant, Michael. *Nero, Emperor in Revolt.* New York: American Heritage Press, 1970.

Scarre, Chris. *Chronicle of the Roman Emperors: The Reign-by-Reign Record of the Rulers of Imperial Rome.* New York: Thames and Hudson, 1995.

Warmington, Brian Herbert. *Nero: Legend and Reality.* New York: Norton, 1970.

Fifth column. ***A clandestine group of subversives who seek to aid an outside enemy.*** This term was coined by General Emilio Mola Vidal, a Nationalist leader during the Spanish Civil War (1936–1939). As he advanced on Madrid with four army columns, he boasted that within Madrid he would find a "fifth column" of sympathetic citizens, who would assist him by undermining the loyalist government from within.

In the 1930s and early 1940s, *fifth column* was also used in Great Britain to describe the surprisingly large number of influential aristocrats who were attracted to the fascist philosophy of the Nazi party. Today the expression is most commonly used in reference to communist or fascist sympathizers who operate within a democratic society. Fifth-column activists function by spreading rumors and misinformation and whipping up the fears of the public. Espionage and sabotage are other standard tools.

Sources

McHenry, Robert, ed. *The New Encyclopedia Britannica*. 15th ed. Chicago: Encyclopedia Britannica, 1992.

Mish, Frederick C. *The Merriam-Webster New Book of Word Histories*. Springfield, IL: Merriam-Webster, 1991.

Safire, William. *Safire's Political Dictionary*. New York: Random House, 1978.

Figurehead. ***Someone who is in a position of nominal leadership but has little actual power.***

A *figurehead* was the ornamental figure on the prow of a ship, and its use dates back to ancient Egypt. Ancient Chinese, Greeks, and Egyptians carved or painted eyes onto the prow of their ships, presumably to help guide the ship across the water. Gods and animals were also popular, but the human form eventually became the favorite subject for figureheads. In the eighteenth and nineteenth centuries, shipping registry firms noted the characteristics of figureheads to help distinguish one vessel from another. Aside from its use in identification, the ornamental carvings had almost no practical value, and by the twentieth century they were no longer common.

The word eventually came to describe a person who is in a position of prominence but has little functional power, such as the queen of England.

Sources

Hendrickson, Robert. *Facts on File Encyclopedia of Word and Phrase Origins*. New York: Facts on File, 1987.

Jeans, Peter D. *Ship to Shore: A Dictionary of Everyday Words and Phrases Derived from the Sea*. Santa Barbara, CA: ABC-CLIO, 1993.

Filibuster. ***A legislative tactic to delay or defeat a bill; in practice, refusing to close debate by not yielding the floor until the opposition grants concessions or withdraws the bill.***

In the seventeenth century, French colonists in the New World used the word *flibustier* ("flyboat") to refer to the pirates who harassed the Gulf Coast. The word eventually came to mean any raiders who made daily life difficult. When the term was adopted into English, the spelling changed to *filibuster*.

By the middle of the nineteenth century, the word was associated with a dilatory practice employed by United States senators. Senatorial rule 22 provides for unlimited debate on any measure before a vote is called. Thus a single member can bring proceedings to a halt by refusing to stop talking. (By contrast, in the U.S. House of Representatives, no member is allowed to speak for more than one hour without unanimous consent.) The typical filibuster tests the endurance of both sides. The minority schedules a long succession of speakers, while their opponents try to wear them down by round-the-clock sessions. Filibuster speeches do not need to relate to the issue at hand, and senators may read from the phone book if they can think of nothing more interesting to say. Filibusters can also be stopped if a three-fifths majority of the Senate votes to bring closure to the debate.

One famous filibuster in recent history was when Senator Strom Thurmond unsuccessfully attempted to defeat the 1957 civil rights bill by speaking for 24 hours straight. Another concerted effort occurred during the debate over the 1964 civil rights bill. This filibuster lasted 82 days, the longest in the Senate's history.

Sources

McHenry, Robert, ed. *The New Encyclopedia Britannica*. 15th ed. Chicago: Encyclopedia Britannica, 1992.

Mish, Frederick C. *The Merriam-Webster New Book of Word Histories*. Springfield, IL: Merriam-Webster, 1991.

Safire, William. *Safire's Political Dictionary*. New York: Random House, 1978.

Simpson, J. A., and E. S. C. Weiner, eds. *The Oxford English Dictionary*. 2d ed. Oxford: Clarendon Press, 1989.

Final solution. ***Eradicating one's enemies.*** In Adolf Hitler's quest to create a pure Aryan nation, he devised a number of "solutions" that would eliminate the Jewish presence in Germany. As early as 1919 Hitler began pondering various methods to drive the Jews out of the country and was already rejecting the use of "emotional anti-Semitism" in favor of systematic legal maneuvers to strip them of their rights and citizenship. Throughout the 1920s Hitler's rhetoric became increasingly ominous, such as when he compared the Jews to a tuberculosis bacillus that had to be destroyed. After becoming chancellor of Germany in 1933, Hitler initially resorted to harassment and population transfers to segregated areas within the country and in newly conquered provinces. However, he eventually decided that the ultimate goal of purging Germany—and ultimately all of Europe that came under German control—of all people of Jewish descent could only be satisfied by the *final solution* of systematic genocide.

The earliest documented appearance of the term was in a bulletin from Gestapo official Adolf Eichmann in March 1941. By June of that year, other approaches to the "Jewish problem" had given way to murder. Jewish men in occupied territories were being apprehended and shot, and the deportation of entire families to death camps began in October. Toward the end of the war, the Nazis stepped up the pace of their ghastly solution, until imminent defeat made it necessary to abandon the operation and instead try to cover up evidence of the slaughter. Although the exact number of Jews who fell victim to the "final solution" will never be known, most estimates place the number at between five million and six million.

Sources

Gutman, Israel, ed. *Encyclopedia of the Holocaust.* New York: Macmillan Publishing Company, 1990.

Safire, William. *Safire's Political Dictionary.* New York: Random House, 1978.

Zentner, Christian, and Friedemann Budurftig, eds. *Encyclopedia of the Third Reich.* New York: Macmillan, 1991.

Flak. ***Excessive criticism or abuse.*** Over half of the pilots in the Royal Air Force were killed or wounded during World War II. This devastating loss was due largely to anti-aircraft weapons. Developed as soon as planes became weapons of war, anti-aircraft guns lacked precision aim during World War I. However, by World War II they could deliver terrible blows to an aerial attack. The Germans had the most effective anti-aircraft device of the war, the 88-millimeter Fliegerabwehrkanone. The Allies abbreviated this tongue-twister to *flak,* which soon became a universal term for all anti-aircraft fire. *Flak-happy* was coined to refer to the mental confusion of airmen who had been exposed to a severe barrage of anti-aircraft gunfire.

By the 1960s the word *flak* had taken on a figurative meaning to denote relentless and annoying criticism.

Sources

Ammer, Christine. *Fighting Words: From War, Rebellion, and Other Combative Capers.* New York: Paragon House, 1989.

McHenry, Robert, ed. *The New Encyclopedia Britannica.* 15th ed. Chicago: Encyclopedia Britannica, 1992.

Simpson, J. A., and E. S. C. Weiner, eds. *The Oxford English Dictionary.* 2d ed. Oxford: Clarendon Press, 1989.

Flash in the pan. ***A person or venture that fails to live up to early promise.*** Hand-held guns were developed in the middle of the fifteenth century, although they were larger, heavier, and far less reliable than the guns designed in later centuries. The wheel lock and flintlock muskets featured a flash pan, a small depression into which gunpowder was loaded. When the trigger was pulled, flint would strike against steel, sending sparks into the flash pan. The powder was supposed to ignite and thus produce the desired explosion. The notorious unreliability of these firearms meant that the powder in the flash pan could ignite but not discharge. These *flashes in the pans* appeared promising but failed to deliver the desired result.

Sources
Ammer, Christine. *Fighting Words: From War, Rebellion, and Other Combative Capers.* New York: Paragon House, 1989.
Diagram Group. *Weapons: An Encyclopedia from 5000 B.C. to 2000 A.D.* New York: St. Martin's Press, 1980.
Reid, William. *The Lore of Arms: A Concise History of Weaponry.* New York: Facts on File, 1984.

Flying colors, to come through with flying colors. *To undertake a difficult task and achieve great success.*

In the era before radio communication or the semaphore system, the primary means of contact between ships at sea was through elementary flag signals, providing such basic information as "enemy in sight" or "give chase." On English ships, specific flags indicated the rank of the commander on board. An admiral was entitled to fly a Saint George's banner from the ship's masthead, while commodores flew a red swallow-tailed pendant. Most important was the national flag, known as the ship's colors, which was flown at all times and was used for identification (see *False colors*).

In battle, a ship signaled defeat by lowering its colors, while victorious ships kept their colors flying high. When returning to port, a ship's raised or lowered flag often provided the first indication of the battle's outcome to those on shore. For ships to return to port with *flying colors* meant that they had been triumphant.

Sources
Jeans, Peter D. *Ship to Shore: A Dictionary of Everyday Words and Phrases Derived from the Sea.* Santa Barbara, CA: ABC-CLIO, 1993.
Masefield, John. *Sea Life in Nelson's Time.* New York: Macmillan, 1937.
McHenry, Robert, ed. *The New Encyclopedia Britannica.* 15th ed. Chicago: Encyclopedia Britannica, 1992.
Whipple, A. B. C. *Fighting Sail.* Alexandria, VA: Time-Life Books, 1978.

Flynn, in like Flynn. *Someone whose position or fortune is assured.*

There are two possible derivations for this expression. The one most commonly cited refers to the screen legend Errol Flynn (1909–1959), who was a ladies' man in both the movies and real life. His promiscuous reputation made him even more appealing to his adoring female fans, at least until 1942, when he was charged with statutory rape. The 33-year-old Flynn was accused of having sex with 17-year-old Betty Hansen and 15-year-old Peggy La Rue Satterlee. California law prohibited sexual relations with anyone under the age of 18, even if the individual consented to the act. The expression *in like Flynn,* which Flynn himself despised, became popular during the 1943 trial, when his sexual adventures were subjected to humiliating public scrutiny. Flynn believed that the Los Angeles district attorney wanted to make him a scapegoat for the sins of Hollywood, and he later admitted that he had made arrangements to flee the country had he not been acquitted. The jury found in Flynn's favor, but the rape charge took some luster off Flynn's golden-boy image. Still, he went on to star in a string of successful movies. Although he was mortified by the attention the scandal had garnered, he continued to enjoy the company of very young women. In his view, "The public has always expected me to be a playboy, and a decent chap never lets his public down."

Other sources contend that though Errol Flynn made the expression popular, it was actually coined years earlier in reference to Ed Flynn, a Democratic machine politician in New York whose candidates invariably won their elections.

Sources
Flynn, Errol. *My Wicked, Wicked Ways.* New York: Buccaneer Books, 1959.
Godfrey, Lionel. *The Life and Crimes of Errol Flynn.* New York: St. Martin's Press, 1977.
Hendrickson, Robert. *Facts on File Encyclopedia of Word and Phrase Origins.* New York: Facts on File, 1987.
Kohn, George C. *The Encyclopedia of American Scandal: From Abscam to the Zenger Case.* New York: Facts on File, 1989.

Forlorn hope. *A vain or faint hope.*

This term emerged in the context of seventeenth-century military ventures. Many soldiers in this era were mercenaries who served whatever leader paid them the most. Not motivated by patriotic devotion to a cause or country, they might quit if treated badly but might also risk great danger if offered sufficient rewards. The elite squads who were willing to undertake potentially suicidal missions were given special treatment and attention. Often these were the men who first charged, scaled a battlement, or stormed a fortification. Given the nature of their tasks, most would never be seen again. The Dutch called such troops the *verloren hoop,* meaning the "lost troop," while both the French *(enfants perdus)* and the German *(verlorner posten)* phrases meant the "lost ones." The English transliteration of *verloren hoop* became "forlorn hope," and the evocative, poetic connotation of the term gave it staying power.

The expression eventually lost its military association. In 1846 the doomed wagon train of American pioneers known as the Donner party became stranded in the Utah mountains by fierce winter blizzards. They sent out a contingent of 17 men, whom they called the "forlorn hope," in an effort to reach civilization. Seven men survived, and rescue squads eventually returned to assist the remaining members of the Donner party. By the end of the nineteenth century, the expression was being used to describe any enterprise that has only a faint chance of success.

Sources

Evans, Ivor H. *Brewer's Dictionary of Phrase and Fable.* 14th ed. New York: Harper and Row, 1989.

Simpson, J. A., and E. S. C. Weiner, eds. *The Oxford English Dictionary.* 2d ed. Oxford: Clarendon Press, 1989.

Fosbury flop. ***A high-jump style in which the jumper leaps backwards over the bar and lands on his or her back; also, a totally new approach to a problem.***

When Dick Fosbury (1947–) began to participate in competitive track meets, the standard form for high jumpers was the straddle method, in which the jumper kicks one leg over the bar and then rolls over the bar face down. At 6′4″ and 183 pounds, Fosbury was described by his high school track coach as a "gangly, gawky, grew-too-fast kid." He was not particularly good in any track event, and his ineptitude at the straddle high jump had almost convinced his coach to move him to the triple jump. In his sophomore year Fosbury began developing his own distinctive style of high jump, in which he twisted his shoulders, kicked his legs up as he cleared the bar, and landed on his back.

This bizarre form of high jumping worked for Fosbury, and he began winning medals. His coaches at Oregon State University were impressed with the height he could clear but thought he would do even better if he just learned to jump the "normal way." All attempts to modify Fosbury's style failed, and he went on to win the gold medal in the 1968 Olympics in Mexico City. The track world quickly took note, and in the 1972 Olympics, 28 of 40 high jump competitors used the Fosbury flop. Since then, no "non-flopper" has won the gold medal for high jumping. The expression *Fosbury flop* has also been used in reference to other instances in which an unorthodox approach to a problem dramatically changes the way something is done.

Sources

Goldberg, Philip. *The Babinski Reflex: And 70 Other Useful and Amusing Metaphors from Science, Psychology, Business, Sports, and Everyday Life.* Los Angeles: J. P. Tarcher, 1990.

Hickok, Ralph. *The Encyclopedia of North American Sports History.* New York: Facts on File, 1992.

Welch, Robert S. "The Fosbury Flop Is Still a Big Hit." *Sports Illustrated* 69, September 12, 1988: 12–15.

Fountain of youth. ***The never-ending search to reverse the ravages of time.***

For centuries before the European discovery of the New World, distant lands were traditionally portrayed as fantastic, populated by monstrous races of people with strange body parts and different social norms. Medieval chronicles told stories of people who lived solely off the smell of apples, and of a headless race whose eyes, nose, and mouth were located on their torso. The Spanish explorers were thus predisposed to believe that equally fantastic wonders awaited in the New World. Nor were the natives averse to telling fabulous tales of riches and treasures, especially if it persuaded the newcomers to head off in some other direction.

Ponce de León (1460–1521) was one of the earliest European explorers of the islands of the West Indies. Although his main quest was for gold, the natives of present-day Puerto Rico told him about a miraculous spring on the island of Bimini to the north. Waters from the spring could restore youth and health to all who would drink from it. For the 53-year old explorer, the tantalizing idea of a *fountain of youth* was irresistible. He outfitted three ships at his own expense and set off in search of the fabled Bimini. He landed on the coast of Florida in 1513, not realizing that he was on a mainland instead of an island. De León explored what appeared to be an untouched paradise. The lush, florid vegetation and mild spring climate lent credibility to the idea that he had entered a land of magical possibilities. No fountain of youth was ever found, but de León continued to explore the Florida Keys and eventually reached the west coast of Florida.

The phrase today has been appropriated by companies selling beauty products and health spas.

Sources

Bedini, Silvio A., ed. *The Christopher Columbus Encyclopedia.* New York: Simon and Schuster, 1992.

McHenry, Robert, ed. *The New Encyclopedia Britannica.* 15th ed. Chicago: Encyclopedia Britannica, 1992.

Mercatante, Anthony S. *Facts on File Encyclopedia of World Mythology and Legend.* New York: Facts on File, 1988.

Stimpson, George. *A Book about American History.* Greenwich, CT: Fawcett Publications, 1960.

Four hundred. *The wealthiest and most exclusive social set in a community.*

During the Gilded Age, Caroline Webster Astor (1830–1908) reigned supreme over the upper echelons of New York society. She came from the old Knickerbocker aristocracy of New York, but her influence skyrocketed when she married William Astor, one of the wealthiest men in the country. However, his family was considered nouveau riche, since his grandfather had been a lowly fur trader. The society's blue bloods were not impressed by her alliance. Perhaps to overcome this stigma, Caroline Astor decided to set herself up as the preeminent social leader of New York City. Using her own impeccable lineage and her husband's staggering fortune, "Mrs. Astor," as she insisted on being called, became the ultimate hostess, and during the 1880s and 1890s, a family's social standing rested almost entirely on her approval.

Assisting her in this project was Ward McAllister (1827–1895), who has been described as "a humorless, indefatigable snob." McAllister had made his fortune as a lawyer, then retired from the bar and devoted himself to pursuing a social life. He traveled, entertained, and contributed articles to newspapers, in the process establishing himself as a self-appointed connoisseur of the social graces. He fully approved of Mrs. Astor's machinations to introduce a hierarchy into New York society. In 1892 he helped with the compilation of the guest list for the Astors' famed annual ball, and he commented that there were really only about 400 people in New York who could be considered high society. The *four hundred* therefore became a term associated with the upper crust of society.

In the early 1980s, the expression gained new life when *Forbes* magazine began to publish its annual list of the four hundred wealthiest people in the United States.

Sources

James, Edward, ed. *Notable American Women, 1607–1950: A Biographical Dictionary.* Cambridge, MA: Belknap Press, 1971.

Sinclair, David. *Dynasty: The Astors and Their Times.* New York: Beaufort Books, 1984.

Stimpson, George. *A Book about a Thousand Things.* New York: Harper and Brothers, 1946.

Fourth estate. *The press.*

The Estates General was a political assembly that participated in governing France from the fourteenth through the eighteenth centuries. Three separate estates, each representing a social class, composed the assembly. The First and Second Estates were the clergy and the nobility. The Third Estate, representing the vast majority, consisted of commoners. In the course of French history the power of the Estates General waxed and waned in relation to the strength or weakness of the monarch. In 1789 the lack of support for the king and the growing unrest among the citizens of France encouraged the Third Estate to seize power and create the National Assembly, which would pave the way for the French Revolution.

The term *fourth estate* is believed to have been coined by Edmund Burke, the great eighteenth-century English statesman. According to a report, Burke once observed, "There are three estates in Parliament, but in the reporters' gallery yonder there sits a fourth estate, more important far than they all." Burke's comment captured the power of the press to influence and shape public opinion.

Sources

Freeman, Morton S. *The Story behind the Word.* Philadelphia: ISI Press, 1985.

Paneth, Donald. *The Encyclopedia of American Journalism.* New York: Facts on File, 1983.

Stimpson, George. *A Book about a Thousand Things.* New York: Harper and Brothers, 1946.

Freudian slip. ***A verbal mistake that is supposed to reveal the speaker's unconscious thought or feeling.***

Sigmund Freud (1856–1939) was an Austrian neurologist whose ground-breaking research into the subconscious shocked, outraged, and intrigued Victorian society. Many of Freud's theories depended on dividing mental life into distinct areas. The id refers to unconscious mental activity that is purely instinctual. Concerned with immediate satisfaction and the release of tension, the id includes aggressive impulses and sexual desires. Setting humans apart from the animals is the ego, which Freud defined as a sense of reason and rationality. Living in civilized society requires that the ego is stronger than the id, although civilization may only be a veneer over the instinctual drives of the id.

The *Freudian slip* occurs when there is a momentary lapse in the ego's control over the id. A person's unconscious attitude spontaneously reveals itself in spite of the conscious desire to keep such feelings hidden. Although everyone commits an occasional Freudian slip, public figures are especially vulnerable to the embarrassment created by such gaffes, which are often immortalized by television cameras. When New York Governor Mario Cuomo, a man who had long had his eye on the White House, was speaking to a group of labor leaders he said, "As I said in my State of the Union speech this year," having intended to refer to his State of the State speech. Republican Senator Alfonse D'Amato referred to his party as "the party of opportunism" rather than "opportunity." When Congresswoman Geraldine Ferraro became the first female vice-presidential candidate chosen by a major party, Republican political consultant Ed Rollins commented that her selection was going to be a "big bust."

Sources

Eysenck, H. J., ed. *Encyclopedia of Psychology.* London: Search Press, 1972.

Hall, Calvin S. *A Primer of Freudian Psychology.* New York: New American Library, 1961.

Simpson, J. A., and E. S. C. Weiner, eds. *The Oxford English Dictionary.* 2d ed. Oxford: Clarendon Press, 1989.

Frisbee. ***A plastic disk that is usually tossed between players.***

The Frisbie Pie Company of Bridgeport, Connecticut, was well known to the nearby students at Yale, who patronized the company for their line of homemade pies. In the 1940s the company noticed that a large percentage of the tin pie plates was no longer being returned for the small deposit offered in exchange for used tins. The students at Yale had discovered that the lightweight tins could float through the air when flung at just the right angle. They called the game "frisbie-ing" in reference to the company logo stamped on the tins.

The pastime would have probably remained a Yale campus fad had it not been for the Wham-O toy company, which released a disk-shaped toy in 1957. At the time, Americans were fascinated with flying saucers, and the company hoped to capitalize on this with the release of a silver, lightweight metal disk that mimicked the alien space ships seen in "B" movies across the country. Named "Flyin' Saucer," the toy sold well in California but not in the rest of the country. Trying to boost sales, a company representative, Richard Knerr, undertook a promotional tour of college campuses. Knerr discovered that the students of Harvard and Yale were already using a similar toy in a popular lawn game. The name Frisbie appealed to Knerr, although he changed the spelling of his product to *Frisbee,* probably to avoid trademark regulations. The Flyin' Saucers were remarketed as Frisbees in 1959, and the toy had nationwide success.

The Frisbie Bakery closed in 1958. Their original pie tins, which cost only a few cents in the 1940s, now sell to collectors for around $100 each.

Sources

Marum, Andrew, and Frank Parise. *Follies and Foibles: A View of Twentieth Century Fads.* New York: Facts on File, 1984.

Panati, Charles. *Panati's Extraordinary Origins of Everyday Things.* New York: Harper and Row, 1987.

Fuchsia. *A vivid, purplish-red color.*

The exploration of the Americas in the seventeenth and eighteenth centuries resulted in the discovery of thousands of previously unknown flora and fauna for European scientists. Armed with reference books and sketch pads, adventurous naturalists trekked into the deserts and jungles to discover and classify new species. Naming what they found was arbitrary, since the Linnaean system of nomenclature was not established until 1750. In many cases discoveries were given the name of an admired person, and this was the case with the Fuchsia plant.

French botanist Charles Plumier found a shrub native to Mexico that had vibrant blossoms in purple, red, yellow, and white. He called the plant *Fuchsia,* in honor of German naturalist Dr. Leonhard Fuchs (1501–1566). Fuchs had been a professor at the University of Tübingen and was famous for his landmark botanical work *Historia Stirpium* (1542), which indexed known medicinal and edible plants. The classic work contained beautiful woodcuts of plants and established the tradition of providing technically detailed and accurate botanical illustrations.

Since Plumier's day, scientific nomenclature has been standardized. Formal codes, such as the International Code of Nomenclature in Botany (1901) and Zoology (1906), dictate how new flora and fauna are named.

Sources

Hendrickson, Robert. *Dictionary of Eponyms: Names That Became Words.* New York: Stein and Day, 1985.

McHenry, Robert, ed. *The New Encyclopedia Britannica.* 15th ed. Chicago: Encyclopedia Britannica, 1992.

G

Garcia, carry a message to Garcia. ***To accept responsibility for a task, no matter how arduous or challenging it may be.***
First Lieutenant Andrew S. Rowan was a junior officer in the army who had spent most of his 17 years of service behind a desk. His one claim to fame was a little book called *The Island of Cuba,* published in 1896. Although Rowan had never been to Cuba, he studied other writers and compiled his own account of the geography and topography of the enchanting island. Rowan's knowledge of Cuba, however limited, brought him to the attention of his superiors when the Spanish-American War broke out in April 1898.

The U.S. military sought to make contact with a powerful Cuban rebel leader, General Calixto Garcia, but had no idea where to find him. Garcia had been fighting in the Cuban mountains and jungles for years and had invaluable insight into the strength of the Spanish forces, the resources needed by the Cubans, and how American troops would be received. Despite the Spanish blockade of Cuba, Rowan was commissioned to find Garcia, although he was given almost no guidance as to how he could accomplish such a daunting task. He went to Jamaica, where he slipped onto a fishing vessel and made his way to Cuba. With nothing but his resourcefulness, determination, and the assistance of sympathetic Cubans, Rowan traveled through swamps and jungles and over mountains to reach Garcia. Messages were exchanged, and Rowan returned to Washington five weeks later.

In the March 1899 issue of the *Philistine,* journalist Elbert Hubbard honored Rowan's feat. He contrasted the soldier's determination to many Americans' complaints about simple tasks, and he posed *carrying a message to Garcia* as an example of resourcefulness and commitment to complete an assignment whatever the odds.

Sources

Hubbard, Elbert. *A Message to Garcia.* New York: Thomas Crowell Company, 1924.

Stimpson, George. *A Book about American History.* Greenwich, CT: Fawcett Publications, 1960.

Garrison finish. ***A race in which the winner comes from behind in the final moments.***
Edward "Snapper" Garrison (1868–1930) was considered to be the best American jockey in the 1890s. As a young man he worked in a blacksmith shop and developed a love of horses. Nicknamed "Jack Snapper" because of his scrappy enthusiasm, he was known to be a fine equestrian. He was attending a race one day when one of the jockeys failed to show up. The horse's owner said, "Let Jack Snapper ride him instead." The track official dutifully entered the name "Jack Snapper" into the roster, thereby giving Garrison an enduring nickname. Garrison rode well that day, and it marked the beginning of his legendary career. By 1894 he was earning $23,000 a year and was the highest-paid jockey in the country.

Garrison was a master at holding the horse in check until the final moments of the race, when he would raise up in his stirrups and bend low over a horse's mane, encouraging the horse to shoot forward. The spectacular, come-from-behind victories were known as *Garrison finishes.* Although the term originally applied only to horse racing, it was eventually picked up and used for other sports and even electoral races.

Sources

Hendrickson, Robert. *The Dictionary of Eponyms: Names That Became Words.* New York: Stein and Day, 1985.

Longrigg, Roger. *The History of Horse Racing.* New York: Stein and Day, 1972.

Porter, David L., ed. *Biographical Dictionary of American Sports: Outdoor Sports.* New York: Greenwood Press, 1988.

-gate. ***Used as a suffix to imply that an enormous scandal lurks beneath the surface.***

Iran-Contragate, Camillagate, Whitewatergate, Billygate, Nannygate. Since the 1970s, adding the suffix *gate* onto the end of a word has been a method of turning an issue into a disgrace. The source is the scandal of the century, Watergate.

In the early morning of 17 June 1972, police arrested five men caught in the act of planting electronic surveillance gear in the headquarters of the Democratic National Committee, located in the Watergate office and apartment complex. Over the next two years, despite a growing stack of evidence, President Richard Nixon and other administration officials repeatedly stated that there was no White House involvement in the break-in. By early 1974 a number of White House aides were either under indictment or had pled guilty to charges surrounding the Watergate affair. Televised hearings held the nation spellbound as charges of misconduct, the purchase of government favors, and "dirty tricks" meant to derail the 1972 Democratic presidential campaign emerged. The president himself tried to undermine the investigation by refusing to turn over recordings of relevant conversations and firing the special prosecutor. Congressional support for Nixon finally collapsed after he was pressured into releasing the transcripts of three tapes that clearly implicated him in the cover-up of the Watergate break-in. Announcing that he "no longer had a strong enough political base," Nixon resigned from office on 9 August 1974.

The Watergate scandal revealed the corruption and misconduct lurking behind a seemingly respectable institution. The suffix *-gate* was soon attached to other improprieties that appear to be just the tip of a devastating iceberg.

Sources

Kohn, George C. *The Encyclopedia of American Scandal: From Abscam to the Zenger Case.* New York: Facts on File, 1989.

Magill, Frank N., and John L. Loos. *Great Events from History: North American Series.* Pasadena, CA: Salem Press, 1997.

McHenry, Robert, ed. *The New Encyclopedia Britannica.* 15th ed. Chicago: Encyclopedia Britannica, 1992.

Gauntlet, run the. ***To expose oneself to danger; to run a great risk.***

The word *gauntlet* in this context is a corruption of the Swedish word *gatlopp,* which means "lane," or course. The Swedish army used the *gatlopp* to punish serious offenders. The guilty soldier was forced to strip naked and run between two rows of fellow soldiers, who used whips and clubs to beat the offender. The more serious the crime, the longer the rows. British soldiers who observed this punishment during the Thirty Years War (1618–1648) brought the expression home.

Gatlopp is awkward for English speakers, but it sounded similar to the English word *gauntlet.* The transliteration is an example of folk etymology, in which a familiar word is substituted for a difficult word.

Sources

Carver, Craig M. *A History of English in Its Own Words.* New York: HarperCollins, 1991.

Holt, Alfred Hubbard. *Phrase and Word Origins.* New York: Dover Publications, 1961.

Lurie, Charles. *Everyday Sayings.* Detroit, MI: Gale Research, 1968.

Simpson, J. A., and E. S. C. Weiner, eds. *The Oxford English Dictionary.* 2d ed. Oxford: Clarendon Press, 1989.

Gauntlet, throw down the gauntlet. ***To issue a challenge; to throw one's hat in the ring.***
A gauntlet was the protective glove worn with a suit of medieval armor, which was usually made of leather and covered with plates of steel. The formal rules of chivalry extended to personal disputes among knights, and it was considered poor form simply to launch into a physical assault against another knight. Instead, a challenge was issued when one knight threw down his gauntlet. If the other knight picked up the glove, the challenge was accepted. Failure to take the glove indicated a refusal to fight and was generally considered an act of cowardice.

The expression *throw down the gauntlet* is often used in a highly figurative sense, as in "the senator threw down the gauntlet by asking the president to debate him."

Sources

Broughton, Bradford. *Dictionary of Medieval Knighthood and Chivalry.* New York: Greenwood Press, 1986.

Simpson, J. A., and E. S. C. Weiner, eds. *The Oxford English Dictionary.* 2d ed. Oxford: Clarendon Press, 1989.

Genghis Khan, to the right of Genghis Khan. ***Someone with extreme right-wing views.***
Genghis Khan (1167–1227) was chief of a petty Mongolian tribe who built the foundations of a world empire through a series of tribal alliances and marriages. While strengthening his own empire, he succeeded in eliminating his enemies through use of cunning and ruthless warfare. He unified the culturally diverse Mongolian tribes into a powerful kingdom that sought to achieve domination over its neighbors. To the east he conquered all of China, and to the west he was able to bring much of Russia under his control.

It is ironic that the name of Genghis Khan is associated with extreme right-wing views. The khan established courts of law that were superior to his own authority, and he was remarkably tolerant of the different religions and cultures absorbed into his empire. Soviet historians were always highly critical of the Mongol raider's achievements, contending that he was a barbarian who helped put a foreign yoke on Russia. Perhaps it was this ardent attack from the left that branded Genghis Khan as a right-winger in contemporary thought.

Sources

Comfort, N. A. *Brewer's Politics: A Phrase and Fable Dictionary.* London: Cassell, 1993.

Davis, Paul K. *Encyclopedia of Invasions and Conquests: From Ancient Times to the Present.* Santa Barbara, CA: ABC-CLIO, 1996.

Hartog, Leo de. *Genghis Khan: Conqueror of the World.* London: Tauris, 1989.

McHenry, Robert, ed. *The New Encyclopedia Britannica.* 15th ed. Chicago: Encyclopedia Britannica, 1992.

Gerber baby. ***The epitome of an attractive, healthy baby.***
Before the development of canned baby food, the preparation of meals for children not capable of digesting regular food was a time-consuming process. This fact was vividly brought home to Daniel Gerber one evening in 1927. As his wife was straining peas to feed their seven-month-old daughter, Gerber impatiently reminded his wife that they were late for an important social engagement. Dumping the bowl on her husband's lap, Mrs. Gerber suggested that he assume the task of straining food three times a day, every day of the week. Gerber's family owned a small cannery, and he quickly recognized that there was an untapped market in prepared baby food. At the time, only pharmacies sold strained baby food, but at 35 cents a can, it was more than the average family could afford. Through mass production, Gerber's baby food sold for 15 cents a can. To add to the convenience, their strained vegetables, soups, and fruits could be purchased in grocery stores.

In 1928, the Gerbers came up with one of the most memorable advertising images of all time when they invited artists from around the country to submit illustrations of happy, healthy babies for use in a marketing campaign. Dorothy Hope Smith submitted a rough charcoal sketch of a baby's smiling face, adding that she would complete the drawing if this was what the company was looking for. The Gerbers decided to use the sketch as it was, believing that any additional work would spoil its fresh innocence. The idealized image of the Gerber baby has become one of the most reproduced faces in history.

Sources

Derdak, Thomas, ed. *International Directory of Company Histories.* Chicago: St. James Press, 1988.

Fucini, Joseph, and Suzy Fucini. *Entrepreneurs: The Men and Women behind Famous Brand Names and How They Made It.* Boston: G. K. Hall, 1985.

Geronimo! ***An exclamation meaning "here goes!"***

Geronimo (1829–1909) was an Apache leader whose Indian name, Goyathlay, actually means "one who yawns." Because he spearheaded his people's defiance of the United States government, his name has become associated with fierce, proud resistance. Geronimo eluded capture for over five months and led troops on a chase that covered over 1,600 miles. It is estimated that some 5,000 soldiers in all were involved in the pursuit and capture of Geronimo. Legend tells of a daring escape in Medicine Bluffs, Oklahoma, when Geronimo leapt off a steep cliff as soldiers were closing in, defiantly shouting his name as he fell.

During World War II American paratroopers shouted *Geronimo!* as they jumped from airplanes. The only explanation for this practice comes from a suggestion that some paratroopers in training camp had watched a movie based on the legend of Geronimo, and the exclamation caught on as a kind of battle cry.

Sources

Ammer, Christine. *Fighting Words: From War, Rebellion, and Other Combative Capers.* New York: Paragon House, 1989.

Markowitz, Harvey, ed. *American Indians.* Pasadena, CA: Salem Press, 1995.

Gerrymander. ***To divide voting districts in a manner that is clearly biased in favor of a particular party or group.***

Although the term did not come into use until the nineteenth century, the practice is as old as popular elections. Elbridge Gerry (1744–1814) was a signer of the Declaration of Independence, governor of Massachusetts, and vice-president of the United States under James Madison. In 1812, while serving as governor of Massachusetts, Gerry approved the redistricting of the state in such a way as to give the Republicans a decided advantage. Voting districts were drawn in bizarre and ungainly shapes to ensure that Federalist strength would be diluted. Outraged Federalists held a series of meetings in an attempt to counter the redistricting measures. At one of the meetings a map of one of the awkward proposed districts was produced, and many commented that the long, skinny shape resembled a salamander. In a light-hearted moment, Gilbert Stuart, the famous presidential portrait painter, rose from the crowd to sketch a head and wings onto the map, completing the proposed district's transformation into a salamander. The lizard was called a "gerrymander" in reference to the governor who had proposed the redistricting. Political cartoonists quickly embraced the term, and caricatures of voting districts shaped like monsters but with the profile of Governor Gerry were widely circulated.

The cartoons damaged Gerry's reputation, but the gerrymandering tactic worked. In the Massachusetts election of 1812, 51,766 Federalist votes and 50,164 Republican votes were cast. Yet the result was 11 Federalist and 29 Republican state senators.

Sources

Johnson, Allen, and Dumas Malone, eds. *Dictionary of American Biography.* New York: Scribner's, 1964.

Mish, Frederick C. *The Merriam-Webster New Book of Word Histories.* Springfield, IL: Merriam-Webster, 1991.

Simpson, J. A., and E. S. C. Weiner, eds. *The Oxford English Dictionary.* 2d ed. Oxford: Clarendon Press, 1989.

Stimpson, George. *A Book about American Politics.* New York: Harper, 1954.

Get one's goat. ***To provoke someone to lose his or her temper.***
Some prominent etymologists contend that this expression arises from the practice of placing a goat inside the stall of a skittish race horse to calm down the high-strung creature. If a rival trainer removed the goat, the horse would become nervous and fail to run well. However, this is a rather improbable explanation, since the phrase did not appear in writing until the early twentieth century. More likely, it is a corruption of the word *goad*.

Sources

Hendrickson, Robert. *Facts on File Encyclopedia of Word and Phrase Origins.* New York: Facts on File, 1987.

Simpson, J. A., and E. S. C. Weiner, eds. *The Oxford English Dictionary.* 2d ed. Oxford: Clarendon Press, 1989.

G.I. ***An enlisted American soldier.***
In the U.S. military, all items carried by the quartermaster, such as food, clothing, and other articles of daily life, were called Government Issue, which was soon shortened to *GI.* During World War II, soldiers extended the definition of the term to include themselves. According to military historian Lee Kennett, referring to soldiers as G.I. may be a holdover from the nineteenth century. Enlisted soldiers in the Regular army were usually able to purchase tailor-made uniforms, while draftees were willing to wear whatever was issued by the government. If true, GI was first used in a derogatory sense. Regardless, the term did not become popularized until the 1940s.

Most military acronyms never circulate in the mainstream, and such might have been the case with GI were it not for the Hasbro toy company. In 1963 Hasbro was impressed by the appeal of a television program about the U.S. Marines called *The Lieutenant*. By creating a military doll, they hoped to capitalize on the show's popularity and at the same time reach the untapped market of dolls for boys. Their concept was G.I. Joe, released in 1964. The figure was a foot tall with articulated limbs and a right hand that was permanently shaped to hold a gun. In its first two years the toy brought in over $35 million and accounted for almost two-thirds of the company's total sales. The popularity of G.I. Joe went into sharp decline during the early 1970s because of antimilitary sentiment and the rising price of plastic. Discontinued in 1975, G.I. Joe was resurrected in 1982 as an antiterrorist commando, complete with comrades and outlandish villains.

Sources

Derdak, Thomas, ed. *International Directory of Company Histories.* Chicago: St. James Press, 1988.

Dickson, Paul. *War Slang: Fighting Words and Phrases of Americans from the Civil War to the Gulf War.* New York: Pocket Books, 1994.

Evans, Ivor H., ed. *Brewer's Dictionary of Phrase and Fable.* 14th ed. New York: Harper and Row, 1989.

Gibson girl. ***An ideal female type—beautiful, refined, and wholesome.***
American illustrator Charles Dana Gibson (1867–1944) set the fashion for young women between 1890–1910. His distinctive pen-and-ink drawings of elegant, well-dressed women with pompadour hairstyles graced the pages of popular magazines and novels. The *Gibson girl* seemed to pass her days in such leisurely activities as tennis, rowing, picnicking, or reading a book beside a lake dotted with sailboats. In the evenings she was the ideal dance partner and dinner companion and was adept at enchanting all the handsome young men who surrounded her. Gibson's drawings influenced women's dress and hairstyles and promoted the idea that young women could ride a bicycle or play tennis and still be utterly charming. The artist was deluged with offers from women eager to pose as his model. However, most of his drawings were inspired by his wife, Irene Langhorn Gibson, and his sister Josephine Gibson Knowlton.

Popularity of the Gibson girl began to fade around 1910. While she waltzed the evening away in an elegantly appointed ballroom, real women were beginning to dance the Turkey Trot and the Charleston. Screen stars Theda Bara, Pola Negri, and Gloria

Swanson vamped and smoldered their way into American consciousness, making the Gibson girl seem hopelessly old-fashioned. Rather than attempt to update his creation, Gibson gracefully retired her and devoted the latter part of his life to painting portraits in oils.

Years later, the U.S. Army dubbed the hand-cranked radio transmitters on life rafts "Gibson girls" because of the wasp-waisted shape of the radio.

Sources

Dickson, Paul. *War Slang: Fighting Words and Phrases of Americans from the Civil War to the Gulf War.* New York: Pocket Books, 1994.

Gibson, Charles Dana. *The Gibson Girl and Her America: The Best Drawings.* New York: Dover Publications, 1969.

Marum, Andrew, and Frank Parise. *Follies and Foibles: A View of Twentieth Century Fads.* New York: Facts on File, 1984.

Gilderoy's kite, higher than Gilderoy's kite. *Something extremely high or extraordinary.*

Gilderoy was a nickname for the notorious Scottish highwayman Patrick MacGregor. Although he had been born into a well-to-do family, within six months of his father's death he had squandered his inheritance. He took to thievery to support his lifestyle. Gilderoy was apparently quite charming and moved easily among the aristocratic classes in France and England. At important social gatherings, people were not generally on guard for pickpockets, so Gilderoy would infiltrate and steal the purses of the wealthy. It is even reported that he lifted the purse of Cardinal Richelieu in the presence of the king of France. Gilderoy's audacity made him popular among the lower classes, but he had a vicious side. He probably murdered his mistress and members of his immediate family when he suspected them of informing the authorities of his whereabouts. He eventually confessed to 37 murders and robberies too numerous to count.

When Gilderoy was finally apprehended, the authorities wanted to make an example of him. An enormous scaffold was built for his execution, and he was hanged in 1636 and left there for weeks. In London slang, a corpse was known as a kite. Thus, to *hang higher than Gilderoy's kite* was soon a grimly colorful expression for something that is very much out of the ordinary.

Sources

Simpson, J. A., and E. S. C. Weiner, eds. *The Oxford English Dictionary.* 2d ed. Oxford: Clarendon Press, 1989.

Vizetelly, Frank H. *The Desk-Book of Idioms and Idiomatic Phrases.* New York: Funk and Wagnalls, 1923.

Whibley, Charles. *A Book of Scoundrels.* London: Constable and Company, 1919.

Gipper, the. *Ronald Reagan.*

Before entering politics, Ronald Reagan (1911–) found fame as a radio sports announcer and as an actor. One of his most famous roles was in *Knute Rockne: All American* (1940), a story about the legendary Notre Dame football coach. Reagan was not a top box-office draw, but he desperately wanted the part of football star George Gipp. He showed the producers photographs of himself playing football in college and told them that his football scholarship had made it possible for him to attend college. Reagan got the part, and he always considered it his favorite role.

George Gipp (1895–1920) had entered Notre Dame on a basketball scholarship but was recruited to play football by head coach Knute Rockne. Gipp, better known to his teammates as the Gipper, played 32 consecutive games for Notre Dame and scored a total of 83 touchdowns. In his final year at Notre Dame, he often played despite injuries or illness. He developed a persistent cold that turned into pneumonia and killed the promising athlete on 14 December 1920. In the movie, there was a sentimental deathbed scene in which Gipp tells Rockne, "Someday, when things look tough for Notre Dame, ask the boys to go out there and win one for the Gipper." The line was the most famous of Reagan's movie career, and when he entered politics, he asked supporters and fellow Republicans to help him "win one for the Gipper." Because of that association, *the Gipper* now invariably refers to Ronald Reagan rather than George Gipp.

Sources

Comfort, N. A. *Brewer's Politics: A Phrase and Fable Dictionary.* London: Cassell, 1993.

Hickok, Ralph. *The Encyclopedia of North American Sports History.* New York: Facts on File, 1992.

McHenry, Robert, ed. *The New Encyclopedia Britannica.* 15th ed. Chicago: Encyclopedia Britannica, 1992.

Go West, young man! ***A call to adventure and setting out on one's own.***

Although frequently attributed to Horace Greeley, the expression *go West, young man!* was coined by John Babson Soule in an 1851 article for the Terre Haute, Indiana, *Express.* Newspaper editor and social commentator Horace Greeley was so impressed with the article that he reproduced it in its entirety in the New York *Tribune.* Since he was more famous than Soule and was known to be an enthusiastic supporter of westward expansion, the phrase was wrongly attributed to Greeley in the minds of the general public.

The expression reflected Greeley's belief in the American West as a safety valve: a land of opportunity for the underemployed and discontented masses who were crowded into the eastern seaboard. Newspapers, especially Greeley's New York *Tribune,* printed stories about the possibilities for mining, fur trading, homesteading, ranching, or simply adventure. As part of his advocacy of western expansion, Greeley lobbied for the establishment of land-grant colleges in the Midwest, the passage of the Homestead Act, and the construction of the transcontinental railroad. However, within forty years of Soule's article, commentators were beginning to herald the "closing of the frontier."

Others have latched on to the spirit of adventure and excitement embodied in the phrase *go West, young man!* Mae West starred in a 1936 film that took that title, which was followed in 1940 by *Go West, Young Woman.* Numerous novels, children's books, movies, and plays have simply been titled *Go West!* Since the collapse of the Soviet Union, the phrase has appeared in connection with Russian entrepreneurs seeking to break into Western-style capitalism.

Sources

Hendrickson, Robert. *The Facts on File Encyclopedia of Word and Phrase Origins.* New York: Facts on File, 1987.

Johnson, Allen, and Dumas Malone, eds. *The Dictionary of American Biography.* New York: Scribner's, 1964.

Magill, Frank N., and John L. Loos. *Great Events from History: North American Series.* Pasadena, CA: Salem Press, 1997.

Titelman, Gregory Y. *Random House Dictionary of Popular Proverbs and Sayings.* New York: Random House, 1996.

Godwin's oath. ***An assertion of innocence that is immediately proven false.***

Godwin (d. 1053) was the earl of Wessex and a close, trusted associate of King Canute of England. A powerful and ambitious man, Godwin was usually able to dodge the charges of treachery and conspiracy that dogged him throughout most of his life. When Edward the Confessor succeeded to the throne, he tried to close the court to Godwin's influence. At some point, the earl was accused of murdering Alfred, the brother of the king. Legend claims that he vehemently protested his innocence and even swore that heaven should strike him dead if he was guilty. He promptly choked to death on a piece of bread. Although it is a fact that Godwin died suddenly during a meal with the king, the exact circumstances (including whether or not he choked to death) are unknown.

Sources

Lurie, Charles. *Everyday Sayings.* Detroit, MI: Gale Research, 1968.

Stephen, Leslie, and Sidney Lee, eds. *The Dictionary of National Biography.* London: Oxford University Press, 1921.

Strayer, Joseph R., ed. *Dictionary of the Middle Ages.* New York: Scribner's, 1982.

Goldwynism. ***Incorrect but humorous use of the English language; a malapropism.***
Samuel Goldwyn (1879–1974) lived the quintessential American dream. Orphaned as a small child in Poland, Goldwyn first emigrated to England, but he discovered that living with his English relatives was not to his taste. At the age of 13 he emigrated alone to New York, where he found work at a glove factory. Learning English at night school, he revealed a talent for salesmanship, and he earned so much money for the company that he was made a partner. Goldwyn had every intention of remaining in the glove business, but in 1910 he was tempted by his brother-in-law, a vaudeville producer, to take part in a daring new venture: motion pictures. Launching his production company with a film by the young Cecil B. deMille in 1913, Goldwyn soon became one of the most influential men in the motion picture industry.

Goldwyn made colorful use of his adopted tongue, and mixed metaphors and grammatically illogical phrases became his trademark. Among the more notable *Goldwynisms:*

Gentlemen, kindly include me out.
A verbal contract isn't worth the paper it's printed on.
You're always taking the bull between the teeth.
Anyone who goes to a psychiatrist should have his head examined.
In two words: Im-possible.

Although Goldwyn was in fact a talented mangler of the English language, many of the so-called Goldwynisms were no doubt apocryphal. Goldwyn allowed his public relations department to circulate phrases attributed to him, in the belief that any publicity was good publicity.

Sources

Berg, A. Scott. *Goldwyn: A Biography.* New York: Knopf, 1989.
McHenry, Robert, ed. *The New Encyclopedia Britannica.* 15th ed. Chicago: Encyclopedia Britannica, 1992.
Simpson, J. A., and E. S. C. Weiner, eds. *The Oxford English Dictionary.* 2d ed. Oxford: Clarendon Press, 1989.

Good Samaritan. ***A helpful person who has no expectation of reward.***
The term *good Samaritan* never appears in the Bible, although it arises from a story in the Gospel of Luke. Jewish law had interpreted the commandment "love your neighbor" as including only fellow Jews. As Jesus was teaching about this directive, a lawyer challenged him on the meaning of neighbor. Jesus replied with the parable known as the Good Samaritan. A man who was traveling through a strange land had been robbed, beaten, and left for dead. A priest and a Levite passed by without stopping to help. A Samaritan, however, treated the man's wounds and took him to safety. "Which of these three, do you think, was a neighbor to the man who fell into the hands of the robbers? The lawyer said, 'The one who showed him mercy.' Jesus said to him, 'Go and do likewise'" (Luke 10:36–37). To make his point clearer, Jesus made the hero of the story a resident of Samaria, whose people were traditionally hostile to the Jews.

Today, most states have what are called Good Samaritan laws, which protect individuals from liability if they attempt to render assistance to someone in distress. Such laws were created after it became evident that passers-by were often reluctant to help accident victims for fear of being held legally responsible if the victim's condition worsened.

Sources

Bromiley, Geoffrey W. *The International Standard Bible Encyclopedia.* Grand Rapids, MI: W. B. Eerdmans, 1988.
Chase, Harold W., ed. *The Guide to American Law: Everyone's Legal Encyclopedia.* St. Paul, MN: West Publishing Co., 1983.
Stimpson, George. *A Book about the Bible.* New York: Harper and Brothers, 1945.

Gordian knot. ***A complex problem that can only be solved by bold action.***
This proverbial tale begins with Gordius, the legendary founder of Phrygia in Asia Minor. During a period of great stress, an oracle proclaimed that the kingdom's savior would arrive riding on a wagon. Soon after,

a peasant named Gordius appeared, riding on a wagon. The people of Phrygia assembled and decided to make Gordius their king. Subsequently the famine and strife that had gripped the land were lifted.

Gordius lashed his wagon to a pole at the acropolis at Gordium and dedicated it to the god Zeus. He used an excessively complicated knot to secure the cart, and over the centuries a legend arose that whoever could untie it would conquer Asia. A thousand years passed, and no one had managed to undo the massive knot. When Alexander the Great reached Phrygia on his march through Anatolia in 333 B.C., he was shown the knot. Ignoring conventional approaches, he drew his sword and sliced the knot open. (Other versions report that Alexander pulled the pole out from the center of the knot.) The phrase *cutting the Gordian knot* has come to mean the solution of perplexing problems by straightforward and daring measures.

Sources

Hornblower, Simon, and Antony Spawforth, eds. *The Oxford Classical Dictionary.* 3d ed. Oxford: Oxford University Press, 1996.

Mercatante, Anthony S. *Facts on File Encyclopedia of World Mythology and Legend.* New York: Facts on File, 1988.

Sacks, David. *Encyclopedia of the Ancient Greek World.* New York: Facts on File, 1995.

Gotham. *New York City.*

During the Middle Ages, the residents of Gotham in Nottinghamshire, England, discovered that King John was thinking of locating a hunting lodge near the town. The Gothamites did not wish to bear the costs of supporting the king and his court whenever they came to the lodge, so the residents pretended to be insane when the king's courtiers scouted the area. They tried to drown fish, trap birds by building hedges around them, and rake the image of the moon's reflection off a pond. The townspeople successfully discouraged the royal presence, but their victory came with a price. Although the king shunned Gotham, the town could not shake the report that it was populated by half-wits.

In 1807 Washington Irving revived the name of Gotham when he used it in his *Salmagundi Papers,* a collection of satirical essays about New York City that was designed to "instruct the young, reform the old, correct the town, and castigate the age." A native of the city, Irving was always chiding his hometown, though with affection and always in a roundabout way (see *Knickerbocker*). He dubbed the city Gotham, an allusion to the old medieval tale that suggested both inane foolishness and clever resourcefulness.

In modern popular culture, Gotham is the city in which Batman resides. As Bill Finger, one of the original creators of the Batman character, explained, "We didn't call it New York because we wanted anybody in any city to identify with it. Of course, Gotham is another name for New York."

Sources

Evans, Ivor H., ed. *Brewer's Dictionary of Phrase and Fable.* 14th ed. New York: Harper and Row, 1989.

Jackson, Kenneth T., ed. *The Encyclopedia of New York City.* New Haven, CT: Yale University Press, 1995.

Mish, Frederick C. *The Merriam-Webster New Book of Word Histories.* Springfield, IL: Merriam-Webster, 1991.

Gothic. *The style of architecture or art that dominated northern Europe during the Middle Ages; also, a type of fiction with brooding, mysterious characters and desolate settings.*

The Goths were a Germanic people whose hostile encroachments into the Roman Empire made them feared and reviled by the "civilized" world. By the fifth and sixth centuries, the Goths were converting to Christianity, settling into their territory, and becoming integrated into European culture. The Goths had little to do with the style that bears their name, yet *gothic* came to be identified with crude barbarism. Coined in the Renaissance, it was used as a derogatory description of medieval architecture and artwork. Renaissance intellectuals sought to break free of what was perceived as the dark ages, and they regarded the pointed arches, flying buttresses, and sacred ornamentation of medieval churches as backward in comparison with the clean, elegant simplicity of classical architecture.

The word was extended to literature when Horace Walpole wrote his novel *The Castle of Otranto: A Gothic Story* in 1765. This tale set in the Middle Ages is filled with gloom and terror and was the forerunner of the gothic genre.

Sources

Davis, Paul K. *Encyclopedia of Invasions and Conquests: From Ancient Times to the Present.* Santa Barbara, CA: ABC-CLIO, 1996.

Lorimer, Lawrence T. *The Encyclopedia Americana.* Danbury, CT: Grolier, 1989.

Simpson, J. A., and E. S. C. Weiner, eds. *The Oxford English Dictionary.* 2d ed. Oxford: Clarendon Press, 1989.

Graham crackers. ***A popular snack cracker made of honey and whole wheat flour.***

The invention of the Graham cracker was but one small brick in the road to dietary and spiritual reform as proposed by the Reverend Sylvester Graham (1794–1851). The New England preacher was convinced that a simple, sparse lifestyle was necessary for moral and physical well-being. He believed in hard mattresses, cold showers, and sleeping with the windows open. Although Graham was married, he disapproved of sexual relations and thought they should be resorted to for procreation purposes only.

Most of Graham's crusade was concerned with dietary reform as a means of improving health and moral character. Convinced that meat consumption led to physical decay and sexual excess, Graham advocated strict vegetarianism. Ham and sausage, for instance, tended to "increase the concupiscent excitability and sensibility of the genital organs." In his dietary regimen, oil was to be used as little as possible, and refined flour, alcohol, coffee, and tobacco were taboo. As an alternative to traditional heavy breakfasts of eggs, bacon, and oatmeal, he invented in 1829 the graham cracker, plain but wholesome crackers made of coarsely ground flour. Although bakers initially regarded Graham crackers as a threat to their bread sales, the public was content to purchase both. Today, Graham crackers are one of the best-selling products of the food conglomerate Nabisco.

Sources

Hendrickson, Robert. *Dictionary of Eponyms: Names That Became Words.* New York: Stein and Day, 1985.

Johnson, Allen, and Dumas Malone, eds. *Dictionary of American Biography.* New York: Scribner's, 1964.

Nissenbaum, Stephen. *Sex, Diet, and Debility in Jacksonian America: Sylvester Graham and Health Reform.* Westport, CT: Greenwood Press, 1980.

Panati, Charles. *Extraordinary Origins of Everyday Things.* New York: Perennial Library, 1987.

Grangerize. ***Tearing illustrations or other valuable material out of books, especially library books.***

In addition to being a clergyman, the Reverend James Granger (1723–1776) was a print collector and biographer. By the time of his death, he had amassed a collection of over 14,000 engraved portraits, many of which he had clipped from books in order to incorporate them into his own publications. In 1769 his *Biographical History of England, From Egbert the Great to the Revolution,* was released. This three-volume set was illustrated with many engravings Granger had filched from other works. Granger saw nothing wrong with this practice, and he recommended that other people take up the hobby as well, since they could only profit from the insight and information that images could provide. A later edition of Granger's *Biographical History* even had blank pages where the reader could insert relevant pictures. This sparked a fad in which people mutilated rare and valuable books in their search for just the right engraving.

Grangerizing is still the bane of libraries. Most libraries allow the public to have open access to their collections so that people may browse at their leisure, but the danger of mutilation remains. Some illustrations are collectors' items worth hundreds or even thousands of dollars. The Library of Congress estimated the loss from vandalism at $1.8 million, which forced the closing of the stacks to the public in 1992.

Sources

Hendrickson, Robert. *Dictionary of Eponyms: Names That Became Words.* New York: Stein and Day, 1985.

Hunt, Cecil. *Word Origins: The Romance of Language.* New York: Philosophical Library, 1962.

Vizetelly, Frank H. *A Desk-Book of Idioms and Idiomatic Phrases in English Speech and Literature.* Detroit, MI: Gale Research, 1970.

Comfort, N. A. *Brewer's Politics: A Phrase and Fable Dictionary.* London: Cassell, 1993.

Magill, Frank N., and John L. Loos. *Great Events from History: North American Series.* Pasadena, CA: Salem Press, 1997.

Grassy knoll. *According to some theorists, the spot from which the fatal shot that killed President Kennedy was fired; implies a wide-ranging conspiracy.*

The belief that Lee Harvey Oswald could not have fired the fatal shots at President Kennedy from the sixth story of the Texas School Book Depository building has kept conspiracy theorists busy for decades. One contention is that a second gunman was involved and that he was located on an open slope, known as the *grassy knoll,* that the president's limousine passed. This was the theory posited in *Rush to Judgment* by lawyer Mark Lane in 1966. Lane interviewed a number of the eyewitnesses to the assassination and claimed that the majority of them had heard the sound of shots being fired from the grassy knoll. Careful examination of the Abraham Zapruder film of the assassination shows that the president's head jerked backward, causing Lane to speculate that Kennedy was shot from the front rather than from behind by Oswald. Lane enjoyed immense publicity from his book, giving lectures at college campuses and appearing on talk shows and in television debates. Some critics questioned Lane's objectivity, since he had been hired by Marguerite Oswald, the alleged assassin's mother, to represent her son.

The debate continues, with exhaustive forensic studies on both sides proving and disproving each other's contentions. The grassy knoll theory persists, and the expression has evolved into a buzzword for sensitive information likely to be suppressed by the government or another powerful organization.

Sources

Callahan, Bob. *Who Shot JFK? A Guide to the Major Conspiracy Theories.* New York: Simon and Schuster, 1993.

Gray eminence. *A powerful advisor who operates in secret or in an unofficial capacity; also known as an éminence grise.*

The life and career of the powerful Cardinal Richelieu has been well documented in books and movies, and Richelieu is often cited as the archetypal "power behind the throne." Less familiar is the life of Richelieu's closest advisor, Father Joseph le Clerc du Tremblay (1577–1638), or Père Joseph, as he was known to contemporaries.

Cardinal Richelieu (1585–1642) was chief minister for Louis XIII of France. He realized his goal of centralizing authority by destroying the power of the Protestant Huguenots and by brilliantly manipulating intricate court politics. In 1612 Richelieu began his close collaboration with Père Joseph, a French mystic and religious reformer who was committed to the conversion of heretics. Père Joseph's ambition extended beyond France, for he envisioned a Counter-Reformation that would bring all of Europe and eventually the Muslim world into the Roman Catholic fold. His vision coincided perfectly with Richelieu's design to force Europe to submit to French domination. Although Père Joseph was officially Richelieu's secretary, his powers were more like those of a foreign minister, and he also dabbled at being a secret agent. At the French court, Richelieu was nicknamed the "red eminence" because of his scarlet cardinal's robes, and Père Joseph's gray habit inspired the name "gray eminence." These labels reflected the resentment and suspicion felt by many in the French court because of the shadowy yet tangible power the two men exerted. The term *gray eminence* fell out of use after Père Joseph's death in 1638. It was revived in 1941 when Aldous Huxley published the definitive biography of the priest, titled *Gray Eminence: A Study in Religion and Politics.*

When the Republic of Zimbabwe was created in 1979 out of the former British colony of Rhodesia, prime minister Ian D. Smith stepped down from office. Smith continued to work as a behind-the-scenes advisor to his successor, Bishop Abel T. Muzorewa, the first black prime minister of the new nation. Smith was sometimes referred to as the *éminence blanche,* or white eminence.

Sources

Huxley, Aldous. *Gray Eminence: A Study in Religion and Politics.* New York: Meridian Books, 1959.

McDonald, William J., ed. *New Catholic Encyclopedia.* New York: McGraw-Hill, 1967.

McHenry, Robert, ed. *The New Encyclopedia Britannica.* 15th ed. Chicago: Encyclopedia Britannica, 1992.

Mish, Frederick C. *The Merriam-Webster New Book of Word Histories.* Springfield, IL: Merriam-Webster, 1991.

Great Scott! ***An exclamation of surprise.*** General Winfield Scott (1786–1866) was a hero of the Mexican War but a terrible presidential candidate. In 1852 the Whig party selected Scott to run against Democrat Franklin Pierce. The general's apparent qualifications were his military record, his lack of political enemies, and the fact that he was a native Southerner who had lived in the North. Regardless, his campaign revealed an extremely vain and arrogant personality. He spoke of himself in the third person and kept a marble bust of his likeness on his desk. When questioned about his suitability for the presidency, he replied by exclaiming "Chapultepec!" and "Lundy's Lane!" as if the names of the battles he had fought required no further comment. His stump speeches were lackluster and focused on accounts of old military engagements. As the nation was preparing to fight new battles over the fugitive slave law and abolitionism, Scott declared that he had no clear opinion on these issues. Franklin Pierce, described as an uncharismatic, third-rate county politician, won the election by a landslide.

The expression *Great Scott!* may have originated with Scott's supporters during the campaign. Others claim that it was a term of derision, used by hecklers. By the 1880s the expression lost its association with Winfield Scott and became merely an exclamation of surprise or wonder.

Sources

Goodheart, Adam. "Would You Vote for These Men?" *Civilization* 3, no. 5 (1996):78–79.

Hendrickson, Robert. *The Facts on File Encyclopedia of Word and Phrase Origins.* New York: Facts on File, 1987.

Levy, Leonard W., and Louis Fisher, eds. *Encyclopedia of the American Presidency.* New York: Simon and Schuster, 1994.

Great White Hope. ***A champion.*** The origins of this phrase are steeped in the racial prejudice of the early twentieth century. When Jack Johnson (1878–1946) became the first black man to win the world heavyweight championship in 1908, white supremacists were unwilling to accept his victory. Their sensibilities were further outraged by Johnson's conduct outside of the ring. The champ indulged in a flamboyant lifestyle and was often seen dating white women. He became a prime target for harassment, and in 1913 he was convicted of violating the Mann Act, which made it illegal for a woman to be transported across state lines for immoral purposes. The woman in question was Johnson's future wife.

Johnson held on to his title for seven years, during which time his detractors eagerly scoured the fighting world for a *great white hope,* a white man who could win back the title. The first candidate was James J. Jeffries, a former heavyweight champion who was persuaded to come out of retirement for the fight. Race riots broke out across the country when Johnson knocked him out in the fifteenth round. In 1915 a strapping wheat farmer from Kansas made the great white hope a reality. In Havana, Cuba, after 26 rounds, Jess Willard knocked out Jack Johnson and became the new heavyweight champion of the world.

Johnson continued fighting in Europe and Mexico and formally retired in 1933. In 1946 he was killed in a car crash while on his way to watch Joe Lewis fight. Lewis was the second black man to win the heavyweight championship.

The term *great white hope* has lost its original racist connotations. It is generally used in a business or technology context, such as "The System X telephone exchange is the great white hope for modernizing Britain's antique telephone Network" (*Economist,* February 12, 1983, p. 27).

Sources

Farr, Finis. *Black Champion: The Life and Times of Jack Johnson.* New York: Scribner's, 1964.

Hickok, Ralph. *The Encyclopedia of North American Sports History.* New York: Facts on File, 1992.

McHenry, Robert, ed. *The New Encyclopedia Britannica.* 15th ed. Chicago: Encyclopedia Britannica, 1992.

Salzman, Jack, ed. *Encyclopedia of African-American Culture and History.* New York: Macmillan Library Reference, 1996.

Greek, it's Greek to me. ***Something that is unintelligible or obscure.***

The Greek language, which dates back to 2000 B.C., is one of the oldest surviving languages of Western civilization. Much of the great literature of the classical period was written in Greek, and after the conquests of Alexander the Great the language spread far outside its original Mediterranean environs.

Most of the earliest Christian gospels were first recorded in Greek, and it was through the influence of the "Greek Jews" that Christianity began to gain strength in the second and third centuries. After the emperor Constantine legalized Christianity in 313, missionaries carried the word throughout the Mediterranean, Europe, and North Africa. The only problem was that the word was still written in Greek, even though Latin was by then the lingua franca of the Western world. It became apparent that the gospels had to be translated into a more common language. Saint Jerome, a scholar who was fluent in several Mediterranean languages, undertook the task, and a Latin version of the New Testament was completed around 405.

Learned people who wished to read the classics in the original version had to wrestle with Greek, which was complex and difficult and used an entirely different alphabet from the Latin-based languages. *Greek* eventually became a byword for unintelligible material.

Sources

Katzner, Kenneth. *The Languages of the World.* London: Routledge, 1995.

Metzger, Bruce M., and Michael D. Coogan, eds. *The Oxford Companion to the Bible.* New York: Oxford University Press, 1993.

Walsh, Michael, ed. *Butler's Lives of the Saints.* San Francisco: Harper and Row, 1985.

Greenland. ***An island in the North Atlantic that is a semiautonomous state of Denmark.***

Even by Viking standards, Eric the Red had a bad reputation. His family had been driven out of Norway "because of some killings," as an old Norse saga states. Eric was able to establish a profitable homestead on the island of Iceland, but he was soon feuding and had to move again. He found a home on one of the tiny islands off the coast of Iceland but had no better luck there. A bloody feud began when one of his neighbors borrowed some boards and failed to return them. When Eric forcefully retrieved them, there was a battle and several men were killed, including the sons of his new neighbors. Eric was judged as an undesirable and was sentenced to three years in exile. He and some of his followers set sail for an island that was rumored to exist farther west.

In 981 or 982 Eric arrived in Greenland. It was a harsh, rugged land, but Eric was no stranger to carving out an existence in semi-Arctic environments. There was ample fishing and grazing land for livestock, and Eric knew that if he could establish a colony on the island he could claim all the privileges associated with being the first settler. After his three years of exile were over, he returned to Iceland to recruit other colonists. To entice homesteaders, he called the land *Greenland* (Groenland, in old Norse), even though it was far less hospitable than the name might suggest. Eric succeeded in attracting 25 ships full of settlers and livestock to follow him to

Greenland. Only 14 ships of the original fleet survived the voyage, but it was enough to start a new colony that would last for several hundred years.

The colony was neglected by Norway, and few additional settlers migrated to what was soon revealed as a barren, desolate environment. The eventual fate of the Norwegian settlement is uncertain, for when the island was rediscovered by British sailors in the sixteenth century, there was no trace. The Viking descendants had either vanished or been assimilated into the Eskimo population.

Sources

Magnusson, Magnus. *Vikings!* New York: Dutton, 1980.

Pulsiano, Phillip, ed. *Medieval Scandinavia: An Encyclopedia.* New York: Garland Publishing, 1993.

Simpson, J. A., and E. S. C. Weiner, eds. *The Oxford English Dictionary.* 2d ed. Oxford: Clarendon Press, 1989.

Gregorian calendar. *The calendar presently used by most of the world.*

From ancient times, various calendars were developed in an attempt to accurately measure the solar year. The purpose of early calendars was almost always related to religious observance, since the determination of the new moon or the shortest day of the year was crucial to the correct celebration of sacred rites. The Julian calendar had been devised under the Roman emperor Julius Caesar, and after working through various problems, the calendar was put into use by A.D. 8. Although the Julian calendar was astonishingly accurate given the resources of the age, it overestimated the length of the year by 11 minutes and 14 seconds. By the mid-sixteenth century this miscalculation had shifted the dates of the seasons by 10 days. The Roman Catholic Church was concerned about the effect of the drift on seasonal church celebrations. In 1545 the Council of Trent authorized the pope to revise the calendar in favor of a more accurate version. The length of the calendar year was redefined to 365.2422 days, which subtracted 0.0078 of a day per year.

It took until 1582 for the astronomers to devise a system for implementing the calendar, which was named for the current pope, Gregory XIII. Gregory announced that the day following October 4 would be October 15. Most of the Catholic countries readily adopted the new calendar, but Protestant countries did not appreciate being told by the pope what day it was. Some resisted embracing the new system until well into the eighteenth century.

Sources

Hendrickson, Robert. *Dictionary of Eponyms: Names That Became Words.* New York: Stein and Day, 1985.

Kelly, John N. *The Oxford Dictionary of Popes.* New York: Oxford University Press, 1986.

McDonald, William J., ed. *New Catholic Encyclopedia.* New York: McGraw-Hill, 1967.

McHenry, Robert, ed. *The New Encyclopedia Britannica.* 15th ed. Chicago: Encyclopedia Britannica, 1992.

Gregorian chant. *A liturgical chant accompanying a mass or the canonical hours.*

Often called Gregory the Great, Pope Gregory (540–604) was one of the preeminent leaders of the early church. Although born into a wealthy family, he abandoned a promising career and gave away his possessions in exchange for monastic austerity. He was motivated by sincere piety and a humble desire to pursue a life of quiet asceticism. His practical and administrative abilities in the founding of additional monasteries brought him to the attention of Pope Pelagius II, who was eager to make use of the talented monk. Gregory's work in Rome throughout a troubled period of flood, famine, and plague earned him the respect of the Catholic hierarchy. When Pope Pelagius died, Gregory learned to his horror that the papal succession appeared to be heading his way. He refused the initial offers, and according to tradition, he even fled Rome and appealed to the emperor Maurice to withhold imperial approval. Despite his preference for a contemplative life, Gregory was eventually persuaded to accept the papal robes.

Gregory reformed many aspects of medieval church life, one of which was the incorporation of music into the liturgical services. Although he approved of the use of chant, its actual invention is inaccurately ascribed to him. Gregory did rearrange the texts of some early chants, and his name was affixed to the prologue of early hymnals. In any event, his name has been firmly associated with this type of singing since the ninth century.

Sources

Kelly, John N. *The Oxford Dictionary of Popes.* New York: Oxford University Press, 1986.

McDonald, William J., ed. *New Catholic Encyclopedia.* New York: McGraw-Hill, 1967.

Sadie, Stanley, ed. *The New Grove Dictionary of Music and Musicians.* Washington, DC: Grove's Dictionaries of Music, 1980.

Gresham's law. ***The economic principle that bad money drives out good money.***
Thomas Gresham (1518–1579) was a financier and agent of the English government for the Tudor monarchs Edward VI and Elizabeth I. During the sixteenth century England borrowed large amounts from the Low Countries and the German states. Gresham spent much of his adult life living in Antwerp negotiating these loans and, on the side, smuggling weapons and coinage to England. As did most European nations, the Low Countries strictly forbade the exportation of bullion in the belief that it would weaken the economy. Gresham sidestepped this by smuggling bullion to England in vats of pepper and bags containing harnesses.

The huge loans negotiated by Gresham eventually had to be repaid, and the fluctuation in exchange rates between the two countries meant that England was frequently at a disadvantage. Gresham sought to alleviate this imbalance by shoring up the British economy. He advised Queen Elizabeth to recoin English currency, which had been devalued during the reign of Henry VIII. Gresham recognized that if two coins have the same nominal value but are made of different metals, the cheaper metal will drive the more valuable metal out of circulation. People will hoard the coin perceived as more valuable and spend only the "cheaper" coins. By advising against the further debasement of English money, Gresham helped put England on a sound economic footing.

Although Gresham was not the first person to observe that *bad money drives out good,* the principle was formally named Gresham's law in 1857 by economist H. D. Macleod.

Sources

Eatwell, John, ed. *The New Palgrave: A Dictionary of Economics.* London: Macmillan, 1987.

Goldberg, Philip. *The Babinski Reflex: And 70 Other Useful and Amusing Metaphors from Science, Psychology, Business, Sports, and Everyday Life.* Los Angeles: J. P. Tarcher, 1990.

Stephen, Leslie, and Sidney Lee, eds. *The Dictionary of National Biography.* London: Oxford University Press, 1921.

Gretna Green marriage. ***A quick elopement.***
In 1753 Parliament passed a law stating that all marriages in England must be presided over by a minister of the Church of England and must be accompanied by a publication of bans. Bans were a declaration of intent to marry that had to be read at church services for at least three consecutive weeks. This law made it virtually impossible for clandestine marriages to take place. As a result, many people who wished to elope headed for Scotland, where the marriage laws were much more relaxed. Scottish law required only that the couple declare their wish to be married in the presence of a witness, and the service did not require a minister. In Scotland the age of consent for marriages was 16, whereas in England it was 21.

Gretna Green was the first Scottish town on the main road from England. As a result, it was to this village that many young lovers eloped. The blacksmith, tollman, and ferryman frequently served as witnesses, and in one year alone, almost 200 marriages took place in the Gretna Green tollhouse. In 1856 the Scottish law was altered to require that at least one partner in a marriage ceremony must have lived in Scotland for at least three weeks. This still did not present too much of an inconvenience, and Gretna Green continued to be popular for quick marriages. In the twentieth century, Scottish marriage laws were again strengthened to insist that marriages be performed by a minister or registrar, and the age of consent was made 18 throughout Great Britain. By 1969 there was no longer any practical advantage in eloping to Gretna Green, but many couples are still married there because of its romantic history.

Sources

McHenry, Robert, ed. *The New Encyclopedia Britannica.* 15th ed. Chicago: Encyclopedia Britannica, 1992.

Outhwaite, R. B. *Clandestine Marriage in England, 1500–1850.* London: Hambledon Press, 1995.

Pool, Daniel. *What Jane Austin Ate and Charles Dickens Knew: From Fox Hunting to Whist: The Facts of Daily Life in Nineteenth Century England.* New York: Simon and Schuster, 1993.

Grog. ***An alcoholic drink, usually rum diluted with water.***

British Admiral Edward Vernon (1684–1757) was regarded by his men as something of a peculiarity because of the distinctive grogram cloak he habitually wore. Grogram is a coarse, stiffened fabric made of wool and mohair, and the admiral was nicknamed "Old Grog" by the sailors under his command. Admiral Vernon was concerned about the amount of alcohol consumed by British sailors. At sea, the available drinking water was usually stale and slimy after months of storage in wooden casks. The water also had a tendency to absorb the odors of whatever cargo the ship carried, making it especially unpleasant. It is therefore little wonder that the sailors preferred alcoholic beverages, and a gallon of beer was the typical daily ration for eighteenth-century British sailors. For ships that took on provisions in the West Indies, rum flowed freely, but sailors very quickly became disorderly when consuming the potent drink. In 1740 Admiral Vernon issued an order to all ships under his command: "The pernicious custom of seamen drinking their allowance of rum in drams, often all at once, is attended with many fatal effects; it impaired their health, ruined their morals, and made them slave to every brutish passion." The rum issued to the men was to be watered down, at a ratio of one quart of water for each pint of rum.

The seamen were disgruntled by the new policy and called the diluted beverage *grog* after the man who issued the order. Despite the resentment of the sailors, the policy was almost universally praised by officers and ship doctors and soon became standard practice in the British navy. *The Dictionary of National Biography* contended that Admiral Vernon's order was "perhaps the greatest improvement to discipline and efficiency ever produced by one stroke of the pen."

Admiral Vernon was also the source of another famous eponym: Mount Vernon, home of George Washington. Originally called Little Hunting Creek Plantation, it was renamed Mount Vernon by Washington's half-brother Laurence, who had admired and served under "Old Grog" in the Caribbean. George inherited the property after Laurence's death in 1751.

Sources

Jeans, Peter D. *Ship to Shore: A Dictionary of Everyday Words and Phrases Derived from the Sea.* Santa Barbara, CA: ABC-CLIO, 1993.

Stephen, Leslie, and Sidney Lee, eds. *The Dictionary of National Biography.* London: Oxford University Press, 1921.

Thrower, William R. *Life at Sea in the Age of Sail.* London: Phillimore, 1972.

Ground zero. ***Dead center of an imperiled area.***

The term *ground zero* refers to the point at which a nuclear weapon makes impact, implying that it is also the place where damage will be the most profound. Ground zero is technically only the area of total vaporization, usually around one-half mile in diameter. However, the detonation of atomic bombs at Hiroshima and Nagasaki resulted in several miles of destruction, which makes a precise measurement of ground zero somewhat specious. Commentators and journalists have latched on to this expression to refer to topics ranging from the site of an airplane crash to the war on drugs in inner cities. In a tongue-in-cheek usage, the name of the snack bar in the courtyard at the center of the Pentagon is Ground Zero, certainly a primary target should a nuclear attack be launched against the United States.

Sources

Dickson, Paul. *War Slang: Fighting Words and Phrases of Americans from the Civil War to the Gulf War.* New York: Pocket Books, 1994.

Glasstone, Samuel. *The Effects of Nuclear Weapons.* Washington, DC: GPO, 1977.

McHenry, Robert, ed. *The New Encyclopedia Britannica.* 15th ed. Chicago: Encyclopedia Britannica, 1992.

Guam, clear out for Guam.
See Clear out for Guam.

Guillotine. ***A mechanical device used for decapitation.***
Dr. Joseph Guillotin (1738–1814) considered himself a humanitarian, and throughout his career he was an ardent advocate of innovations to improve the life of the common man. An anatomy professor at the University of Paris, Guillotin introduced a number of reforms into the teaching of medicine, and in 1788 he was one of the first to call for increased representation of the Third Estate in the Estates General. He was elected to represent Paris, and in 1789 he proposed that all persons who had been sentenced to death should meet their end in the same manner: swift decapitation on a machine. Before this, persons without aristocratic rank were sentenced to hanging, which can be a long and agonizing death. Decapitation for all condemned prisoners, regardless of their social standing, was perceived as an act of mercy.

Dr. Guillotin did not invent the machine that bears his name. It was in fact a collaborative effort by Dr. Antoine Louis and a harpsichord maker, Tobias Schmidt, and the device was initially called *La Louisette.* Its first use was on the afternoon of 25 April 1792, when a notorious highwayman, Nicolas Pelletier, was executed before an enthusiastic crowd of 3,000 people. The machine was an instant hit and spawned miniature models, toys, and even tiny earrings in the shape of the machine. Children were known to experiment with slicing off the heads of mice and other small animals. Finally, the authorities in Arras banned the sale of these toys lest they corrupt the youth. Guillotin's name came to be associated with the device after remarks he made in the assembly. The doctor claimed that execution by the machine was completely painless. "The victim does not suffer at all. He is conscious of nothing more than a slight chill on the neck."

During the French Revolution, the machine was heavily used, and it was popularly known as Madame Guillotine. Before the Terror was over, more than 2,000 heads would roll, including that of its creator, Dr. Louis. Even Guillotin came close to losing his head. Condemned to death as an enemy of Robespierre, Guillotin was spared when Robespierre himself was executed. Nevertheless, rumors persist to this day that Guillotin was a victim of the machine that took his name. In fact, he died peacefully in his bed in 1814. After his death his children unsuccessfully lobbied to have the name of the decapitation device changed. When their petition was rejected, they changed their own name instead.

Sources

Arasse, Daniel. *The Guillotine and the Terror.* London: Lane, 1989.

Beeching, Cyril Leslie. *Dictionary of Eponyms.* London: Clive Bingley, 1979.

McHenry, Robert, ed. *The New Encyclopedia Britannica.* 15th ed. Chicago: Encyclopedia Britannica, 1992.

Mish, Frederick C. *The Merriam-Webster New Book of Word Histories.* Springfield, IL: Merriam-Webster, 1991.

Panati, Charles. *Panati's Extraordinary Endings of Practically Everything and Everybody.* New York: Perennial Library, 1989.

Gung ho. ***Unbridled enthusiasm and willingness to work cooperatively toward an objective.***
In 1938 the Chinese Industrial Cooperatives Society was formed with initial funding from British and American businessmen living in China. The objective was to improve

the working conditions for Chinese laborers and so help counter the threats of civil war and Japanese invasion. The Chinese nicknamed the society *Gung Ho,* meaning "work together." By 1940, about 30,000 Chinese laborers had formed themselves into 1,200 individual cooperatives.

During World War II Colonel Evans Carlson of the U.S. Marine Corps was so impressed with what he saw of the Gung Ho societies that he advocated its principles to his men. Carlson held meetings at which the men were encouraged to voice concerns, give opinions, and thrash out their problems in groups. In a 1943 interview, Carlson said: "I was trying to build up the same sort of working spirit I had seen in China where all the soldiers dedicated themselves to one idea and worked together to put that idea over. I told the boys about it again and again. I told them of the motto of the Chinese Cooperatives, Gung Ho. It means Work Together—Work in Harmony. It was hard at first to make them understand since we are essentially a selfish people. But gradually, the longer we were together and the more I had a chance to talk with them, they began to feel it."

Colonel Carlson's idea eventually caught on, and his battalion began calling themselves the Gung Ho battalion. Other marines also began using the expression *gung ho* in reference to the positive spirit of working together. During the Korean War, however, the term lost its positive connotation and was used in a disparaging sense to refer to people perceived as overzealous and obnoxious. This expression can still be used as either a compliment or insult, depending on the context.

Sources

Dickson, Paul. *War Slang: Fighting Words and Phrases of Americans from the Civil War to the Gulf War.* New York: Pocket Books, 1994.

Mish, Frederick C. *The Merriam-Webster New Book of Word Histories.* Springfield, IL: Merriam-Webster, 1991.

Safire, William. *Safire's Political Dictionary.* New York: Random House, 1978.

Wales, Nym. *The Chinese Labor Movement.* Freeport, NY: Books for Libraries Press, 1945.

Guns before butter. ***Government policy that gives priority to military armament over domestic needs.***

This expression arose in Germany during the 1930s, although it is uncertain who actually coined it. After World War I Germany was plunged into an economic depression from which it seemed incapable of emerging. Inflation spun out of control in the 1920s, and there were stories of German housewives using worthless currency to light fires in ovens because coal was too expensive. Some people survived on turnips for months on end. After Adolph Hitler became the chancellor of Germany in 1933, he embarked on an aggressive policy to reassert German power in the international arena. He was determined to regain industrial territories that had been ceded to France and to cease payment of heavy war reparations. This could be done only by convincing the rest of the world that Germany was again a military force to be reckoned with.

In 1936, Joseph Goebbels, the Nazi minister of propaganda, said, "We can do without butter, but despite all our love of peace, not without arms. One cannot shoot with butter, but with guns." Later that same year, Hermann Goering declared in a radio broadcast that "guns will make us powerful, butter will only make us fat." Rudolf Hess has also been credited with coining the expression by some historians.

In the United States, critics of administration policies during the 1960s charged that the government was bent on a guns *and* butter program. They warned that attempting to meet both demands would lead to bankruptcy. Economists use the term *guns versus butter* to describe the budgetary conflict between spending for both military and domestic programs.

Sources

Pickering, David, ed. *Brewer's Dictionary of Twentieth Century Phrase and Fable.* Boston: Houghton Mifflin Company, 1992.

Safire, William. *Safire's Political Dictionary.* New York: Random House, 1978.

Zentner, Christian, and Friedemann Budurftig, eds. *The Encyclopedia of the Third Reich.* New York: Macmillan, 1991.

Guy. ***In American slang, a man or fellow; in Britain, a person of ridiculous or bizarre appearance.***

In American slang, *guy* has been completely severed from its origins, which were somewhat sinister. It derives from Guy Fawkes (1570–1606), an English Catholic living in an age when being Catholic was hazardous to one's health. Fawkes's religious zeal prompted him to leave England and seek adventure on the Continent, where he joined the Spanish army and fought against Protestants in the Netherlands.

Meanwhile in England, James I took the throne, amid hopes from English Catholics that he would rescind some of the more punitive anti-Catholic legislation. Parliament as a whole did not share the king's interest in greater religious toleration. Since Parliament held the purse strings, James, who was always in desperate need of funds, was forced to compromise his ideals. The maxim that fanatic persecution breeds fanatic retaliation proved to be true, and in 1605 a group of militant Catholics devised a scheme to assassinate the king, the queen, and the entire Parliament. The conspirators felt that they needed a man with military training to mastermind the plan, and Guy Fawkes was persuaded to return to England to assist the plotters. The idea was to pack a tunnel underneath Parliament with gunpowder and ignite it on 5 November 1605, when the king was scheduled to open Parliament. Most of the important Protestant leaders of the country would be present at this grand ceremony. On the eve of the scheduled day, the tunnel was loaded with 36 barrels of gunpowder, with Fawkes standing guard.

One of the conspirators, Francis Tresham, had warned his brother-in-law, Lord Monteagle, not to attend Parliament on November 5, and Monteagle relayed the information to the authorities. At 2:00 A.M., Fawkes was arrested. Under torture he revealed the names of his fellow conspirators, and all were arrested and sentenced to death. Public outrage over the attempt on the king's life, combined with anti-Catholic hysteria, guaranteed that the execution of the Gunpowder Plot conspirators would draw huge crowds. Grotesque effigies of Guy Fawkes were paraded through the streets and ritualistically tortured and burned. The condemned suffered the traditional death of traitors: they were carried through the streets, hanged, cut down while still living, disemboweled, and quartered.

Parliament subsequently declared November 5 "a holiday for ever in thankfulness to God for our deliverance and detestation of the Papists." It is still celebrated in England, and grotesquely garbed effigies are burned in conjunction with a huge fireworks display. Other effigies of unpopular persons have been traditionally displayed during Guy Fawkes Day, and by extension they were also called "guys." In England, the word *guy* gradually came to mean any man of gaudy, obnoxious appearance. By the 1840s the word had crossed the Atlantic to the United States, but it then lost its negative association.

Sources

Fraser, Antonia. *Faith and Treason: The Story of the Gunpowder Plot.* New York: Doubleday, 1996.

Fritze, Ronald H., and William B. Robison. *Historical Dictionary of Stuart England: 1603–1689.* Westport, CT: Greenwood Press, 1996.

McHenry, Robert, ed. *The New Encyclopedia Britannica.* 15th ed. Chicago: Encyclopedia Britannica, 1992.

Mish, Frederick C. *The Merriam-Webster New Book of Word Histories.* Springfield, IL: Merriam-Webster, 1991.

Simpson, J. A., and E. S. C. Weiner, eds. *The Oxford English Dictionary.* 2d ed. Oxford: Clarendon Press, 1989.

H

Hair shirt. ***Self-imposed penance.***

Penance has been variously expressed in different times and in different cultures. In the twentieth century most penance takes the form either of service, such as assisting the infirm, or meditation and prayer. In the early days of the Christian church, physical mortification was a highly respected form of penance and could include fasting, self-flagellation, and sleeping on boards. A popular kind of penance was wearing a *hair shirt,* which was a sleeveless garment made of coarse animal hair, usually goat or camel. Worn next to the skin, it was extremely uncomfortable and was described as agonizing by those who donned it for more than a few hours. During the Middle Ages wearing a hair shirt became standard penance during Lent and Advent. Many who were not up to the challenge of acute physical discomfort for weeks on end instead tied a narrow strip of hair cloth around their waist. One of the dangers of public penance was the tendency for overzealous individuals to become focused on physical mortification and neglect the spiritual component of penance. Saint Cassian, the fifth-century monk and theologian, denounced the wearing of hair shirts as a form of monastic exhibitionism.

The expression *wearing a hair shirt* is used to refer to someone who is indulging in excessive austerity or self-denial. In the 1980s the term *hair shirt economics* was used in reference to a policy of strictly balanced budgets and diminished expectations from the public for maintaining a comfortable lifestyle.

Sources

Fehren, Henry. "For Sale: One Hair Shirt." *US Catholic* 56, no. 2 (1991): 38–40.

McDonald, William J., ed. *New Catholic Encyclopedia.* New York: McGraw-Hill, 1967.

Hara-kiri. ***To commit suicide or some other self-destructive act.***

Although the term *hara-kiri* (belly-cutting) is familiar to Americans, it is rarely used by the Japanese, who prefer the Chinese word *seppuku.* Both refer to a form of ritual suicide, in which a sword is plunged into the left side of the abdomen and drawn across to the right. The moment the knife has been pulled across the belly, a person acting as the victim's second was permitted to cut off the head of the victim as an act of mercy. Hara-kiri arose from the principles of bushido, a code of chivalry that guided the behavior of the warrior class. Bushido required self-discipline, honor, loyalty, and skill in martial arts. If a person had been indelibly stained by dishonor or humiliation, hara-kiri was considered to be the only honorable choice. Warriors killed themselves to prevent being captured after a battle, to atone for failure in duties, and occasionally to demonstrate loyalty to a deceased overlord.

The practice of hara-kiri was probably established in Japan during the Ashi-kaga dynasty (1336–1568). It has been estimated that up to 1,500 of these suicides occurred annually. The formal ritual of hara-kiri involving disembowelment and beheading was officially abolished in 1868. After a number of Japanese soldiers resorted to suicide near the end of World War II, the word entered the English language. It is generally used in a figurative sense for any self-destructive act undertaken by a person or organization.

Sources

Itaska, Gen, ed. *Kodansha Encyclopedia of Japan*. Tokyo: Kodansha International, 1983.

Perkins, Dorothy. *Encyclopedia of Japan: Japanese History and Culture, from Abacus to Zori*. New York: Facts on File, 1991.

Haussmannization. ***To restore and upgrade deteriorating urban areas.***
Baron Georges-Eugene Haussmann (1809–1891) was a French administrator who undertook the monumental task of modernizing Paris in the 1850s and 1860s. Paris was essentially a medieval city, with narrow, twisting streets and no proper sewage or water systems. The need for an overhaul was driven home in the revolution of 1848, when mobs of angry citizens crowded the streets, pulled down trees to block roadways, and brought the city to its knees. The army was rendered useless by the roadblocks, and the rebels succeeded in forcing the abdication of King Louis-Philippe. When Louis-Napoleon became emperor of the French in 1852, he was determined that the army would never again be disabled because of the poor layout of the streets.

Haussmann was appointed to launch an ambitious public works program. He tore down a number of buildings to construct wide, straight avenues over what had been a chaotic mass of small lanes. New water supply and sewage systems were built. A train system was incorporated into the overall plan to facilitate public transportation. Parks, streetlamps, and sidewalks made the city a more pleasant place to live. However, Haussmann's improvements generated an enormous amount of controversy. The razed buildings left people homeless, and some thought the new broad avenues were utilitarian and unattractive. It was the huge cost overruns that finally sank Haussmann, and he was dismissed in 1870.

In the United States, the gentrification of urban areas, with all its benefits and problems, has been referred to as *Haussmannization.*

Sources

Jordan, David P. *Transforming Paris: The Life and Labors of Baron Haussmann*. New York: Free Press, 1995.

McHenry, Robert, ed. *The New Encyclopedia Britannica*. 15th ed. Chicago: Encyclopedia Britannica, 1992.

Saalman, Howard. *Haussmann: Paris Transformed*. New York: Braziller, 1971.

Trahair, R. C. *From Aristotelian to Reaganomics: A Dictionary of Eponyms with Biographies in the Social Sciences.* Westport, CT: Greenwood Press, 1994.

Hays code. ***A code that regulated the moral content of films produced in Hollywood.***
In the early 1920s the Hollywood community was reeling from bad publicity in the wake of the Fatty Arbuckle scandal, in which one of Hollywood's most popular comedic actors was accused of raping and murdering a young actress. Hollywood notables decided that a little self-policing was in order, and to that end they selected Will H. Hays (1879–1954) as head of the Motion Picture Producers and Distributors Association. A Presbyterian lawyer and former chairman of the Republican National Committee, Hays claimed that he represented "Middle America" and would defend its values. In his view, films had a duty to educate and protect the minds of the young, and they should "reflect aspiration, achievement, optimism, and kindly humor" while they entertained.

The major principles of the regulatory code he devised were (1) No picture shall be produced which will lower the moral standards of those who see it. Hence the sympathy of the audience shall never be thrown to the side of crime, wrong-doing, evil, or sin. (2) Correct standards of life, subject only to the requirements of drama and entertainment, shall be presented. (3) Law, natural or human, shall not be ridiculed, nor shall sympathy be created for its violation.

A jury composed of the heads of production from Hollywood movie companies would decide if a movie was consistent with the spirit and letter of the Hays code. Knowing that their work would be submitted to such a review panel, directors often filmed alternative versions of specific scenes in case of trouble with the Hays jury. The effect of the code was to stifle creativity and to discourage films that dealt with hard-hitting, realistic issues. It would take the cultural revolution of the 1960s to shake the influence of the Hays code over Hollywood.

Sources

Carmen, Ira H. *Movies, Censorship, and the Law.* Ann Arbor: University of Michigan Press, 1966.

Gardner, Gerald C. *The Censorship Papers: Movie Censorship Letters from the Hays Office, 1934–1968.* New York: Dodd, Mead, 1987.

Green, Jonathon. *The Encyclopedia of Censorship.* New York: Facts on File, 1989.

Hendrickson, Robert. *Dictionary of Eponyms: Names That Became Words.* New York: Stein and Day, 1985.

Hegira. ***A flight to escape danger.***

Like many religious visionaries, the prophet Muhammad (570–632) found himself in dangerous situations throughout his life. He first began gathering converts in about 613 in Mecca, the city of his birth. Although his following was small, their passionate beliefs and practices attracted suspicion from some of the established clans in Mecca. After about seven years, men from the city of Medina came to hear Muhammad and were converted to Islam. They carried the message back to their home city, where they succeeded in gaining more adherents. Because Medina welcomed the new religion, many of Muhammad's followers migrated there, and eventually only his family and a few close advisors remained in Mecca. Hostility from the Mecca clans had continued to escalate, and a number of plots to murder Muhammad began taking shape. Using various ruses Muhammad and his remaining band safely escaped from Mecca and arrived in Medina in 622. To the Muslims, this *hegira,* or emigration, by the prophet does not signify flight but was rather a decisive break with the past and a step forward into a new future.

The term *hegira* is often used in a broader sense to mean any move, especially a political one, that places someone in a more desirable setting.

Sources

Eliade, Mircea, ed. *The Encyclopedia of Religion.* New York: Macmillan, 1986.

Glasse, Cyril. *The Concise Encyclopedia of Islam.* London: Stacey International. 1989.

Hendrickson, Robert. *The Facts on File Encyclopedia of Word and Phrase Origins.* New York: Facts on File, 1987.

Irving, Washington. *Mahomet and His Successors.* Madison: University of Wisconsin Press, 1970.

Heidi Award. ***A tongue-in-cheek recognition of a terrible programming decision in television broadcasting.***

One Sunday night in 1968, millions of Americans were engrossed in the televised broadcast of an exciting football game between the New York Jets and the Oakland Raiders. With one minute and five seconds left to play, the Jets were winning, 32–29, but the Raiders were closing in on a touchdown. The game was about to overrun its time slot, and NBC made the decision to pull the plug on the game in order to air the scheduled Sunday night movie, *Heidi.* The network was flooded with thousands of angry phone calls from football fans. The deluge of calls to the NBC office in New York City caused its switchboard to short out. Some desperate fans called the New York City Police Department, tying up the emergency lines. Oakland Raider fans were no doubt further irritated by the news that their team was able to pull off a sensational last-minute victory by scoring two touchdowns in the final 65 seconds.

A few hours after the game an NBC spokesman delivered a public apology to the fans. "It was a forgivable error by humans who were concerned about the children who were expecting to see *Heidi.*"

NBC no longer preempts the final minutes of sporting events to return to regularly scheduled programming. The dubious honor of a Heidi Award has since been used to describe a really bad programming decision by a network.

Sources
Schuster, Joe. "Jets vs. Raiders: Great Games" *Sport.* November 1993, 22.
Taaffe, William. "There's No Hiding from Heidi." *Sports Illustrated,* 21 December 1987, 80.

Hemlock, to drink hemlock. ***To self-destruct; to resign; to be forced to take a fall.*** The great Athenian philosopher Socrates (469–399 B.C.) was one of the seminal figures in the history of thought, but his emphasis on ethics and his methodology represented a threat to some of the political elite of Athens. During his life, he challenged, angered, and frustrated many of the city's leaders. Moreover, two of his pupils, Alcibiades and Critias, had engaged in ambitious power plays that threatened the democratic principles of Athens, and it was this association that provided Socrates' opponents with the ammunition they needed. He was charged with the vague crime of "corrupting the young," or impiety.

Socrates treated the trial with contempt. He refused to answer specific charges and instead relied on a recitation of the facts of his life and his basic philosophy. He argued that his actions had always been consistent with the cause of justice, but the Athenians were not swayed. A narrow margin of the 501 jurors found him guilty, and he was condemned to death. It is likely he could have avoided the sentence had he been willing to compromise. As it was, Socrates chose to commit suicide by drinking hemlock, one of the most violent of poisons. The symptoms of hemlock poisoning—abdominal pain, respiratory problems, and violent convulsions—start soon after ingestion and result in death in about an hour.

Socrates took his stand not because he was suicidal but because the alternatives were unacceptable to him. A person who makes a decision that seems self-destructive but is the only honorable option may be said in a metaphorical sense to be *drinking hemlock.*

Sources
McHenry, Robert, ed. *The New Encyclopedia Britannica.* 15th ed. Chicago: Encyclopedia Britannica, 1992.
Sacks, David. *Encyclopedia of the Ancient Greek World.* New York: Facts on File, 1995.
Turkington, Carol. *Poisons and Antidotes.* New York: Facts on File, 1994.

Herod, to out-Herod Herod. ***To be surpassingly cunning and wicked.*** Herod the Great (73–4 B.C.) was of Arab descent, although he was a practicing Jew. His close connection with the ruling class in Rome was rewarded when he was appointed king of Judea in 37 B.C. Herod attempted to win the favor of his Jewish subjects through elaborate building projects, including theaters, aqueducts, and fortifications. He built the port city of Caesarea, rebuilt the city of Samaria, and constructed the second Temple in Jerusalem. Despite these achievements and the general prosperity during Herod's reign, he remained unpopular with the Jews, who regarded him as a foreigner. Surrounded by Greek counselors and indulging in Greek customs, Herod outraged the conservative Jewish population.

In his later years Herod became increasingly unstable and suspicious. For example, he repeatedly altered his will to benefit whichever of his children he currently favored, he killed his innocent wife and most of her family, and he had three of his own sons executed by strangulation. His most infamous act was the massacre of newborn children, which is recounted in the Gospel of Matthew (2: 16). Although no source other than the Bible records this slaughter, it is entirely consistent with Herod's irrational and brutal policies during this time. Despite his violent life, he died of natural causes, and his kingdom was divided among his three surviving sons. The expression *to out-Herod Herod* was coined by Shakespeare, and became popular by the nineteenth century.

Sources
Harris, Roberta L. *The World of the Bible.* New York: Thames and Hudson, 1995.
Jones, A. H. M. *The Herods of Judaea.* Oxford: Clarendon Press, 1938.
Metzger, Bruce M., and Michael A. Coogan, eds. *The Oxford Companion to the Bible.* New York: Oxford University Press, 1993.

Roth, Cecil E., ed. *Encyclopedia Judaica.* New York: Macmillan, 1971.
Sandmel, Samuel. *Herod: Profile of a Tyrant.* Philadelphia: Lippincott, 1967.
Simpson, J. A., and E. S. C. Weiner, eds. *The Oxford English Dictionary,* 2d ed. Oxford: Clarendon Press, 1989.

Hippocratic oath. *An oath of ethical professional conduct sworn by physicians.*

Hippocrates (c. 460–370 B.C.) was a Greek physician born and raised on the island of Cos. Few biographical details are certain, but it is known that he was a teacher, traveled widely throughout Greece, and was one of the most famous physicians of his day. Although an extensive collection of manuscripts, called the Hippocratic collection, has survived to this day, it is not known if any of these were actually written by Hippocrates. Some of the essays in the collection give considerable attention to the respect for moral values. These writings have formed the basis for an ethical code of conduct for physicians. The first section of the code details the obligations between the practitioner of medicine and the student, the second is the pledge of the physician to practice only beneficial medicine and lead a respectable lifestyle. It is uncertain whether Hippocrates penned the oath that bears his name, although it does represent his principles as embodied by the surviving Hippocratic manuscripts.

Sources

Gillispie, Charles Coulston, ed. *Dictionary of Scientific Biography.* New York: Scribner's, 1970.
McHenry, Robert, ed. *The New Encyclopedia Britannica.* 15th ed. Chicago: Encyclopedia Britannica, 1992.
Sacks, David. *Encyclopedia of the Ancient Greek World.* New York: Facts on File, 1995.

Hobson's choice. *Making do with what is offered, or doing without.*

Thomas Hobson, who lived in Cambridge, England, in the last half of the sixteenth century, was one of the first men in England to rent horses. He kept a stable of over 40 horses and hired them out to students at nearby Cambridge University. Fearing his best horses would suffer from overuse, Hobson insisted that the horses be let out in rotation. The stall nearest the stable door was always occupied by the horse that would be ridden next, and Hobson allowed the customer no opportunity to request a different mount. *Hobson's choice* meant making do with what was offered.

Sources

Evans, Ivor H., ed. *Brewer's Dictionary of Phrase and Fable.* 14th ed. New York: Harper and Row, 1989.
Simpson, J. A., and E. S. C. Weiner, eds. *The Oxford English Dictionary.* 2d ed. Oxford: Clarendon Press, 1989.
Stimpson, George. *A Book about a Thousand Things.* New York: Harper and Brothers, 1946.

Honeymoon. *A vacation taken by a newlywed couple immediately following their wedding.*

The word *honeymoon* was coined in the Middle Ages, when it certainly bore no resemblance to the contemporary practice of indulging in a relaxing vacation following the stress of a wedding. In an age when the vast majority of people never traveled more than a few miles from the spot where they were born, the idea of risking life, limb, and possessions on unsafe roads for a superfluous trip was unthinkable. The most common way a newly married couple celebrated their marriage was by drinking mead, a fermented liquor made from honey. Such alcoholic beverages were common in areas where the climate did not favor grapevines. Mead could be sweet or dry, and in the Middle Ages it was usually similar to a sparkling table wine. It could be spiced with the addition of herbs such as cloves, thyme, and ginger, and it was believed to have medicinal benefits. Mead was far more costly than ale, which was the standard drink of peasants. As such, common people rarely indulged except on special occasions, such as a wedding. A supply of mead for one month (or cycle of the moon) was standard fare for the newlyweds, giving rise to the expression *honeymoon*.

Sources
Panati, Charles. *Extraordinary Origins of Everyday Things.* New York: Perennial Library, 1987.
Simpson, J. A., and E. S. C. Weiner, eds. *The Oxford English Dictionary.* 2d ed. Oxford: Clarendon Press, 1989.
Trench, Richard Chenevix, ed. *Origin of Things Familiar: Sketches on the Origin of Common Things.* Cincinnati, OH: United Book Corporation, 1934.

Hook or by crook. ***To obtain something by any means necessary.***
In feudal times, peasants who owned no land had difficulty obtaining sufficient firewood. It was the custom on many estates to allow peasants to collect wood lying on the ground as well as any branches they could gather from the trees using a bill-hook or a shepherd's crook. The expression *by hook or by crook* originally implied that there are limitations on how a goal could be achieved. No such constraints apply to the contemporary phrase, which implies the use of fair means or foul to accomplish a deed.

Sources
Evans, Ivor H., ed. *Brewer's Dictionary of Phrase and Fable.* 14th ed. New York: Harper and Row, 1989.
Morris, William, and Mary Morris. *Morris Dictionary of Word and Phrase Origins.* New York: Harper and Row, 1977.
Vizetelly, Frank H. *A Desk-Book of Idioms and Idiomatic Phrases in English Speech and Literature.* Detroit, MI: Gale Research, 1970.

Hooker. ***A prostitute.***
A very tempting theory about the origin of this word associates it with Joseph Hooker (1814–1879), a Union general in the Civil War. Hooker's finest achievement was his successful reorganization of the Army of the Potomac. Although the soldiers heeded Hooker's leadership in military matters, in their off-hours their priorities were hard liquor and loose women. The Army of the Potomac was so notorious for giving business to prostitutes that the red-light district in Washington, D.C., was dubbed "Hooker's Division."

In fact, the term predates the Civil War, and references appear in the 1840s and 1850s. Its origin is unknown, but it may derive from the manner of a prostitute's solicitation, in which she "hooks" her client. Nevertheless, the word entered widespread usage beginning in the 1860s, which may owe something to the exploits of Hooker's Army of the Potomac after all.

Sources
Hendrickson, Robert. *The Dictionary of Eponyms: Names That Became Words.* New York: Stein and Day, 1985.
Johnson, Allen, and Dumas Malone, eds. *The Dictionary of American Biography.* New York: Scribner's, 1964.
Simpson, J. A., and E. S. C. Weiner, eds. *The Oxford English Dictionary.* 2d ed. Oxford: Clarendon Press, 1989.

Hoosier. ***A native or resident of Indiana.***
There are a number of thoroughly unsatisfying explanations for the origin of this term. The word dates at least to the early nineteenth century, when it was used in reference to backwoods people. The most commonly cited origin is that it is a contraction of "who's there," a standard, gruff reply in answer to a knock on the door. Another suggestion associates it with Samuel Hoosier, who contracted a number of Indiana laborers to work on the Louisville and Portland canal. These laborers were referred to as "Hoosier's men." The most likely explanation is that it is a derivation of *hoojee,* which meant a dirty or vagrant person. The word eventually lost its negative connotation and assumed the more flattering implication of someone from the unspoiled heartland of the country. It was eventually used specifically in reference to people from Indiana, although there is no clear reason for this.

Sources
Mish, Frederick C. *The Merriam-Webster New Book of Word Histories.* Springfield, IL: Merriam-Webster, 1991.
Stimpson, George. *A Book about American History.* New York: Harper and Brothers, 1962.

Horatio Alger story. ***A rags-to-riches story.***
Most of Horatio Alger's novels received excruciatingly bad reviews, but that seemed

to have no effect on the wild popularity of the rags-to-riches novels he pounded out every few months. Horatio Alger (1832–1899) was the son of a Unitarian minister and was reluctantly persuaded to follow in his father's footsteps. After graduating from Harvard Divinity School in 1860, he moved to New York, but he preferred to write stories rather than minister to a flock.

Alger's stories all bore a remarkable similarity: Young, ragged boy rises to the top through plucky determination, hard work, and virtuous deeds. The titles of his books illustrate the distinctive Alger stamp:

Ragged Dick; or Streetlife in New York with the Bootblacks (1868)
Tattered Tom; or the Story of a Street Arab (1871)
Strive and Succeed; or the Promise of Walter Conrad (1872)
Brave and Bold; or the Fortunes of a Factory Boy (1874)
Sam's Chance; and How He Improved It (1876)

Alger wrote over 130 books in his lifetime. All of them imply that through hard work and determination, anyone can succeed. These books were extraordinarily popular during Alger's lifetime, and this is often credited to Americans' desire to believe that the Horatio Alger scenario is possible—and that it could happen to them.

Sources

Estes, Glenn E. *American Writers for Children before 1900.* Detroit, MI: Gale Research, 1985.
Johnson, Allen, and Dumas Malone, eds. *The Dictionary of American Biography.* New York: Scribner's, 1964.

Horse latitudes. ***Subtropical belts that circle the earth between the latitudes 30 degrees north and 30 degrees south.***

The belts within these latitudes tend to have calm weather, which was a disadvantage to ships that relied solely on wind power to cross the ocean. Sailors on a becalmed ship were in mortal danger if their supply of water ran out. Stills that could desalinate water were invented in the eighteenth century, but the enormous amount of fuel they required made them impractical for use at sea. The expression *horse latitudes* may have arisen from the practice of eating or throwing horses overboard while ships were dead in the water in order to conserve water and lighten the vessel. Memoirs of sailors who had been becalmed include accounts of eating sawdust, rats, and the leather fittings of the ship. The horses didn't stand a chance.

Sources

Jeans, Peter D. *Ship to Shore: A Dictionary of Everyday Words and Phrases from the Sea.* Santa Barbara, CA: ABC-CLIO, 1993.
Stimpson, George. *A Book about a Thousand Things.* New York: Harper and Brothers, 1946.
Thrower, William R. *Life at Sea in the Age of Sail.* London: Phillimore, 1972.

Horse's mouth, straight from the horse's mouth. ***To hear something from the most knowledgeable authority.***

In the days when horses were the primary means of transportation, knowing a horse's age was as important to the buyer as knowing a used car's mileage is today. There was no reliable way to determine the age of a horse, but examining the teeth could give the purchaser a rough idea. For a horse under five years old, the counting of teeth is an accurate measure of age. A horse's first permanent teeth begin to appear at two and a half years, and all permanent teeth will be present in five years. However, the potential life span of a horse is 30 years, and teeth could offer few guides to pin down the age of an older horse, except perhaps by inspecting the degree of wear on the surface of the teeth. Despite the drawbacks, finding needed information *straight from the horse's mouth* was still the most reliable method of approximating a horse's age.

Sources

Hendrickson, Robert. *The Facts on File Encyclopedia of Word and Phrase Origins.* New York: Facts on File, 1987.
Nowak, Ronald D. *Walker's Mammals of the World.* Baltimore, MD: Johns Hopkins University Press, 1991.

How the other half lives. ***Refers to the lack of understanding that economically privileged people have about the condition of the poor.***

How the Other Half Lives is the title of a ground-breaking book by Danish immigrant Jacob Riis (1849–1914). For several years after Riis emigrated to New York City, he lived in poverty as he drifted from one job to another. In 1873 he landed steady work as a police reporter and was assigned to the Lower East Side, which he described as "the foul core of New York's slums." Riis was appalled by the grinding poverty he witnessed. The infant death rate in the tenements was one in ten, and several families shared one-room apartments that lacked plumbing or ventilation.

How the Other Half Lives was a powerful indictment of slum conditions. It was illustrated with bleak photographs showing, in the starkest possible manner, the despair and filth in which the poor, particularly the new immigrants, lived. The book sent shock waves through American society. Future Secretary of Labor Frances Perkins read the book while still a student and "straightaway felt that the pursuit of social justice" would be her vocation. Theodore Roosevelt, then a prestigious member of the U.S. Civil Service Commission, was so affected by the book that he sought out Riis out, saying, "I have read your book, and I have come to help." Later, as president of the New York City Board of Police Commissioners, Roosevelt continued to acquaint himself with the condition of the slums by visiting them with Riis. The book proved to be a major inspiration for the social reform movement that flourished around the turn of the century.

The phrase *how the other half lives* refers to the difficulty a privileged group has in understanding the plight of a less fortunate group. It is also used by commentators to draw the distinction between men and women, straight and gay, and blue-collar and white-collar workers.

Sources

Riis, Jacob. *How the Other Half Lives.* New York: Hill and Wang, 1957.

Simpson, J. A., and E. S. C. Weiner, eds. *The Oxford English Dictionary.* 2d ed. Oxford: Clarendon Press, 1989.

Hoyle, according to Hoyle. ***According to the rules; also, referring to an authority to ensure correctness.***

Very little is known about the life of Edmond Hoyle (1671–1769) except that he was an avid whist player. He may have been a barrister, although he probably never practiced, since he merely styled himself "Edmond Hoyle, Gentleman," in his book. Whist, the forerunner of bridge, was a phenomenally popular game in the eighteenth century. People played it in coffeehouses, at parties, and at home. Hoyle decided to capitalize on the craze and offered his services as an expert tutor. He gave private lessons to people in their homes, in the same way that a dancing master or piano teacher might provide services to wealthy clients. Hoyle furthered his career by publishing a book on the game in 1741, which was soon considered to be the definitive guide to whist. Other gaming books followed, and before Hoyle died at the ripe old age of 98, he had produced instruction guides to backgammon, piquet, chess, quadrille, and a general rule book called *Hoyle's Standard Games.* He was the first person to publish game rules, and so he was considered the grand old man of card playing, and his word was law. Soon the expression *according to Hoyle* came to mean an authoritative standard for any behavior or activity.

Sources

Evans, Ivor H., ed. *Brewer's Dictionary of Phrase and Fable.* 14th ed. New York: Harper and Row, 1989.

McHenry, Robert, ed. *The New Encyclopedia Britannica.* 15th ed. Chicago: Encyclopedia Britannica, 1992.

Simpson, J. A., and E. S. C. Weiner, eds. *The Oxford English Dictionary.* 2d ed. Oxford: Clarendon Press, 1989.

Humble pie, to eat humble pie. ***To be forced to acknowledge one's error in humiliating circumstances.***

The expression *humble pie* is an example of folk etymology, a process by which a perfectly good word is altered to resemble a more familiar word. In this case, the original word was *umble,* a medieval word that referred to an animal's edible organs. Since the prime cuts from an animal were usually reserved for wealthy consumers, peasants made do with what was left over: the head, liver, lungs, kidneys, and so on. The best way to prepare these rather undesirable cuts was to stew them and then bake the mixture in a doughy crust. The crust on a medieval pie was usually a mixture of flour and water, and the absence of fat would have made it rather hard, edible only after it had been softened by the juices of the filling.

Umble pie was a standard dish for the common people of medieval society. By the sixteenth century *umble* was being pronounced as the more familiar *humble,* a word derived from the Latin *humilis,* or "earth." Although there was nothing shameful about eating humble pie, it was associated with the impoverishment of the lower classes. As standards of living rose in later centuries, fewer people had to resort to organ meat, and the expression *humble pie* was inaccurately presumed to refer to a humiliating experience.

Sources

Henisch, Bridget Ann. *Fast and Feast: Food in Medieval Society.* University Park: Pennsylvania State University Press, 1976.

Mish, Frederick C. *The Merriam-Webster New Book of Word Histories.* Springfield, IL: Merriam-Webster, 1991.

Simpson, J. A., and E. S. C. Weiner, eds. *The Oxford English Dictionary.* 2d ed. Oxford: Clarendon Press, 1989.

I

"I shall return." ***A reference to a bleak situation from which one still hopes to triumph.***

Shortly after the U.S. entry into World War II, the Japanese began their drive in the Philippines to force American troops south toward the Bataan peninsula. There were 80,000 American troops and 26,000 civilian refugees but less than a month's supplies. The commanding officer, General Douglas MacArthur, received orders to take command of American forces in Australia, which meant that he would be leaving in the middle of a desperate situation. In any event, there was little that could stop the Japanese onslaught at that time. MacArthur's parting pledge was, "I shall return." Most of the troops left behind became prisoners of the Japanese. Three years later, MacArthur made good on his promise when in October 1944 the army stormed the east coast of Leyte in the central Philippines. They met with little resistance, and after wading through knee-deep water to reach the shores, MacArthur emotionally declared, "People of the Philippines, I have returned."

In the decades since World War II, the phrase *I shall return* has often been used when it appears that an individual has met his match. Politicians, sports figures, and Wall Street brokers have all been known to fall back on the well-used phrase. Perhaps the most ironic allusion to MacArthur's pledge occurred in 1986, when Philippine president Ferdinand Marcos and his wife were driven into exile by their own people. The disgraced president claimed, "We shall return."

Sources

Comfort, N. A. *Brewer's Politics: A Phrase and Fable Dictionary.* London: Cassell, 1993.

Manchester, William R. *American Caesar: Douglas MacArthur, 1880–1964.* Boston: Little, Brown, 1978.

Titelman, Gregory. *Random House Dictionary of Popular Proverbs and Sayings.* New York: Random House, 1996.

Iron curtain. ***A barrier to the exchange of people and information that existed along the border of the nations controlled by the former Soviet Union.***

This expression was popularized by Winston Churchill in a speech at Westminster College in Fulton, Missouri, on 5 March 1946: "From Stettin in the Baltic to Trieste in the Adriatic, an iron curtain has descended across the continent. Behind that line lie all the capitals of the ancient states of central and eastern Europe." This speech marked the end of the alliance between the Soviet Union and the Western nations, which had continued uneasily after the conclusion of the war. Thereafter the expression *iron curtain* was used to refer to the grim, impermeable wall that Stalin was creating to stop the influx of culture and ideas into the Eastern European nations now under his control.

The term *iron curtain* first appeared in the eighteenth century to refer to a curtain of metal that was put in theaters as a precaution against fire. In the nineteenth century, it came to mean any impenetrable barrier. The expression was initially used in the context of the Soviet Union by the Viscountess Snowden. In her 1920 memoir

Through Bolshevik Russia, she wrote, "We were behind the 'iron curtain' at last!"

Variations on the term include *bamboo curtain* to apply to the wall of secrecy that surrounds communist China; and *tortilla curtain,* to describe the increased—if inadequate—security along the Mexico-U.S. border to prevent illegal immigration.

Sources

Arms, Thomas S. *Encyclopedia of the Cold War.* New York: Facts on File, 1991.

McHenry, Robert, ed. *The New Encyclopedia Britannica.* 15th ed. Chicago: Encyclopedia Britannica, 1992.

Safire, William. *Safire's Political Dictionary.* New York: Random House, 1978.

Ishmael. ***An outcast; also, the progenitor of the Islamic religion.***

In the Old Testament, Abraham's wife Sarah could not conceive children, so she encouraged him to take her servant Hagar as his concubine. Hagar bore Ishmael, Abraham's first-born son. After Sarah miraculously conceived a child, her jealousy drove Abraham to expel Hagar and Ishmael. They lived in the wilderness and eventually settled in Egypt, where Ishmael married a woman from the tribe of Jurhum. Islamic tradition claims that among their descendants was the prophet Muhammad, and Ishmael is considered the ancestor of Islam.

Sources

Bromiley, Geoffrey W., ed. *The International Standard Bible Encyclopedia.* Grand Rapids, MI: W. B. Eerdmans, 1988.

Glasse, Cyril. *The Concise Encyclopedia of Islam.* London: Stacey International. 1989.

Metzger, Bruce M., and Michael A. Coogan, eds. *The Oxford Companion to the Bible.* New York: Oxford University Press, 1993.

J

Jack Ketch. ***A public executioner.***

Jack Ketch (d. 1686) became the public executioner in London around 1663, and within a decade, his name was already being used as an eponym for executioner. Except for a few years, he held the post until shortly before his death. Ketch was notorious for his antics on the scaffold, which included rifling through his victim's pockets and displaying any findings to the assembled crowd. He was also famous for his bungled executions. In 1683 he was to behead Lord William Russell. Just before the axe fell, Russell moved slightly, and it took Ketch several blows to complete the job. Two years later the duke of Monmouth, the illegitimate son of Charles II, was scheduled to meet his death for attempting to seize the throne from his uncle, James II. As the duke approached the block, he warned Ketch not to bungle the job as he had with Russell. The first blow was ineffectual, and Monmouth turned to glare at Ketch. Two more blows failed to sever the head, and Ketch threw down his ax saying he could not continue. The attending sheriffs forced him to proceed, and after two more blows the job was completed.

A rumor circulated that Ketch was a tool of the pope, since most of his bungled executions occurred with Protestants, but there is no evidence to support this. In 1686 Ketch indulged in a drinking binge, during which he beat a woman to death. Thus, the executioner met his end on his own scaffold, hanged in a public execution in November 1686.

Sources

Clifton, Robin. *The Last Popular Rebellion: The Western Rising of 1685.* New York: St. Martin's Press, 1984.

Cyriax, Oliver. *Crime: An Encyclopedia.* London: Andre Deutsch, 1993.

McHenry, Robert, ed. *The New Encyclopedia Britannica.* 15th ed. Chicago: Encyclopedia Britannica, 1992.

Jacquard. ***A fabric with an intricately woven pattern.***

Joseph Marie Jacquard (1752–1834) was a French silk weaver who preferred tinkering with mechanical devices. Although he was a young man with a wife and child to support, he became absorbed by the challenge of creating a machine that could weave silk and other fabrics more efficiently than the labor-intensive looms of the day. He neglected his business, went broke, and had to sell his house and household goods. The family's struggle to survive was interrupted by the French Revolution. Jacquard joined the Republican ranks, but by the end of the tumult both his wife and son were dead.

Jacquard went back to the seclusion of invention. By 1805 he had developed a punch card system that was able to control individual skeins of thread and produce richly textured fabrics, such as tapestry, paisley prints, and damask fabrics. He was stunned, however, when his revolutionary device, which had the potential to produce beautiful fabric at a fraction of the usual cost, was greeted with hostility and suspicion by the textile workers of France. Jacquard's loom required less skill and could be operated with far fewer employees than traditional methods. Fearing depressed wages and unemployment, silk weavers rioted, broke into factories, and smashed the looms in the public square. On one occasion Jacquard was attacked and beaten by a mob and would have been killed had he not been rescued by police.

Dissatisfied workers could not halt the adoption of such a useful invention. By 1812 there were over 11,000 Jacquard looms in France. The price of fabric did fall, but instead of leading to massive unemployment, it ushered in a boom for the textile industry. Future inventors Charles Babbage and Herman Hollerith later modified Jacquard's punch card concept and used it in mechanical calculators.

Sources

Kidwell, Peggy Aldrich, and Paul E. Ceruzzi. *Landmarks in Digital Computing: A Smithsonian Pictorial History.* Washington, DC: Smithsonian Institution Press, 1994.

McHenry, Robert, ed. *The New Encyclopedia Britannica.* 15th ed. Chicago: Encyclopedia Britannica, 1992.

Jacuzzi. ***A hot bath with air pumps to swirl water.***

Candido Jacuzzi (1903–1986) became an inventor in the process of trying to help his severely arthritic son Kenny cope with his pain. The Jacuzzis regularly took Kenny for hydrotherapy treatments at a local hospital, where the boy was able to find some measure of comfort in the warm, swirling waters of the institution's whirlpool tub. Jacuzzi noticed that the pumps powering the tub were very similar to the ones his company manufactured for use in the drilling industry. He set his engineers to work designing a smaller version of the pump that might be used in a home bathtub.

Jacuzzi originally marketed his creation as a medical device for the relief of arthritis or muscle and joint disorders, to be sold primarily at a doctor's recommendation and in medical supply stores. Soon athletes and others began to use it for sheer relaxation, and Jacuzzi realized that the market for his invention was potentially huge. In the mid-1950s, movie stars Randolph Scott and Jayne Mansfield were recruited to endorse the Jacuzzi, which was now promoted as a luxury for pampering oneself. Jacuzzis gained national attention when one was offered as a prize on the television game show *Queen for a Day.* Sales continued to grow throughout the 1960s and 1970s, and the family sold the company in 1979 for $70 million. Incidentally, Kenny Jacuzzi grew up to be a healthy man and headed the European division of the family firm in Italy.

Sources

Fucini, Joseph J., and Suzy Fucini. *Entrepreneurs: The Men and Women behind Famous Brand Names and How They Made It.* Boston: G. K. Hall, 1985.

Hendrickson, Robert. *Dictionary of Eponyms: Names That Became Words.* New York: Stein and Day, 1985.

Jeep. ***A general-purpose army vehicle known for its sturdy durability.***

Although this is a relatively new word, there is great debate about its derivation. Most sources indicate that it is a contraction of the acronym G.P., meaning "general purpose." During World War I, automobiles became hopelessly bogged down in the muddy roads of France, and it was determined that the military needed rugged four-wheel-drive vehicles. A prototype was designed by Karl K. Pabst, and in 1940 Willys-Overland Motors and the Ford Motor Company won contracts to produce the vehicles. By 1941 the name for them, *Jeep,* was firmly entrenched among servicemen. Within the next five years over 649,000 Jeeps were manufactured in the United States.

The *Oxford English Dictionary* and other sources trace the word to a cartoon character in the strip "Popeye." In 1936 cartoonist E. C. Segar introduced Eugene the Jeep, an amazing dog Olive Oyl gave to Popeye for a pet. Known simply as The Jeep, the dog had amazing powers, such as the ability to walk through walls, appear and disappear at will, foretell the future, and shoot sparks from his tail. The amazing "go anywhere, do anything" abilities of The Jeep may have been the original inspiration for the name of the sturdy army vehicles that were so highly touted during World War II.

Sources

Dickson, Paul. *War Slang: Fighting Words and Phrases of Americans from the Civil War to the Gulf War.* New York: Pocket Books, 1994.

Grandinetti, Fred. *Popeye: An Illustrated History of E. C. Segar's Character in Print, Radio, Television, and Film Appearances, 1929–1993.* Jefferson. NC: McFarland, 1994.

Simpson, J. A., and E. S. C. Weiner, eds. *The Oxford English Dictionary.* 2d ed. Oxford: Clarendon Press, 1989.

Jehu. *A reckless driver.*

Wild driving occurred even in biblical times, and Jehu had a well-known reputation for it. He lived during the reign of Jezebel, the notorious Phoenician princess who sought to introduce the worship of pagan gods in the Temple at Jerusalem. This, combined with some infamous behavior (see *Jezebel*), sparked a rebellion against Jezebel and her son, King Jehoram. Jehu was a commander in the Hebrew army, and he took to his chariot to lead a march against the city to overthrow the king. Jehoram sent out messengers to determine the intentions of the army, but instead of reporting back, they switched allegiance. Still not certain about the loyalties of the approaching force, the king consulted a watchman, who told him: "The driving is like the driving of Jehu, son of Nimshi, for he drives furiously" (II Kings 9: 20).

Jehu succeeded in his quest to overthrow Jezebel and Jehoram and was crowned king in their place. However, he is remembered more for his driving than for anything that happened during his reign, which lasted from 842–815 B.C. The first recorded use of *Jehu* to refer to a reckless driver is in 1682.

Sources

Bromiley, Geoffrey W., ed. *The International Standard Bible Encyclopedia.* Grand Rapids, MI: W. B. Eerdmans, 1988.

Metzger, Bruce M., and Michael D. Coogan, eds. *The Oxford Companion to the Bible.* New York: Oxford University Press, 1993.

Stimpson, George. *A Book about the Bible.* New York: Harper and Brothers, 1945.

Jeremiad. *A complaining tirade; a prolonged lamentation.*

Jeremiah the prophet was born a few miles north of Jerusalem, in about 650 B.C., and he lived during one of the most troubling periods in Hebrew history. He believed that Jews were being seduced by pagan religions and that straying from the Hebrew law would mean the downfall of his people. As recorded in the Bible in the books of Jeremiah and Lamentations, his doleful teachings were full of anguished warnings, tirades, complaints, and despair. As might be expected, Jeremiah was not very popular among his contemporaries. Because of his unceasing criticism of the political and religious policies of his day, he was viewed as both a traitor and a heretic and was repeatedly persecuted.

In the end Jeremiah's warnings were vindicated. After Jerusalem was destroyed in 587 B.C. by Babylonian invaders, he and other Hebrew refugees fled to Egypt. However, many of the exiles blamed their defeat on their failure to worship the "Queen of Heaven," a Near Eastern mother goddess. Jeremiah continued his somber tirades against this sort of pagan worship, and, according to legend, he was finally stoned to death.

Sources

Beeching, Cyril Leslie. *A Dictionary of Eponyms.* London: Clive Bingley, 1979.

Bromiley, Geoffrey W., ed. *The International Standard Bible Encyclopedia.* Grand Rapids, MI: W. B. Eerdmans, 1988.

Metzger, Bruce M., and Michael D. Coogan, eds. *The Oxford Companion to the Bible.* New York: Oxford University Press, 1993.

Stimpson, George. *A Book about the Bible.* New York: Harper and Brothers, 1945.

Jericho, walls of Jericho. *Something that appears sturdy but that can be toppled.*

According to the famous Old Testament story, Joshua and a band of Israelites returned to their ancient homeland after years of exile in the desert, persuaded that

God intended them to take possession of it once more. The Israelites began their conquest at the walled city of Jericho. They spent six days circling the city and blowing trumpets. On the seventh day Joshua instructed his people to shout as well as sound the trumpets. "So the people shouted and the trumpets were blown. As soon as the people heard the sound of the trumpets, they raised a great shout, and the walls fell down flat; so the people charged straight ahead into the city and captured it" (Joshua 6: 20).

Twentieth-century historians and archaeologists have attempted to determine if there could be a scientific basis to the collapse of Jericho's walls. During its 10,000-year history, many cultures, including Mesolithic hunters, Hebrews, and Canaanites, occupied the area of Jericho. The accumulated debris formed a *tell,* or raised mound of earth, on which the ancient city was built. Although the harsh desert climate took its toll on structures made of stones, clay, and sun-baked mud, Jericho's earliest walls, dating to around 8000 B.C., were made of boulders dragged from outside the town and resisted erosion. The archaeological record provides some indication of how the inhabitants lived, and it appears that Jericho was subjected to a number of catastrophic events, including earthquakes. If Joshua did attack the city, it would have occurred around 1500 B.C. There is no way to determine how the walls of Jericho from this period were destroyed.

Sources

Buttrick, George Arthur, ed. *The Interpreter's Dictionary of the Bible.* New York: Abingdon Press, 1962.

Hamblin, Dora Jane. *The First Cities.* New York: Time-Life Books, 1973.

McHenry, Robert, ed. *The New Encyclopedia Britannica.* 15th ed. Chicago: Encyclopedia Britannica, 1992.

Metford, J. C. J. *Dictionary of Christian Lore and Legend.* London: Thames and Hudson, 1983.

Neev, David. *The Destruction of Sodom, Gomorrah, and Jericho: Geological, Climatological, and Archaeological Background.* Oxford: Oxford University Press, 1995.

Stimpson, George. *A Book about the Bible.* New York: Harper and Brothers, 1945.

Jezebel. ***A scheming, wicked woman; often carries an implication of sexual promiscuity.*** Jezebel was the daughter of the king of Sido (presently Sayda in Lebanon) and was married to Ahab, king of Israel. This politically motivated marriage brought Israel Phoenician wealth and power but also an influx of new religious and cultural influences. Ahab allowed Jezebel a great deal of freedom in instituting foreign religious practices. She not only fostered the worship of the Canaanite god Baal but actively tried to suppress the worship of the Hebrew god. The unfavorable connotation of her name derives particularly from her role as the prototypical enemy of the Israelites, but she was undoubtedly a strong-willed woman who used her power as queen to destroy any opponents. One vivid example was the stoning of the commoner Naboth, who refused to part with a vineyard she coveted.

After Ahab's death, Jezebel's son Jehoram ruled for approximately ten years, during which time the queen continued to exert tyrannical control. In 843 B.C. a civil war broke out in which the Hebrews set out to overthrow Jezebel and all the followers of Baal. Her son Jehoram was killed, and when the mob descended on her palace, Jezebel reportedly painted her face, adorned herself in her best finery, then shouted insults to the crowd from her window. Regally defiant to the end, she was hurled out of the window by her own eunuchs.

Sources

Bromiley, Geoffrey W., ed. *The International Standard Bible Encyclopedia.* Grand Rapids, MI: W. B. Eerdmans, 1988.

Hendrickson, Robert. *Dictionary of Eponyms: Names That Became Words.* New York: Stein and Day, 1985.

Kam, Rose. *Their Stories, Our Stories: Women of the Bible.* New York: Continuum, 1995.

Metzger, Bruce M., and Michael A. Coogan, eds. *The Oxford Companion to the Bible.* New York: Oxford University Press, 1993.

Stimpson, George. *A Book about the Bible.* New York: Harper and Brothers, 1945.

Jim Crow laws. ***Laws in the southern United States that required the separation of the races in private and public institutions.***
Although the *Negro Yearbook* for 1925–26 indicates the existence of an emancipated slave named Jim Crow who emigrated to England, it is unlikely that he is the source of the eponym Jim Crow. It is most likely derived from a popular minstrel show performed in the 1830s by Thomas Dartmouth Rice (1808–1861). Rice was one of the first white entertainers to impersonate African Americans as part of a vaudeville performance, and Jim Crow was one of his most popular characters. The chorus of one song and dance was:

> First on de heel tap, den on de toe,
> Ebery time I wheel about I jump Jim Crow.
> Wheel about and turn about and do jis so,
> And ebery time I wheel about I jump Jim Crow.

Rice's show was so well-known that *Jim Crow* became a slang term for an African-American. In 1839 a British antislavery book detailing the plight of the American slaves was titled *The History of Jim Crow,* thus suggesting that the term was fairly familiar by then.

In the 1880s, Jim Crow laws enacted in the southern states were motivated by a desire to limit the freedom of the black population, to ensure a cheap labor supply to southern farms, and to separate the races. The effect of the laws was to segregate residential areas, restaurants, workplaces, public parks, and cemeteries. In 1883 the Supreme Court ruled that segregation in privately owned institutions did not violate the Fourteenth Amendment, and in 1896 *Plessy v. Ferguson* approved segregation of public facilities as long as they were "separate but equal." Not until the landmark case of *Brown v. Topeka Board of Education* in 1954 were Jim Crow laws finally ruled unconstitutional.

Sources

Bessette, Joseph M. *American Justice.* Pasadena, CA: Salem Press, 1996.

McHenry, Robert, ed. *The New Encyclopedia Britannica.* 15th ed. Chicago: Encyclopedia Britannica, 1992.

Salzman, Jack, ed. *Encyclopedia of African-American Culture and History.* New York: Macmillan Library Reference, 1996.

Stimpson, George. *A Book about a Thousand Things.* New York: Harper and Brothers, 1946.

Joe Miller. ***A stale joke.***
In his day, Joe Miller (1684–1738) was one of England's most celebrated actors and humorists. A popular man, he was on friendly terms with many famous playwrights and intellectuals of early eighteenth-century England. When he died in 1738 he would undoubtedly have slipped into obscurity had it not been for the posthumous publication of a book of jokes that was attributed to the actor. In 1739 John Mottley published a collection whose complete title was: *Joe Miller's Jests; or the Wits Vade-mecum. Being a Collection of the most Brilliant Jests; the Politest Repartees; the most elegant Bon-Mots, and most pleasant short Stories in the English Language. First carefully collected in the company, and many of them transcribed from the mouth of the Facetious Gentleman whose name they bear; and now set forth and published by his lamentable friend and former companion, Elijah Jenkins, Esq*. Most of the material was in fact lifted from other books, and Mottley was merely taking advantage of the dead man's popularity. Although the insipid writing style aroused the disdain of the educated classes, the book was a hit with the rest of society, and by 1751 it had gone through ten editions, with each subsequent edition including more jokes, anecdotes, and short stories.

In spite of the popularity of these books, the term *Joe Miller* soon became synonymous with a tired, overused joke.

Sources

Hunt, Cecil. *Word Origins: The Romance of Language.* New York: Philosophical Library, 1962.

Lurie, Charles. *Everyday Sayings.* Detroit, MI: Gale Research, 1968.

Stephen, Leslie, and Sidney Lee, eds. *The Dictionary of National Biography.* London: Oxford University Press, 1921.

John Bull. *A personification of England as a bluff, prosperous man.*

Just as Uncle Sam personifies the United States, John Bull represents the English people. He was the creation of Scottish satirist and physician John Arbuthnot in 1712. Arbuthnot published a series of pamphlets that had a distinct political slant, and the image of portly, honest John Bull represented the idealized English country gentleman. Bull's friend, linen merchant Nicholas Frog, was the personification of Holland. Both Bull and Frog were allied against Lewis Baboon, who symbolized France and interference in trade. The pamphlets were an enormous success and were collectively published as *The History of John Bull.*

John Bull became a favorite of cartoonists both in Great Britain and abroad. Hostile caricatures portrayed him as a rather dull, overweight, and stupid figure, but favorable representations depicted him as a good-natured, honest farmer wearing a Union Jack waistcoat.

Sources

Isaacs, Alan, and Jennifer Monk, eds. *The Cambridge Illustrated Dictionary of British Heritage.* Cambridge: Cambridge University Press, 1986.

McHenry, Robert, ed. *The New Encyclopedia Britannica.* 15th ed. Chicago: Encyclopedia Britannica, 1992.

Stimpson, George. *A Book about a Thousand Things.* New York: Harper and Brothers, 1946.

John Hancock. *A signature.*

John Hancock (1737–1793) is probably best remembered for his large, bold signature on the Declaration of Independence. Hancock was a wealthy and popular Boston merchant who stood to lose a huge fortune, not to mention his life, if the rebel cause did not succeed. Extant speeches and writings by Hancock reveal the idealistic convictions that motivated his opposition to British actions. His prestige was such that he was elected president of the Continental Congress, which stepped into history by declaring the American colonies independent from Great Britain. Hancock was the only person to sign the Declaration of Independence on 4 July 1776. The other 55 signatures were gradually added between then and November 4. When others commented on the unusually large size of Hancock's signature, he reportedly said that he did it so King George could read the name without his spectacles and then double the reward placed on his head. Hancock's proud flourish made his name a byword for signature.

Sources

Fowler, William M. *The Baron of Beacon Hill: A Biography of John Hancock.* Boston: Houghton Mifflin, 1980.

Umbreit, Kenneth B. *Founding Fathers: Men Who Shaped Our Tradition.* Port Washington, NY: Kennikat Press, 1969.

Jolly roger.

See False colors.

Judas. *A traitor.*

Almost nothing is known about the early life of Judas Iscariot beyond the supposition that he came from the city of Carioth, since his last name means *man of Carioth* in Hebrew. Judas was one of the twelve disciples of Jesus, but he betrayed the Nazarene to the Jewish authorities. The elders feared that Jesus' electrifying effect on the people of Israel would provoke trouble with the Romans. To avoid any public disturbance, they needed to apprehend him with few of his followers around him. In exchange for 30 pieces of silver, Judas suggested that the arrest take place at the garden of Gethsemane, and he offered to identify Jesus by a kiss.

There are varying accounts of Judas's death. Most say that he immediately repented, returned the money, and hanged himself. The Jewish elders used the 30 pieces of silver to purchase a field in which paupers could be buried (see *Potter's field*). In the Acts of the Apostles (1: 18), Peter claimed that with the money, Judas bought a field, but on taking possession, he was seized with an illness, swelled up, and burst open. The spot on which he died was thereafter known as the field of blood.

Judas is thus the quintessential traitor, and in Dante's *Inferno,* he is portrayed in the deepest pit of Hell along with the assassins of Julius Caesar. A number of eponymous terms have been derived from Judas's name:

Judas goat: An animal that has a calming effect on other animals and is used to lead them to their death.

Judas kiss: An outward sign of loyalty that masks treachery and betrayal.

Judas tree: A type of tree in the *circis* family on which Judas supposedly hanged himself. The trees bear a dark purple flower reminiscent of blood.

Judas hole: A small opening in a door of a prison cell, through which guards can surreptitiously observe prisoners.

Sources

McDonald, William J., ed. *New Catholic Encyclopedia.* New York: McGraw-Hill, 1967.

Metzger, Bruce M., and Michael D. Coogan, eds. *The Oxford Companion to the Bible.* New York: Oxford University Press, 1993.

Simpson, J. A., and E. S. C. Weiner, eds. *The Oxford English Dictionary.* 2d ed. Oxford: Clarendon Press, 1989.

Stimpson, George. *A Book about the Bible.* New York: Harper and Brothers, 1945.

Juggernaut. *A powerful force that crushes whatever is in its path.*

In Hinduism, Juggernaut is a sacred image of the god Krishna. The Hindu religion claims that when Krishna was accidentally killed by a hunter, his bones were collected and placed inside a huge statue named Juggernaut, which had been created specifically for that purpose. One of the most important Hindu festivals of the year occurs in the spring when the statue is moved to its summer home. The Juggernaut is placed on a large cart and dragged through the sand on a journey that takes several days and is accompanied by drumbeats, clashing cymbals, and the incantations of priests. The task requires the strength of thousands of pilgrims, and the crush of the crowds has resulted in people being caught and killed under the cart. Reports of frenzied worshippers eagerly throwing themselves beneath the cart as an expression of devotion have been greatly exaggerated.

The English use of *juggernaut* refers to any situation in which people are at the mercy of a powerful force that rolls over whatever lies in its path.

Sources

Mish, Frederick C. *The Merriam-Webster New Book of Word Histories.* Springfield, IL: Merriam-Webster, 1991.

Stutley, Margaret, and James Stutley. *Harper's Dictionary of Hinduism: Its Mythology, Folklore, Philosophy, Literature, and History.* New York: Harper and Row, 1977.

Walker, Benjamin. *The Hindu World: An Encyclopedic Survey of Hinduism.* New York: Praeger, 1968.

Julian calendar. *Often referred to as "old style," the standard calendar in the Christian era until the sixteenth century.*

The Julian calendar was devised under the Roman emperor Julius Caesar and implemented A.D. 8. It was revolutionary for its time because it was based on the solar year rather than the lunar month. Although the Julian calendar was astonishingly accurate given the resources of the ancient world, it overestimated the length of the year by 11 minutes and 14 seconds. It was gradually phased out in favor of the Gregorian calendar (see *Gregorian calendar*), although there are a few countries (such as Ethiopia) that still operate under the Julian system.

Great Britain and its colonies finally adopted the Gregorian calendar in the eighteenth century. Because of the 11-day discrepancy, eighteenth-century dates often record both versions: for example, George Washington, born 22 February (11 February, old style) 1732.

Sources

Adkins, Lesley, and Roy A. Adkins. *Handbook to Life in Ancient Rome.* New York: Facts on File, 1994.

Hendrickson, Robert. *Dictionary of Eponyms: Names That Became Words.* New York: Stein and Day, 1985.

McHenry, Robert, ed. *The New Encyclopedia Britannica.* 15th ed. Chicago: Encyclopedia Britannica, 1992.

Jump the broom.
See Broom, jumping the.

Juneteenth. ***An African-American celebration of emancipation.***
On 1 January 1863, Abraham Lincoln issued the Emancipation Proclamation, a historic edict that freed the slaves of the Confederate states. No slaves were freed as a direct result of this proclamation, since the Confederacy did not recognize Lincoln's authority. However, the edict had a great symbolic import.

More than two years passed before news of the Emancipation Proclamation reached the slaves in the southern states. The most obvious explanation for this delay is that it was in the interest of white southerners to keep the slaves in ignorance of the decree. On 19 June 1865, two months after the surrender of the Confederacy, General Gordon Granger landed in Galveston, Texas, with a troop of Union soldiers and read General Order Number 3, which stated:

> The people of Texas are informed that in accordance with a Proclamation from the Executive of the United States, all slaves are free. This involves an absolute equality of rights and rights of property between former masters and slaves, and the connection heretofore existing between them becomes that between employer and free laborer.

The day on which the slaves of Texas learned of their liberation became an annual celebration called *Juneteenth,* a blend of the words "June" and "nineteenth." The holiday was quickly adopted by African Americans in the neighboring states of Louisiana and Arkansas. As southern blacks migrated to northern and western states in the latter half of the nineteenth century, the observance of Juneteenth traveled with them. The day was traditionally celebrated with a country picnic.

Following World War II commemoration of Juneteenth declined. According to one commentator, "The younger generation of blacks have been taught that they're part of this country and that the Fourth of July is the day for them to celebrate." During the civil rights movement of the 1960s and 1970s there was a reawakening of cultural pride among African Americans, and the celebration of Juneteenth has been enjoying a slow but steady resurgence.

Sources

Cohen, Hennig. *America Celebrates! A Patchwork of Weird and Wonderful Holiday Lore.* Detroit, MI: Visible Ink Press, 1991.

Taylor, Charles A. *Juneteenth: A Celebration of Freedom.* Madison, WI: Praxis Publications, 1995.

Wiggins, William. "Juneteenth." *American Visions* 8, no. 3 (1993): 28–31.

Wilson, Charles Reagan, and William Ferris, eds. *Encyclopedia of Southern Culture.* Chapel Hill: University of North Carolina Press, 1989.

K

Kamikaze. ***Behavior so reckless as to be suicidal.***

The Japanese word *kamikaze,* meaning "divine wind," dates back to the thirteenth century. Mongol forces had attempted to invade Japan in 1281, but a violent typhoon damaged their ships so badly that they were forced to withdraw. The Japanese regarded these storms as divine intervention and called the winds *kamikaze.*

Seven hundred years later, the Japanese hoped for another divine wind to repel the Allied forces from retaking the Philippine Islands. By 1944 Japanese military strategists knew that they did not have the manpower or traditional weaponry to block the inevitable Allied attempt to storm the Philippines. Vice Admiral Ōnishi Takijirō of the First Air Fleet designed a plan to damage and demoralize the Allied forces. Earlier in the war several Japanese pilots had impulsively crash-dived into enemy vessels when it appeared they were outnumbered. Now specially trained Japanese pilots were ordered to make suicide dives on Allied ships. One successful suicide plane loaded with extra bombs and gasoline could do far more damage than an entire squadron of planes flown by men whose goal was to return to base in one piece. On 19 October 1944, the admiral announced his to plan "to organize suicide attack units of Zero fighters armed with 550-pound bombs, with each plane to crash dive into an enemy carrier."

The shocking kamikaze strategy attracted more than twice as many volunteer pilots as there were available planes. Most of the pilots selected were young and inexperienced, since expert fliers were too valuable to expend on such missions. Ultimately, over 200 Allied ships were damaged in the attacks, and 34 ships were sunk. Japanese records indicate that 2,198 pilots met their death in these suicide missions.

By the 1960s the word *kamikaze* was also used in a more general sense to describe reckless and potentially self-destructive actions.

Sources

McHenry, Robert, ed. *The New Encyclopedia Britannica.* 15th ed. Chicago: Encyclopedia Britannica, 1992.

Millot, Bernard. *Divine Thunder: The Life and Death of the Kamikazes.* New York: McCall Publishing Co., 1971.

Perkins, Dorothy. *Encyclopedia of Japan: Japanese History and Culture, from Abacus to Zori.* New York: Facts on File, 1991.

Warner, Denis Ashton, and Peggy Warner. *The Sacred Warriors: Japan's Suicide Legions.* New York: Van Nostrand Reinhold, 1982.

Kentucky colonel. ***An honorary appointment.***

Most state governors also serve as commanders of the state militia. In this capacity he or she may appoint a pseudomilitary staff. Such appointments are purely honorary, as the recipients need have no military training, do not wear uniforms, and have no official duties. In many states their primary responsibility is to serve as members of the governor's inaugural party. The governors of Kentucky have a long tradition of liberally dispensing commissions as colonels.

For example, Governor Isaac Shelby, who commanded a brigade of Kentucky volunteers during the War of 1812, made all the men who served under him honorary colonels. Kentucky has literally thousands of honorary colonels, which is why citizens of Kentucky are sometimes referred to as "colonels."

Nebraska has a similar though less well-known practice, in which the governor may appoint "Nebraska admirals."

Sources

Kleber, John E., ed. *The Kentucky Encyclopedia.* Lexington: University Press of Kentucky, 1992.

Stimpson, George. *A Book about American History.* Greenwich, CT: Fawcett Publications, 1962.

Kilkenny cats, to fight like Kilkenny cats. ***To engage in fierce, bloodthirsty brawling.***

There are two possible explanations for the origin of this expression. One story arose from the Hessian troops stationed in County Kilkenny, Ireland, in the late seventeenth century. These soldiers supposedly amused themselves by tying cats together by their tails, draping them over a clothesline, and watching the animals fight to death. One fabled pair fought so hard that only their tails remained slung over the clothesline.

A more probable explanation was cited by Jonathan Swift, who believed that *cats* was merely slang for the pugnacious young men of Kilkenny. A number of English settlements had begun taking hold within the region, which was primarily Irish Catholic, and violent skirmishes between the inhabitants were commonplace. *Fighting like Kilkenny cats* refers to the notorious enmity between Irish Catholics and English Protestants.

Sources

Lurie, Charles. *Everyday Sayings.* Detroit, MI: Gale Research, 1968.

Simpson, J. A., and E. S. C. Weiner, eds. *The Oxford English Dictionary.* 2d ed. Oxford: Clarendon Press, 1989.

King James version of the Bible. ***The most popular of the English language translations of the Bible, completed in 1611.***

Until the Protestant Reformation, ecclesiastic authorities did not believe that the Bible needed to be in any other language than Latin, even though Latin was understood by only a tiny fraction of the population. As Pope Gregory VII (1073–1085) had stated, "Not without reason has it pleased Almighty God that Holy Scripture should be a secret in certain places, lest, if it were plainly apparent to all men, perchance it would be little esteemed and subject to disrespect; or it might be falsely understood by those of mediocre learning, and lead to error." This attitude persisted until the fifteenth century, when reformers began to propose that all people should have access to the Bible in the vernacular.

In England, translating the Bible smacked of heresy. The English biblical scholar William Tyndale was among the victims of the controversy and was executed in 1536. A change of heart (and of wives) on the part of Henry VIII opened the way for an English version of the Bible. Although in the coming decades a handful of translations appeared, none carried the official sanction of the Church of England. James I, who fancied himself a scholar, decided to sponsor an authorized version. Forty-seven of the most respected scholars in England were assembled for the task, and with the king's input, the *King James version* was completed in 1611. Its poetic style, rhythmic prose, and scholarly credentials won the translation wide and lasting acceptance.

Sources

Fritze, Ronald H., and William B. Robison, eds. *Historical Dictionary of Stuart England, 1603–1689.* Westport, CT: Greenwood Press, 1996.

Hendrickson, Robert. *Dictionary of Eponyms: Names That Became Words.* New York: Stein and Day, 1985.

Metzger, Bruce M., and Michael A. Coogan, eds. *The Oxford Companion to the Bible.* New York: Oxford University Press, 1993.

King's English. ***Properly spoken English.***
For such a small island, Great Britain has incorporated a remarkably large number of linguistic influences. English as we know it today has its roots in the sixth century, when the Jutes, Angles, and Saxons began to immigrate to the island from Denmark and Germany. The dialects of Old English (Northumbrian, Mercian, West Saxon, and Kentish) were formed. The Viking invasions and the Norman Conquest brought Scandinavian and French influences into the language. As a result of the Norman Conquest in 1066, French became the language spoken at court and by the upper class. Dialects continued to develop along geographic and class lines and were so distinct that people from different parts of the island were unlikely to understand one another. King's English as the "official" dialect began to develop in the fourteenth century. It was the tongue spoken in and around London by the well-to-do but could be grasped by the majority of the population. Official proclamations and edicts were issued in this language.

Ironically, some later English kings were unable to speak English at all. William of Orange (1689–1702) was of Dutch descent and spoke very limited English. When the throne of England passed to the German Hanoverians, many of these monarchs considered themselves primarily German. George I, king of England from 1714 to 1727, never made any attempt to learn to speak or read English. His son, George II (1727–1760), spoke halting, imperfect English and was never comfortable with the tongue. The inability of the Hanoverians to understand their subjects played an important role in weakening the power of the monarchy. Earlier kings had presided over meetings of the cabinet, but between 1714 and 1760 this did not occur owing to George I and George II's inability to understand English. Only George III was sufficiently fluent to participate in such deliberations. However, by the time he took the throne in 1760, the precedent of independent cabinet meetings outside the presence of the king had been established.

Sources

Bryson, Bill. *The Mother Tongue: English and How It Got That Way.* New York: William Morrow, 1990.
Classen, Ernest. *Outlines of the History of the English Language.* New York: Greenwood Press, 1969.
McCrum, Robert. *The Story of English.* New York: Viking, 1986.
Simpson, J. A., and E. S. C. Weiner, eds. *The Oxford English Dictionary.* 2d ed. Oxford: Clarendon Press, 1989.

King's evil. ***Scrofula.***
Scrofula is a tubercular disease of the lymph nodes. It was once a common disorder caused primarily by drinking contaminated milk. Tumors would form under the jaw and swell until bursting, leaving disfiguring scars on the neck. Although the disease is now rare in developed nations, it still occurs in Asian and African countries.

Beginning in the Middle Ages the disease was called the *King's evil* because it was believed that the touch of a king could cure it. The tradition began in England with Edward the Confessor (1003–1066). Edward had a well-deserved reputation for kindness and piety and is one of the few members of royalty to be declared a saint. According to his biographers, there was once a young woman who was so badly infected with scrofula that she was hardly able to speak. She was advised in a dream that if the king bathed her tumors, she would be cured of the disease. The woman traveled to London and made an appeal to Edward, who consented to her request. The king dipped his finger in water and touched the sores several times, making the sign of the cross over her neck throughout the procedure. The sores began to soften and separate and then fell off completely.

The story spread throughout England, and others who suffered from the disease came to the king for help. The belief that the monarch could heal by touch alone continued after Edward's death. Charles II was believed to have touched nearly 100,000 people in his lifetime, and in 1682 alone he touched over 8,000 diseased people. On the other hand, William III called it a "silly superstition." Queen Anne, who reigned from 1702 to 1714, was the last English monarch to perform the practice.

Sources

Barlow, Frank. *The Life of King Edward Who Rests at Westminster.* Oxford: Clarendon Press, 1992.

Evans, Ivor H., ed. *Brewer's Dictionary of Phrase and Fable.* 14th ed. New York: Harper and Row, 1989.

Hazlitt, William C. *Faiths and Folklore of the British Isles.* New York: B. Blom, 1965.

Wagner, Leopold. *Manners, Customs, and Observances: Their Origin and Signification.* London: William Heinemann, 1894.

King's ransom. ***A huge financial commitment.***

Although the intense security that insulates twentieth-century royalty makes the threat of kidnapping all but obsolete, this was certainly not the case in the Middle Ages, when kings were expected to fight alongside their men in battle. The possibility of capture was very real and often resulted in huge ransom demands in exchange for the king's release. There were formal rules governing hostage situations. Prisoners being held for ransom were under protection of law and could not be killed, although conditions of imprisonment were set by the captor. Ransoms could not be set so high that they could never be met and were usually equal to the annual revenue from the hostage's estate. The hostage must agree not to attempt an escape, and if the hostage was rescued, the ransom remained as an outstanding debt. Prisoners who were released in order to make arrangements for raising the ransom were honor-bound to return, and the captor could appeal to the prisoner's sovereign for restitution should he fail to do so.

One of the best-known cases of a king taken hostage was that of Richard the Lion-Heart. Richard was returning to England after a crusade in the Holy Land when his ship was blown off course in the Adriatic. He was captured in Venice and handed over to Duke Leopold in 1192. An enormous ransom of 150,000 marks (equivalent to $35 million in today's currency) was demanded from Richard's mother, Eleanor of Aquitaine. Over a year passed, and Richard was released upon payment of the bulk of the sum, with the promise that his honor depended on meeting the rest of the debt as soon as possible.

Another illustration of a king's ransom was that of John II of France. In 1356 John lost a disastrous battle to the English and was captured. His ransom was set at 3 million gold écus and a portion of southwestern France. The king was released conditionally to raise the colossal sum, and hostages were sent in his place. One of the hostages, John's own son, escaped. The king was so mortified by this breach of honor that he returned to London of his own free will. Special taxes had to be levied on the sale of salt and wine in an attempt to raise the ransom. When the king died in 1364, his successor, Charles V, refused to complete payment of the ransom, resulting in a renewed war with England.

Sources

Broughton, Bradford. *Dictionary of Medieval Knighthood and Chivalry.* New York: Greenwood Press, 1986.

Strayer, Joseph R., ed. *Dictionary of the Middle Ages.* New York: Scribner's, 1982.

Kiss the blarney stone.

See Blarney stone, kissing the.

Knickerbocker. ***A New Yorker of Dutch descent; also, full breeches that are gathered and banded just below the knee.***

In 1809 *A History of New York from the Beginnings of the World to the End of the Dutch Dynasty* was published, supposedly written by Deidrich Knickerbocker, elderly bachelor and long-time resident of New York. Deidrich Knickerbocker was a pseudonym for Washington Irving (1783–1859), and the book became so popular that it was not long before the true identity of the author was known. The work was a parody of the pretentious histories of New York and a good-natured satire of its Dutch roots. Old Dutch legends, traditions, and history were interspersed with some irreverent passages about the Dutch founders of the city. Irving acknowledged that his book had offended some of the "Dutch worthies," although most had taken the jibes with good humor. The book was an immediate success, and the word *knickerbocker* was soon being used to describe anything of Dutch origin. Before long there were knickerbocker societies, a knickerbocker baseball club, and knickerbocker magazines. The term was successful in marketing as well, with companies adopting the name for use with steamboats, bakeries, ice, and insurance. The word still survives in New York City's basketball team, the Knicks.

An illustrated edition of Irving's history was published in the 1850s, featuring exaggerated drawings by George Cruikshank of sixteenth-century Dutchmen dressed in baggy knee breeches and smoking long clay pipes. Ironically, knee breeches had recently come back into fashion as a result of interest in outdoor sports such as tennis and bicycle riding. These short trousers were dubbed *knickerbockers,* or as they are now known, knickers.

Sources

Irving, Washington. *A History of New York: From the Beginning of the World to the End of the Dutch Dynasty.* Philadelphia: J. B. Lippincott and Co., 1871.

Jackson, Kenneth T., ed. *The Encyclopedia of New York City.* New Haven, CT: Yale University Press, 1995.

Mish, Frederick C. *The Merriam-Webster New Book of Word Histories.* Springfield, IL: Merriam-Webster, 1991.

Knock on wood. ***A superstitious practice performed immediately after stating a hope.***
The ancient Romans believed that spirits lived in trees, and this belief evolved through the centuries into the superstition that spirits or goblins lurked in wood, even after the tree had been cut down. If these spirits heard someone make a boastful remark or speculate about coming good fortune, a malicious spirit might decide to make its presence known by spoiling the luck of the speaker. *Knocking on wood* served to acknowledge and placate the mischievous spirit.

Sources

Panati, Charles. *Extraordinary Origins of Everyday Things.* New York: Perennial Library, 1987.

Tallman, Marjorie. *Dictionary of American Folklore.* New York: Philosophical Library, 1960.

Kowtow. ***A display of servile deference and submission.***
Traditional Chinese protocol required that individuals of lesser birth perform elaborate demonstrations of servility and supplication when appealing to a person of higher status. This rigid protocol was epitomized by the *kowtow,* a ceremony in which the supplicant knelt on the floor and pressed his or her forehead to the ground. A total of three kneelings and nine prostrations was required to complete the ritual

Before the seventeenth century, the Chinese emperor only received envoys from tributary states—subjects who did not find the kowtow offensive or unreasonable. By 1655 Dutch and Russian envoys were making inroads into China, and these representatives of mighty trading nations raised loud and vehement objections to the ceremony. Several delegations were turned away from the Chinese court as a result of their refusal to submit. The demand that Western diplomats perform the kowtow made the ritual an international symbol of servility and served to exacerbate relations between China and the Western world until the mid-nineteenth century. Europeans considered genuflection before the emperor not only galling but inappropriate, because it implied that China was superior to the Western powers.

In 1793 British envoy Lord Macartney was sent to China to negotiate trading rights between the two countries. Macartney let it be known that he would refuse to accede to the ceremony when he was received by the emperor unless a Chinese diplomat performed the kowtow before a portrait of George III of England. This request gave rise to considerable discussion, and in the end it was decided that Lord Macartney would go down on one knee before the emperor. The Chinese emperor was not impressed, and very few trading concessions were granted.

As late as 1840 the former American president John Quincy Adams referred to the kowtow as an "arrogant and insupportable pretension" of the Chinese court, and he charged that China's insistence on maintaining the ritual was responsible for its strained relations with Great Britain. After the Opium Wars of the mid-nineteenth century, the kowtow requirement for Western diplomats was abolished, and after the fall of the Ch'ing dynasty in 1912, the Chinese were no longer required to perform it.

Sources

Eames, James B. *The English in China: Being an Account of the Intercourse and Relations between England and China from the Year 1600 to the Year 1843 and a Summary of Later Developments.* London: Pitman and Sons, 1909.

Hevia, James L. *Cherishing Men from Afar: Qing Guest Ritual and the Macartney Embassy of 1793.* Durham, NC: Duke University Press, 1995.

McHenry, Robert, ed. *The New Encyclopedia Britannica.* 15th ed. Chicago: Encyclopedia Britannica, 1992.

O'Neill, Hugh B. *Companion to Chinese History.* New York: Facts on File, 1987.

L

Labyrinth. ***A maze; an intricate structure that is difficult to navigate.***

Greek legend tells of a famous labyrinth at Crete that was built to hold the ferocious minotaur. King Minos of Crete demanded an annual tribute of fourteen young men and women from Athens.

Sent into the maze, the youth would become lost and would continue to wander in the labyrinth until they were devoured by the beast. When the daughter of the king, Ariadne, fell in love with Theseus, who had volunteered to be one of the intended victims, she gave him a sword to slay the minotaur and a skein of thread so that he could find his way out of the labyrinth. He did, then he proceeded to abandon the princess on the island of Naxos.

This tale had always been regarded as pure fiction until 1900, when Sir Arthur Evans of England excavated an enormous Cretan palace at Knossos that was built around 1700 B.C. The huge complex contained hundreds of rooms, balconies, hallways, and storage areas. The Minos legend may have been inspired by this palace, given its labyrinthine network of corridors, rooms, atriums, and staircases.

Sources

Cottrell, Leonard. *The Concise Encyclopedia of Archaeology.* New York: Hawthorn Books, 1960.

Ingpen, Robert R. *Encyclopedia of Mysterious Places: The Life and Legends of Ancient Sites around the World.* New York: Viking Studio Books, 1990.

McHenry, Robert, ed. *The New Encyclopedia Britannica.* 15th ed. Chicago: Encyclopedia Britannica, 1992.

Laconic. ***Concise, terse speech.***

Laconia was an ancient country of the Peloponnesus, and its most famous city was its capital, Sparta. The citizens of Laconia valued the spare, military lifestyle that featured few embellishments or comforts (see *Spartan*). While the rest of the Greek world delighted in poetry, drama, and artistry, the Laconians developed a reputation for secrecy, austerity, and anti-intellectualism. Hostile to outsiders, their characteristic manner of speech was terse, abrupt, and to the point.

One famous example of Laconic rhetoric emerged from the long-standing Spartan rivalry with Macedonia. As hostilities mounted, Philip II of Macedonia sent a message to the elders of Sparta, stating, "If I enter Laconia, I will level it to the ground." The reply consisted of one word: "If."

Sources

Evans, Ivor H., ed. *Brewer's Dictionary of Phrase and Fable.* 14th ed. New York: Harper and Row, 1989.

Hornblower, Simon, and Antony Spawforth, eds. *The Oxford Classical Dictionary.* 3d ed. Oxford: Oxford University Press, 1996.

Sacks, David. *Encyclopedia of the Ancient Greek World.* New York: Facts on File, 1995.

Lafayette, we are here. ***To acknowledge and return a favor.***

In 1777 eleven men set sail from France for the American colonies, led by the idealistic young Marquis de Lafayette (1757–1834). Lafayette had recently graduated from the French military academy and was eager to lend his services to the fledgling American rebellion against the British. He served on

General Washington's staff without pay and eventually commanded French troops allied with the Continental army. Lafayette succeeded in winning a series of impressive victories, and was one of the most colorful, popular, and respected leaders of the American Revolution.

Almost 50 years later the aging Marquis de Lafayette made one last visit to the United States and was received with wild adulation. His 15-month tour took him across the country and included visits to old compatriots such as Thomas Jefferson and James Madison. When he left in 1826, he took home a large cask of earth collected from Bunker Hill. Lafayette died in 1834 and was buried in the Picpus Cemetery. He was covered by the soil that he had carried from the United States, a country he referred to as the sacred land of liberty.

One hundred and forty years later, during World War I, American soldiers began landing on the coast of France to lend assistance to the besieged country. The American Expeditionary Force was under the command of General John Pershing, and he chose Colonel Charles E. Stanton to give an address at the Picpus Cemetery on 4 July 1917. Standing at the base of Lafayette's tomb, Stanton declared: "Here and now, in the presence of the illustrious dead, we pledge our hearts and our honor in carrying this war to a successful issue. Lafayette, we are here!" The phrase has often been mistakenly attributed to Pershing, although the general denied ever having said "anything so splendid." As relations between France and the United States cooled noticeably in the second half of the twentieth century, commentators have often asked where the spirit of "Lafayette, we are here" has gone.

Sources

Bernier, Oliver. *Lafayette: Hero of Two Worlds.* New York: E. P. Dutton, 1983.

Greene, Jack P., and J. R. Pole, eds. *The Blackwell Encyclopedia of the American Revolution.* Cambridge, MA: Blackwell Reference, 1991.

Rees, Nigel. *Sayings of the Century.* London: Allen and Unwin, 1984.

Stimpson, George. *A Book about American History.* Greenwich, CT: Fawcett Publications, 1960.

Lame duck. ***An elected official who has failed to win reelection but must serve out the remaining days of his or her term.***

This expression comes from British stock exchange slang. The London stock market, located in Exchange Alley, was the site of some wild stock speculation during the eighteenth and nineteenth centuries. Optimists who bought heavily when they believed that prices were about to rise were called bulls, while those who held a more conservative outlook were called bears. Depending on the vagaries of the market, most people were able to ride the waves of the market and make a profit. However, some speculators were not so lucky. Those who went bankrupt were called dead ducks, and others having difficulties meeting their obligations were called *lame ducks,* because they were said to "waddle out of the alley like a lame duck."

When this expression was transplanted to the United States, it initially referred to stock market dealers. By the mid-nineteenth century it was commonly associated with politics, as when President Abraham Lincoln used it to refer to a number of Republican senators who had lost in the 1864 elections. The discredited President Andrew Johnson was portrayed as a dead duck in a famous cartoon by Thomas Nast.

At that time, elections were held in November, with the newly elected legislators not taking office until the following March. This five-month period was helpful in an age when travel and communications were slow, but by the twentieth century this lag time was no longer necessary. The Twentieth Amendment to the Constitution, ratified in 1933, stipulated that terms of the president and congressmen will begin in January, thereby reducing the lame-duck period to three months.

Sources

Nelson, Michael. *The Presidency A to Z: A Ready Reference Encyclopedia.* Washington, DC: Congressional Quarterly, 1992.

Safire, William. *Safire's Political Dictionary.* New York: Random House, 1978.

Stimpson, George. *A Book about American Politics.* New York: Harper, 1954.

Lamourette's kiss. ***An insincere or short-lived reconciliation.***
Factionalism plagued the leaders of the French Revolution. Although a coalition had swept away the ancien régime, rivalries escalated to such a point that people were willing to execute anyone who disagreed with them. In particular, militants who had risen to positions of power within the legislative assembly feared that moderation would imperil the revolution, and they considered even the slightest objection to the course of events as a counterrevolutionary threat.

In 1792, in the midst of the assembly's raging factionalism, a voice of reason and forgiveness briefly rose to prominence. Abbé Adrien Lamourette was one of the few clerics who had succeeded in riding the tide of the revolutionaries' resentment of the Catholic church. Lamourette was willing to swear allegiance to the principle of a constitutional government and was therefore accepted into the assembly. On 7 July 1792, after a particularly acrimonious debate, Abbé Lamourette took the floor and spoke of the need for love between men engaged in a common cause. The priest must have been very persuasive, as it was said that the speech moved some people to tears. The factions exchanged what was called *Lamourette's kiss* and set aside their differences for the rest of the day.

The truce was short-lived, and the abbé, horrified by the violent events of late 1792, returned to his home in Lyon in despair. He was executed in 1794 by people who did not share his views on tolerance.

Sources
Darnton, Robert. *The Kiss of Lamourette: Reflections in Cultural History.* New York: Norton, 1990.
Evans, Ivor H., ed. *Brewer's Dictionary of Phrase and Fable.* 14th ed. New York: Harper and Row, 1989.
Jones, Colin. *The Longman Companion to the French Revolution.* London: Longman, 1988.

Land-office business. ***When a business is doing extremely well.***
In 1812 the U.S. government established the General Land Office to survey, manage, and control the dispersal of land in the public domain. The Midwest was beginning to be opened to settlement, and land was inexpensive and plentiful. Land offices were set up to administer the claims of miners and the sale of land to settlers. In control of more than a billion acres, the General Land Office was one of the largest and most important federal bureaus. Throughout the nineteenth century, whenever new territory was to be made available, eager citizens lined up at the land offices well before they were open for business. This practice gave rise to the expression *doing land-office business,* as the kind of bustling business every company hopes for.

Sources
Chase, Harold W., ed. *Dictionary of American History.* New York: Charles Scribner's Sons, 1976.
Claiborne, Robert. *Loose Cannons and Red Herrings: A Book of Lost Metaphors.* New York: Norton, 1988.
Hendrickson, Robert. *The Facts on File Encyclopedia of Word and Phrase Origins.* New York: Facts on File, 1987.

Laodicean. ***Being apathetic or indifferent, especially in matters of religion or politics.***
Laodicea, in present-day Turkey, was a prosperous town built in the third century B.C. Although it was an early center of Christianity, the church there grew lazy and indifferent, which led to the severe reprimand in Revelation (3: 14–16): "I know that you are neither cold nor hot. How I wish you were either one or the other! But because you are lukewarm, neither hot nor cold, I am going to spit you out of my mouth!"

The word *Laodicean* evolved into a term for anyone who displays a lack of interest in religion, current events, politics, or life itself.

Sources
Hendrickson, Robert. *Facts on File Encyclopedia of Word and Phrase Origins.* New York: Facts on File, 1987.
Simpson, J. A., and E. S. C. Weiner, eds. *The Oxford English Dictionary.* 2d ed. Oxford: Clarendon Press, 1989.

Laurels, to rest on one's laurels. ***To be satisfied with past accomplishments and unwilling to expend time or effort to achieve additional success.***

The laurel is a Mediterranean evergreen tree that was considered sacred by the ancient Greeks. In Greek mythology, Apollo was hopelessly in love with the nymph Daphne, but when she refused his advances, he transformed her into a laurel tree. A wreath of laurels was therefore awarded as the highest honor at festivals held in Apollo's name and was conferred upon victors of athletic contests as well as poets and war heroes. At Apollo's temple at Delphi, the oracles chewed laurel leaves to bring on their powers of prophecy.

As early as the fourteenth century, the word *laureate* was in circulation to refer to those who had attained the highest possible honor in a field, such as a poet laureate. Today, winners of the coveted Nobel prizes, established in 1901, are called "Nobel laureates." This honor can be a double-edged sword for those who fail to maintain their momentum. By the nineteenth century, "resting on one's laurels" became a mild slur for those who were no longer living up to their potential.

Sources

Evans, Ivor H., ed. *Brewer's Dictionary of Phrase and Fable.* 14th ed. New York: Harper and Row, 1989.
Sacks, David. *Encyclopedia of the Ancient Greek World.* New York: Facts on File, 1995.
Whittick, Arnold. *Symbols, Signs, and Their Meaning.* Newton, MA: C. T. Branford, 1960.

Lazy as Lawrence. ***Too lazy even to move.***

Saint Lawrence, martyred in 258, was an actual person, but the wealth of stories that surround his death may be apocryphal. According to tradition, Lawrence was known for his kindness, humility, and gracious demeanor. When the emperor Valerian published edicts against Christians in 257, a wave of executions swept through Rome. Lawrence sensed that he would be caught up in the massacres and began distributing what little wealth he had to the poor. This prompted rumors that Lawrence was in possession of the church's treasures. The prefect of Rome informed Lawrence that he had to surrender the riches to the emperor. When Lawrence arrived, he brought with him a great number of people: beggars, lepers, orphans, the blind, and the lame. These, Lawrence declared, were the treasures of the church.

Needless to say, this response did not please the prefect, who ordered the slow torture and execution of Lawrence. The legend is that he was slowly roasted on a gridiron, and at one point he said to his executioner: "You have done me on one side, turn me over so that you may eat me well done." Rather perversely, this unwillingness to roll over by his own strength gave Lawrence the reputation for laziness.

Lawrence was one of the most venerated saints of the early church, and he is usually portrayed holding a gridiron. When the pious Phillip II of Spain defeated the French in 1557, his victory fell on the feast day of Saint Lawrence. The king paid his respects to the saint by designing his palace, the Escorial, in a gridiron shape and repeating a gridiron motif in windowpanes and on wrought-iron fences.

Sources

Lozoya, Juan C. *The Escorial: The Royal Palace at La Granja de San Ildefonso.* New York: Meredith Press, 1967.
McDonald, William J., ed. *New Catholic Encyclopedia.* New York: McGraw-Hill, 1967.
Walsh, Michael, ed. *Butler's Lives of the Saints.* San Francisco: Harper and Row, 1985.

Leave no stone unturned. ***To spare no effort in accomplishing a goal.***

Delphi was the most influential of all ancient Greek shrines (see *Delphic*), but the oracle's prophecies had a reputation for being vague, ambiguous, or mere common sense. One such prophecy was given to the general Polycrates. Following a massive defeat of the Persian army at the battle of Plataea (479 B.C.), one of the fleeing Persian generals, Mardonius, was rumored to have hidden a splendid treasure, but the Greeks could not locate it. In frustration, the Theban leader

Polycrates turned to the oracle at Delphi in hopes of learning the whereabouts of the treasure. He was merely told to "leave no stone unturned." Polycrates returned to the site of the battle and renewed his efforts. A treasure was soon discovered buried at the spot where Mardonius's tent had been.

Despite this legend, some experts have speculated that the expression *leave no stone unturned* was a Greek cliché and was already well-known before Polycrates' fateful trip to the oracle.

Sources

Dempsey, T. *The Delphic Oracle: Its Early History, Influence, and Fall.* New York: B. Blom, 1972.

Parke, H. W., and D. E. W. Wormell. *The Delphic Oracle.* Oxford: Basil Blackwell, 1956.

Sacks, David. *Encyclopedia of the Ancient Greek World.* New York: Facts on File, 1995.

Lebensraum. ***An excuse for territorial expansion.***

The nineteenth century witnessed a frantic rush by the European nations to acquire colonies in Africa, Asia, and India. The word *lebensraum,* or "living space," was coined by Swedish scientist Rudolf Kjellen and initially referred to the desire of European nations to gain status and natural resources through colonial expansion. Nazi ideologues latched onto the term and used it to justify Germany's territorial ambitions. However, to Hitler, colonial holdings were of limited value, and he wanted to acquire land "where geographical contiguity with the motherland is assured." He was strongly influenced by Hans Grimm's 1926 book *A People without a Space.* This became a classic justification of the German craving for more territory.

Use of force is the natural corollary to the acquisition of lebensraum. Although the Nazi plunder of Eastern Europe was the most obvious example of lebensraum expansionism, the word subsequently has been used in a broader sense to refer to multinational companies that seek to expropriate and exploit the resources of Third World nations for their own benefit.

Sources

Gutman, Israel. *The Encyclopedia of the Holocaust.* New York: Macmillan, 1990.

Safire, William. *Safire's Political Dictionary.* New York: Random House, 1978.

Zentner, Christian, and Friedemann Budurftig, eds. *Encyclopedia of the Third Reich.* New York: Macmillan, 1991.

Legionnaire's disease. ***A potentially fatal flulike illness caused by the bacterium*** **legionella pneumophila.**

In 1976, medical science's goal of conquering bacterial disease was set back by the outbreak of a dangerous flulike illness in a Philadelphia hotel. As an American Legion state convention drew to a close, many of the participants began to fall severely ill. One hundred and seventy-nine cases were reported, and 26 legionnaires died. Health authorities eventually determined that the disease was spread through the hotel's air conditioning system. The previously unknown bacterium was named *legionella pneumophila* after its first victims. Subsequent outbreaks of the disease have also been blamed on air-conditioning systems in older buildings.

Sources

Evans, Ivor H., ed. *Brewer's Dictionary of Phrase and Fable.* 14th ed. New York: Harper and Row, 1989.

Kohn, George C. *Encyclopedia of Plague and Pestilence.* New York: Facts on File, 1995.

Thomas, Gordon, and Max Morgan-Witts. *Anatomy of an Epidemic.* Garden City, NJ: Doubleday, 1982.

Leotard. ***A snug-fitting, elasticized garment.***

In the world of the circus, the most glamorous performers are the flying trapeze artists. The elegantly costumed acrobats display feats of grace, dexterity, and strength as they swing high above the circus floor. One particularly renowned trapeze artist was Jules Léotard (1830–1870), who inspired the song "That Daring Young Man on the Flying Trapeze." Léotard was the son of a physical education instructor who owned a gymnasium in Toulouse, France. One day while practicing on a trapeze bar, the young

Léotard decided to suspend an additional trapeze several feet away, allowing him to switch from one to the other while performing. As he developed his technique, he moved so gracefully between bars that he gave the appearance of flying through the air. His skill was recognized by a traveling circus, and in 1859 he made his debut before a Paris audience. The act became such a sensation that he received the immense salary of 500 francs a day.

The next ten years were spent dazzling audiences throughout Europe and inspiring other circus performers to follow suit, although none rivaled Léotard in popularity. In addition to his acknowledged superiority on the trapeze, Léotard wore a most shocking costume. Circus performers in the early eighteenth century wore outlandish and colorful outfits, with exotic capes, sashes, hats, and scarves. Léotard instead adopted a skintight suit of clothes that left little to the imagination—the ancestor of the modern leotard. This was partly due to the danger of his act, in which flapping clothing could prove fatal, but also because Léotard enjoyed displaying his magnificent physique before thousands of spectators. Unfortunately, his fame and fortune were brief, since his life was cut short by smallpox.

Sources

Croft-Cooke, Rupert. *Circus: A World History.* London: Elek, 1976.

Hendrickson, Robert. *Dictionary of Eponyms: Names That Became Words.* New York: Stein and Day, 1985.

Ogden, Tom. *Two Hundred Years of the American Circus: From Aba-Daba to the Zoppe-Zavatta Troupe.* New York: Facts on File, 1993.

Lesbian. ***A female homosexual.***

Sappho (fl. 580 B.C.) was the most famous female poet among the ancient Greeks, and she lived on the island of Lesbos in the Aegean Sea, not far from present-day Turkey. Lesbos was a center of cultural achievement and counted Aristotle and Epicurus among its inhabitants. Sappho was believed to have been married to Cercolas, a wealthy man from the island of Andros. Writing and reciting poetry was considered an appropriate pastime for well-to-do women, and Sappho's lyrical verse, which was intensely passionate, was highly regarded. Her ardent friendships with other women were the most common theme of her work, and the turbulence, jealousy, and desire that is revealed in this poetry have led people to believe that these friendships were not merely platonic. From reading between the lines of her poetry, scholars have concluded that Sappho was a homosexual, although she herself never made any public statement to that effect.

Although the origin of *lesbian* clearly derives from Sappho's association with the island of Lesbos, the word itself is very recent. *The Oxford English Dictionary* cites 1890 as the earliest recorded use in the context of homosexual relations. Before this there was no standard term to refer to a female homosexual. Verbal ploys such as "the nameless sin" or "the crime against nature" were adopted until the Victorians created a word from a classical allusion.

Sources

Dynes, Wayne R., ed. *Encyclopedia of Homosexuality.* New York: Garland Publishers, 1990.

Hendrickson, Robert. *Facts on File Encyclopedia of Word and Phrase Origins.* New York: Facts on File, 1987.

McHenry, Robert, ed. *The New Encyclopedia Britannica.* 15th ed. Chicago: Encyclopedia Britannica, 1992.

Mish, Frederick C. *The Merriam-Webster New Book of Word Histories.* Springfield, IL: Merriam-Webster, 1991.

Simpson, J. A., and E. S. C. Weiner, eds. *The Oxford English Dictionary.* 2d ed. Oxford: Clarendon Press, 1989.

Let them eat cake. ***Implies the wealthy have no understanding of the plight of the poor.***

Marie Antoinette (1755–1793) will forever be associated with this callous remark, but it is highly unlikely that she ever said it. Like many rumors that circulated about this frivolous queen, it was probably fabricated by her enemies to whip up animosity toward the French monarchy. The expression was common in France even before Marie Antoinette was born. According to Jean Jacques Rousseau, a member of the aristocracy had uttered the flippant remark in the context of an incident in 1740. Also, shortly before the French Revolution, Joseph François Foullon, an unpopular royal financial administrator, was supposed to have said, "If the people cannot get bread, let them eat hay." Again, there is little evidence Foullon ever spoke the words, but he later paid for them with his life.

The notoriously extravagant Marie Antoinette became the favorite target on which to pin the inflammatory remark. Born into the Austrian royal family, she married the heir to the throne of France at the age of 15, which placed her in a position to freely indulge fantasies of glamour and vanity. The French people were hesitant to embrace an Austrian consort as their queen, and Marie's extravagance quickly sealed their dislike. At fancy court balls, Marie draped her hair, clothes, and person in sparkling jewels, which earned her the nickname Madame Deficit. When she withdrew to the countryside, she had a small village, La Trianon, constructed, with artificial ponds and brooks and an operating mill. Small farmhouses painted to look old were built, and cows and sheep dotted the hastily cleared pastures. Exotic trees were imported from all over the world to complete the picture. Marie and her friends from court dressed in extravagant versions of milkmaids' costume. This play village cost the crown millions of francs and did nothing to endear Marie to the French people.

As the story goes, when the revolution began in 1789, Marie asked why the people were unhappy. When told that they had no bread to eat, she carelessly replied, "Let them eat cake!" The French were eager to believe the tale, and other rumors testifying to her villainy circulated: that she slept with a cardinal in exchange for a diamond necklace, and that she even sexually "corrupted" her own son. Although these charges have long since been dismissed, the comment *let them eat cake* remains linked to Marie Antoinette.

Sources

Erickson, Carolly. *To the Scaffold: The Life of Marie Antoinette.* New York: W. Morrow and Co., 1991.

Platt, Suzy. *Respectfully Quoted: A Dictionary of Quotations from the Library of Congress.* Washington, DC: Congressional Quarterly, 1992.

Scott, Samuel F., and Barry Rothaus, eds. *Historical Dictionary of the French Revolution 1789–1799.* Westport, CT: Greenwood Press, 1985.

Levittown. ***Housing developments that are mass-produced and monotonous but also new and affordable.***

The first Levittown project was begun in 1947 by the firm of Levitt and Sons. New home construction had plummeted during the Depression and World War II, but the sharp increase in marriage and birthrates following the war resulted in an unprecedented demand for affordable housing. William J. Levitt's dream was to bring Ford Motor Company's techniques for mass production to the housing business. A site for a planned community was selected in southeastern New York, and over 17,000 homes were rapidly built using prefabricated parts and assembly-line techniques. The modest two-bedroom, one-bathroom homes were quickly constructed and just as quickly purchased by eager buyers. Because the land selected had previously been a potato farm, the terrain was flat, treeless, and stark. The monotony was made worse by the gridlike street pattern and the uniform plots and house design. In spite of the bland, "vanilla" appearance of Levittown, the price was right for many Americans struggling to buy their first home. Houses were initially priced at $7,900, with no down payment required. A second Levittown was built in Pennsylvania in the 1950s.

Levittown became a byword for the type of standardized housing development that lacks character, privacy, or individuality. Despite the scorn heaped on them—often by snobbish, more affluent people—they were innovative projects for their time, and they attempted to build community through public parks, swimming pools, and community centers. Many Americans unable to break into established neighborhoods or to purchase custom-made houses had the opportunity to be homeowners. Future planned communities learned from the mistakes of Levittown by curving the street patterns, incorporating more trees, and varying house size and design.

Sources

Halberstam, David. *The Fifties.* New York: Villard Books, 1993.

Kelly, Barbara M. *Expanding the American Dream: Building and Rebuilding Levittown.* Albany: State University of New York Press, 1993.

McHenry, Robert, ed. *The New Encyclopedia Britannica.* 15th ed. Chicago: Encyclopedia Britannica, 1992.

West, Elliot. *Growing Up in Twentieth Century America: A History and Reference Guide.* Westport, CT: Greenwood Press, 1996.

Wilkes, Joseph A., ed. *Encyclopedia of Architecture: Design, Engineering, and Construction.* New York: Wiley, 1988.

Lick into shape. ***To make presentable; to eradicate undesirable behavior by disciplined training.***
This expression derives from the antiquated belief that newborn bears enter the world as a shapeless mass and that careful tending by the mother forms the tiny baby bear into the correct shape. Pliny the Elder, an ancient source for this contention, included it in his naturalist observations in the first century. The idea persisted through the Renaissance, and the French poet Guillaume du Bartas (1544–1590) even put it into verse:

> Not unlike the bear which bringeth forth
> In the end of thirty days a shapeless birth;
> But after licking, it in shape she draws,
> And by degrees she fashions out the paws,
> The head, and neck, and finally doth bring
> To a perfect beast that first deformed thing.

By the eighteenth century the expression "lick into shape" was a common reference for the process of training and molding a person's behavior.

Sources

Evans, Ivor H., ed. *Brewer's Dictionary of Phrase and Fable.* 14th ed. New York: Harper and Row, 1989.

Nowak, Ronald M. *Walker's Mammals of the World.* Baltimore, MD: Johns Hopkins University Press, 1991.

Limelight. ***Public scrutiny.***
Until the nineteenth century, lighting for theaters was much the same as it had been in ancient times. Torches and candles were the primary means of illumination. The development of gaslight in the 1810s was an improvement over candles, but gas had a number of problems, including the excessive heat, potentially unsafe conditions, and dimness. In 1816 Thomas Drummond came up with a method of obtaining a bright light using lime. If a piece of lime was heated by an oxy-hydrogen flame, it became highly luminescent. Introduced into the theater in 1837, limelight was most useful when it was focused and projected into a spotlight. This produced light far brighter than had ever been seen before, and the phrase *in the limelight* originally referred to the area of the stage where the light was the strongest. Limelight was rendered obsolete in the late nineteenth century by the incorporation of electric lighting into theaters.

Sources

Law, Jonathan, ed. *Brewer's Theater: A Phrase and Fable Dictionary.* New York: HarperCollins, 1994.

Lorimer, Lawrence T., ed. *The Encyclopedia Americana.* Danbury, CT: Grolier, 1989.

Stimpson, George. *A Book about a Thousand Things.* New York: Harper and Brothers, 1946.

Limey. ***A British citizen.***
By the eighteenth century, Great Britain was acknowledged as possessing one of the finest navies in history. In the course of establishing trading connections around the world, British sailors would be at sea for months at a time and became highly susceptible to scurvy. Seaboard diets excluded fresh fruit and vegetables, resulting in vitamin C deficiency and scurvy. Characterized by loose teeth, anemia, and bleeding under

the skin, scurvy was a painful and potentially fatal disease. Leaking blood vessels gave its victims an appearance of bruising, even in the absence of injury. When hemorrhaging occurred in the brain, death quickly followed.

In 1753 the Scottish naval surgeon James Lind published the results of a carefully controlled study indicating that scurvy could be prevented through the consumption of citrus juice. The British navy was slow to adopt this remedy, since supplying fresh citrus fruit would be expensive and other remedies, such as the sauerkraut cure advocated by Captain Cook, had not yet been discounted. By 1795 the British Admiralty was convinced, and lime juice was selected as the most economical and practical solution for scurvy prevention. It is from this practice of dispensing limes to British sailors that they earned the nickname *limeys,* and the word later embraced British citizens in general.

Ironically, the variety of West Indian limes used by the Admiralty, selected because they were inexpensive, lacked many of the nutrients essential in scurvy prevention. As a result, scurvy outbreaks continued until the late nineteenth century.

Sources

Dawson, Dawn P. *Magill's Medical Guide: Health and Illness.* Pasadena, CA: Salem Press, 1995.

Jeans, Peter D. *Ship to Shore: A Dictionary of Everyday Words and Phrases Derived from the Sea.* Santa Barbara, CA: ABC-CLIO, 1993.

Kiple, Kenneth F., ed. *Cambridge World History of Human Disease.* Cambridge: Cambridge University Press, 1993.

McHenry, Robert, ed. *The New Encyclopedia Britannica.* 15th ed. Chicago: Encyclopedia Britannica, 1992.

McNeill, William Hardy. *Plagues and Peoples.* Garden City, NY: Anchor Press, 1976.

Listerine. *The first over-the-counter mouthwash.*

Listerine was named after Baron Joseph Lister, the British surgeon whose pioneering research in antiseptic surgery paved the way to modern practices. As a young doctor, Lister (1827–1912) worked in the Male Accident Ward of the Glasgow Royal Infirmary, where he performed numerous amputations. His mortality rate was around 50 percent as a result of sepsis, an infection of the wound. Lister began to search for a preventive measure, an antisepsis. He was able to adapt some of Louis Pasteur's theories to the treatment of wounds in danger of infection. Convinced that sepsis was caused by the fermentation of either invisible microorganisms or dust in the air, he sought a method of creating a barrier between the wound and the air. The antiseptic he first used was carbolic acid, which had already been proven effective in cleaning foul sewers. Use of this technique was immediately effective, and the mortality rate from his amputations dropped to 15 percent. In 1870 the German physicians working in the Franco-Prussian War adopted Lister's ideas. Eventually sterile operating procedures became universally accepted.

In the late nineteenth century the American company Lambert Pharmacal marketed an antiseptic mouthwash using Lister's name. *Listerine* was advertised as being effective in the fight against bad breath, sore throats, and dandruff. One magazine ad depicted a woman massaging her husband's scalp with Listerine. The caption read, "Tear into it honey—it's infectious dandruff!" Other advertisements focused on portraying bad breath as a social disgrace. Largely because of the success of Listerine, Lambert Pharmacal's profits increased 60-fold. Meanwhile, Joseph Lister, who had been made a baron in 1883, tried unsuccessfully to remove his name from the product, which went on to become a mainstay of the Warner-Lambert pharmaceutical conglomerate.

Sources

Derdak, Thomas, ed. *International Directory of Company Histories.* Chicago: St. James Press, 1988.

Hendrickson, Robert. *Dictionary of Eponyms: Names That Became Words.* New York: Stein and Day, 1985.

McHenry, Robert, ed. *The New Encyclopedia Britannica.* 15th ed. Chicago: Encyclopedia Britannica, 1992.

Stephen, Leslie, and Sidney Lee, eds. *The Dictionary of National Biography.* London: Oxford University Press, 1921.

Little Red Book. ***The collected quotations of Mao Zedong, often cited as an example of something that demands rigid conformity.***
The collected *Quotations* of Mao Zedong (1893–1976) are better known in the Western world as the *Little Red Book.* The pocket-sized work was bound in red plastic and distributed by the millions to stimulate revolutionary commitment. Some of Mao's assistants compiled excerpts of the writings that were thought to best express the communist ideology Mao wished China to adopt. The book became a symbol of China's "Great Proletarian Cultural Revolution," which began in 1966, and was especially important to China's Red Guard, the politically active students who were the driving force behind the Cultural Revolution. Historian Stewart Fraser claimed that the book was used by the Red Guards as "their bible, prayer book, and catechism." In a compelling photo image, thousands of zealous Red Guards held up the little books as they demanded that revisionists be booted out of the Communist party. Western commentators began associating the books with blind conformity. The Chinese Communists hoped that the work, with its easily quoted bits of Mao's writings, would be exported to other nations and assist in a worldwide revolution. It was briefly in vogue among radical American students but is now a symbol of mindless obedience.

Sources

Arms, Thomas S. *Encyclopedia of the Cold War.* New York: Facts on File, 1991.

Cohen, Arthur Allen. *The Communism of Mao Tse-Tung.* Chicago: University of Chicago Press, 1964.

Comfort, N. A. *Brewer's Politics: A Phrase and Fable Dictionary.* London: Cassell, 1993.

Mao Zedong. *Mao Zedong's Quotations: The Red Guard's Handbook.* Nashville, TN: George Peabody College for Teachers, 1967.

Lone star state. ***Texas.***
Six separate nations have flown their flags over the territory encompassed by Texas. Spain claimed the region from 1519 to 1821, except for a brief five-year period beginning in 1685 when France tried to add the territory to its other New World claims. From 1821 to 1836 Texas was part of the Mexican nation. After the war with Mexico, Texas declared its independence in 1836 and established the Republic of Texas. The republic's flag had a single star on it. Just as the United States designed their first flag with 13 stars to represent the original 13 colonies, Texas needed only one star to signify its nationhood. Texas became part of the United States in 1845, as the twenty-eighth state.

The flag of the Confederate States of America was the sixth flag to fly over Texas, lasting until 1865 when it was replaced by the flag of the United States once again.

Sources

Day, James M. *Six Flags of Texas.* Waco: Texian Press, 1968.

Simpson, J. A., and E. S. C. Weiner, eds. *The Oxford English Dictionary.* 2d ed. Oxford: Clarendon Press, 1989.

Lost tribes of Israel. ***Something lost without a trace.***
According to Hebrew tradition, after Moses led the Jews out of Egypt, they reestablished themselves in the promised land, and the sons and grandsons of Jacob formed the twelve tribes of Israel. Although the tribes were bound together by their monotheism, clannishness prevented them from developing a lasting union. After the death of Solomon, the tribes split into two kingdoms. The southern kingdom of Judah included only the tribes of Judah and Benjamin. The northern kingdom of Israel included the other ten tribes of Asher, Dan, Ephrain, Gad, Issachar, Manasseh, Naphtali, Reuben, Simeon, and Zebulun.

In 722 B.C. the northern kingdom was conquered by the Assyrians, and the ten tribes were exiled. All that is known for certain about their fate is that they disappeared from history as distinct groups. It is believed that some were forced into slavery and others may have become refugees in the southern kingdom of Judah. Throughout the Middle Ages and into the modern era a number of theories emerged to explain what happened to the missing tribes. Some of those identified as possible descendants of the tribes include the Japanese, the American Indians, and the Falashas of Ethiopia.

Sources

Roth, Cecil E., ed. *Encyclopedia Judaica.* New York: Macmillan, 1971.

Stimpson, George. *A Book about the Bible.* New York: Harper and Brothers, 1945.

Lou Gehrig's disease. ***A degenerative disease of the nervous system that results in wasting muscles and paralysis; officially known as amyotrophic lateral sclerosis (ALS).***

A quiet and unassuming man, Lou Gehrig (1903–1941) was in the shadow of his flamboyant teammate Babe Ruth for much of his professional baseball career. Nevertheless, Gehrig eventually won the admiration of New York Yankee fans and colleagues for his consistently good performances. He set a major league record for playing in 2,130 consecutive games, which earned him the nickname "the Iron Horse." With a batting average of .373, he was named the American League's Most Valuable Player in 1927. However, in 1939 it became apparent that there was something wrong. Gehrig had lost weight, appeared slow and clumsy on the field, and was batting only .143. On May 2, he told his manager, "I think I'm hurting the team. Maybe it would be better if I took a rest for a while." He never played baseball again. In June, Gehrig was diagnosed with amyotrophic lateral sclerosis (ALS), a rare and debilitating disease that was almost unheard-of at that time.

Gehrig's prognosis was not good, since most people afflicted with ALS usually die within two to five years. When the Yankees realized that Gehrig would not be returning to baseball, they held a game in his honor on 4 July 1939. The packed stadium heard Gehrig deliver his famous and moving statement: "I may have been given a bad break, but I have an awful lot to live for. With all this, I consider myself the luckiest man on the face of the earth." He died less than two years later.

Sources

Hickok, Ralph. *A Who's Who of Sports Champions: Their Stories and Records.* Boston: Houghton Mifflin Co., 1995.

McHenry, Robert, ed. *The New Encyclopedia Britannica.* 15th ed. Chicago: Encyclopedia Britannica, 1992.

Porter, David L., ed. *Biographical Dictionary of American Sports: Baseball.* New York: Greenwood Press, 1987.

Lucy Stoner. ***A woman who keeps her maiden name after marriage.***

Lucy Stone (1818–1893) was one of nine children born into a farming family just outside Brookfield, Massachusetts. As a girl Lucy was appalled at her mother's unceasing toil. She also developed a keen sense of injustice when she and her sisters were asked to use their free time sewing clothes in order to raise money to send her brothers to school. Lucy's father refused to pay for her education, so she put herself through college, graduating at the age of 29. She immediately plunged into the abolition and women's rights movements, becoming prominent in both crusades. At the age of 38 Lucy married a fellow abolitionist, Henry Blackwell, who supported her right to maintain her own identity. Marriage in the nineteenth century was often regarded as "civil death" for the woman because she lost rights to her property and custody of her children. On the day of their marriage in 1855, Stone and Blackwell issued a statement, which began:

> While acknowledging our mutual affection by publicly assuming the relationship of husband and wife, yet in justice to ourselves and a great principle, we deem it a duty to declare that this act on our part implies no sanction of, nor promise of voluntary obedience to such of the present laws of marriage, as refuse to recognize the wife as an independent, rational being, while they confer upon the husband an injurious and unnatural superiority, investing him with legal powers which no honorable man would exercise, and which no man should possess.

Lucy Stone maintained her own name for the rest of her life as a symbol of her independence.

Sources

Cullen-DuPont, Kathryn. *The Encyclopedia of Women's History in America.* New York: Facts on File, 1996.

James, Edward T., ed. *Notable American Women, 1607–1950: A Biographical Dictionary.* Cambridge, MA: Belknap Press, 1971.

Johnson, Allen, and Dumas Malone, eds. *Dictionary of American Biography.* New York: Scribner's, 1964.

Trahair, R. C. *From Aristotelian to Reaganomics: A Dictionary of Eponyms with Biographies in the Social Sciences.* Westport, CT: Greenwood Press, 1994.

Luddite. ***Someone who resists technological innovations.***

The early nineteenth century was an era of tremendous technological advance in Europe, but there was a concurrent decline in working and living conditions for the laboring classes. Factories for the production of cloth and other textiles employed unskilled workers at oppressively low wages and put traditional artisans out of work. Disaffected laborers destroyed the machines they believed were the cause of unemployment. The English protesters called themselves *Luddites* after the story of Ned Ludd, a slow-witted knitting apprentice who became so frustrated with his knitting frame that he smashed it. Whenever a machine had been inexplicably damaged, people would say that Ned Ludd had been there.

The Luddite movement began in Nottingham in 1811 but soon spread to the rest of England. Disguised men would descend on factories at night and smash whatever machinery they could find. Wooden pieces were brought outside to light bonfires in the middle of the street. Luddites occasionally gave advance warning, tacking notes to factory doors stating that if machines were not removed, the task would be handled by King Ludd. Although damage to property was heavy, the Luddites did not harm people until one of their own was shot by a soldier during a raid. In retaliation, the Luddites killed the factory owner who had summoned the soldiers. In 1813 a number of Luddites were apprehended and hanged, and a vigorous campaign of repression began. Within a few years the movement sputtered out. The Luddites succeeded in calling attention to the plight of the working poor, but their protest is generally regarded as a failure, since they made no dent in either the factory system or working conditions.

The information age has spawned a new version of Luddites—people who denounce computer technology for the dehumanizing effects it has on society. Bumper stickers proclaiming "The Luddites were right" are seen even in Silicon Valley. Given the pervasive presence of the computer in American culture, it is likely that the twentieth-century Luddites will meet with no more success than their nineteenth-century counterparts.

Sources

Hendrickson, Robert. *Dictionary of Eponyms: Names That Became Words.* New York: Stein and Day, 1985.

Reid, Robert William. *Land of Lost Content: The Luddite Revolt, 1812.* London: Heinemann, 1986.

Sale, Kirkpatrick. *Rebels against the Future: The Luddites and Their War on the Industrial Revolution.* Reading, PA: Addison-Wesley Publishing Co., 1995.

Thomis, Malcolm I. *The Luddites: Machine-breaking in Regency England.* Hamden, CT: Archon Books, 1970.

Lurch, to leave in the lurch. ***To leave someone or something in an awkward position.***

Lurch is derived from an old French game called *lourche,* which was brought to England in the seventeenth century. The rules of the game have been lost, but it was probably similar to backgammon. To achieve a lurch in the game, the winner had to accumulate a significant number of points at the opponent's expense.

The word *lurch* was adapted in whist, cribbage, and other card games. It refers to a lopsided score, in which one player is extremely far ahead of the others. By the seventeenth century, *leaving someone in the lurch* was used in a general sense, as being isolated in a position of difficulty.

Sources
Carver, Craig. *A History of English in Its Own Words.* New York: HarperCollins, 1991.
McHenry, Robert, ed. *The New Encyclopedia Britannica.* 15th ed. Chicago: Encyclopedia Britannica, 1992.

Lynch. ***To execute an individual without due process of law, usually by hanging.*** For many years it was believed that Captain Charles Lynch (1736–1796) was the most likely candidate for this eponym. Captain Lynch was a justice of the peace in Bedford County in southwestern Virginia. Certain serious crimes could only be tried by the court in Williamsburg, which was over 200 miles away. During the closing years of the American Revolution, Lynch decided it was too risky to transport defendants across the state, much of which was threatened by the British. Incidents involving collusion with the British were especially sensitive, so Captain Lynch proceeded to hear these cases without benefit of official imprimatur. His typical punishment for guilty parties consisted of fines or flogging, but there is no evidence that he ever sentenced anyone to death.

A more likely contender for the origin of the word *lynch* is William Lynch (1742–1820) of Pittsylvania County, Virginia. In 1780 Pittsylvania County was disrupted by the war and plagued by a number of lawless men who escaped any sort of punishment. Lynch and his followers resolved amongst themselves that any man who was apprehended in the commission of a crime would be given "such corporeal punishment on him or them, as to us shall seem adequate to the crime committed or the damage sustained." Two other contemporary sources point to William Lynch: the diary of surveyor Andrew Ellicott, and the testimony of a longtime resident of the county that was published in an 1859 issue of *Harper's Weekly.*

The practice of lynching is often associated with racial violence, although Jews, Catholics, communists, pacifists, and white criminal suspects have also been its targets. African Americans have suffered the most, with an estimated 5,000 lynching victims, of whom about 100 were women. Nearly all states have lynchings on record. The only four that do not are Massachusetts, New Hampshire, Rhode Island, and Vermont.

Sources
Hendrickson, Robert. *Dictionary of Eponyms: Names That Became Words.* New York: Stein and Day, 1985.
Mish, Frederick C. *The Merriam-Webster New Book of Word Histories.* Springfield, IL: Merriam-Webster, 1991.
Panati, Charles. *Panati's Extraordinary Endings of Practically Everything and Everybody.* New York: Perennial Library, 1989.

M

Machiavellian. ***Actions characterized by deceit, cunning, and intrigue.***

Niccolo Machiavelli (1469–1527) was an Italian statesman, historian, and playwright, but he is primarily remembered for his work as a political theorist. He was born in Florence to a noble but impoverished family, and as such, he was forced to earn a living in a variety of intellectual endeavors. Despite an unexceptional education, his mind was brilliant, and he moved into positions of influence within Florence.

Machiavelli formed a mental picture of an ideal Italian republic and formulated theories he thought would realize that vision. He believed that the society of sixteenth-century Florence suffered from too much corruption, moral weakness, and threats from foreign invasions. His most famous work, *The Prince,* was written to address these problems. Dedicated to Lorenzo de Medici, the book advocated a cold, cunning, and ruthless approach in which all generous impulses were subordinated to the demands of statecraft. Philosophers regard Machiavelli as the first political thinker who drew a distinction between political morality and everyday ethical norms.

Machiavelli had hoped that his bold and shocking recommendations would catch the attention of Lorenzo de Medici and result in a lucrative position in the Florentine government. This ambition was never achieved, and the man whose name was synonymous with amoral cynicism eventually found a position working for the church.

Sources

Bergin, Thomas G. *Encyclopedia of the Renaissance.* New York: Facts on File, 1987.

Hendrickson, Robert. *Dictionary of Eponyms: Names That Became Words.* New York: Stein and Day, 1985.

Miller, David, ed. *The Blackwell Encyclopedia of Political Thought.* Oxford: Basil Blackwell, 1968.

Ridolfi, Roberto. *The Life of Niccolo Machiavelli.* Chicago: University of Chicago Press, 1963.

Mad as a hatter. ***An off-beat, eccentric, or irrational individual.***

In the seventeenth century, European hatmakers began using felt because it could be shaped and steamed into a variety of fashions. To make felt, fur or wool is pressed into a fabric through the application of heat and moisture. Hatters used mercury nitrate to treat the raw wool or fur fibers before pressing. Exposure to the toxic elements of mercury, either by inhalation or absorption through the skin, can result in depression, sleeplessness, tremors, eating disorders, and hallucinations. Prolonged contact can cause strong muscular spasms, severe facial twitches, and tremors of the limbs, while chronic mercury poisoning results in psychosis and damage to the central nervous system.

The phrase *mad as a hatter* is believed to have first been used in reference to the seventeenth-century hatter Robert Crab, who gave all his possessions to the poor and lived on a diet of leaves and grass. The expression was in vogue well before Lewis Carroll's 1865 classic *Alice in Wonderland.*

Although the dangers of mercury poisoning were known in the nineteenth century, the use of mercury in the hat-making industry was not banned in the United States until 1941. The legislation may have been prompted by the wartime shortage of mercury rather than concern for a health hazard.

Sources

Evans, Ivor H., ed. *Brewer's Dictionary of Phrase and Fable.* 14th ed. New York: Harper and Row, 1989.

Neal, Paul A. *Mercurialism and Its Control in the Felt Hat Industry.* Washington, DC: GPO, 1941.

Sayers, R. R. *A Study of Chronic Mercurialism in the Hatters' Fur-Cutting Industry.* Washington, DC: GPO, 1937.

Turkington, Carol. *Poisons and Antidotes.* New York: Facts on File, 1994.

Mafia. ***Organized criminal societies.***
Mafia is an Arabic word meaning "place of refuge." It slipped into the Italian language during the ninth century, when Sicily was subjected to a series of Muslim raids. At first the Muslim incursions were simply looting raids, but expeditions to establish a long-term foothold on the island began in 827, and by 902 the Muslims had control of most of Sicily.

Some of the Sicilian natives found refuge in the hills, where they became peasant bandits and carried out resistance activities. Their enclaves were referred to as *mafias,* or refuges. Over the next several centuries successive waves of foreign invaders gained control of the island, including the Normans and the Spanish. The mafia organizations continued their clandestine exploits throughout these various occupations. They developed their own unique code of private justice, which centered on the concept of *omertá:* a pledge never to apply to the legal authorities for redress. Justice was to be determined and administered only by members of the mafia, and no member could assist in an official investigation of a crime or cooperate in any way. In later centuries, absentee landlords hired members of the mafia to help protect their estates from bandits. Investing these ruffians with so much unsupervised power was a dangerous gamble, and soon mafia groups formed themselves into private armies. Turning against the landlords, they extorted money and branched out into other forms of organized crime.

When waves of Italian immigrants came to the United States in the late nineteenth century, members of the mafia made their way to New York, Chicago, and other major American cities. There they set about reproducing the criminal patterns that had worked so effectively in Italy. In contemporary usage, *mafia* refers to organized crime societies of any nationality, including Russian and Chinese, which operate in the United States and elsewhere.

Sources

Evans, Ivor H., ed. *Brewer's Dictionary of Phrase and Fable.* 14th ed. New York: Harper and Row, 1989.

McHenry, Robert, ed. *The New Encyclopedia Britannica.* 15th ed. Chicago: Encyclopedia Britannica, 1992.

Strayer, Joseph R., ed. *Dictionary of the Middle Ages.* New York: Scribner's, 1982.

Magazine. ***A periodical containing a selection of stories, articles, and other features.***
Most of the English-language borrowings from Arabic occurred as a result of the Crusades. The Crusaders admired the Muslims' military planning and especially their use of *makhazins,* or huge fortresslike storage facilities that held tremendous amounts of military equipment and provisions but only required a few soldiers on guard.

Upon their return to Europe, the Crusaders began to build their own magazines for military provisions and, in times of peace, for many types of goods. By the seventeenth century the word *magazine* was being used in a general sense to represent any miscellaneous collection of items. In 1639 a book titled *Militarie Magazine of the Truest Rules for the Managing of Warre* was published, followed in 1669 by the *Mariner's Magazine,* with the implication that these books contained a "storehouse of information." The word acquired its modern connotation in 1731, with the launch of *The Gentleman's Magazine* (1731–1914). The first periodical in England designed for the general reader, the monthly magazine reprinted essays and articles that had first appeared in books, pamphlets, or broadsides. When Dr. Samuel Johnson joined the staff of the magazine in 1738, it began to publish original essays as well as parliamentary reports. The success of *The Gentleman's Magazine* inspired a number of contemporary imitators and created a genre.

Sources

McHenry, Robert, ed. *The New Encyclopedia Britannica.* 15th ed. Chicago: Encyclopedia Britannica, 1992.

Mish, Frederick C. *The Merriam-Webster New Book of Word Histories.* Springfield, IL: Merriam-Webster, 1991.

Simpson, J. A., and E. S. C. Weiner, eds. *The Oxford English Dictionary.* 2d ed. Oxford: Clarendon Press, 1989.

Maginot mentality. ***Belief in outmoded methods of defense and protection.***

During World War I much of eastern France was crisscrossed with miles of trenches in which thousands of troops attempted to fend off a German invasion. Life in the trenches was appalling and drove many soldiers into mental illness. Despite the fact that trench warfare had produced grotesque casualty rates and resulted in years of deadlock, many French strategists believed that it had successfully achieved its objective of halting the German advance. After the war, the French were determined never again to be subjected to another German invasion and decided to invest in an elaborate defensive barrier called the Maginot Line.

Named after a defense minister, André Maginot (1877–1932), the barrier stretched for 87 miles along the French-German border and cost over $200 million to build. With enormous mounds of earth covering underground tunnels, concrete bunkers, storage compartments, and heavy artillery, it was a masterpiece of static defense. There were air-conditioned living quarters for troops, recreation areas, and underground rail lines to transfer supplies to various locations. Rows of automatic weapons, heavy guns, artillery, and barbed wire topped the thick concrete fortifications. The Maginot Line appeared to be impregnable.

As it turned out, it was almost useless in France's next conflict with Germany. Airplanes, which had not been a significant factor in World War I, were a key part of Hitler's military strategy, and they flew right over the Maginot Line. The barrier looked to the French-German frontier, so when German troops invaded, they came by way of Belgium, simply walking around the Maginot Line. Not only was the ultimate defensive weapon ineffective, but according to some historians, it gave the French a false sense of security that encouraged complacency in the face of increasing German militancy during the 1930s.

Commentators often refer to the Maginot Line as an example of foolish reliance on outmoded means to halt an inevitable tide. The French desire to insulate its culture by outlawing the use of English has also been likened to *Maginot mentality.*

Sources

Evans, Ivor H., ed. *Brewer's Dictionary of Phrase and Fable.* 14th ed. New York: Harper and Row, 1989.

Hughes, Judith M. *To the Maginot Line: The Politics of French Military Preparation in the 1920s.* Cambridge: Harvard University Press, 1971.

McHenry, Robert, ed. *The New Encyclopedia Britannica.* 15th ed. Chicago: Encyclopedia Britannica, 1992.

Polmar, Norman, and Thomas B. Allen. *World War II: The Encyclopedia of the War Years, 1941–1945.* New York: Random House, 1996.

Maid of Orleans. ***Joan of Arc.***

At once controversial and inspirational, Joan of Arc (1412–1431) was born into a peasant family in Lorraine, France. She was a pious but otherwise entirely normal child until the age of 13, when she claimed to hear the voices of Saint Michael, Saint Catherine, and Saint Margaret. The voices indicated that Joan should take part in the great national struggle to expel the English from French soil. In what was later known as the Hundred Years War, the French nobility had been struggling for over 70 years to regain control of their lands. When Joan was 17, she left her village, donned male clothing, and set out to find the dauphin, the crown prince of France, in order to offer her assistance. She gradually worked her way into the dauphin's inner circle by first persuading the guards that hers was a holy mission, then responding convincingly to three weeks of intense questioning from the prince's counselors and ecclesiastical advisors. Joan requested permission to render assistance to the besieged city of Orleans, which had been surrounded by English troops for over seven months. When she arrived at Orleans, wearing a suit of armor and ardently proclaiming the justice of the French cause, the troops were inspired and reclaimed the city from the English. Joan played a crucial role in other military campaigns, but it was the triumph at Orleans for which she is best remembered. These victories helped turn the tide for the French, and a few short months later Charles was crowned king of France with Joan standing nearby.

Joan was subsequently captured by French forces hostile to the new king, and they ransomed her to the English. Tried for heresy, Joan defended herself brilliantly, frustrating the arguments of some of England's most respected theologians. The fact that an illiterate peasant girl with no formal education was able to confound and thwart these ecclesiastical authorities added to her mystique, as did her execution at the stake. Her controversial role in history, which had political as well as spiritual ramifications, delayed her canonization until 1920.

Sources

Clifton, Chas. *Encyclopedia of Heresies and Heretics.* Santa Barbara, CA: ABC-CLIO, 1992.

Walsh, Michael, ed. *Butler's Lives of the Saints.* San Francisco: Harper and Row, 1985.

Wheeler, Bonnie, and Charles T. Wood, eds. *Fresh Verdicts on Joan of Arc.* New York: Garland Publishing, 1996.

Manna from heaven. ***An unexpected but cherished gift.***

According to the Old Testament book of Exodus, in the second month of the Jewish migration out of Egypt, the Israelites appealed to Moses about the lack of food. He replied that the Lord had heard their complaints and would provide for his people. When the morning dew lifted, the ground was covered by a fine, flaky substance. The Israelites called the substance manna, and it was described as tiny, pale amber particles with the flavor of honey that could be pounded into a meal and made into cakes. There are many theories about what manna was. One explanation suggests that it was the sweet resin exuded from the tamarisk tree, while another posits that the substance was a type of insect excretion containing large quantities of sap. In both cases, the phenomenon occurs only in the first few weeks of June.

Sources

Achtemeier, Paul J. *Harper's Bible Dictionary.* San Francisco: Harper and Row, 1985.

Bromiley, Geoffrey W., ed. *The International Standard Bible Encyclopedia.* Grand Rapids, MI: W. B. Eerdmans, 1979.

Metzger, Bruce M., and Michael D. Coogan, eds. *The Oxford Companion to the Bible.* New York: Oxford University Press, 1993.

Stimpson, George. *A Book about the Bible.* New York: Harper and Brothers, 1945.

Marathon. ***A cross-country foot race of 26 miles 385 yards; also, an event that requires endurance or lasts for a long time.***

Marathon was a village in Attica, northeast of Athens. In the fifth century B.C. the Persian empire began a series of offensives against mainland Greece. Although the Persians boasted the strongest military force of the time, the Greek city-states were able to withstand their assault at Marathon. According to Herodotus, in 490 B.C. the Persians landed with a force of 25,000 men on the plains outside Marathon in preparation for an assault on the prize city of Athens. The Athenians appealed to Sparta for help, but the Spartans claimed that a religious festival prevented them from assisting. With a force of only 11,000 men, the Athenians faced the Persians alone. Although outnumbered at least 2 to 1, the Greeks had better armor and military organization, and they seized the initiative while the Persian cavalry was at ease. They won the battle and lost only 192 men, compared with 6,400 Persian dead. As the extent of the damage to their army became evident, the Persians began a massive, disorganized retreat. The Greeks feared that the Persians would try to find another harbor from which to launch an assault on Athens, and the runner Pheidippides was dispatched from Marathon to warn the city. Pheidippides ran 26 miles to carry the news, which foiled the Persian hopes of surprising the Athenians.

The contemporary marathon race commemorates Pheidippides' heroic run. In 1896 the first modern Olympiad was held in Athens, and the marathon was won by a Greek shepherd, Spiridon Loues.

Sources

Hornblower, Simon, and Antony Spawforth, eds. *The Oxford Classical Dictionary.* 3d ed. Oxford: Oxford University Press, 1996.

Levinson, David, and Karen Christensen, eds. *The Encyclopedia of World Sport: From Ancient Times to the Present.* Santa Barbara, CA: ABC-CLIO, 1996.

Margiotta, Franklin D. *Brassey's Encyclopedia of Military History and Biography.* Washington, DC: Brassey's, 1994.

Sacks, David. *Encyclopedia of the Ancient Greek World.* New York: Facts on File, 1995.

Maroon. ***To intentionally isolate or abandon someone in a place from which there is little hope of rescue.***

The word *maroon* is now a verb and is most commonly used in tales of the sea in which unfortunate individuals have been abandoned on desert islands. The word first came into use during the seventeenth century in South America and the West Indies, when it referred to African slaves who had escaped into the wilds. Slaveowners were reluctant to pursue fugitives into inhospitable environments, and the slaves who succeeded in reaching the jungles and swamps were able to establish independent communities. As long as they remained segregated from the rest of the population, they were generally left undisturbed.

There are two possible explanations for the derivation of the term. The French word for runaway slave is *marron,* and the word may have made its way into the English language via the slave society in the Caribbean. An alternative explanation comes from Guiana, a region in northeast South America. Many escaped slaves found refuge in the low-lying swamps of the Morony River, which may have evolved into *maroon.*

Sources

Cordingly, David. *Under the Black Flag: The Romance and Reality of Life among the Pirates.* New York: Random House, 1996.

Mish, Frederick C. *The Merriam-Webster New Book of Word Histories.* Springfield, IL: Merriam-Webster, 1991.

Simpson, J. A., and E. S. C. Weiner, eds. *The Oxford English Dictionary.* 2d ed. Oxford: Clarendon Press, 1989.

Martinet. ***A rigid disciplinarian; someone who demands puppetlike obedience from subordinates.***

After the decline of the Roman Empire, the disciplined drill techniques that had made its armies so formidable practically disappeared for over a thousand years. Most warfare degenerated into disorganized brawling in which battles were determined more by sheer numbers and luck than by prowess. The seventeenth century witnessed a revival of respect for military drills. A regimen designed by Gustavus Adolphus of Sweden was emulated by a number of European nations. However, the development of the modern standing army was spearheaded by Louis XIV of France, the Sun King. In the 1660s France's army was embarrassingly disorganized and had no identifiable uniform, except a white sash tied across whatever clothes the soldier was wearing. Louis believed that a force of well-disciplined, visually impressive soldiers carried great potential for intimidation, and he entrusted the task of remaking his army to Jean de Martinet (d. 1672).

Martinet was lieutenant-colonel of the Régiment du Roi, which was a model of discipline and regularity. To bring the rest of the army into line with strict military practice, Martinet implemented exacting standards, and his tedious drills soon made his name a byword for rigid and annoying adherence to even the most minute rules. Martinet was killed by his own troops at the siege of Duisberg in 1672. Although it was declared an accident, many historians have suggested that some of Martinet's soldiers were willing to resort to foul play in order to secure a new commander.

Sources

Chartrand, Rene. *Louis XIV's Army.* London: Osprey Publishers, 1988.

Hendrickson, Robert. *Dictionary of Eponyms: Names That Became Words.* New York: Stein and Day, 1985.

McHenry, Robert, ed. *The New Encyclopedia Britannica.* 15th ed. Chicago: Encyclopedia Britannica, 1992.

Masada complex. ***Religiously motivated inflexibility in the face of a hostile force; a willingness to commit suicide rather than surrender.***

Masada is an ancient mountaintop fortress built by Herod the Great around 30 B.C. The isolated stronghold stands in the middle of the Judean Desert and has been a symbol of Jewish resistance to Roman power since it was besieged A.D. 72–73. It is uncertain what the name Masada means, but it may derive from *mezad* ("stronghold" in Aramaic).

After Herod's death in 4 B.C. a Roman garrison took possession of the fort. In A.D. 66 a group of Zealots—a Jewish sect violently opposed to Roman rule—took the fortress by surprise. For several years Masada served as a refuge for Jews, but in 70 the Romans launched a major offensive in which Jerusalem was sacked and the Temple destroyed. A legion of Roman soldiers were dispatched to Masada to stamp out the last of the Jewish resistance. After a prolonged siege, the Romans made a breach in the wall of Masada, and it was apparent that the fortress would soon fall to the conquerors. In response, the Jewish leader Eleazar persuaded the 960 men, women, and children in Masada to commit suicide rather than submit to the Roman yoke. Two women and five children survived by hiding in a water conduit.

The historian Josephus described the last dramatic hours of Masada. Lots were drawn to determine which ten men would serve as the executioners. When all were dead but the executioners, one man was selected by lot to cut the throats of the others. Then he too committed suicide. Excavations of Masada in the 1960s uncovered potsherds inscribed with Hebrew names, tantalizing archaeologists with the possibility that these may have been the lots cast on the final day of resistance at Masada.

Today Masada stands as a symbol of Jewish heroism but is also used to describe religious fanaticism.

Sources

Harris, Roberta L. *The World of the Bible.* New York: Thames and Hudson, 1995.

Josephus, Flavius. *The Jewish War.* Baltimore, MD: Penguin Books, 1959.

Roth, Cecil E., ed. *Encyclopedia Judaica.* New York: Macmillan, 1971.

Masochist. ***A person who derives sexual satisfaction from being subjected to pain.***

Although the psychological disorder of masochism doubtless dates back thousands of years, it received its name in the late nineteenth century. Leopold Sacher-Masoch (1835–1895) was an Austrian writer who reveled in the thrill of ritual humiliation at the hands of domineering women. His detailed exploration of the subject in his books created an association between this fetish and his name.

From an early age Sacher-Masoch had a fascination with pain and cruelty. His childhood nurse was a strong Ruthenian peasant who enjoyed telling the boy fearsome tales of Ivan the Terrible and a wicked czarina who threw her captives into dark torture chambers. Sacher-Masoch was enthralled by these stories and fantasized about being the victim of the cruel czarina. According to psychologists, masochistic tendencies form during adolescence, when experiencing pain is associated with the awakenings of sexual desire. Such an incident occurred in Sacher-Masoch's case. He hid in his closet spying on his paternal aunt, the countess Zenobia, as she toyed with a much younger lover. When the closet door slipped open and revealed the boy's presence, the countess turned on him in a rage and beat him. The linkage of sexual desire and physical abuse remained with him from that time.

As an adult Sacher-Masoch made a reputation for himself by writing novels and short stories. He became a "slave" of two wives and a number of mistresses, often drawing up contracts that specified the nature of the dominatrix relationship. He eventually suffered a nervous breakdown, and his second wife had him committed to an asylum. Consistent with her total control over Sacher-Masoch, his wife announced to the public that he had died, although he lived another ten years in confinement.

Sources

Bullough, Vern, and Bonnie Bullough, eds. *Human Sexuality: An Encyclopedia*. New York: Garland Publishing, 1994.

Cleugh, James. *The First Masochist*. New York: Stein and Day, 1967.

McHenry, Robert, ed. *The New Encyclopedia Britannica*. 15th ed. Chicago: Encyclopedia Britannica, 1992.

Mish, Frederick C. *The Merriam-Webster New Book of Word Histories*. Springfield, IL: Merriam-Webster, 1991.

Mason-Dixon line. ***A figurative dividing line between the North and the South in the United States.***

Established in 1768, the 233-mile Mason-Dixon line was drawn by the English surveyors Charles Mason and Jeremiah Dixon. Its purpose was to define the boundary between Maryland and Pennsylvania, which had long been the subject of dispute. The Maryland and Pennsylvania charters were so loosely worded that they were each subject to various interpretations. Maryland declared that its rightful area encompassed Philadelphia, while Pennsylvania claimed a huge chunk of northern Maryland. The two colonies finally agreed to submit to the boundary determined by Mason and Dixon.

During the nineteenth century, as tensions between the North and South escalated, the line became a symbolic boundary between the differing culture, economy, climate, and temperament of the people in the two regions.

Sources

Greene, Jack P., and J. R. Pole, eds. *The Blackwell Encyclopedia of the American Revolution*. Cambridge: Blackwell Reference, 1991.

McHenry, Robert, ed. *The New Encyclopedia Britannica*. 15th ed. Chicago: Encyclopedia Britannica, 1992.

Stimpson, George. *A Book about American History*. Greenwich, CT: Fawcett Publications, 1960.

Wilson, Charles Reagan, and William Ferris, eds. *Encyclopedia of Southern Culture*. Chapel Hill: University of North Carolina Press, 1989.

Mata Hari. ***An alluring woman who uses her sexuality to coax secrets from the enemy.***

Mata Hari is considered to be one of the most famous spies in history, yet 75 years after her execution historians are still not certain who she was spying for or exactly what her crime was. She was born Margaretha Gertruida Zelle in Holland on 7 August 1876. At the age of 17 she answered a personal ad from a Dutch soldier looking for a wife. Although he was twenty years her senior, she married him, and the couple moved to Java and Sumatra. After five years, the marriage ended badly, and Margaretha returned to Europe. With no means of support, she became a courtesan and an exotic dancer in Paris. Changing her name to Mata Hari, she claimed to be a native of the Far East who had been raised to be a sacred dancer in a Hindu temple. Her dark coloring and exotic looks made this claim not entirely implausible. Throwing together a mixture of dance styles, theatrical gestures, and flimsy costumes, she declared that her near-nude performance was a "sacred oriental art," which enabled her to dodge charges of lewdness.

By 1915, the 39-year-old dancer was no longer in high demand, and even her services as a prostitute did not bring in enough money to support the grandiose lifestyle to which she had become accustomed. It is at this point that her activities become obscure. According to many of her biographers, she met a German diplomat in the Hague who offered to pay her for any information she could glean from her French lovers. When she was arrested in 1917, she claimed that she was working for the French as a double agent, but the French denied the association. Most historians believe that Mata Hari was probably working for the Germans in a free-lance capacity. In any event, the famous courtesan was tried by a French military court and shot by a firing squad on 17 October 1917.

Sources

Keay, Julia. *The Spy Who Never Was: The Life and Loves of Mata Hari.* London: Michael Joseph, 1987.

Polmar, Norman, and Thomas B. Allen. *Spy Book: The Encyclopedia of Espionage.* New York: Random House, 1997.

Tucker, Spencer C., ed. *The European Powers in the First World War: An Encyclopedia.* New York: Garland Publishers, 1996.

Mau Mau. ***The use of harassment and intimidation for political ends.***

The Mau Mau was a militant African nationalist organization in the British crown colony of Kenya that advocated violence in pursuit of its anticolonialist objectives. The group launched a rebellion in 1952 and directed its terrorist activities primarily toward the white settlers of Kenya. The government declared a state of emergency, and over the next three years, 12,000 Africans were killed and another 80,000 were placed in detention camps. Although the name of Mau Mau instilled terror in the hearts of the white minority, fewer than 100 whites were killed during the war. The insurrection collapsed in 1956 with the capture of Dedan Kimathi, one of the rebel leaders. Kenya finally became a fully independent nation in 1963.

In 1970 Tom Wolf renovated the term in his essay "Mau Mauing the Flak Catchers," in which a minority group harasses bureaucrats in the San Francisco welfare program. More recently the term has been applied to racial politics in South Africa.

Sources

McHenry, Robert, ed. *The New Encyclopedia Britannica.* 15th ed. Chicago: Encyclopedia Britannica, 1992.

Simpson, J. A., and E. S. C. Weiner, eds. *The Oxford English Dictionary.* 2d ed. Oxford: Clarendon Press, 1989.

Throup, David. *Economic and Social Origins of Mau Mau, 1945–1953.* Athens: Ohio University Press, 1988.

Mausoleum. ***A large, stately tomb for honoring the dead.***

Mausolus (d. 353 B.C.) was a satrap in the Persian empire. When the great Persian king Darius I (522–486 B.C.) conquered Mesopotamia, Syria, India, and Egypt, he found he could no longer wield direct control over his colossal empire. He established twenty satrapies, or provinces, whose administrators would maintain order and collect tribute. Satraps were usually members of the royal family, appointed for life, and had complete authority over the province. Mausolus apparently became weary of his subordination, and in 362 he plotted with other satraps to declare their provinces as their own kingdoms. When it was evident that the revolt would not succeed, he abandoned his plans but was able to keep the favor of the king.

Mausolus would have been forgotten by history had it not been for his tomb, which was so splendid that his name became an eponym for any grand, imposing burial structure. Plans for the tomb were begun by Mausolus himself and completed after his death by Artemisia, a woman who was both his sister and his wife. Located in Bodrum (formerly known as Halicarnassus) in southwestern Turkey, the tomb was 140 feet high and built in the classical style, featuring a colonnade and Greek sculptures. Inside were colossal figures of Mausolus and his wife. Considered one of the Seven Wonders of the Ancient World, the Mausoleum at Halicarnassus was destroyed by a series of earthquakes between the eleventh and fifteenth centuries. When the Knights of Saint John of Malta invaded the region in the early fifteenth century, they used stones from the mausoleum to build a massive castle. The polished marble blocks of the mausoleum can still be seen in the castle walls.

Sources

Clayton, Peter A., and Martin J. Price. *The Seven Wonders of the Ancient World.* London: Routledge, 1988.

Hornblower, Simon, and Antony Spawforth, eds. *The Oxford Classical Dictionary.* 3d ed. Oxford: Oxford University Press, 1996.

Mercer, Cathy. "Mausoleum of Halicarnassus." *History Today* 45, no. 9 (1995): 62–63.

Mish, Frederick C. *The Merriam-Webster New Book of Word Histories.* Springfield, IL: Merriam-Webster, 1991.

Maverick. ***Someone who refuses to abide by the dictates of a group; a nonconformist.***
Samuel A. Maverick (1803–1870) was a successful soldier and politician who served in the Mexican War, signed the Texas Declaration of Independence, became mayor of San Antonio, and was elected to the Texas state legislature. In 1845 he received a herd of cattle as payment for a debt. Absorbed with his political career, Maverick had no interest in ranching and simply allowed the cattle to roam free on his Matagorda Island estate. When he sold the property ten years later, the contract included all the cattle on the estate. Since Maverick had never bothered to brand his cattle, the new owner began to refer to unbranded cattle as *mavericks.*

As early as the 1880s, the word had evolved into a description of a person who stands out from the pack and follows his or her own brand of individualism.

Sources

Beeching, Cyril Leslie. *Dictionary of Eponyms.* London: Clive Bingley, 1979.

Johnson, Allen, and Dumas Malone, eds. *Dictionary of American Biography.* New York: Scribner's, 1964.

Slatta, Richard W. *The Cowboy Encyclopedia.* Santa Barbara, CA: ABC-CLIO, 1994.

McCarthyism. ***The use of intrusive investigations into someone's background, political inclinations, or social connections in order to damage that person's reputation.***
As the political fortunes of Senator Joe McCarthy (1908–1957) declined in 1949, he eagerly cast about for an issue he could champion in order to bolster his sagging career. Anticommunism provided the perfect cause. McCarthy embarked on a reckless campaign of vilification and unfounded accusations against his political enemies that captured the public's attention. According to McCarthy, communism was no longer just a foreign policy concern, since American government itself was being sabotaged from within by carefully placed communist sympathizers. Fears were heightened with the outbreak of the Korean War in 1950, which seemed to confirm that communism was advancing and only dedicated vigilance would halt its spread.

McCarthy officially began his anticommunist crusade in February 1950 when he delivered a speech before the Republican Women's Club in Wheeling, West Virginia. Waving a piece of paper, he claimed that he had "in his hand" a list of 205 communist sympathizers who worked for the State Department. In fact, no such list existed. Over the next four years McCarthy would rely on rumor, innuendo, and character assassination to fuel his crusade. Elected officials were reluctant to challenge him, knowing that to do so might imply that they harbored communist sympathies, and senatorial immunity protected McCarthy from legal action from his victims.

A turning point in the frenzy was reached on 9 June 1954, during the nationally televised hearings of McCarthy's Senate committee. McCarthy had mistakenly decided to turn his attentions to the U.S. Army and was firing off charges of communist affiliation against a congressional assistant, a man who had briefly flirted with communism in college over 15 years earlier. In the midst of McCarthy's abusive denunciation, Joseph Welch, the elderly, dignified attorney representing the army, said in a weary voice: "Until this moment, Senator, I think I have never really gauged your cruelty or your recklessness. Let us not assassinate this lad further, Senator. You have done enough. Have you no sense of decency, sir, at long last? Have you no sense of decency?" The wind was taken out of McCarthy's sails, and he suffered an abrupt fall from grace. He was politically ostracized, and in December 1954 the Senate voted 67–22 to condemn him for contempt and abuse of power.

The term *McCarthyism* was coined by Herb Block in a 1950 editorial cartoon. It has subsequently been used to refer to activities that bear a greater resemblance to witch-hunts than to official legal proceedings.

Sources

Caute, David. *The Great Fear: The Anti-Communist Purge under Truman and Eisenhower.* New York: Simon and Schuster, 1978.

Johnson, Allen, and Dumas Malone, eds. *Dictionary of American Biography.* New York: Scribner's, 1964.

Klingaman, William K. *Encyclopedia of the McCarthy Era.* New York: Facts on File, 1996.

Melba toast. ***Thin, crisp wafers of toast.***
Dame Nellie Melba (1861–1931) was one of the most popular opera singers of her day. She was born in Melbourne, Australia, and took her stage name from her hometown. Performing throughout Europe in the 1880s, her beauty and talent made her a huge success, but like many opera singers she constantly battled her weight. Chef George Auguste Escoffier, one of Europe's best chefs, was also an avid admirer of Dame Melba. Escoffier was the head chef at the Savoy Hotel in London, where the opera diva often resided. In an effort to maintain her figure, she usually abstained from the delicacies prepared by Escoffier in favor of simple, plain toast. One day an inexperienced cook prepared the toast, and it turned out extremely thin and overtoasted. Mortified, Escoffier rushed to the dining room to make amends to Dame Melba, but he found that the dry, crisp toast was much to her liking. She thereafter requested that her toast be prepared in this fashion, and it was consequently named for her. Although Escoffier cannot claim credit (nor did he want to) for these dry pieces of toast, he did name one of his other masterpieces, Peach Melba, after the great soprano (see *Peach Melba*).

Sources

Hunt, Cecil. *Word Origins: The Romance of Language.* New York: Philosophical Library, 1962.

McHenry, Robert, ed. *The New Encyclopedia Britannica.* 15th ed. Chicago: Encyclopedia Britannica, 1992.

Panati, Charles. *Panati's Extraordinary Origins of Everyday Things.* New York: Harper and Row, 1987.

Wechsberg, Joseph. *Red Plush and Black Velvet: The Story of Melba and Her Times.* Boston: Little, Brown, 1961.

Melting pot. ***The blending of various ethnic heritages into an American identity.***
In the late nineteenth century, the explosion of industrial development in the United States created an unprecedented demand for cheap labor. Immigrants from Europe arrived in droves—over 8 million people between 1901 and 1910 alone. Their natural inclination was to seek out enclaves of people with similar ethnic backgrounds, with the result that many eastern cities had a "Little Italy," or "Germantown," or districts whose residents were overwhelmingly from a specific nationality.

Among the nation's intellectuals and political leaders, there was a strong feeling that the new immigrants should become "Americanized" in order to avoid the ethnic fragmentation that had fostered centuries of war in Europe. Names were changed, so that an immigrant who entered Ellis Island as "Powalski" might leave it as a "Powell." There was a cultural stigma associated with not speaking English or maintaining ethnic styles of dress and food. Given the influence of the public school system and social pressures, immigrants were usually assimilated into American life within two or three generations.

The expression *melting pot* was used in the nineteenth century, but it gained widespread currency in 1908 when the English-Jewish author Israel Zangwill wrote the play *The Melting Pot* about the lives of Jewish immigrants. Especially among Progressives, melting-pot assimilation was touted as preserving the best of a variety of cultures yet still shaping the diverse American people into a unified and stronger nation. In 1915 President Woodrow Wilson proclaimed, "There is here a great melting pot in which we must compound a precious metal. That metal is the metal of nationality."

Sources

Miller, Willard E., and Ruby M. Miller. *United States Immigration: A Reference Handbook*. Santa Barbara, CA: ABC-CLIO, 1996.

Stimpson, George. *A Book about American Politics.* New York: Harper, 1952.

West, Elliot. *Growing Up in Twentieth Century America: A History and Reference Guide.* Westport, CT: Greenwood Press, 1996.

Mending fences. ***Strengthening a political position by forming alliances with various factions.***

This phrase was coined by reporters covering a speech by John Sherman (1823–1900), then secretary of the Treasury in the administration of Rutherford B. Hayes. Sherman was the younger brother of General William Tecumseh Sherman and had high ambitions. At one time he even considered running for the presidency of the United States. A native of Ohio, Sherman had returned home to visit his family and attend to his property. There was a great deal of speculation as to whether he would enter the Ohio gubernatorial race, and many reporters were predicting that his trip might have an ulterior motive. After being deluged with questions from reporters regarding his political ambitions, Sherman repeatedly told them that he had merely returned home to look after his neglected property and mend his fences. In his 1895 memoir, *Recollections of Forty Years in the House, Senate and Cabinet,* Sherman reports how his remarks were misinterpreted: "The reporters seized upon the reference to my fences, and construed it as having a political significance. The phrase mending fences became a byword, and every politician engaged in strengthening his position is still said to be *mending fences.*"

Sherman never did run for governor of Ohio, and it is probably safe to take him at his word that the casual remark was not originally intended to have political significance.

Sources

Johnson, Allen, and Dumas Malone, eds. *Dictionary of American Biography.* New York: Scribner's, 1964.

Safire, William. *Safire's Political Dictionary.* New York: Random House, 1978.

Stimpson, George. *A Book about American Politics.* New York: Harper, 1954.

Mercator projection. ***The most famous system for mapping the world, in which the spherical surface of the earth is presented as a flat rectangle divided by lines of longitude and latitude.***

Before the Renaissance, maps of the world were largely dictated by biblical mythology, with Jerusalem depicted in the center of a flat earth. By the late sixteenth century, new insights into the shape of the world were pushing cartography into a revolutionary era of scientific precision.

Gerardus Mercator (1512–1594) tackled the problem of how to represent the spherical world on a flat map. Although his depiction distorted the size of land masses, the *Mercator projection* could be counted on to provide an accurate ratio of latitude to longitude. This type of map gave navigators greater precision in plotting their travels, and the map was eagerly embraced by explorers who were charting new routes around the world.

The Mercator projection is still the image of choice for popular maps and for scientists. Modern navigators use it in more than 90 percent of their work.

Sources

Boorstin, Daniel J. *The Discoverers.* New York: Random House, 1983.

Hendrickson, Robert. *Dictionary of Eponyms: Names That Became Words.* New York: Stein and Day, 1985.

McHenry, Robert, ed. *The New Encyclopedia Britannica.* 15th ed. Chicago: Encyclopedia Britannica, 1992.

Mesmerize. ***To enthrall, or to hypnotize.***

Franz Anton Mesmer (1734–1815) was a flamboyant German healer whose unconventional practices inspired the word *mesmerize.* As a young man he had studied science and mathematics, and like other scientists of the era, he was intrigued by magnetism. By 1765 Mesmer, now a qualified physician, began to experiment with the possibility of using magnets for the cure of physical ailments. He was convinced that laying magnets on afflicted areas would ease the pain. Many of his patients agreed with him, and Mesmer's clinic became one of the most popular in Vienna. As Mesmer's fame grew, so did his ego. He moved to Paris and set up a bizarre clinic that had all the trappings of a seance parlor. The rooms were decorated with mirrors, crystals, ornate furniture, and special lighting, and Mesmer dressed in flowing purple robes and carried a wand of iron. His patients submerged themselves in oversized tubs of water and joined hands to form a large circle. Mesmer and his assistants moved around the tub waving wands and magnets. Many patients lapsed into convulsions or succumbed to fits of crying or laughter. Periods of lethargy usually followed. Despite these unconventional techniques, many patients claimed that they were cured.

In 1784 the medical community of France decided to launch a formal investigation of Mesmer's clinic. A commission of notable scientists, which included Benjamin Franklin and the French chemist Antoine Lavoisier, published a damning report that contained the testimony of people who had faked illnesses in order to gain access to Mesmer's "treatments." The doctor's reputation plunged, but some devoted followers kept him in business until 1789, when he fled the country at the outbreak of the French Revolution.

Sources

Guiley, Rosemary. *Harper's Encyclopedia of Mystical and Paranormal Experience.* San Francisco: HarperSanFrancisco, 1991.

Hendrickson, Robert. *Dictionary of Eponyms: Names That Became Words.* New York: Stein and Day, 1985.

Melton, Gordon, ed. *Encyclopedia of Occultism and Parapsychology.* Detroit, MI: Gale Research, 1996.

Mish, Frederick C. *The Merriam-Webster New Book of Word Histories.* Springfield, IL: Merriam-Webster, 1991.

Messalina. ***A sexually voracious woman.*** History has not been kind to Messalina Valeria (d. A.D. 48) She is remembered as a malicious and sexually voracious woman who used her power to obliterate her enemies and kept a legion of lovers at her beck and call. She was probably only 15 years old when she married the insecure Claudius, a man in his late forties who was completely infatuated with her. Three years later, in 41, Claudius became emperor of the Roman Empire, and this teenage girl became the most powerful woman in the Roman world. Messalina wielded immense influence, especially since she was the mother of Britannicus, the heir to the throne. She apparently abused this power, insisting on the appointment of close friends to important political positions, then arranging for their murder if they fell out of favor with her. To establish the paternity of her children, she was scrupulously faithful in the early years of her marriage, but then she began to take a string of lovers and became infamous for her lascivious appetites.

Messalina's most infamous exploit occurred as a result of her infatuation with a young consul-designate named Gaius Silius. While Claudius was at the port city of Ostia overseeing the construction of a new harbor, Messalina engaged in a mock wedding ceremony with Silius. She may also have tried to arrange for Silius to adopt Britannicus. These activities were seen as treasonous, and as soon as Claudius learned of them, he hurried back to Rome. Messalina's death warrant was signed, and she was promptly executed in her garden by the praetorian guard.

After her death, Claudius had her name stricken from all documents, monuments, and inscriptions. As a consequence, piecing together Messalina's story is a challenge for historians. Some revisionists have recently claimed that Messalina was more canny than lewd and that she carefully chose her lovers to help secure her position should Claudius die before Britannicus had reached his manhood. By taking key political and military figures as lovers, Messalina could manipulate them into supporting her in the event of the emperor's death. Whether or not this is true, her name remains synonymous with unfaithfulness and lust.

Sources

Bunson, Matthew. *Encyclopedia of the Roman Empire.* New York: Facts on File, 1994.

Hornblower, Simon, and Antony Spawforth, eds. *The Oxford Classical Dictionary.* 3d ed. Oxford: Oxford University Press, 1996.

Levick, Barbara. *Claudius.* London: Batsford, 1990.

Mickey Finn. ***A knockout drink.***
Mickey Finn was a notorious Chicago bartender during the 1890s who supplemented his income by drugging his customers and robbing them while they lay unconscious. Finn operated the Lone Star Saloon in a seedy neighborhood. Customers who entered the bar alone were served drinks laced with a drug that caused the individual to first become highly restless and talkative, then suddenly drop off into a deep sleep from which they could not be roused until the drug had worn off. The victim would be hauled into a back room, whereupon Finn would rob him of money, valuables, and even his clothes. The person would be dumped in an alley and, upon waking, would have little recollection of the previous events.

A special Chicago crime commission persuaded two of Finn's employees, Gold Tooth Mary Thornton and Isabelle Ffyffe, to expose his practices. Finn lost his license to operate a saloon and went out of business. He thereafter sold his infamous recipe for *Mickey Finns* to other unscrupulous barkeeps.

Sources

Hendrickson, Robert. *Dictionary of Eponyms: Names That Became Words.* New York: Stein and Day, 1985.

Sifakis, Carl. *The Encyclopedia of American Crime.* New York: Facts on File, 1982.

Milliner. ***Maker or retailer of hats.***
Since the Renaissance, the Italian city of Milan has been known as one of the premier cities for textiles and fashion. Its strategic geographic location in northern Italy also made it a natural commercial crossroads. When the Sforza family rose to prominence in the fifteenth century, they helped build a thriving silk industry to supply an international market. Merchant houses throughout Europe were eager to acquire silk from Italy, and Milan gloves, hats, ribbons, lace, and scarves represented the height of Renaissance splendor. These luxurious accessories were so closely associated with the city that the people who produced them were known as *milaners,* no matter what city the craftsmen resided in. That this was commonplace by the end of the century was revealed in the 1592 memoir, *A Quip for an Upstart Courtier,* by Robert Greene. The author commented about a Frenchman who was "a Millaner in Saint Martins, and sells shirts, bands, bracelets, jewels and such pretty toys for Gentle women."

The spelling of the word was eventually standardized to *milliner,* and by the nineteenth century it had come to refer exclusively to the makers and sellers of hats.

Sources

Hendrickson, Robert. *Business Talk: The Dictionary of Business Words and Phrases.* New York: Stein and Day, 1984.

McHenry, Robert, ed. *The New Encyclopedia Britannica.* 15th ed. Chicago: Encyclopedia Britannica, 1992.

Mish, Frederick C. *The Merriam-Webster New Book of Word Histories.* Springfield, IL: Merriam-Webster, 1991.

Miranda rights. ***A passage read to all criminal suspects at the time of their arrest that informs them of their right to remain silent.***
Ernesto Miranda (1940–1975) was a convicted robber with little education or understanding of the legal system. When he was arrested in 1963 under suspicion of kidnapping and rape, Miranda initially proclaimed his innocence, but after a two-hour interrogation he was willing to sign a confession. He was later convicted of the charges.

Although everyone present at the interrogation agreed that Miranda had not been physically threatened or coerced, it was not clear that the suspect knew he did not have to incriminate himself by answering questions. The Fifth Amendment to the Constitution guarantees that a person cannot be forced into testifying against him/herself. Because the police could not prove that Miranda had been informed of his right to remain silent, the Supreme Court ruled in a 5 to 4 vote that Miranda had been denied the protection of the Fifth Amendment. As a result of this case, criminal suspects are now immediately informed of their right to remain silent, that anything they say can be used against them in court, and that they have a right to be represented by an attorney.

Miranda's conviction was overturned as a result of the 1966 Supreme Court ruling, but he was retried and convicted even without the earlier confession. After being released on parole, he was killed in a knife fight in a Phoenix bar. His assailant was duly read his Miranda rights upon arrest.

Sources

Bessette, Joseph M. *American Justice.* Pasadena, CA: Salem Press, 1996.

Milner, Neal A. *The Court and Local Law Enforcement: The Impact of Miranda.* Beverly Hills, CA: Sage Publications, 1971.

Trahair, R. C. *From Aristotelian to Reaganomics: A Dictionary of Eponyms with Biographies in the Social Sciences.* Westport, CT: Greenwood Press, 1994.

Missouri, I'm from Missouri; also, Show me, I'm from Missouri. ***Indicates a no-nonsense skepticism.***

The best explanation for the origin of this expression derives from an event in 1899 at the Five O'Clock Club in Philadelphia. Some congressmen were delivering typical political speeches, and one overly enthusiastic speaker from Iowa bragged in extravagant terms about the prosperity of his state. Willard Vandiver (1854–1932) was less than impressed. Seeking to put the hyperbole into perspective, Vandiver said, "I come from a country that raises corn, cotton, cockleburs, and Democrats. I'm from Missouri, and you've got to show me."

A less well-documented but frequently cited story dates from the Civil War, when a troop of Union soldiers came across a small group of Confederate soldiers. The Union commander demanded that the Confederates surrender, claiming that he had one thousand troops ready to attack. One Confederate refused to believe the Northerner's boast and countered, "I'm from Missouri; you'll have to show me." Since the *Oxford English Dictionary* indicates that the expression became popular around 1900, shortly after the event at the Five O'Clock Club, it is unlikely that the phrase emerged during the Civil War and then lay dormant for 35 years. Thus the Philadelphia incident certainly seems to deserve the credit for the popular maxim.

The down-to-earth attitude embodied in the expression appealed to the people of Missouri, who soon adopted "Show Me" as a state slogan. The phrase *I'm from Missouri* was subsequently used by people, whether from Missouri or not, to demand that someone validate a claim.

Sources

Hendrickson, Robert. *The Facts on File Encyclopedia of Word and Phrase Origins.* New York: Facts on File, 1987.

Simpson, J. A., and E. S. C. Weiner, eds. *The Oxford English Dictionary.* 2d ed. Oxford: Clarendon Press, 1989.

Stimpson, George. *A Book about American History.* Greenwich, CT: Fawcett Publications, 1962.

Titelman, Gregory Y. *Random House Dictionary of Popular Proverbs and Sayings.* New York: Random House, 1996.

Mitford funeral. ***An inexpensive funeral.***

Jessica Mitford (1917–1996) was an English-born investigative writer whose topics included animal research, civil rights, and childbirth practices. In 1963 she wrote an exposé of the funeral industry titled *The American Way of Death.* The book was a scathing condemnation of practices at funeral homes, which often exploited and bullied grieving family members into paying exorbitant sums for funerals. Americans spend $9 billion each year on funeral expenses, and it is estimated that almost half goes for unnecessary extras, such as protective vaults, specially sealed caskets, and embalming. Vulnerable families are told that some items are mandated by law, when in fact very few states have such requirements. Because funeral homes traditionally do not advertise prices for any of their services, it is difficult to compare costs. As Mitford observed, there is no reluctance to advertise in Europe, and Europeans pay on average half as much for funerals as Americans do.

Mitford's book generated a wave of anger toward the funeral industry, and consumers began to take more responsibility in uncovering deliberate misrepresentation and asserting their preferences. People who elect to buy simple caskets, headstones, and flowers are said to be having a *Mitford funeral*.

Sources

Mitford, Jessica. *The American Way of Death*. New York: Simon and Schuster, 1963.

Roberts, Darryl. *Profits of Death: An Insider Exposes the Death Care Industries*. Chandler, AZ: Five Star Publications, 1997.

Modest proposal. ***An audacious, shocking suggestion, not meant to be taken literally.***

Jonathan Swift (1667–1745) is considered one of the greatest satirists in the English language. His fictional works included *Gulliver's Travels* (1726) and *A Tale in a Tub* (1704), but his biting satire is best reflected in his essay *A Modest Proposal* (1729). The Anglo-Irish Swift shocked European society when he published a thin pamphlet advocating the use of cannibalism as a means of solving the problem of starvation in Ireland. The proposal outlines the plight of the hungry and the poor of Ireland, advocates the selling of Irish infants as meat, highlights the advantages to the suggestion, and refutes possible arguments against it:

> I do therefore humbly offer it to public consideration that of the one hundred and twenty thousand children already computed, twenty thousand be reserved for breed, whereof only one-fourth part to be males; which is more than we allow to sheep, black cattle, or swine; and my reason is, that these children are seldom the fruits of marriage, a circumstance not much regarded by our savages, therefore one male will be sufficient to serve four females. That the remaining hundred thousand may, at a year old, be offered in the sale to persons of quality and fortune through the kingdom; always advising the mother to let them suck plentifully in the last month, so as to render them plump and fat for a good table. I grant this food will be somewhat dear, and therefore very proper for landlords, who, as they have already devoured most of the parents, seem to have best title to the children.

The essay is presented in a logical, unemotional tone that deliberately dehumanizes the Irish. Swift was keenly aware of the exploitation of Irish laborers by the English, and by literalizing the metaphor of England devouring Ireland, his pamphlet rocked polite society.

The phrase *a modest proposal* has subsequently been used by individuals who exaggerate the positions of their opponents in order to draw attention to an issue.

Sources

McHenry, Robert, ed. *The New Encyclopedia Britannica*. 15th ed. Chicago: Encyclopedia Britannica, 1992.

Siebert, Donald T., ed. *British Prose Writers, 1660–1800*. Detroit, MI: Gale Research, 1990.

Stephen, Leslie and Sidney Lee, eds. *The Dictionary of National Biography*. London: Oxford University Press, 1921.

Mohammed. If the mountain will not come to Mohammed, Mohammed must go to the mountain. ***Being forced to make concessions to an opponent.***

After the prophet Mohammed began seeking converts to his new religion, some skeptical Arabs demanded proof that his revelation was divinely inspired. They claimed that Moses, Jesus, and the other great prophets were capable of performing miracles as proof of their supernatural connection to the divine. Mohammed replied, "What greater miracle could they have than the Koran itself; a book revealed by means of an unlettered man; so elevated in language, so incontrovertible in argument, that the united skill of men and devils could compose nothing comparable. The Koran itself is a miracle."

The doubting Arabs would not accept this reply and wished for more tangible evidence, such as healing the blind or the creation of a spring in the midst of the desert. The prophet finally acquiesced and commanded Mount Safa to come to him. When the mountain remained firmly in place, the prophet said, "God is merciful. Had the mountain obeyed my words, it would have fallen on us to our destruction. I will therefore go to the mountain and thank God that He has had mercy on a stiffnecked generation." The episode demonstrated Mohammed's reliance on reason and eloquence, rather than miracles, to awaken listeners to the logic of the Koran.

Sources

Evans, Ivor H., ed. *Brewer's Dictionary of Phrase and Fable.* 14th ed. New York: Harper and Row, 1989.

Irving, Washington. *Mohamet and His Successors.* Madison: University of Wisconsin Press, 1970.

Molotov cocktail. *A homemade grenade, easily produced by amateurs.*

Civilians engaged in violent protests against their own or a foreign government generally must manufacture their own weapons, which have to be inexpensive, produced from common materials, and difficult to trace. Molotov cocktails fit this bill perfectly. The weapon is usually a glass bottle filled with a flammable liquid and stoppered with a gasoline-soaked rag and fuse. Immediately after lighting the fuse the bottle is thrown at a target, whereupon it shatters and ignites. The first users of these homemade grenades were probably the Loyalists in the Spanish Civil War (1936–1939). During the 1940s the Finns also deployed them against Russian troops. Hastily organized, Finnish resistance was resourceful: The state liquor board provided 70,000 empty bottles to protesters. It was the Finns who gave the weapon the name *Molotov cocktail,* after the hated Soviet foreign minister Vyacheslav Molotov (1890–1986). The ease with which these devices can be manufactured has made them a civilian favorite around the world.

Sources

Arms, Thomas S. *Encyclopedia of the Cold War.* New York: Facts on File, 1994.

Frankland, Noble, ed. *The Encyclopedia of Twentieth Century Warfare.* New York: Orion Books, 1989.

Hendrickson, Robert. *Dictionary of Eponyms: Names That Became Words.* New York: Stein and Day, 1985.

Montezuma's revenge. *Diarrhea.*

Montezuma (1467–1520) was the ninth Aztec ruler of Tenochtitlan, the area near present-day Mexico City. He was something of a puzzle to his subjects. Well-known for his humility and religiosity in his youth, after his coronation he displayed a proud and arrogant character and required all his subjects, even those of noble birth, to treat him with slavish deference.

Montezuma ruled a vast empire, but it was weakened by the resentment of conquered tribes who were forced to send heavy tribute and sacrificial victims. In the last years of his reign, Montezuma was haunted by a fear of approaching doom. Omens had foretold the return of Quetzalcoatl, a white, bearded god who would wrest control of the empire away from the Aztec ruler. When the white, bearded Cortez appeared, Montezuma's fatalism led to his downfall. He was taken hostage in 1519 by Cortez, and he lost his hold over his kingdom. At this point, history becomes clouded by differing accounts. The Spaniards claimed that Montezuma was assaulted by his own subjects and died three days later. The Aztecs believed that the emperor had been murdered while under Spanish guard. Regardless, accompanied by only 800 soldiers, Cortez was able to gain control of an empire of over 20 million people. Montezuma's capitulation was reinforced by the superior technology, ships, and horses of the Spanish, but the most significant factor was the deadly smallpox virus carried by the Europeans, which wiped out approximately 18 million Aztecs but did not affect the Europeans, who were generally immune to the disease.

Centuries later the biological advantage has shifted to the Mexicans. When visitors travel to Mexico, they are usually advised not to drink tap water, as it is likely to cause diarrhea. Even fruits and vegetables washed in tap water may result in a nasty case of the traveler's complaint. Longtime residents of Mexico are able to drink the water with no problem. This reversal of biological immunity is called poetic justice by some, and *Montezuma's revenge* by others.

Sources

Bedini, Silvio A. *The Christopher Columbus Encyclopedia.* New York: Simon and Schuster, 1992.

Davis, Paul K. *Encyclopedia of Invasions and Conquests: From Ancient Times to the Present.* Santa Barbara, CA: ABC-CLIO, 1996.

McHenry, Robert, ed. *The New Encyclopedia Britannica.* 15th ed. Chicago: Encyclopedia Britannica, 1992.

Panati, Charles. *Panati's Extraordinary Endings of Practically Everything and Everybody.* New York: Perennial Library, 1989.

Morse code. ***A system for representing letters of the alphabet with a series of dots and dashes that can be transmitted through wires or with flashing lights.***

Samuel Morse (1791–1872) began life as a portrait painter. Disappointing his austere family, Morse traveled to England after college to study with the great artists of the day. On returning to the United States he scratched out a living as an itinerant portrait painter in New England. Although he was poor, he was an interesting character, and he moved with ease in the intellectual circles of his day, counting the Marquis de Lafayette and James Fenimore Cooper among his close friends.

While he was in college, Morse had evinced an interest in electricity but had never pursued it. In 1832 he learned about the discovery of the electromagnet. His curiosity was rekindled, and he began toying with the idea of using electromagnetic impulses to transmit coded messages. Although other inventors were already working on similar projects, it is believed that Morse arrived at his system independent of other researchers. By 1835 he had sketched a rough outline for his idea, but as an amateur inventor and penniless artist, he was in desperate need of funding to test his invention. After much effort he was awarded a $30,000 grant by Congress to build an experimental line from Washington, D.C., to Baltimore. In 1844 the line was completed and he sent the first message: "What hath God wrought!" Morse was immediately deluged with legal claims from rival inventors. He successfully defended himself against rival claims and was awarded full patent rights, which would ultimately make him a very wealthy man.

As Morse code was adopted by other nations, it became apparent that Morse's original system was not suitable for languages other then English, as it lacked a method of indicating diacritic markings. A conference of European nations was called, and in 1851 the International Morse Code was put into use, although the United States still uses the original code.

Sources

Beeching, Cyril Leslie. *A Dictionary of Eponyms.* London: Clive Bingley, 1979.

Coe, Lewis. *The Telegraph: A History of Morse's Invention and Its Predecessors in the United States.* Jefferson, NC: McFarland, 1993.

McHenry, Robert, ed. *The New Encyclopedia Britannica.* 15th ed. Chicago: Encyclopedia Britannica, 1992.

Motown. ***A style of music that blends rhythm and blues, soul, rock, and gospel.***

In 1959 songwriter Berry Gordy (1929–) obtained an $800 loan to start a recording company in Detroit. The city's nickname is "Motor town" due to its long association with the automobile industry, and Gordy named his company *Motown* as a contraction of this nickname. Motown became *the* place for rising black musicians to get their start. The distinctive musical style used large studio orchestras and blended mainstream music with rhythm and blues, which made the records popular with both black and white audiences. The company launched some of the biggest recording stars of the 1960s, including Diana Ross and the Supremes, Smokey Robinson, the Four Tops, Marvin Gaye, Stevie Wonder, and the Jackson Five. By 1970 the Motown sound was so distinctive that the word was synonymous with urban, rhythm-and-blues music.

Sources

Early, Gerald Lyn. *One Nation Under a Groove: Motown and American Culture.* Hopewell, NJ: Ecco Press, 1995.

Hitchcock, H. Wiley, ed. *The New Grove Dictionary of American Music.* London: Macmillan, 1986.

Moxie. ***Courage or spunk, especially in the face of difficult situations.***

Moxie was a soft drink created by Dr. Augustine Thompson in 1884 and touted as a patent medicine that would cure almost anything. The origin of the name itself is something of a mystery, but it may have a Native American derivation, since it appears in many place names throughout Maine, Thompson's home state. The bittersweet beverage was initially advertised as a remedy for sleep disorders, loss of manhood, paralysis, and softening of the brain, which was accomplished through Moxie's amazing ability to "feed the nerves." With the passage of the Pure Food and Drug Act in 1906, manufacturers could no longer make fantastic claims for medicinal products without validating their assertions. The producers of Moxie therefore had to develop an alternative advertising campaign, and they hit upon the slogan "What this country needs is plenty of Moxie." Moxie became a household word across the country and took on the connotation of spunk and courage under fire.

In 1923, the reputation of the drink soared when a famous incident was publicized. Vice-president Calvin Coolidge was awakened at his family home in Vermont with the news that President Warren G. Harding had died. Coolidge's father was a notary public, so he administered the presidential oath of office to his son in the family living room. Following the solemn event, the new president said, "Guess we better have a drink." The group adjourned to Miss Cilley's Store across the street where Coolidge asked for a Moxie.

Moxie sales declined in the 1940s because of a sharp rise in sugar prices and increased national competition from Coca-Cola. The drink still has an ardent following in New England. "Moxie Days," an annual festival in celebration of the soft drink, is held on the second Saturday in July at Lisbon Falls, Maine. Acknowledging that the strong, bittersweet beverage is not to everyone's taste, even the organizer of Moxie Days offers the following advice: "On the first taste, you may want to spit it out. Don't! On the second taste, you may want to do the same. Don't! Wait for the third taste, to allow the true flavor of Moxie to tickle the taste buds."

Sources

Bowers, David Q. *The Moxie Encyclopedia.* Vestal, NY: Vestal Press, 1985.

Hendrickson, Robert. *The Facts on File Encyclopedia of Word and Phrase Origins.* New York: Facts on File, 1987.

Mrs. Lincoln. Aside from that, Mrs. Lincoln, how was the play? ***A macabre, rhetorical question used to imply that something has been irredeemably flawed.***

On the evening of 14 April 1865, Abraham Lincoln and his wife, Mary, attended a play, *Our American Cousin,* at Ford's Theater. The war had ended only five days earlier, and the couple welcomed the rare opportunity to relax and enjoy themselves. The shot fired by John Wilkes Booth put an abrupt end to the evening, and the president died at 7:22 the following morning. Mary Lincoln (1818–1882) never fully recovered from this blow. Already emotionally frail after the death of her son William and the strains of the White House, she became increasingly neurotic and obsessed with attempts to contact the dead through mediums.

The lowest point for Mrs. Lincoln came in 1875 when her only surviving son put her on trial for incompetence, a polite word for insanity. The all-male jury deliberated less than fifteen minutes before ordering her confined to a mental institution outside of Chicago. She remained there for four months before obtaining her release. The allusion to the Lincoln shooting has become popular among political pundits who wish to sarcastically draw attention to an enormous, overwhelming flaw in a supposition. "To evaluate Alger Hiss's life with regard to anything except his espionage is to beg the question: Aside from the shooting, Mrs. Lincoln, how was the play?" *New York Times,* 22 November 1996, p. A30.

Sources

Gould, Lewis L., ed. *American First Ladies: Their Lives and Their Legacy.* New York: Garland Publishers, 1996.

James, Edward T., ed. *Notable American Women, 1607–1950: A Biographical Dictionary.* Cambridge, MA: Belknap Press, 1971.

Neely, Mark E. *The Abraham Lincoln Encyclopedia.* New York: McGraw-Hill, 1982.

Mrs. O'Leary's cow. ***Something seemingly harmless that causes a major catastrophe.***
The Chicago Fire of 1871 was a tragedy of monumental proportions. At that time the city was a dense mass of buildings that had been constructed with no thought of fire control. Wooden sidewalks lined the streets, and only a single pumping station supplied the mains with water. The hot, dry weather and strong winds whipped the fire into a conflagration that could not be stopped. The roof of the pumping station collapsed, leaving the city without water. Two-thirds of the city's buildings were constructed of wood, and the majority of these went up in flames. After consuming five square miles of Chicago, the fire burned itself out after two days. One hundred thousand people were homeless, and 17,500 buildings had been destroyed. Three hundred people were killed, but since most people had to escape on foot in mass confusion, it is surprising that the death toll was not higher.

The cause of the fire will never be known for certain, but the flames had not been entirely extinguished before suspicion began to center on the barn used by the O'Leary family, which was located on the block where the fire started. Mrs. O'Leary testified that she had milked the cow early in the evening, then returned to the house and gone to bed. Newspaper reporters speculated that she had left a kerosene lamp in the barn, which the cow must have subsequently kicked over. Members of the O'Leary family denied the cow story, and a reporter, Michael Ahern, later said that he had fabricated these details to make the story more interesting. Noting that members of the O'Leary family often used the barn for smoking and playing cards, most writers believe that the fire began as the result of a carelessly extinguished cigar butt that smoldered and ignited the barn.

Sources

Adams, J. T. *Dictionary of American History.* New York: Scribner's, 1976.

Cromie, Robert. *The Great Chicago Fire.* New York: McGraw Hill, 1958.

Miller, Ross. *American Apocalypse: The Great Fire and the Myth of Chicago.* Chicago: University of Chicago Press, 1990.

Stimpson, George. *A Book about a Thousand Things.* New York: Harper and Brothers, 1946.

Mrs. Wilson's regency. ***The seventeen-month period between October 1919 and March 1921 when it is believed that Woodrow Wilson's wife was the primary decision maker in the Oval Office.***
Edith Boling Gault (1872–1961) was born into an aristocratic Virginia family that had been devastated by the Civil War. Her first marriage to a jewelry-store owner was unhappy, and when she was widowed in 1908 she resolved never to marry again. That changed when she had a chance encounter in March 1915 with the widowed president of the United States, Woodrow Wilson. During their three-month courtship, Wilson wrote daily letters to Gault, but she was reluctant to accept his offer of marriage and thereby become First Lady. Wilson convinced her that she was indispensable as a helpmate, and they were married.

On 2 October 1919 Edith found her husband unconscious on the floor of the bathroom, having suffered a massive stroke. Bypassing the White House switchboard for fear of being overheard, she placed a call on a private phone to summon a physician. The president's condition was a secret to everyone but his doctors and his wife. Over the next few months little information was forthcoming, except that the president was suffering from "nervous exhaustion." Edith vetoed suggestions that the president consider resigning, contending that it would impair his recovery. All matters of state requiring the president's attention were submitted to her in writing, and she decided which documents would be forwarded to the president. She had sole responsibility for determining and relaying the president's wishes to the rest of the government. Since their sessions were strictly private, the extent of her regency may never be known, and Edith Wilson later referred to her role in terms of "stewardship." However, even members of the cabinet suspected that Wilson's signature on official appointments and policy decisions may have been forged.

Woodrow Wilson died in February 1924, three years after leaving office. In 1967, provisions for succession in the event of presidential disability were formalized in the Twenty-fifth Amendment to the Constitution.

Sources

Gould, Lewis L., ed. *American First Ladies: Their Lives and Their Legacy.* New York: Garland Publishers, 1996.

James, Edward T., ed. *Notable American Women, 1607–1950: A Biographical Dictionary.* Cambridge, MA: Belknap Press, 1971.

Panati, Charles. *Panati's Extraordinary Endings of Practically Everything and Everybody.* New York: Perennial Library, 1989.

Mud, his/her name is Mud. *When a person has disgraced him/herself.*

This phrase has often been inaccurately attributed to the actions of Dr. Samuel Mudd (1833–1883), who treated John Wilkes Booth's broken leg after Booth assassinated President Lincoln. Booth arrived at Mudd's house at 4 A.M. the morning after the shooting, and the doctor set his leg and sent him on his way. Mudd reported the event to investigators the following day. Suspicious over the delay in reporting such a peculiar incident, authorities arrested Mudd nine days after the crime and charged him with conspiracy in the assassination. The doctor certainly had no role in the crime, but his ardent pro-Southern sympathies and dilatory cooperation were enough to condemn him. It was also revealed that Mudd had met Booth previously. On this scanty evidence Mudd was convicted and sentenced to hard labor for life. Although he was pardoned by President Andrew Johnson in 1869, neither his reputation nor his medical practice ever entirely recovered.

The expression is so closely associated with Dr. Mudd that it sometimes appears as *his name is Mudd.* Nevertheless, this phrase was common by the early nineteenth century, decades before Lincoln's assassination, and probably originated simply as a colorful analogy.

Sources

Neely, Mark E. *The Abraham Lincoln Encyclopedia.* New York: McGraw-Hill, 1982.

Simpson, J. A., and E. S. C. Weiner, eds. *The Oxford English Dictionary.* 2d ed. Oxford: Clarendon Press, 1989.

Weckesser, Elden C. *His Name Was Mudd: The Life of Dr. Samuel A. Mudd, Who Treated the Fleeing John Wilkes Booth.* Jefferson, NC: McFarland, 1991.

Mugwump. *A big-shot; also, someone who abandons an affiliation with a political party.*

John Eliot (1604–1690) coined the word *mugwump* as part of his effort to make the Bible understandable to the American Indians he hoped to convert to Christianity. Eliot emigrated to Massachusetts in 1631 and became the pastor of a church. Eliot had a natural facility with languages, and he knew that he would have a better chance of converting the Indians if he could preach in their native tongue. He studied with a man who had once been a captive of the Indians, and by 1649 he was able to communicate well enough to preach. Villages of "praying Indians" were established for new converts.

Eliot's next objective was to translate the Bible. His Indian version of the New Testament was published in 1661, and the Old Testament followed in 1663. These were the first Bibles printed in North America. One of the difficulties Eliot faced in completing his translations was finding words for concepts for which the Indians had no equivalent. The word *duke* is used several times in the book of Genesis, and Eliot lit upon the Algonquian term *mukquomp* to describe this type of important leader. New Englanders later latched onto this word to refer to arrogant, puffed-up individuals, and it was in common use by the early nineteenth century.

A secondary meaning emerged in 1884 when a number of Republicans bolted from their party rather than support the presidential candidacy of James Blaine. Newspapers and commentators referred to these defectors as *mugwumps,* implying that they felt they were too superior to be associated with Blaine. Some mugwumps even went so far as to vote for the Democratic candidate, Grover Cleveland, who won the election.

Sources

Johnson, Allen, and Dumas Malone, eds. *Dictionary of American Biography.* New York: Scribner's, 1964.

McHenry, Robert, ed. *The New Encyclopedia Britannica.* 15th ed. Chicago: Encyclopedia Britannica, 1992.

Mish, Frederick C. *The Merriam-Webster New Book of Word Histories.* Springfield, IL: Merriam-Webster, 1991.

Winslow, Ola Elizabeth. *John Eliot: Apostle to the Indians.* Boston: Houghton Mifflin, 1968.

Munchausen syndrome. ***A psychological disorder in which a patient feigns or self-inflicts an illness to gain the attention of medical practitioners. Also, Munchausen syndrome by proxy. A psychological disorder in which a parent induces illness in his or her child to gain the attention and sympathy of medical practitioners.***

Once while hunting in Africa, the Baron von Munchausen was chased by a ferocious lion. Barely able to outdistance the hungry lion, the baron came upon a giraffe that was quietly grazing on the leaves of a tree. Springing up the giraffe's back into the tree, the baron then conked the giraffe on the head and knocked the creature out, thereby preventing the lion from following him into his lofty refuge.

This tall tale was typical of the extravagant and preposterous stories that the Baron Karl Munchausen (1720–1797) enjoyed telling the neighborhood children. In his youth Munchausen had served with the Russian cavalry and fought against the Turks, and in his later years he enjoyed life as a country gentleman and hunter. He probably would have slipped into obscurity after his death were it not for a small volume published by one of his acquaintances, Rudolf Erich Raspe (1737–1794). Raspe had fled Germany to avoid prosecution as a jewel thief, and in desperate need of funds he penned an outrageous novel: *Baron Munchausen's Narrative of His Marvelous Travels and Campaigns in Russia.* The word *Munchausen* eventually became synonymous with someone who tells exaggerated stories in order to draw attention to himself.

Psychologists attached the name to a syndrome to describe a person who enjoys the attention received upon checking into a hospital. Such individuals may feign hallucinations, delusions, and suicidal thoughts or may claim to suffer from physical maladies, which are either self-inflicted, self-maintained, or simulated. Once a Munchausen patient has been treated at one hospital, he or she may repeat the process at other medical facilities. In the 1980s a new and more sinister variant of the disorder known as *Munchausen syndrome by proxy* was identified by health practitioners. This is a form of child abuse in which a parent derives satisfaction from assuming the role of devoted caretaker to an ailing child. The parent may inflict physical symptoms, alter lab specimens, or induce disorders in the child to create a medical condition that requires attention and treatment.

Sources

Clark, Robin E., and Judith Freeman Clark. *The Encyclopedia of Child Abuse.* New York: Facts on File, 1989.

McHenry, Robert, ed. *The New Encyclopedia Britannica.* 15th ed. Chicago: Encyclopedia Britannica, 1992.

Raspe, R. E. *Singular Travels, Campaigns, and Adventures of Baron Munchausen.* New York: Dover Publications, 1960.

Munich syndrome. ***A belief that a government should permit zero tolerance of totalitarian dictators in order to avoid the mistakes embodied in the 1938 Munich Pact.***

In the late 1930s Adolph Hitler set into motion a plan for acquiring more "living space" (see *Lebensraum*) for Germany. By 1938 he had achieved a political union between Austria and Germany, and he began laying plans to absorb Czechoslovakia. On the pretense that the Czechs were persecuting German minorities in Czechoslovakia, Hitler ordered his troops to prepare for an invasion. Hitler's bombastic statements and audacious behavior alarmed politicians in England and France, who did not feel prepared to take on Germany in the event of war. British Prime Minister Neville Chamberlain summed up the mood of many of his countrymen: "How horrible, fantastic, incredible it is that we should be digging trenches and trying on gas masks here because of a quarrel in a far-away country between people of whom we know nothing."

It could not have been reassuring to the people of Czechoslovakia to know that the man who uttered this statement was on his way to Munich to attempt to arrive at a peaceful solution to this crisis. Chamberlain met with Hitler and French officials in Germany, where the infamous Munich Pact was signed on 30 September 1938. Czechoslovakia was partitioned, and most of its area was ceded to Hitler in return for his pledge to make no further territorial demands in Europe. Chamberlain returned to England in triumph, proudly displaying the agreement that was supposed to avert another war. The prime minister declared that he had achieved "peace for our time." Less than a year later Hitler invaded Poland, and Europe was again plunged into war. The Munich agreement is now regarded as an act of appeasement to the point of betrayal. In 1942 Franklin Roosevelt used it to rebuke isolationists who did not want the United States involved in the war. The *Munich syndrome* has been cited to portray dovish-isolationists as cowards in the face of international villains. In the words of writer Philip Goldberg, "The Munich Syndrome assumes that it is categorically dangerous to think that your opponent shares your views of honor, trust and peaceful coexistence."

Sources

Comfort, N. A. *Brewer's Politics: A Phrase and Fable Dictionary.* London: Cassell, 1993.

Safire, William. *Safire's Political Dictionary.* New York: Random House, 1978.

Zentner, Christian, and Friedemann Budurftig, eds. *Encyclopedia of the Third Reich.* New York: Macmillan, 1991.

Murphy's law. ***If anything can go wrong, it will.***

There are dozens of variations on Murphy's law, but the most frequently cited of the cynical maxims is *If anything can go wrong, it will.* Exactly who Murphy was is a mystery that has etymologists eagerly searching the lives of prominent individuals named Murphy for clues. All that is known for certain is that the expression is of American origin and started to be quoted in the middle of the twentieth century. Only one theory seems credible.

In the late 1940s Captain Ed Murphy was a development engineer at the Wright Patterson Air Force Base near Dayton, Ohio. Murphy was working on the MX981 project that was studying human tolerance to high decelerative forces in order to design proper aircraft and protective equipment. Murphy experienced considerable frustration with one of his technicians who had repeatedly miswired a strap transducer and caused it to malfunction. The captain commented that "if there is any way to do it wrong, he will." Observers immediately dubbed this Murphy's law, and the expression was disseminated a few weeks later when it was alluded to in a press conference. Over the years Murphy's law has grown to include a number of variations. The following is a list culled from Paul Dickson's *The Official Rules:*

1. If anything can go wrong, it will.
2. Nothing is ever as simple as it seems.
3. Everything takes longer than you expect.
4. If there is a possibility of several things going wrong, the one that will go wrong first will cause the most damage.
5. Left to themselves, all things go from bad to worse.
6. If you play with something long enough, you will surely break it.
7. If everything seems to be going well, you have obviously overlooked something.
8. Nature always sides with the hidden flaw.

Sources

Dickson, Paul. *The Official Rules.* New York: Delacorte Press, 1978.

Pickering, David, ed. *Brewer's Dictionary of Twentieth Century Phrase and Fable.* Boston: Houghton Mifflin Company, 1992.

N

Namby-pamby. *Something that is sickeningly sweet and sentimental.*

In the early eighteenth century there was a rivalry between the followers of Alexander Pope and Joseph Addison, two of the great British writers of the day. Pope was a poet whose verses favored classical, balanced rules of composition. He had a wicked sense of satire that often shone through in his writing. Joseph Addison was primarily an essayist, and his poetry tended to be emotional and patriotic. Each writer inspired a camp whose members scorned the opposing style. When one of Addison's admirers, "Namby" Philips, wrote a sentimental and hackneyed poem, it was ripe for skewering by the followers of Pope.

Henry Carey accepted the challenge. He wrote a poem called *Namby-Pamby* that ridiculed the insipid effort of the unfortunate Namby Philips:

Namby Pamby's Little Rhymes
Little Jingle, Little Chimes
To repeat to Little Miss,
Piddling Ponds of Pissy-Piss;
Cacking-packing like a lady,
or Bye-bying in the Crady.
Namby Pamby will never die
While the Nurse sings Lullaby.

Within a few years, literary critics were using the expression *namby-pamby* in connection with writing that was either childishly simple or cloyingly sweet. By the nineteenth century namby-pamby referred more generally to anything that was overly sentimental.

Sources

Backscheider, Paula R., ed. *Restoration and Eighteenth-Century Dramatists.* 2d ser. Detroit, MI: Gale Research, 1989.

Lurie, Charles. *Everyday Sayings: Their Meanings Explained, Their Origins Given.* Detroit, MI: Gale Research, 1968.

Mish, Frederick C. *The Merriam-Webster New Book of Word Histories.* Springfield, IL: Merriam-Webster, 1991.

Nation of shopkeepers. *England.*

The phrase *nation of shopkeepers* was popularized by Adam Smith's *Wealth of Nations.* As he wrote, "To found a great empire for the sole purpose of raising up a people of customers may at first sight appear a project fit only for a nation of shopkeepers. It is, however, a project altogether unfit for a nation of shopkeepers; but extremely fit for a nation whose Government is influenced by shopkeepers." Smith did not intend this statement to be derogatory, but rivals of England seized on it to deride the character of the small island nation, whose citizens were portrayed as parochial, greedy people with no military sense. Both Napoleon and Kaiser Wilhelm hurled the accusation at England, although the British consider the phrase to be a testament to their industry rather than an insult.

Sources

Hendrickson, Robert. *Facts on File Encyclopedia of Word and Phrase Origins.* New York: Facts on File, 1987.

Safire, William. *Safire's Political Dictionary.* New York: Random House, 1978.

Stimpson, George. *A Book about a Thousand Things.* New York: Harper and Brothers, 1946.

Nelson's blood. ***Rum.***
Admiral Horatio Nelson (1758–1805) is one of England's greatest national heroes. Born into a genteel but poor family, Nelson went to sea at an early age. His bright mind and unflagging diligence caused him to be promoted up through the ranks, and he was appointed captain of a ship by age 20. Nelson's career was unexceptional until Napoleon began to cast his shadow over Europe. During the Napoleonic Wars, Nelson's flare for tactical maneuvers won him world renown. Shot by a sniper in the midst of his greatest victory at the Battle of Trafalgar, Nelson died on 21 October 1805. It would be another month before his body was brought up the Thames to Greenwich where he would lie in state. On board the ship his body was preserved in a cask of rum. Since then, dark rum has been called *Nelson's blood* by British seamen.

Sources
Beeching, Cyril Leslie. *Dictionary of Eponyms.* London: Clive Bingley, 1979.
Jeans, Peter D. *Ship to Shore: A Dictionary of Everyday Words and Phrases Derived from the Sea.* Santa Barbara, CA: ABC-CLIO, 1993.
Walder, David. *Nelson: A Biography.* New York: Dial Press, 1978.
Whipple, Addison B. *Fighting Sail.* Alexandria, VA: Time-Life Books, 1978.

Nepotism. ***The practice of awarding jobs and other favors to friends or family members.***
This word is derived from the Italian *nepote,* meaning nephew. During the Renaissance many popes had a seemingly inexplicable number of nephews—in reality, their bastard sons who were smuggled into the family as "nephews." Some popes compounded their indiscretion by heaping ecclesiastical offices on their nephews. The practice was so flagrant that the word *nepotism* was coined. In one blatant example, the notorious Borgia pope Alexander VI (1492–1503) made his 17-year-old son Cesare a cardinal of the church. Cesare had never shown any pious inclinations and was far better known for his magnificent wardrobe, hunting parties, and scandalous love life. Pope Paul III (1468–1549) was another infamous nepotist. In 1534 he made cardinals out of two of his grandsons, who were only 14 and 16 years old. Sixtus IV (1414–1484) was more liberal in his appointments. Only 6 of the 34 cardinals he appointed were his nephews; the others were simply friends.

In modern times, nepotism in government agencies and private companies takes the form of awarding contracts or jobs to family members of employees.

Sources
Hendrickson, Robert. *Facts on File Encyclopedia of Word and Phrase Origins.* New York: Facts on File, 1987.
Kelly, J. N. D. *The Oxford Dictionary of Popes.* New York: Oxford University Press, 1986.

Next year in Jerusalem. ***A toast given on the first night of Passover that speaks to the Jewish desire to end their exile and reclaim the city of Jerusalem.***
Passover is the Jewish festival that celebrates the deliverance of the Israelites from Egypt. Scripture tells that the angel of death who had been sent to kill the firstborn children of Egypt "passed over" the Jewish households whose doors had been marked with lamb's blood. To commemorate this event, the Jews were commanded to make pilgrimages to the Temple in Jerusalem. After the destruction of the Temple A.D. 70, the Jews were driven into exile, and the seder, a home ceremony, was instituted to replace the temple celebration. The seder involves several special dishes, readings, and rituals. The evening concludes with the traditional toast *next year in Jerusalem,* which is a reference to the desire to reclaim the Holy Land and celebrate the festival in its appointed place. The toast continues in use despite the creation of the Jewish state of Israel in 1948.

Sources
Panati, Charles. *Sacred Origins of Profound Things.* New York: Penguin Arcana, 1996.
Roth, Cecil E., ed. *Encyclopedia Judaica.* New York: Macmillan, 1972.
Wigoder, Geoffrey, ed. *The Encyclopedia of Judaism.* New York: Macmillan, 1989.

Nicotine. ***A highly addictive alkaloid derived from the tobacco plant.***

Nicotine has been described as one of the most addictive drugs in the world, and so perhaps it is no surprise that there has been a great deal of controversy surrounding the tobacco plant since its introduction to Europeans over four hundred years ago.

André Thevet (b. 1502) was a French monk and adventurer who first brought the tobacco plant into Europe from the New World. However, the book he wrote recounting his experiences and discoveries was so bizarre and poorly written that it barely made an impact among the Europeans. Jean Nicot (1530–1600) was a far more memorable individual. Although he came from an impoverished family, he acquired a good education and had an ingratiating personality. Traveling to the court of Henry II of France, he so impressed the members of the court that he was appointed ambassador to Portugal. While in Lisbon he came into contact with a Flemish merchant who gave him some tobacco seeds. He grew the seeds in his garden and carried out a variety of experiments with the leaves. He used them as a poultice for skin ailments, pressed them into a juice for a tonic, and smoked them as a stimulant. Nicot was so impressed with the uses of the plant he sent the seeds and instructions for their growth to the French court.

The popularity of tobacco spread quickly, and in 1573 a French dictionary recorded the word *nicotiane* with the following definition: "This is an herb of marvelous virtue against all wounds, ulcers, lupis, or other eroding ulcers of the face, herpes, and other such like things." Jean Nicot was a contributing editor to the dictionary, which probably accounts for the creation of the word. In any event, by the end of the 1570s the word *nicotine* was in heavy use throughout much of Europe. André Thevet bitterly resented the fame that tobacco had brought to Nicot. In a 1575 book Thevet wrote: "I can boast of having been the first in France who brought the seed of this plant in question *herbe Angoulmoisine* [named after the place of Thevet's birth]. Since then, a certain individual who never made any voyage has given it his name, some ten years after my return." This was only the first of many controversies that would surround the history of tobacco.

Sources

Beeching, Cyril Leslie. *Dictionary of Eponyms.* London: Clive Bingley, 1979.

Billings, E. R. *Tobacco: Its History, Varieties, Culture, Manufacture, and Commerce, with an Account of Its Various Forms of Use, from Its First Discovery Until Now.* Hartford, CT: American Publishing Company, 1875.

Laufer, Berthold. *Introduction of Tobacco into Europe.* Chicago: Field Museum of Natural History, 1924.

Night of the long knives. ***A surprise political attack launched by one's supposed allies.***

The Night of the Long Knives occurred on 30 June 1934 and was the moment when Adolph Hitler cemented his control over the Nazi party by eliminating rival Ernst Röhm (1887–1934). Röhm had been a member of the Nazi party from its earliest days, and he considered Hitler a close personal friend. In 1923 Röhm took part in Hitler's Beerhall Putsch, an unsuccessful attempt to start an insurrection against the German government. Both men were sentenced to serve time in prison, which further solidified the bond between them. After their release, they began to differ on how the Nazi party should be run. Röhm grew impatient with what he perceived to be the slow progress of the party, so he went to Bolivia to serve as a military advisor. In 1930 Hitler summoned him back to Germany to assume command of the Nazi Storm Troopers, known as the SA.

Still disagreeing on policies, relations between Hitler and Röhm further deteriorated. By 1934 Hitler wanted to purge the Nazi party of anyone who seemed more loyal to Röhm than to him, and Heinrich Himmler's Gestapo troops began arresting and executing people identified by Hitler. Röhm and 83 other leaders of the SA were shot, and Hitler's power over the Nazi party was uncontested. Himmler presented the men who had carried out the assassinations with inscribed daggers to commemorate the night's work.

The phrase *night of the long knives* was coined by Hitler himself. It has subsequently been used to describe surprising and drastic political reorganizations, such as when British Prime Minister Harold Macmillan instituted a wholesale reorganization of his cabinet in 1962.

Sources

Comfort, N. A. *Brewer's Politics: A Phrase and Fable Dictionary.* London: Cassell, 1993.

Safire, William. *Safire's Political Dictionary.* New York: Random House, 1978.

Zentner, Christian, and Friedemann Budurftig, eds. *Encyclopedia of the Third Reich.* New York: Macmillan, 1991.

Nine days' wonder. ***Something that causes a sensation for a brief time, then fades into obscurity.***

The origin of this phrase is uncertain, but it probably refers to the nine-day reign of Lady Jane Grey (1537–1554) as queen of England. The death of the young Protestant king Edward VI raised difficult questions of succession. The logical candidate was Edward's oldest sister, Mary Tudor, but her ardent Catholicism was repugnant to the high-placed advisors who surrounded the throne. A series of political machinations put Lady Jane on the throne. Jane was the niece of Henry VIII, but most important to her supporters, a Protestant. The 15-year-old Jane fainted upon being informed of her impending role and accepted the crown with great reluctance. The people of England generally supported Mary Tudor, as King Henry's natural heir, and the tide quickly turned against young Queen Jane. Her supporters melted away, and she relinquished the crown. She pled guilty to treason and was beheaded on 12 February 1554.

Another possible explanation for this phrase is that it refers to the first nine days of a puppy's life when it is blind.

Sources

McHenry, Robert, ed. *The New Encyclopedia Britannica.* 15th ed. Chicago: Encyclopedia Britannica, 1992.

Phyfe, William H. *5000 Facts and Fancies.* Detroit, MI: Gale Research, 1996.

Stimpson, George. *A Book about a Thousand Things.* New York: Harper and Brothers, 1946.

Williamson, David. *Brewer's British Royalty.* London: Cassell, 1996.

Not worth a continental. ***Something that is worthless.***

In 1776 the Continental Congress was eager to demonstrate to the world that the United States was a sovereign nation. One way to do this was to issue its own currency. In anticipation of a massive loan of silver bullion from France, Congress commissioned its own currency, both paper money and coins, which were called continentals. Unfortunately, the French loan did not arrive, and the value of the money began to depreciate. To make matters worse, the British began to circulate counterfeit continentals, which further eroded the value of the original currency. In 1779 George Washington wrote: "A wagon-load of money will scarcely buy a wagon-load of provisions."

By the end of the war the money was literally useless, and it took the financial wizardry of Alexander Hamilton in the 1790s to create a legitimate currency for the United States. When that occurred, the exchange rate at the Treasury was $100 in continentals for $1 in gold.

Sources

Breen, Walter H. *Complete Encyclopedia of U.S. and Colonial Coins.* Garden City, NJ: Doubleday, 1988.

Stimpson, George. *A Book about American History.* Greenwich, CT: Fawcett Publications, 1960.

Nuremberg defense. ***The claim that a perpetrator of a heinous act is not liable if the action was ordered by a commanding officer.***

The Nuremberg trials of Nazi leaders after World War II were an unprecedented attempt to hold individuals legally responsible for atrocities committed during war. Leaders of the Nazi movement were charged under three main headings: 1) crimes against peace and waging an aggressive war, 2) conventional war crimes including wanton destruction of nations conquered by Germany, and 3) crimes against humanity. The trial began in November 1945 in the Nuremberg courthouse. The site was selected because it was one of the few large public buildings still standing in Germany and because Nuremberg had great symbolic significance as a birthplace of Nazism.

The prosecution had an astounding amount of evidence to document each of the charges. Proving that the accused had committed the crimes was not difficult. The real challenge would be to convince an international tribunal and public opinion that the defendants could be held responsible for acts that were ordered by their superior officers. The defense argument was that the orders came from the German government and were legal at the time they were issued. Therefore, responsibility rested with the man giving the orders, Adolph Hitler.

Despite the controversy, 16 of the 19 defendants were found guilty. Additional proceedings continued until 1949, and over 200 Nazis were found guilty of war crimes. The objective of the Nuremberg trials was to show that some crimes are so heinous they cannot be dismissed by citing obedience to authority.

Sources

Gutman, Israel. *The Encyclopedia of the Holocaust.* New York: Macmillan, 1990.

Persico, Joseph E. *Nuremberg: Infamy on Trial.* New York: Viking, 1994.

Zentner, Christian, and Friedemann Budurftig, eds. *The Encyclopedia of the Third Reich.* New York: Macmillan, 1991.

O

Ockham's Razor. ***The belief that the best theory is usually the simplest one.***
William of Ockham (1285–1347) valued simplicity. This English philosopher and theologian lived in an era when puzzling natural phenomena were often explained by exotic theories of demons or other unprovable notions. Ockham was convinced that reason must rely on observable facts and experience. Rather than reach for improbable explanations, the simplest one was usually the best. This was known as the law of parsimony, or *Ockham's razor,* which could be used to slice away the deliberately complex and unnecessary facets of an argument or operation. Ockham's razor is now a guiding principle in modern science.

Sources

Goldberg, Philip. *The Babinski Reflex: And 70 Other Useful and Amusing Metaphors from Science, Psychology, Business, Sports, and Everyday Life.* Los Angeles, 1990.

McDonald, William J., ed. *New Catholic Encyclopedia.* New York: McGraw-Hill, 1967.

McHenry, Robert, ed. *The New Encyclopedia Britannica.* 15th ed. Chicago: Encyclopedia Britannica, 1992.

Old Contemptibles. ***The British army.***
During World War I, the British expeditionary force named themselves the *Old Contemptibles,* which derived from a slur attributed to Kaiser Wilhelm. The kaiser supposedly ordered the commander of the First German Army to "walk over General French's contemptible little army." Kaiser Wilhelm was well known for his militaristic and bombastic posturing, and such a statement was not inconsistent with his comportment during the war. However, the kaiser denied ever having made this statement, and the evidence seems to point to British propagandists as the actual source. Regardless of the truth, British soldiers were eager to believe that the kaiser insulted them, and they proudly adopted the nickname *Old Contemptibles.*

Sources

Messenger, Charles. *History of the British Army.* Novato, CA: Presidio, 1986.

Pickering, David, ed. *Brewer's Dictionary of Twentieth Century Phrase and Fable.* Boston: Houghton Mifflin Company, 1992.

Old Lady of Threadneedle Street. ***The Bank of England.***
The Bank of England has been located on Threadneedle Street since 1734. In 1797 it acquired its nickname, the *Old Lady of Threadneedle Street,* from a political cartoon by satirist James Gilray. The Bank of England had always enjoyed an unshakable reputation for solid investments. In particular, the bank loaned money to the government for its wars, and as the wars increased Britain's commercial influence, the bank reaped the profits. By the end of the eighteenth century this strategy backfired. Expensive military operations against the American colonies and France drained the resources of the bank, and in 1797 it was announced that the bank would be unable to convert notes into gold. In the context of this potential crisis, Gilray drew a cartoon in

which an elderly, respectable-looking matron personified the Bank of England. A young politician reached into the pockets of grande dame. Outraged, she cried out, "Rape! Murder! Oh you villain! Have I kept my honor so long to have it broken by you at last? Rape! Ravishment! Ruin! Ruin! Ruin!"

A run on the bank was averted when 4,000 wealthy people signed a declaration of confidence in the bank. The image of the Old Lady of Threadneedle Street was so apt that it has remained associated with the bank ever since.

Sources

Evans, Ivor H., ed. *Brewer's Dictionary of Phrase and Fable.* 14th ed. New York: Harper and Row, 1989.
Lurie, Charles. *Everyday Sayings.* Detroit, MI: Gale Research, 1968.
Roberts, Richard, and David Kynaston. *The Bank of England 1694–1994: Money, Power, and Influence.* Oxford: Clarendon Press, 1995.
Simpson, J. A., and E. S. C. Weiner, eds. *The Oxford English Dictionary.* 2d ed. Oxford: Clarendon Press, 1989.

Olive branch. ***A symbol of peace.***
Since ancient times, the olive branch has represented a peace offering. Olive trees require many years of careful tending before they bear fruit. In periods of stress or drought they are barren. Consequently, a healthy olive branch came to be associated with the flourishing times of peace. According to legend, the ancient Greeks had to decide whether Poseidon or Athena should be the patron of their city. Poseidon offered a horse, symbolizing strength and courage. Athena offered the gift of an olive tree, representing peace and plenty. The Greeks opted for Athena's gift and gave Athens its name. At games held in Athena's honor, victors were crowned with olive wreaths.

The olive branch also has meaning in the Judeo-Christian tradition. According to Genesis, after Noah had sailed for 40 days, a dove carrying an olive branch in its beak brought him hope. "And the dove came to him in the evening; and, lo, in her mouth was an olive leaf plucked off; so Noah knew that the waters were abated off the earth"(Genesis 8: 11).

Depictions of a dove with an olive branch were very popular during World War I and continue to represent the hope for world peace.

Sources

Evans, Ivor H., ed. *Brewer's Dictionary of Phrase and Fable.* 14th ed. New York: Harper and Row, 1989.
Whittick, Arnold. *Symbols, Signs, and Their Meaning.* Newton, MA: C. T. Branford Co., 1960.

Orangemen. ***Those in Ireland who support a political union with Great Britain.***
Throughout the sixteenth and seventeenth centuries, the throne of England was contested ground for the religious conflict between Catholics and Protestants. By the 1680s, the majority of the English people and Parliament supported a Protestant monarchy. When James II took the throne, his Catholic sympathies were cause for concern, but since his daughters were loyal Protestants, it was widely believed that the succession would reaffirm the nation's Protestant identity. Then, in 1688, the king's new Catholic wife gave birth to a son. It was widely believed that the king intended to raise his new heir in the Catholic faith. Amid increasing antagonism toward the king, Parliament claimed that James II had "abdicated" and offered the throne to William of Orange (1650–1702), the staunch Protestant husband of James's daughter Mary and prince of the Dutch province of Orange. The Glorious Revolution, in which William and Mary were proclaimed the joint monarchs of Britain, was accomplished with very little bloodshed in England. This was not the case in Ireland, where the Catholic majority bitterly resented the forced abdication of King James and were willing to fight on his behalf.

The decisive battle was fought on 12 July 1690, along the banks of the Boyne River in Ireland. James's army of 21,000 was routed by William's 35,000 men, and James was driven into exile. The Battle of the Boyne marked the triumph of a Protestant monarchy, and its

Irish supporters adopted the color orange to symbolize their patriotism. In Northern Ireland, July 12 is still celebrated annually, and parades of Protestants wend their way through the streets of Belfast waving orange banners.

Sources

Ashley, Maurice. *The Glorious Revolution of 1688.* London: Hodder and Stoughton, 1966.

Fritze, Ronald H. *Historical Dictionary of Stuart England, 1603–1689.* Westport, CT: Greenwood Press, 1996.

Grell, Ole Peter, ed. *From Persecution to Toleration: The Glorious Revolution and Religion in England.* Oxford: Clarendon Press, 1991.

McHenry, Robert, ed. *The New Encyclopedia Britannica.* 15th ed. Chicago: Encyclopedia Britannica, 1992.

Oscar. ***Annual award given by the Academy of Motion Picture Arts and Sciences for achievement in film; generally considered the most prestigious of film awards.***

The Academy of Motion Picture Arts and Sciences was organized in 1927 and within a year had begun its annual tradition of granting awards in twelve categories for motion picture excellence. The golden statuette was designed by MGM art director Cedric Gibbons in 1928 and represents a knight holding a crusader's sword. The figure stands on a reel of film, whose five spokes represent the five original branches of the academy: actors, directors, technicians, producers, and writers.

For several years the statue had no name, but by the 1930s it had been dubbed *Oscar.* A number of people have been credited with coining the name, but the most likely source rests with the academy's librarian Margaret Herrick. When first shown the trophy, she remarked, "Why, it looks like my uncle Oscar." Actress Bette Davis also claimed credit. According to her story, she commented at the time that the backside of the statuette reminded her of her husband, Harmon Oscar Nelson. Hollywood columnist Sidney Skolsky also nominated himself as the originator of the name. The true source will probably never be known.

Sources

Holden, Anthony. *Behind the Oscar: The Secret History of the Academy Awards.* New York: Simon and Schuster, 1993.

Hunt, Cecil. *Word Origins: The Romance of Language.* New York: Philosophical Library, 1962.

Levy, Emanuel. *And the Winner Is . . . : The History and Politics of the Oscar Awards.* New York: Ungar Publishing Company, 1987.

Shale, Richard. *The Academy Awards Index: The Complete Categorical and Chronological Record.* Westport, CT: Greenwood Press, 1993.

Ostracism. ***To banish or exclude someone from a group as a form of punishment.***

The citizens of Athens jealously guarded their democracy and were willing to go to extreme measures to preserve it. During the sixth century B.C., Athens had fallen under control of the dictators Pisistratus and Hippias and only regained a democratic form of government after Hippias had been driven into exile. In order to prevent such ambitious men from ever again acquiring a strong foothold, the procedure of ostracism was developed.

Once a year a vote was held to single out individuals who, while not guilty of any wrongdoing, were considered too powerful and ambitious to be allowed to continue living in Athens. Each citizen of Athens was permitted to write the name of one person on a broken piece of pottery, the ancient equivalent of scrap paper. These potsherds were known as *ostraka.* The man who had received the most votes was required to leave the city for a period of ten years, during which time any dangerous political objectives he might have been harboring would have subsided or lost their momentum. Unlike exile or banishment, there was no disgrace associated with ostracism. Individuals voted out of the city were allowed to keep all personal property, and their families continued to enjoy their previous social position.

Over the course of the fifth century, ostracism became a tool by which the major political parties attacked the most prominent men from opposing factions. The last ostracism occurred in 417 B.C., when Hyperbolus, a member of a radical pro-war party, sought to remove either Alcibiades or Nicias. Instead, the two men secretly joined forces and engineered the ostracism of Hyperbolus himself. The practice fell out of use after this highly partisan incident. In later years the word *ostracism* became associated with shame and disgrace, which was not an aspect of its original meaning.

Sources

Carver, Craig. *A History of English in Its Own Words.* New York: HarperCollins, 1991.

Mish, Frederick C. *The Merriam-Webster New Book of Word Histories.* Springfield, IL: Merriam-Webster, 1991.

Sacks, David. *Encyclopedia of the Ancient Greek World.* New York: Facts on File, 1995.

Over the top. ***To launch an assault; to undertake a difficult task and succeed.***

This expression refers to one of the most difficult and terrifying aspects of trench warfare, the dominant military strategy during World War I. As both sides hunkered down in trenches, the war ground to a stalemate. The primary duties of the soldiers were to guard and maintain the trenches and to construct new trenches during the night. The war was one of attrition, which would gradually destroy the strength and morale of the opposing soldiers. Snipers took shots at any heads that might appear over the enemy trenches; throwing grenades into trenches was another favorite technique.

Given the cost in human lives, mass charges over the parapet of a trench were relatively rare. However, officer training manuals spoke of mentally preparing the soldiers for the terrifying experience of climbing over the edge of the trench and rushing forth into no man's land. A few minutes before the assault, the men were positioned at the launching points, where they affixed bayonets to the ends of their rifles. They had to maintain absolute silence so the command to attack could be heard. Once the signal was given, the men surged over the top of the trench and tried to plow through the intervening space of 200 to 300 yards (known as no man's land) in order to capture an enemy trench. Second and third waves of soldiers followed within moments of the first group. Barbed wire, land mines, and enemy fire kept casualties high.

These attacks rarely accomplished any objective, but going *over the top* was long perceived as a valid tactic to try to break out of the trench-warfare deadlock. The current connotation of *over the top* almost always implies a daring success.

Sources

Bertrand, Georges, and Oscar Solbert. *Tactics and Duties for Trench Fighting.* New York: G. P. Putnam and Sons, 1918.

Dickson, Paul. *War Slang: Fighting Words and Phrases of Americans from the Civil War to the Gulf War.* New York: Pocket Books, 1994.

Messenger, Charles. *Trench Fighting, 1914–1918.* New York: Ballantine Books, 1972.

P

Pale, beyond the pale.
See Beyond the pale.

Panjandrum, a grand panjandrum. ***A self-important person.***
The eighteenth-century Irish actor Charles Macklin once made the dangerous boast that his memory was so well trained that he could repeat any passage after hearing it once. The playwright Samuel Foote (1720–1777) took the challenge and composed the following nonsense selection:

> So she went into the garden to cut a cabbage leaf to make an apple pie; and at the same time a great she-bear, coming up the street, pops its head into the shop, 'What, no soap?' So he dies, and she very imprudently married the barber; and there were present the picninnies, and the Joblillies, and the Garyulies, and the Grand Panjandrum himself, with the little round button at top, and they all fell to playing the game of catch as catch can, till the gunpowder ran out at the heel of their boots.

Evidently Macklin was so outraged that he refused to attempt to repeat the lines. The passage subsequently became a brain-teaser and a test of memory. The term *grand panjandrum* was adopted by writers to refer to any person possessing a pompous demeanor.

Sources
Funk, Charles E. *Thereby Hangs a Tale.* New York: Harper, 1950.

Simpson, J. A., and E. S. C. Weiner, eds. *The Oxford English Dictionary.* 2d ed. Oxford: Clarendon Press, 1989.

Vizetelly, Frank H. *A Desk-Book of Idioms and Idiomatic Phrases in English Speech and Literature.* Detroit, MI: Gale Research, 1970.

Paper chase. ***A negative term for the deluge of bureaucratic paper work.***
Since the fifteenth century, the English upper class has traditionally sent its sons to boarding schools for their education. One game devised by the boys was called the *paper chase* and closely resembled the classic English fox hunt, in which a fox was chased across the countryside by dozens of eager bloodhounds. In the boarding school version, one boy was given a ten-minute lead to head out into the country with a bag of paper pieces and lay a "scent," or trail, for the other boys to chase. The pursuers followed the paper trail and attempted to overtake the lead boy, who was at liberty to lay false trails. The game was essentially a variation of cross-country running and usually covered eight to ten miles. Paper chases date back to the eighteenth century and are still played in some English schools.

After these boys left school and took positions in business and government, the term began to have a different meaning for them. Observing how operations could grind to a halt under the burdensome weight of paperwork and bureaucratic hoop-jumping, the term *paper chase* seemed perfectly appropriate. The expression entered the mainstream in 1973 with the release of *The Paper Chase,* a popular movie adapted from John Jay Osborne's novel. It dramatized the high-pressure world of students at the Harvard Law School, an intellectual boot camp where students chase after the most coveted of law degrees.

Sources

Arlott, John, ed. *The Oxford Companion to World Sports and Games.* New York: Oxford University Press, 1975.

Cole, Sylvia, and Abraham Lass. *Facts on File Dictionary of Twentieth-Century Allusions: From Abbott and Costello to Ziegfeld Girls.* New York: Facts on File, 1991.

Pariah. ***A social outcast.***

There are over 3,000 castes in India, divided into four major classifications. At the top of the hierarchy are the brahmans (priests and scholars), followed by the kshatriyas (rulers and warriors), then the vaishyas (merchants and farmers). At the bottom are the sudras (laborers, servant, and slaves), whose members are called untouchables, or *pariahs.* A primary tenet of the caste system is that contact with someone in the untouchable class pollutes anyone in a higher caste. Physical encounters or social discourse with a pariah are therefore strictly forbidden.

Attempts have been made in the twentieth century to modify the ancient caste system. Mahatma Gandhi renamed the untouchables *harijans,* meaning "children of God." The legal system has been modified to remove outright discrimination against this class of people, but embedded social customs cannot be easily changed by the stroke of a pen.

During the colonial era many of the British who had settled in India had servants from the pariah caste. This close association may have facilitated the incorporation of the word into the English language, and it was in common usage by the eighteenth century.

Sources

Kolenda, Pauline. *Caste in Contemporary India: Beyond Organic Solidarity.* Menlo Park, CA: Benjamin Cummings Publishing Company, 1978.

McHenry, Robert, ed. *The New Encyclopedia Britannica.* 15th ed. Chicago: Encyclopedia Britannica, 1992.

Rice, Stanley. *Hindu Customs and Their Origins.* London: G. Allen and Unwin, 1937.

Walker, Benjamin. *The Hindu World: An Encyclopedic Survey of Hinduism.* New York: Praeger, 1968.

Parthian shot. ***A parting shot, delivered so as to leave one's opponent little opportunity to respond.***

Parthia was a region between the Euphrates River, the Oxus River, and the Caspian Sea. The inhabitants were of Persian descent but were subjected to a succession of foreign invasions from Assyria, Media, and Macedonia. A nomadic people, their skill with horses was their greatest strength in battle. When outnumbered by a superior force, the Parthians did not attempt to win by outright confrontation but would encircle the hostile army and rapidly fire a shower of arrows. As quickly as they appeared, they would retreat, continuing to fire arrows behind them as they fled.

This tactic was novel for the ancient world and worked well for the Parthians for a while, but ultimately they could not withstand the sheer numbers of the invading armies.

Sources

Evans, Ivor H., ed. *Brewer's Dictionary of Phrase and Fable.* 14th ed. New York: Harper and Row, 1989.

Hornblower, Simon, and Antony Spawforth, eds. *The Oxford Classical Dictionary.* 3d ed. Oxford: Oxford University Press, 1996.

Stimpson, George. *A Book about a Thousand Things.* New York: Harper and Brothers, 1946.

Pasquinade. ***A witty satire, usually posted in a public place.***

In 1501 an ancient statue was unearthed by Italian citizens, who were eager to celebrate their classical heritage from the golden days of the Roman Empire. The statue had been badly damaged, and little remained other than a fine torso. Nevertheless the torso was proudly displayed outside the palace of Cardinal Caraffa, near the Piazza Navona in Rome. Under the cardinal's patronage, it became an annual custom to "restore" the statue on Saint Mark's day, usually by dressing it to represent some great historical or mythological person. The sight of a torso wrapped in an extravagant costume complete with feathers and flowers became a source of amusement, and people began to post comical messages on the statue. The lampoons ranged in content from ecclesiastical commentary to social satire. Eventually the statue became a year-round site for posted commentary.

By 1509 the statue was being called Pasquino, probably because that was the name of a caustic old man who lived just opposite the statue. This Pasquino was said to be a schoolteacher, although later traditions made him a barber or a shoemaker. The word *pasquinade* spread to other countries and referred generally to anonymous, satirical lampoons posted in a public place.

Sources

Funk, Charles E. *Thereby Hangs a Tale.* New York: Harper, 1950.

Hendrickson, Robert. *The Facts on File Encyclopedia of Word and Phrase Origins.* New York: Facts on File, 1987.

Simpson, J. A., and E. S. C. Weiner, eds. *The Oxford English Dictionary.* 2d ed. Oxford: Clarendon Press, 1989.

Pasteurization. ***To subject a liquid to heat in order to kill all or part of the bacteria it contains.***

Although *pasteurization* is usually associated with making milk safe to drink, Louis Pasteur (1822–1895) first developed his process for use with the French national beverage, wine. For centuries scientists had been battling with the concept of spontaneous generation, the belief that living creatures could arise from nonliving matter. Before microscopes enabled people to see tiny microorganisms, scientists had no idea how living matter such as insects could suddenly appear in a bin of sealed flour. As early as the fourth century B.C., Aristotle endorsed the theory of spontaneous generation. This concept was generally accepted until the seventeenth century, and for two hundred years thereafter, scientists attempted to prove or disprove the postulate.

Pasteur, a chemist and microbiologist, believed in the existence of creatures too small to be seen even through a microscope. In 1861 he proved that exposing meat to sustained heat killed any minute bacteria the meat contained, thereby preventing the decay of the meat after it had been sealed in an airtight container. He was then approached by representatives of the wine industry, which had recently been embarrassed by the widespread spoilage of French wines. Costly bottles of wine were turning into vinegar before they were even uncorked, causing severe economic loss and damaging the reputation of the wineries. After examining the wine, Pasteur discovered minute yeast cells that were causing the wine to ferment and spoil. He recommended gently heating the wine to 120 degrees, which should kill the yeast and allow the wine to age properly. Although some wine makers were appalled at the thought of subjecting their precious vintages to such treatment, it solved the problem with no noticeable effect on the wine.

After the success of this enterprise, Pasteur devised a modified technique for beer, milk, and other beverages that were being bottled for public consumption. He went on to other avenues of microscopic research, inventing a vaccine for anthrax, a treatment for rabies, and procedures for the sterilization of surgical equipment. He was elected to the Académie Française in 1881, and in 1883 the Pasteur Institute was established. By the time of his death in 1895 he was one of the most highly honored scientists in history.

Sources

Dubos, Rene J. *Louis Pasteur: Free Lance of Science.* New York: Scribner's, 1976.

Gillispie, Charles Coulson, ed. *Dictionary of Scientific Biography.* New York: Scribner's, 1970.

Nicolle, Jacques. *Louis Pasteur: The Story of His Major Discoveries.* New York: Basic Books, 1961.

Travers, Bridget, and Jeffrey Muhr, eds. *World of Scientific Discovery.* Detroit, MI: Gale Research, 1994.

Pay the piper. ***To pay for services rendered.*** The phrase derives from the story of the Pied Piper of Hamelin. German legend claims that during the rat plague of 1284 a man wearing strange, multicolored clothes appeared in the town of Hamelin and offered to drive out the town's rats. The town fathers agreed, and the man began playing music on a pipe. The rats came swarming out to follow the piper into a river, where they were drowned. When he returned to collect his fee, the villagers refused to pay. The Pied Piper began to play again, but this time it was the children of the village who were coaxed out and followed him out of town. The piper led the children to Kippenberg Hill, where they vanished.

This tale may have responded to the numerous stories of missing children in medieval Germany, or to the claim that there was a mass migration of young men to the east at this time. Others have linked the Pied Piper to Nicholas of Cologne, a boy who led an estimated 7,000 German youths in a Children's Crusade. Proponents hoped that the children could convert the Muslims by a demonstration of love and innocence, since the use of force had failed so often in the past. The religious fervor generated by the Crusade encouraged thousands of children to leave home and follow the charismatic young Nicolas. After crossing the Alps into Italy, the children split up into groups and were subsequently exploited by unscrupulous merchants. Many of them were sold into slavery, and very few ever found their way home.

Sources

McHenry, Robert, ed. *The New Encyclopedia Britannica.* 15th ed. Chicago: Encyclopedia Britannica, 1992.

Mercatante, Anthony S. *Facts on File Encyclopedia of World Mythology and Legend.* New York: Facts on File, 1988.

Peach Melba. ***Vanilla ice cream, topped with peaches and raspberry.***

The great French chef George Auguste Escoffier was a tremendous fan of Dame Nellie Melba (1861–1931), the most popular soprano of her day (see *Melba toast*). In 1892 Dame Melba delivered a magnificent portrayal of Elsa in Wagner's *Lohengrin,* and Escoffier wished to commemorate her performance. In one scene, Lohengrin, a knight of the Holy Grail, arrives to meet his lover Elsa in a boat pulled by a swan, so Escoffier used this scene as the inspiration for his culinary masterpiece. He created an ice sculpture of the swan, coated the wings with iced sugar, and filled the space in between with vanilla ice cream, with peaches and raspberry sauce ladled on top. Dame Melba was impressed, although she would have doubtless preferred to be remembered for her fine voice rather than for this dessert.

Sources

Hendrickson, Robert. *Dictionary of Eponyms: Names That Became Words.* New York: Stein and Day, 1985.

McHenry, Robert, ed. *The New Encyclopedia Britannica.* 15th ed. Chicago: Encyclopedia Britannica, 1992.

Panati, Charles. *Panati's Extraordinary Origins of Everyday Things.* New York: Harper and Row, 1987.

Peeping Tom. ***A voyeur; a person who derives sexual pleasure from secretly observing others.***

Peeping Tom is a seventeenth-century embellishment to the medieval legend of Lady Godiva. There is little factual information about Lady Godiva, but it is known that by the year 1040 she was married to Leofric, earl of Mercia. She and her husband founded the monastery at Coventry, and she was considered a woman of sincere religious devotion and great beauty. The earliest surviving record of Lady Godiva's story is from the writings of Roger of Wendover (d. 1236). He claimed that Lady Godiva had frequently pleaded with her husband to reduce the heavy taxes imposed on the people of Coventry. In exasperation the earl replied that he would do so only if she rode naked through the streets of the town. Lady Godiva took her husband at his word and made her famous ride, with her long hair covering most of her body. A fourteenth-century version added that as a result of the ride, the earl lifted all taxes on the town except those on horses. An even later chronicle reported that all the townspeople kept indoors during the ride as a sign of respect for Lady Godiva. Only the foolhardy Peeping Tom disobeyed and spied on the lady. Most accounts say that he was struck blind because of his misdeed.

Sources

Hazlitt, William Carew. *Faiths and Folklore of the British Isles.* New York: B. Blom, 1965.
Stephen, Leslie, and Sidney Lee, eds. *The Dictionary of National Biography.* London: Oxford University Press, 1921.
Stimpson, George. *A Book about a Thousand Things.* New York: Harper and Brothers, 1946.

Pharisee. ***A self-righteous hypocrite.***

The Pharisees were members of a Jewish religious movement that flourished around 160 B.C. to A.D. 70. Unlike some of the more orthodox Jewish sects, the Pharisees believed that the law God gave to Moses was twofold. There was the traditional written law, but also a law of reason that unfolds over time. Man must use reason, wisdom, and experience learned over time to discern the unwritten law and apply it to contemporary problems. Believing that too much power was in the hands of a small class of Temple priests, the Pharisees sought to democratize the Jewish religion. They wanted to de-emphasize the rigid procedures and bloody sacrifices of the Temple and devote greater reliance to prayer and the study of God's law.

Although to the modern observer the Pharisees seemed to represent a remarkably liberated and humanistic movement, their name became synonymous with sanctimonious bigotry. The explanation lies in the Pharisees' opposition to Jesus. Many of the Pharisees denounced Jesus for consorting with prostitutes and sinners, while others criticized the early Christians for breaking with traditional Hebrew dietary laws and circumcision. The New Testament is richly laden with diatribes against the Pharisees, such as that in Matthew 23: 27: "Woe to you, scribes and Pharisees, hypocrites! For you are like the white-washed tombs, which on the outside look beautiful, but inside they are filled with the bones of the dead and of all kinds of filth. So you also on the outside look righteous to others, but inside you are full of hypocrisy and lawlessness."

Sources

Bromiley, Geoffrey W., ed. *The International Standard Bible Encyclopedia.* Grand Rapids, MI: W. B. Eerdmans, 1988.
Buttrick, George Arther. *The Interpreter's Dictionary of the Bible.* New York: Abingdon Press, 1962.
McHenry, Robert, ed. *The New Encyclopedia Britannica.* 15th ed. Chicago: Encyclopedia Britannica, 1992.
Metzger, Bruce M., and Michael D. Coogan, eds. *The Oxford Companion to the Bible.* New York: Oxford University Press, 1993.
Stimpson, George. *A Book about the Bible.* New York: Harper and Brothers, 1945.

Philadelphia lawyer. ***A lawyer with great ability, especially one who is proficient in exploiting legal technicalities.***

When John Peter Zenger (1697–1746) launched a barrage of inflammatory articles condemning William Cosby, the colonial governor of New York, he set into motion one of the greatest free speech cases in history. Zenger was an immigrant from Germany and had founded the *New York Weekly Journal.* After a year-long attack on the governor through the magazine, Crosby brought charges of seditious libel against Zenger in 1743. Zenger had initially obtained very good lawyers, but when they became too ardent in the defense of their client during pretrial hearings, they were disbarred. A well-meaning but inexperienced lawyer was appointed by the court to serve as Zenger's counsel, and his chances for acquittal looked bleak. On the day of the trial, observers were shocked when Andrew Hamilton of Philadelphia rose from the audience and introduced himself as Zenger's new counsel. Hamilton was rumored to be the finest lawyer in the colonies, and Zenger eagerly accepted his help.

Hamilton conceded that Zenger was the author of the offensive pieces, but he claimed that since the articles were true, his client could not be found guilty for simply printing the truth. Despite the judge's instructions that the articles were inherently libelous and that if Zenger had written them, he should be convicted, the jury refused to return a guilty verdict. Zenger was freed, and a new standard was set for the principle of free speech.

Hamilton's skillful engineering of the trial gave rise to the expression *Philadelphia lawyer* as a term for an unusually keen attorney. The expression was in wide use by the end of the eighteenth century, when it was said that three Philadelphia lawyers were a match for the devil.

Sources

Bessette, Joseph M. *American Justice.* Pasadena, CA: Salem Press, 1996.

Evans, Ivor H., ed. *Brewer's Dictionary of Phrase and Fable.* 14th ed. New York: Harper and Row, 1989.

Levy, Leonard W. *Emergence of a Free Press.* New York: Oxford University Press, 1985.

Rutherford, Livingston. *John Peter Zenger: His Press, His Trial, and a Bibliography of Zenger Imprints.* New York: Arno, 1970.

Simpson, J. A., and E. S. C. Weiner, eds. *The Oxford English Dictionary.* 2d ed. Oxford: Clarendon Press, 1989.

Philip sober, to appeal from Philip drunk to Philip sober. *To delay a difficult task until a more favorable time.*

The Macedonian king Philip II (d. 336 B.C.) is best remembered as the father of Alexander the Great, although in his own time he was known as a brilliant diplomat and warrior. Philip turned the backward Greek province of Macedonia into the mightiest kingdom in the Mediterranean world by implementing military reforms and by subjugating or creating alliances with all of his Greek neighbors. Using marriage as a diplomatic weapon, Philip married a total of seven well-connected women from various noble families, resulting in a consolidation of his control over much of the Mediterranean.

Ancient historians depict Philip II as a shrewd, hard-drinking man who was famous for his monumental rages. One story involved a Macedonian noblewoman who had turned to the king seeking justice for her husband. Philip was in a drunken, ill-tempered mood and refused to grant her request, prompting her to proclaim angrily, "I shall appeal this judgment!" The inebriated king roared in reply, "Appeal! And to whom shall you appeal?" The woman declared, "To Philip sober!" According to the historian Valerius Maximus, she won her case.

Sources

Hendrickson, Robert. *Facts on File Encyclopedia of Word and Phrase Origins.* New York: Facts on File, 1987.

Sacks, David. *Encyclopedia of the Ancient Greek World.* New York: Facts on File, 1995.

Philippics. *A speech that sharply criticizes an opposing viewpoint.*

Demosthenes (384–322 B.C.) was a great Athenian orator, living at a time when Greece was waning as Macedonia to the north was waxing. Although King Philip of Macedonia was gradually annexing Greek cities into his kingdom, many Greeks failed to recognize the threat that this posed to their independence. Demosthenes was the fiercest critic of Macedonian ambitions. Beginning in 351 B.C. he delivered a series of three *Philippics,* or speeches that denounced Philip in scathing terms and attempted to rouse Athenian resistance. These speeches were not able to halt the tide of Macedonian conquests in Asia and the Mediterranean. In 322 the Macedonian regent Antipater vowed to silence the voice that had been a thorn in the side of his kingdom's ambitions. He sent messengers to seize Demosthenes, but the great orator escaped to the island of Calauria and committed suicide to avoid capture.

Today, the word *philippic* refers to any speech that excoriates the opposition in harsh, unflinching language.

Sources

Adams, Charles Darwin. *Demosthenes and His Influence.* New York: Cooper Square Publishers, 1963.

Hornblower, Simon, and Antony Spawforth, eds. *The Oxford Classical Dictionary.* 3d ed. Oxford: Oxford University Press, 1996.

Sacks, David. *Encyclopedia of the Ancient Greek World.* New York: Facts on File, 1995.

Safire, William. *Safire's Political Dictionary.* New York: Random House, 1978.

Philistine. ***An ignorant, uncultured individual.***

The Philistines were a people of Aegean origin who arrived in the coastal areas of Palestine in the twelfth century B.C. They came into conflict with the Hebrews, who were moving into the area at approximately the same time. The territorial rivalry between the Jews and the Philistines was well documented in the Old Testament, especially in the stories of Samson, Saul, and David, each of whom conquered Philistine enemies. Jewish hostility extended to Philistine culture as well, and the Philistines were condemned as ignorant, unsophisticated pagans. The Bible contains more than 250 references to the Philistines, most of which are unfavorable. By the seventeenth century, the word *philistine* had evolved to refer to any group considered an enemy. It eventually became associated with ignorant, uninformed, and complacent traits.

The blackened reputation of the Philistines is a good example of the power of the written word, which can continue to shape attitudes in the absence of any countervailing record. According to archaeologists, the Philistines were actually skilled architects and metalworkers and created some of the most beautiful pottery in the ancient world. They also played an important and influential role in the commercial and political organization of the Near East.

Sources

Bromiley, Geoffrey W., ed. *The International Standard Bible Encyclopedia.* Grand Rapids, MI: W. B. Eerdmans, 1988.

Buttrick, George Arther. *The Interpreter's Dictionary of the Bible.* New York: Abingdon Press, 1962.

Meyers, Eric. *The Oxford Encyclopedia of Archaeology in the Near East.* New York: Oxford University Press, 1997.

Roth, Cecil E., ed. *Encyclopedia Judaica.* New York: Macmillan, 1971.

Sasson, Jack M. *Civilizations of the Ancient Near East.* New York: Scribner's, 1995.

Picayune. ***Something of little value or importance; petty.***

During the Revolutionary War, the Continental Congress began to issue American money. However, continental currency was very vulnerable to inflation, and many people refused to accept it, preferring to use British, Spanish, or French coins. In 1792 Congress prohibited the use of foreign coins as legal tender, with the exception of Spanish money. Because of the substantial commerce with the Spanish territories that bordered the United States, it was impractical to outlaw the use of Spanish money. A *picayune* was a small Spanish coin that was equivalent to the American nickel. It circulated in the southern United States until 1857, when Spanish money was no longer considered legal tender.

The word *picayune* came to mean anything that was small or of trifling value.

Sources

Breen, Walter H. *Walter Breen's Complete Encyclopedia of U.S. and Colonial Coins.* Garden City, NJ: Doubleday, 1988.

Evans, Ivor H., ed. *Brewer's Dictionary of Phrase and Fable.* 14th ed. New York: Harper and Row, 1989.

Mish, Frederick C. *The Merriam-Webster New Book of Word Histories.* Springfield, IL: Merriam-Webster, 1991.

Simpson, J. A., and E. S. C. Weiner, eds. *The Oxford English Dictionary.* 2d ed. Oxford: Clarendon Press, 1989.

Pillar to post, to wander from pillar to post. ***To wander back and forth, accomplishing little.***

The earliest form of tennis was a thirteenth-century French game called *jeu de paume* (game of the palm), which had spread to Italy and England by the fourteenth century. The fittings on the court were known as the pillar and the post. The repetitive movements of the players between these two points gave rise to the expression *from pillar to post* (or, as it was first coined, *from post to pillar*). The earliest recorded use of the expression was in 1420: "Thus fro poost to pylour was he made to daunce."

Sources

Arlott, John, ed. *The Oxford Companion to World Sports and Games.* New York: Oxford University Press, 1975.

Holt, Alfred H. *Phrase and Word Origins: A Study of Familiar Expressions.* New York: Dover Publications, 1961.

Simpson, J. A., and E. S. C. Weiner, eds. *The Oxford English Dictionary.* 2d ed. Oxford: Clarendon Press, 1989.

Pink triangles. ***A symbol of solidarity within the homosexual community.***

Under Adolf Hitler's Third Reich (1933–1945), the German government adopted virulent policies of discrimination toward selected groups of people, including homosexuals. Nazi ideology favored a strong division between male and female roles, and homosexuals seemed to blur this distinction. Moreover, in a society that equated population growth with military strength, homosexuals were perceived as a threat to German survival and morality.

When Nazi soldiers began herding "undesirables" into concentration camps at the start of World War II, homosexuals were among the groups targeted. Within the camps prisoners were forced to wear badges that distinguished their particular offense. Homosexuals wore pink triangles, Jews wore the yellow star of David, communists wore red badges, green was for criminals, violet for Jehovah's Witnesses, and brown for gypsies. It is estimated that between 10,000 and 25,000 homosexuals were sent to the concentration camps, but an accurate count is no longer possible.

In the early 1970s a gay pride movement began to gather momentum in the United States. The pink triangle was adopted by activists as a symbol of solidarity and to commemorate the homosexuals who perished in the Nazi concentration camps. The pink triangle has since become a worldwide emblem of the gay liberation movement.

Sources

Dynes, Wayne R., ed. *Encyclopedia of Homosexuality.* New York: Garland Publishing, 1990.

Plant, Richard. *The Pink Triangle: The Nazi War Against Homosexuals.* New York: Henry Holt, 1986.

Rector, Frank. *The Nazi Extermination of Homosexuals.* New York: Stein and Day, 1981.

Zentner, Christian, and Friedemann Budurftig, eds. *Encyclopedia of the Third Reich.* New York: Macmillan, 1991.

Pinkerton. ***A detective.***

Allan Pinkerton (1819–1884) had never planned to be a detective, and indeed, most of his early life was guided by unexpected twists. He was born in Glasgow, Scotland, into a working-class family. When Allan was 10, his father became crippled, and the boy had to quit school to work as an apprentice to a cooper. When he was 23, he became involved in the Chartist organization, a working-class movement that demanded social and economic reforms. Fearing arrest because of his activism, he fled to the United States, settled near Chicago, and opened his own cooper shop. One day while he was making hoops for his barrels on a remote island in the Fox River, he chanced to stumble on evidence of a counterfeiting ring. He gathered a party together and succeeded in capturing the criminals.

So began Pinkerton's long career in detection. He was soon hired by the Chicago police department to be its one and only detective. He then went into business for himself, working mostly for the railroads. He gained a national reputation after he solved a number of sensational railway robberies. Before the Civil War, while working for the Philadelphia, Wilmington and Baltimore Railroad, he learned of an assassination plot on Abraham Lincoln's life. The conspirators planned to shoot the recently elected Lincoln as he traveled from Baltimore to the inauguration ceremony in Washington, D.C. With the support of the president's advisors, Pinkerton succeeded in persuading Lincoln to alter his plans and accept protection.

During much of the war, Pinkerton headed the Union's counterintelligence program, and at its conclusion, he resumed control of his now-famous Pinkerton National Detective Agency. By the 1890s the word *Pinkerton* was being used as a synonym for detective. The agency's logo, "the eye that never sleeps," gave rise to the term *private eye.* After Pinkerton's death in 1884, his sons took over the business. The agency is still active today.

Sources
Hendrickson, Robert. *Dictionary of Eponyms: Names That Became Words.* New York: Stein and Day, 1985.
Johnson, Allen, and Dumas Malone, eds. *Dictionary of American Biography.* New York: Scribner's, 1964.
Rowan, Richard Wilmer. *The Pinkertons: A Detective Dynasty.* Boston: Little, Brown, and Company, 1931.

Play in Peoria, will it play in Peoria? ***To question whether mainstream Americans will accept an innovative position or product.***
Peoria is a town of about 115,000 in central Illinois and is the transportation hub for the region's livestock, produce, and coal. It has a reputation for being the quintessential middle American town, representing old-fashioned values and traditions.

The phrase *play in Peoria* comes from the vaudeville circuit, as performers discussed how their acts would be received in small towns. Risqué performances could find an audience in large cities, but shows destined for the hinterland might need to be altered. In that context, Peoria was cited as the typical middle American town, probably for its alliterative value, since there is no evidence that vaudeville acts ever traveled to Peoria specifically to try out their shows.

Politicians and campaign consultants, isolated in Washington D.C., and other large cities from their ordinary constituents, have employed the concept of *playing in Peoria* as a reminder of the need to appeal to middle American values.

Sources
Safire, William. *Safire's Political Dictionary.* New York: Random House, 1978.
Webber, Elizabeth. *Grand Allusions.* Washington, DC: Farragut Publishing Company, 1990.

Plimsoll mark. ***A line drawn on the hull of a ship to indicate the maximum load a ship can safely carry; officially known as the International Load Line.***
Samuel Plimsoll (1824–1898) served in the British Parliament and was known as a champion of the common sailor. The second half of the nineteenth century was an era of peace and prosperity in which trade flourished. Businessmen resisted government interference in their operations, and the government complied by permitting a great deal of freedom to commercial concerns. To maximize profits, merchants tried to load the ships with as much cargo as possible, greatly increasing the likelihood of a wreck. Ships could be fully insured, so even if the ship sank and all the sailors were drowned, the merchants could still turn a healthy profit.

Samuel Plimsoll was determined to improve the working conditions for sailors. In 1873 he published a book called *Our Seamen: An Appeal,* which detailed the deadly scenario that resulted when merchants gambled with their employees' lives. A map was published the same year that illustrated the shocking number of shipwrecks along the British coast. As a result of Plimsoll's efforts, a commission was appointed to investigate the conditions of the shipping industry, and in 1876 use of *Plimsoll lines* was declared mandatory on British ships. The markings appeared on the hull of ships, with differing lines to indicate the maximum safe loads for ocean service, coastal service, and freshwater travel. If the Plimsoll line slipped below the surface of the water, the ship was not permitted to leave port. In 1930 54 nations signed a treaty to adopt the Plimsoll mark.

Sources
Jeans, Peter D. *Ship to Shore: A Dictionary of Everyday Words and Phrases Derived from the Sea.* Santa Barbara, CA: ABC-CLIO, 1993.
Masters, David. *The Plimsoll Mark.* London: Cassell, 1955.
Plimsoll, Samuel. *Our Seamen: An Appeal.* London: Virtue and Co., 1873.
Stimpson, George. *A Book about a Thousand Things.* New York: Harper and Brothers, 1946.

Pompadour. ***A woman's hairstyle in which the hair is swept away from the forehead and arranged in large curls.***
Madame de Pompadour, born Jeanne-Antoinette Poisson (1721–1764), was the most famous royal mistress of the eighteenth century. Although she was born into a poor family, her mother's wealthy lover gave her

the means to acquire an outstanding education. By the time she was of marriageable age she was a beautiful, intelligent, and charming companion, and she managed to marry a member of the nobility. Three years later she caught the eye of Louis XV of France. After obtaining a legal separation from her husband, she moved to Versailles and became mistress to the king. Within a few years he had bestowed on her the title of duchess of Pompadour.

For the next 20 years Madame de Pompadour played a major role in the royal court. She was the king's private secretary and advisor. She also set the fashion at court, in everything from furnishings to apparel, but her coiffure was her most lasting contribution to style. The *pompadour* featured large, loose curls around the face but swept high off the forehead. The style was copied by men as well as women and lasted well into the next century.

Sources

Hendrickson, Robert. *Dictionary of Eponyms: Names That Became Words.* New York: Stein and Day, 1985.

McHenry, Robert, ed. *The New Encyclopedia Britannica.* 15th ed. Chicago: Encyclopedia Britannica, 1992.

Mitford, Nancy. *Madame de Pompadour.* New York: Random House, 1954.

Pony Express. *Very fast delivery service.*

Although the Pony Express was only in business for 18 months, it has assumed a significant place in American legend and imagination. It was founded in April 1860 by the freighting firm of Russell, Majors, and Waddell, which promised to deliver mail from Missouri to California in ten days. This was a marked improvement over the three-week average of their competitor, the Overland Mail Company. The federal government had granted a lucrative contract to the Overland Mail Company, and Russell, Majors, and Waddell hoped to steal it away by demonstrating their superior service.

Four hundred fast horses were purchased and 80 riders hired, both selected for their speed and stamina. Riders for the Pony Express were usually lean teenage boys who were willing to ride day and night in any sort of weather. Way stations were established approximately every 30 miles, and riders exchanged horses at each station. Letters were carried in specially designed pouches slung over the saddle, with only the rider's weight to hold the bag in place. This meant that the bag could be easily shifted from one horse to another, and changing horses could be accomplished in around two minutes. Most riders carried a pair of pistols and a knife. Despite the danger of attack, only one rider was killed by Indians.

Businesses were pleased with the speed of the Pony Express, although the service was expensive. The initial fee was $5 per letter, which translates to about $75 today. The price proved to be prohibitive and was dropped to $1 per one-ounce letter. When the transcontinental telegraph began operation in October 1861, the Pony Express was doomed, and the operation closed just a few days later. Russell, Majors, and Waddell lost over $100,000 in the venture and were forced to declare bankruptcy the following year.

Sources

Adams, J. T. *Dictionary of American History.* New York: Scribner's, 1976.

Bloss, Roy S. *Pony Express: The Great Gamble.* Berkeley, CA: Howell-North, 1959.

Chapman, Arthur. *The Pony Express: The Record of a Romantic Adventure in Business.* New York: Cooper Square, 1971.

Philips, Charles, and Alan Axelrod, eds. *Encyclopedia of the American West.* New York: Simon and Schuster, 1996.

Pope Joan. *A card game in which the eight of diamonds is removed.*

Contemporary scholars deny that a female pope ever existed, but in the Middle Ages it was widely believed that a woman was elected to the papacy in the ninth century under the name Pope John VIII. According to legend, Joan was born in Germany to English parents. Using the name Johannes Anglicus she disguised herself as a man and traveled to Rome and Athens to study scripture. After the death of Pope Leo she was chosen to be pope based on her wisdom and knowledge of the Bible. She held the papacy for two years. Impregnated by a servant, she was seized with labor pains during a ceremonial procession, and her deception was revealed. She died in childbirth.

The tenacious legend entered the medieval historical record in Thomas de Elmham's official list of the popes, in which it is written: "A.D. 855, Joannes. This doesn't count; she was a woman." A rhyme from seventeenth-century England reflected the usefulness of the legend in discrediting the papacy and catering to anti-Catholic sentiments:

> A woman Pope, as history doth tell
> In high procession, she in labor fell
> And was delivered of a bastard son;
> Thence, Rome some call the whore
> of Babylon.

Tales of Pope Joan flourished in Protestant nations during the Reformation, and most of them had a scandalous and salacious flavor. Thus it has been argued that the perpetuation of the Pope Joan story was motivated by the anti-Catholicism of the Reformation.

Sources

Evans, Ivor H., ed. *Brewer's Dictionary of Phrase and Fable.* 14th ed. New York: Harper and Row, 1989.

Metford, J. C. J. *The Dictionary of Christian Lore and Legend.* London: Thames and Hudson, 1983.

Walker, Barbara G. *The Women's Encyclopedia of Myths and Secrets.* San Francisco: Harper and Row, 1983.

Pork-barrel politics. ***The practice of allocating government funding to favored constituencies, particularly when the projects are only marginally important or completely pointless.***

The expression *pork barrel* derives from the Old South, when plantation slaves gathered at the pork barrel, where their weekly ration of meat was stored. By the second half of the nineteenth century, *pork* had come to mean government funds doled out to eager congressional districts. An issue of the 1879 *Congressional Record* reported that "St. Louis is going to have some of the 'pork' indirectly; but it will not do any good." Early references to pork and pork-barrel funding do not have the negative connotation that the terms later acquired.

In the late twentieth century, Senator Robert Byrd from West Virginia has frequently been cited as an egregious example of pork-barrel politics. During the five years he served as chairman of the Senate Appropriations Committee, he sent more than $1 billion of federal funding to his home state by transferring pieces of federal agencies to West Virginia. Important offices of the FBI, the CIA, the Treasury Department, and the Bureau of Alcohol, Tobacco, and Firearms were all relocated to West Virginia. At Senator Byrd's request, even the Coast Guard had its national computer operations moved to the landlocked state. Such flagrant abuses of dispensing government money have permanently made *pork-barrel politics* a derogatory expression.

Sources

Comfort, N. A. *Brewer's Politics: A Phrase and Fable Dictionary.* London: Cassell, 1993.

Patterson, Eugene, ed. *Congressional Quarterly's Guide to Congress.* Washington, DC: Congressional Quarterly, 1982.

Safire, William. *Safire's Political Dictionary.* New York: Random House, 1978.

Posh. ***Stylish, classy, first-rate.***

The origin of this word is uncertain, but it has been ascribed to the very elegant P&O (Peninsular and Oriental) steamship line. In the days when intercontinental travel could consume weeks or months, the well-to-do transformed these journeys from a tedious burden into a luxury. Oceangoing liners had all the amenities of a first-class hotel. Well-dressed patrons dined in tasteful, chandelier-decked rooms while orchestras played soft music in the background. Although the public areas bespoke of luxury, the quality of private accommodations varied widely. Some of the cabins had only the basic amenities: a bed, table, and tiny closet. Others were larger, furnished with expensive oriental rugs and antique furniture and offering a window.

According to one source, on voyages between England and India, wealthy travelers requested cabins that were *P*ort *O*utward, *S*tarboard *H*omeward. This meant that on the outgoing journey their cabins would be located on the port side of the ship, which took advantage of the cooler prevailing winds. On the return journey, booking a cabin on the starboard side gave access to those same breezes. Thus, the acronym *posh* was used to describe the travelers who were savvy and wealthy enough to afford such arrangements.

Etymologists have not confirmed this explanation for the word. The archivist of the P&O has observed that return tickets were usually not issued at the time that outward-bound tickets were purchased. Also, it was not the practice of the P&O to assign cabin numbers based on port and starboard designations. Although *The Oxford English Dictionary* and *Webster's Dictionary* have refused to accept the acronymic derivation, some etymologists are still working to prove the connection.

Sources

Chowdharay-Best, G. "Notes," *Mariner's Mirror* 57 (1971): 91–92.

Jeans, Peter D. *Ship to Shore: A Dictionary of Everyday Words and Phrases Derived from the Sea.* Santa Barbara, CA: ABC-CLIO, 1993.

Mish, Frederick C. *The Merriam-Webster New Book of Word Histories.* Springfield, IL: Merriam-Webster, 1991.

Simpson, J. A., and E. S. C. Weiner, eds. *The Oxford English Dictionary.* 2d ed. Oxford: Clarendon Press, 1989.

Potemkin village. ***An attractive facade that disguises social and economic decay.***

Prince Grigory Potemkin (1739–1791) was Catherine the Great's lover and most trusted advisor. Their partnership worked well because they shared the same ambitious vision for Russia. They wanted to attract foreign trade, extend agriculture, increase manufacturing capabilities, build towns, create universities, and enlarge the physical boundaries of Russia. Catherine relied on the prince to implement this daunting agenda.

Potemkin took a personal interest in making the Ukrainian steppes a productive part of the empire, and he embarked on a monumental scheme to colonize the region. When Catherine toured the region in 1787, Potemkin had to disguise his slow progress. Hastily planted crops covered areas that had previously been wasteland. Enormous sums of money were expended to create grand spectacles for Catherine's entertainment. There were military reviews featuring thousands of troops fitted out in extravagant uniforms and sumptuous banquets in newly erected buildings. When Catherine visited one of the Black Sea ports, Potemkin created a battalion of "Amazons"—a hundred Greek women dressed in gold-trimmed military uniforms with spangles, turbans, and ostrich feathers. Catherine was delighted.

Potemkin's enemies at the Russian court circulated rumors to discredit him, including the apocryphal tale that the prince had constructed entire villages out of cardboard and paste to give Catherine the impression that he had fully colonized the region with prosperous, happy peasants. According to the story, peasants, wearing their best clothing, were imported into the sham villages to wave gaily at Catherine as her carriage rolled past. The peasants would then be carted to the next sham village in time to repeat the performance.

Catherine herself was unmoved by the slanderous stories told about her favorite advisor. Despite her insulated, regal life, she would never have been fooled by a *Potemkin village*. She seems to have treated the rumors in the same way she handled other disagreeable aspects of life: she ignored them.

Sources

Alexander, John T. *Catherine the Great: Life and Legend.* New York: Oxford University Press, 1989.

Kochan, Miriam. *Life in Russia under Catherine the Great.* London: Batsford, 1969.

McHenry, Robert, ed. *The New Encyclopedia Britannica.* 15th ed. Chicago: Encyclopedia Britannica, 1992.

Mish, Frederick C. *The Merriam-Webster New Book of Word Histories.* Springfield, IL: Merriam-Webster, 1991.

Potter's field. ***A cemetery in which paupers and unclaimed bodies are buried.***
According to the Gospel of Matthew (27: 7), after Judas betrayed Jesus for thirty pieces of silver, he was so racked with guilt that he returned the coins and hanged himself. The priests of the temple thought it bad luck to return blood money to the treasury, so they purchased a piece of ground outside of Jerusalem to be used for the burial of paupers and the unidentified dead. It was known as *potter's field* because local potters had obtained their clay from this field. Towns and cities frequently establish *potter's fields* for families who cannot afford the cost of burial and for unidentified bodies.

Sources

Achtemeier, Paul J. *Harper's Bible Dictionary.* San Francisco: Harper and Row, 1985.

Bromiley, Geoffrey W., ed. *The International Standard Bible Encyclopedia.* Grand Rapids, MI: W. B. Eerdmans, 1988.

Stimpson, George. *A Book about the Bible.* New York: Harper and Brothers, 1945.

Praetorian guard. ***An elite military unit that serves, and sometimes manipulates, a government.***
During military campaigns, it was often the practice of Roman generals to have a group of personal soldiers serve as bodyguards. The tent of the commanding general on a campaign was called the *praetorium,* and it is from this word that the praetorian guards drew their name. After Augustus became emperor in 27 B.C., he decided to keep the guard as part of his palace household. Totaling 9,000 men, the praetorian guard patrolled the imperial palace, public buildings, and much of Rome. The men selected to become praetorians were the best trained and most elite, and they were fiercely loyal to Augustus. Subsequent emperors were never able to command the same degree of loyalty. As the strength of the guard increased, the members had the power to control as well as "undo" the appointment of an emperor. Between A.D. 41 and 282 it is believed that the praetorian guard murdered at least nine emperors and participated in deposing several others. In 79 Titus became the first of several praetorians who became emperor with the fearsome backing of the guard.

In the twentieth century, military regimes in Iraq, Pakistan, and Paraguay have been described, sometimes by the governments themselves, as *praetorian.*

Sources

Adkins, Lesley, and Roy A. Adkins. *Handbook to Life in Ancient Rome.* New York: Facts on File, 1994.

Bunson, Matthew. *Encyclopedia of the Roman Empire.* New York: Facts on File, 1994.

Ranlov, Boris. *The Praetorian Guard.* London: Osprey, 1994.

Prester John, the land of Prester John. ***A legendary enclave of Christianity in the midst of uncharted wilderness; an idyllic land ardently hoped for, yet unlikely to exist.***
Stories of Prester John, a mystical warrior-priest, began to circulate in the twelfth century, as the Holy Land and North Africa came increasingly under Islamic control. In 1145 Bishop Hugh of Gebal in Syria reported that Prester John was a Christian king whose empire lay somewhere deep in Asia. Supposedly a descendant of one of the three wise men, Prester John ruled over a large kingdom that was believed to possess amazing natural riches. The king's scepter was said to be of solid emerald. The land was at peace, the leaders were wise, and justice was administered by a court of archbishops and Prester John himself.

For the next two centuries, accounts of Prester John turned up at different times and in different geographic regions. Sometimes his kingdom was in the Middle East, sometimes India, sometimes North Africa. Prester John did not seem to suffer from old age. During the Crusades it was said that if Prester John could be located, he would lend assistance to the cause. There were other motivations for finding the elusive kingdom. Prince Henry the Navigator took great personal interest in attempting to locate the mysterious priest in order to help secure Portugal's maritime empire. Marco Polo was instructed to be on the lookout for any signs of Prester John during his travels. By the early Renaissance many were convinced that Prester John's kingdom was located in northern Africa, and the discovery of the Coptic Christians, an ancient enclave, seemed to lend credence to its existence.

Medieval and Renaissance maps often labeled uncharted territory as "the Kingdom of Prester John." As late as the sixteenth century many of the finest Dutch maps identified various regions of India and Africa as Prester John's realm. Such a designation was synonymous with *terra incognita* or *Here be Dragons.*

Sources

Boorstin, Daniel J. *The Discoverers.* New York: Random House, 1983.
Lurie, Charles. *Everyday Sayings.* Detroit, MI: Gale Research, 1968.
Mercatante, Anthony S. *The Facts on File Encyclopedia of World Mythology and Legend.* New York: Facts on File, 1988.
Silverberg, Robert. *The Realm of Prester John.* Garden City, NJ: Doubleday, 1972.

Propaganda. ***Highly partisan material distributed in order to promote a doctrine or cause.***

Although the word *propaganda* has a negative connotation, it had no such pejorative meaning when it was coined in the seventeenth century. In 1622 Pope Gregory XV proclaimed the establishment of *De Propaganda Fide,* or the Congregation for the Propagation of the Faith. Its two primary objectives were to support a seminary for the training of missionaries and to create a publishing house that would produce materials for distribution in foreign missions. The pope believed that such a group was necessary in order to make doctrine and procedures uniform among the missions scattered throughout the world. There was concern that Spain and Portugal, who had almost complete control of missions in the Americas and much of Africa, were converting native peoples to an Iberian strain of Catholicism. Rome wished to bring these missions back in line with standard Catholic theology.

Another motivation behind the formation of the group stemmed from the difficulty missionaries experienced with new languages. Learning indigenous tongues was time-consuming, and the task of producing printed literature in native languages was too onerous for most to attempt. The Congregation for the Propagation of the Faith set up its own printing press in 1622 to fill that void, and by end of the eighteenth century they possessed specialized fonts for 44 Asian and African languages. By that time, some anticlerical writers in England and France had latched onto the publications of the group as proof that the Vatican was attempting to brainwash unsuspecting natives. The negative implications of *propaganda* persisted, although the word lost its connection to Catholicism. In the early twentieth century, it was used to describe the highly charged literature produced during World War I and during the Bolshevik Revolution.

Sources

McDonald, William J., ed. *New Catholic Encyclopedia.* New York: McGraw-Hill, 1967.
Mish, Frederick C. *The Merriam-Webster New Book of Word Histories.* Springfield, IL: Merriam-Webster, 1991.
Safire, William. *Safire's Political Dictionary.* New York: Random House, 1978.

Public enemy number one. ***A policy, individual, or trend identified as a malignant force in society.***

FBI director J. Edgar Hoover invented the generic term *public enemies* in hopes of dampening the glamorous appeal of gangsters and thugs such as Bonnie and Clyde in the poverty-stricken 1930s. Creating a new genre of criminals would garner media attention, which would boost FBI investigations by distributing photographs of suspects and publicizing the rewards being offered for bank robbers and con artists. The idea of singling out *public enemies* eventually evolved into the FBI's Ten Most Wanted list.

The notorious John Dillinger (1902–1934) was the first person ever designated *public enemy number one.* U.S. Attorney General Homer Cummings granted him the dubious honor in an attempt to publicize Dillinger's many crimes. Dillinger was the superstar gangster of the Depression years, although his heaviest crime spree lasted a mere 11 months during 1933–1934. He robbed from 15 to 20 banks, engaged in three spectacular jail breaks, and murdered ten people while attempting to elude capture. His audacity caught the public's imagination. Dillinger's lighthearted bantering with customers at banks he was robbing sealed his image as a Depression-era Robin Hood, and the public noted that he never robbed individuals, just banks. He was eventually cut down in a blaze of gunfire as he left a Chicago movie theater.

The use of *public enemy number one* was expanded by journalists and commentators as a way to call attention to malignant social problems. The tobacco industry, teenage pregnancy, cholesterol, inflation, and bureaucratic procedures have all been named as targets.

Sources

Cromie, Robert. *Dillinger: A Short and Violent Life.* New York: McGraw-Hill, 1962.

Pickering, David, ed. *Brewer's Dictionary of Twentieth Century Phrase and Fable.* Boston: Houghton Mifflin Company, 1992.

Sifakis, Carl. *The Encyclopedia of American Crime.* New York: Facts on File, 1982.

Punch's advice. *Don't get married.*

Punch was a British periodical published between 1841 and 1992 that was noted for its wicked sense of humor, caricatures, and satire. In 1845 the magazine's publishers perpetrated one of its most famous jokes. They announced that all young men who were contemplating marriage could write to the magazine and receive free advice. The eager young bridegrooms received a one-word reply: "Don't." To be told to *heed* Punch's *advice* was a roundabout way of expressing disapproval of a potential marriage without bluntly saying so.

Sources

Holt, Alfred H. *Phrase and Word Origins.* New York: Dover Publications, 1961.

McHenry, Robert, ed. *The New Encyclopedia Britannica.* 15th ed. Chicago: Encyclopedia Britannica, 1992.

Punic faith. *Deceitful, fraudulent, and dishonest.*

Rome and Carthage fought three wars in the second and third centuries B.C., collectively known as the Punic Wars (named after the Latin word for Carthaginian, *Punicus*). In the time-honored tradition of ascribing dastardly characteristics to one's enemies, the Romans referred to any dishonest and treacherous behavior as *punic.* This association may have been reinforced by the Carthaginians' annoying habit of refusing to be vanquished. After each Roman conquest, the Carthaginians rose with renewed vigor to challenge the Republic. Many Roman statesmen believed that the continued existence of Carthage presented a serious threat to Roman power, and Cato the Elder ended every senate speech with the declaration, "Carthage must be destroyed."

Rome finally gained a lasting victory at the close of the Third Punic War in 146 B.C., and the conditions imposed on Carthage were so stringent that it created another historical allusion: Carthaginian peace (see *Carthaginian peace*).

Sources

Caven, Brian. *The Punic Wars.* New York: St. Martin's Press, 1980.

Crowley, Robert, and Geoffrey Parker, eds. *The Reader's Companion to Military History.* New York: Houghton Mifflin, 1996.

Evans, Ivor H., ed. *Brewer's Dictionary of Phrase and Fable.* 14th ed. New York: Harper and Row, 1989.

Hornblower, Simon, and Antony Spawforth, eds. *The Oxford Classical Dictionary.* 3d ed. Oxford: Oxford University Press, 1996.

Purple, born to the purple. *A mark of royalty, wealth, or power.*

Since antiquity, the color purple has been a mark of highest distinction, most likely because of the difficulty of making purple dye. The famous Tyrian purple, the dye used by the Romans, was produced at enormous expense from a Mediterranean shellfish. The amount of purple in a toga indicated status. Well-to-do equestrians were permitted a narrow purple stripe in their otherwise white togas. Senators had a broad purple stripe, and the emperor's toga was entirely purple. It is said that Cleopatra's luxurious barge had gold fittings and silver oars, but the most obvious sign of grandeur was its purple sails.

Dyes made from natural substances were not only expensive but had a limited range of color and tended to fade after prolonged exposure to sunlight. Throughout the Middle Ages and Renaissance, the richness of color in a fabric was a mark of luxury. It was not until the nineteenth century that synthetic dyes were developed to produce a range of vibrant colors. In 1856 an 18-year-old chemistry student, William Perkin, created the first synthetic purple dye from coal tar. Thereafter, the colors in fabrics were no longer directly related to their cost.

Sources

Adkins, Lesley, and Roy A. Adkins. *Handbook to Life in Ancient Rome.* New York: Facts on File, 1994.
Vries, Ad de. *Dictionary of Symbols and Imagery.* London: North-Holland Publishing Co., 1976.
Whittick, Arnold. *Symbols, Signs, and the Meaning.* Newton, MA: C. T. Branford Co., 1960.

Pyrrhic victory. ***A victory that costs the winner as much or more than the loser.***
Pyrrhus (c. 318–272 B.C.) was king of Epirus, an ancient country in western Greece. Described as a brilliant tactician, Pyrrhus was accustomed to fighting against the odds. Driven from his throne at the age of 16, he was sent as a hostage to Egypt. He gained the trust of the Egyptian king Ptolemy I, married the king's stepdaughter, and was eventually able to recapture his throne in 297 B.C. After he secured and enlarged his own kingdom, he was prepared to lend aid to his neighboring allies. To assist the Tarentines in their battle to resist Roman colonization, Pyrrhus invaded Italy with approximately 25,000 men and 20 elephants. In 280 he defeated the Romans at Heraclea and Asculum, but his army incurred such heavy casualties that he declared, "One more such victory and I am lost." By the time he returned to Epirus in 275, he had lost two-thirds of his original force. He was later killed in a street fight in Argos.

Sources

Evans, Ivor H., ed. *Brewer's Dictionary of Phrase and Fable.* 14th ed. New York: Harper and Row, 1989.
Hornblower, Simon, and Antony Spawforth, eds. *The Oxford Classical Dictionary.* 3d ed. Oxford: Oxford University Press, 1996.
Sacks, David. *Encyclopedia of the Ancient Greek World.* New York: Facts on File, 1995.
Stimpson, George. *A Book about a Thousand Things.* New York: Harper and Brothers, 1946.

Q

Quarantine. ***A period during which a person or conveyance is isolated in an attempt to halt the spread of an infectious disease.***
The word *quarantine* means 40 days, and this was a number with great symbolic meaning for the Hebrews and early Christians. Moses spent 40 days and nights on Mount Sinai, the Israelites wandered in the wilderness for 40 years, and Jesus spent 40 days in the desert during his temptation. Given this sacred import, the number became a cultural signifier as well. Lent was defined as 40 days, a widow was permitted to remain in the house of her deceased husband for 40 days, and the right of sanctuary as a protection from civil persecution lasted 40 days as well. It is therefore not surprising that the isolation period for people suffering from unknown diseases would also be set at 40 days.

Isolation as a means of dealing with disease dates back to biblical times. The Book of Leviticus, for example, specified segregation as the primary way of "treating" those with leprosy. During the Renaissance quarantines were instituted when a number of highly contagious diseases spread throughout Europe. Since the understanding of disease transmission was limited, officials were guided by biblical tradition in choosing 40 days as the duration of time for a disease to run its course.

The most common use of quarantines was in relation to the shipping trade. Ships arriving from a port at which an outbreak of plague was suspected were forced to weigh anchor in an isolated place and have no communication with the shore for 40 days. Quarantines were not always successful. For example, the plague was transmitted through the fleas of rats, and rats were sometimes able to get ashore on their own. Aside from this, 40 days proved to be an adequate period of isolation, and quarantine rules, first instituted in Venice, soon spread to other Mediterranean ports. Nineteenth-century scientists had a better understanding of the nature of communicable diseases, and international conferences attempted to formulate more effective public health measures. By 1907 the International Office of Public Health, the forerunner of the World Health Organization, had been established. This organization recommended sanitation and vaccination as more effective than quarantine at halting disease, although quarantines are still used in a few rare instances.

Sources

Kiple, Kenneth F. *The Cambridge World History of Human Disease.* Cambridge: Cambridge University Press, 1993.

McHenry, Robert, ed. *The New Encyclopedia Britannica.* 15th ed. Chicago: Encyclopedia Britannica, 1992.

McNeill, William Hardy. *Plagues and Peoples.* Garden City, NJ: Anchor Press, 1976.

Quarter, to grant quarter. ***To grant mercy to a failed or defeated individual.***
This curious expression may derive from an agreement struck by Spanish and Dutch officers during the wars between their nations in the sixteenth and seventeenth centuries. Captured officers were often ransomed back to their families, and it was agreed that the

ransom should be set at one-quarter of the officer's annual pay. *Asking for quarter* became standard practice upon capture. However, if an officer was believed to possess significant knowledge about his nation's military strength or strategy, it was unlikely that he would be traded so casually.

This explanation is disputed by some authorities, most notably *The Oxford English Dictionary.* In their view, *quarter* in this context was probably a reference to the lodgings a prisoner received. If prisoners were given quarter, they were granted mercy in that they received lodgings instead of execution.

Sources

Evans, Ivor H., ed. *Brewer's Dictionary of Phrase and Fable.* 14th ed. New York: Harper and Row, 1989.

Lurie, Charles. *Everyday Sayings.* Detroit, MI: Gale Research, 1968.

Simpson, J. A., and E. S. C. Weiner, eds. *The Oxford English Dictionary.* 2d ed. Oxford: Clarendon Press, 1989.

Queer as Dick's hat-band. ***Something very awkward or strange.***

After the execution of Charles I, Oliver Cromwell assumed leadership of England as lord protector and wielded his authority with a stern and sometime ruthless hand. In stark contrast to his father, Richard Cromwell (1626–1712) was a pleasant and gentle man with little interest in politics. He preferred to lead the life of a country squire, indulging his love of hunting and horses. Considering his father's role in overthrowing an English monarch, Richard also had an embarrassing fondness for royalty. When in his cups, he was even known to raise a toast to the beheaded King Charles.

When Oliver Cromwell died unexpectedly in 1658, the mantle of lord protector fell to Richard by default, although there was immediate opposition to his appointment. The country was again splitting into political, military, and religious factions, and Richard lacked the ability to reconcile these groups. He was branded "Queen Dick" by the increasingly contemptuous populace. As a nonmilitary man, Richard could not command the respect of the army, and after eight months, he was driven out of office. He fled the country and lived in France under the assumed name John Clarke. In 1680 he returned to England and lived quietly under the same pseudonym until his death in 1712.

Hat-band is a British slang word for crown. *Queer as Dick's hat-band* was an allusion to the awkward nature of Richard Cromwell's brief regime and was a common expression by the eighteenth century.

Sources

Fritze, Ronald H., and William B. Robison, eds. *Historical Dictionary of Stuart England, 1603–1689.* Westport, CT: Greenwood Press, 1996.

Hause, Earl Malcolm. *Tumble-Down Dick: The Fall of the House of Cromwell.* New York: Exposition Press, 1972.

Hendrickson, Robert. *Facts on File Encyclopedia of Word and Phrase Origins.* New York: Facts on File, 1987.

Simpson, J. A., and E. S. C. Weiner, eds. *The Oxford English Dictionary.* 2d ed. Oxford: Clarendon Press, 1989.

Quintessence. ***The purest and most refined essence of an object.***

This word derives from the scientific philosophy of ancient Greece. The Greeks believed that all substances were composed of some combination of the four essences, or elements: earth, air, fire, and water. None of the four existed in a totally pure state but were always a mixture of two or more elements. Moreover, the four elements obeyed laws of motion. It was the nature of earth and water to move downward, to seek the lowest possible point. It was the nature of fire to fly upward. Air was the wild card because it moved in a random and unpredictable manner. All objects behaved in some combination of these movements, depending on their elemental composition.

The Greeks noticed that there was one part of nature that did not fit into these laws of motion. Celestial bodies moved in a curved pattern and never varied, year after year. Because they behaved in a consistently predictable manner, unlike the four essences, it was conjectured that the heavenly bodies must be made of another essence—a pure, fifth essence, containing no earth, fire, water, or air. This unknown element was named the *quintessence,* and the Greeks believed it was the only unadulterated substance that existed.

The word *quintessence* in popular usage means the embodiment or most extreme example of something, such as the quintessence of evil, joy, or beauty.

Sources

Mish, Frederick C. *The Merriam-Webster New Book of Word Histories.* Springfield, IL: Merriam-Webster, 1991.

Phyfe, William H. *5000 Facts and Fancies.* Detroit, MI: Gale Research, 1996.

Van Doren, Charles L. *A History of Knowledge: Past, Present, and Future.* New York: Carol Publishing Group, 1991.

Quisling. *A traitor who acts as a puppet for the enemy.*

Vidkun Quisling's role as a Nazi collaborator made him one of the most despised figures of World War II. Quisling (1887–1945) was a Norwegian but betrayed his country in order to be appointed to a high position in the Nazi regime. His name is now synonymous with the most loathsome of traitors.

Quisling's fascist leanings began to emerge in the late 1920s, and in 1933 he was appointed to head the National Union Party, whose platform included suppressing revolutionary activity and freeing the workers from union control. The Norwegian people soundly rejected the National Unionists, and throughout the decade the party received little more than 1 percent of the vote. Quisling believed that his destiny was linked with the Nazi party, and when Norway was invaded by the Germans in 1940, Quisling impulsively declared himself premier of Norway. Hitler refused to support the opportunist. A week later, Quisling was compelled to renounce his claim. However, after spending a year helping the Germans demobilize Norway, he was finally appointed "minister president" in February 1942. A megalomaniac who issued a postage stamp in his likeness and ordered pictures of himself displayed throughout Norway, Quisling brutally suppressed all opposition to the Nazi party. He participated in the deportation of over 1,000 Jews to concentration camps and attempted to convert the church, schools, and youth of Norway to Nazism.

After the liberation of Norway in May 1945, Quisling was arrested and found guilty of treason, murder, theft, and illegally changing the constitution. The Norwegian civilian courts had not ordered an execution since 1876, but they resorted to a military penal code, which permitted capital punishment, in order to have Quisling shot by a firing squad.

Sources

Hendrickson, Robert. *Dictionary of Eponyms: Names That Became Words.* New York: Stein and Day, 1985.

Hewins, Ralph. *Quisling: Prophet without Honor.* New York: John Day Co., 1966.

Hoidal, Oddvar K. *Quisling: A Study in Treason.* Oxford: Oxford University Press, 1989.

Nordstrom, Byron J., ed. *Dictionary of Scandinavian History.* Westport, CT: Greenwood Press, 1986.

Safire, William. *Safire's Political Dictionary.* New York: Random House, 1978.

Zentner, Christian, and Friedmann Budurftig, eds. *Encyclopedia of the Third Reich.* New York: Macmillan, 1991.

Quiz. *To test knowledge by posing a series of questions.*

The origin of the word *quiz* is uncertain, but one widely circulated story points to a Dublin theater manager named James Daly. Sometime in the late 1700s Daly made a wager with his drinking companions that he would be able to create a new and meaningless word overnight. There were takers for his bet, so Daly paid a number of street urchins to scrawl the word *quiz* on walls throughout Dublin. Previously unknown, the word was a curiosity because it began and ended with two of the least-used letters in the alphabet. Within days people all over the city were wondering what it meant, and Daly won his bet.

Sources

Carver, Craig M. *A History of English in Its Own Words.* New York: HarperCollins, 1991.

Evans, Ivor H., ed. *Brewer's Dictionary of Phrase and Fable.* 14th ed. New York: Harper and Row, 1989.

Hendrickson, Robert. *The Facts on File Encyclopedia of Word and Phrase Origins.* New York: Facts on File, 1987.

R

Rasputin. ***A trusted advisor who is ultimately a destructive influence.***
Grigory Yefimovich Novykh (c.1872–1916), destined to play a significant role in Russian history, was born into a Siberian peasant family and remained mostly illiterate throughout his life. As a young man he entered a monastery and was converted to a philosophy that advocated shedding the passions as the prelude to spiritual enlightenment. Grigory decided that the best way to achieve this "holy passionless" state was through sexual exhaustion. His reputation for licentiousness earned him the nickname Rasputin, meaning *the debauched one* in Russian. A favorite maxim of Rasputin's was "Sin in order that you may obtain forgiveness." He eventually left the monastery and became a wandering holy man, with a reputation for being able to cure people who could not be helped by traditional medicine.

In 1905 rumors of his mystical healing powers reached the ears of the czarina Alexandra, who was desperately seeking help for her hemophiliac son, Alexei. By all accounts Rasputin eased the boy's suffering to a remarkable extent, possibly using hypnotism to calm Alexei. In any event, Rasputin convinced the royal family that he was vital to the continued health of the young prince. When the czar left the court in September 1915 to assume personal command of the Russian forces, his wife depended on Rasputin as her most trusted advisor. He reinforced her ultraconservative beliefs, and as a result she became even more despised by the increasingly frustrated Russian populace.

While in the presence of the fanatically religious czarina, Rasputin maintained the appearance of a pious holy man. Outside the court, Rasputin quickly resumed his debauched, scandalous lifestyle. There were several attempts on his life, and finally in 1916 a group of young aristocrats succeeded at the task. They invited Rasputin to a small gathering and fed him poisoned wine and tea cakes. When this had no apparent effect, they shot him twice. Rasputin escaped from the house, but the assassins brought him down with a third shot. They bound him and dumped him in a frozen river. When his body was later retrieved, an autopsy revealed that drowning was the actual cause of the mad monk's death. Under Rasputin's spell, the royal family's reputation had declined so precipitously that the country was soon plunged into civil war. The Romanovs were overthrown and eventually murdered.

Sources

De Jong, Alex. *The Life and Times of Grigorii Rasputin.* London: Collins, 1982.

McHenry, Robert, ed. *The New Encyclopedia Britannica.* 15th ed. Chicago: Encyclopedia Britannica, Inc., 1992.

Pares, Bernard. *The Fall of the Russian Monarchy: A Study of Evidence.* London: J. Cape, 1939.

Rastafarian. ***A member of a religious and cultural movement founded in Jamaica.***
Ras Tafari (1892–1975) was born Tafari Makonnen but assumed the title *ras* (prince) when he married the daughter of the emperor of Ethiopia and became the heir to the throne. Tafari was a Coptic Christian,

had a progressive outlook, and was idolized by the younger generation in Ethiopia. When he was crowned in 1930, he took the name Haile Selassie, meaning "might of the Trinity." Haile Selassie's accomplishments were many. He succeeded in obtaining Ethiopia's admission to the League of Nations in 1923, personally led troops against Italian invaders in 1935–1936, established provincial schools throughout Ethiopia, and helped ease the burden of taxation for the poor. He played a major role in the Organization of African Unity in 1963. In spite of his many achievements, by 1974, worsening famine, poverty, and unemployment resulted in an army coup. Haile Selassie was deposed and died a year later under mysterious circumstances.

Cults dedicated to Haile Selassie developed in many countries, but the most devoted following arose in Jamaica. The Rastafarians of Jamaica believe that Haile Selassie was a divine being and a savior for the black race, and that Africa is the promised land. Rastafarian lifestyle includes wearing the colors yellow, green, and black (the colors of the Ethiopian flag), long hair, and beards and observing dietary rules.

Sources

Jacobs, Virginia Lee. *Roots of Rastafari.* San Diego: Avant Books, 1985.

Lockot, Hans Wilhelm. *The Mission: The Life, Reign, and Character of Haile Selassie.* London: Hurst, 1989.

Ofosu-Appiah, L. H., ed. *Dictionary of African Biography.* New York: Reference Publications, 1977.

Schwab, Peter. *Haile Selassie I: Ethiopia's Lion of Judah.* Chicago: Nelson-Hall, 1979.

Real McCoy. ***The genuine article.***
The origin of this expression is unclear, but most word-sleuths give the credit to "Kid" McCoy, a popular welterweight boxer who lived in the Chicago area in the 1890s. One day McCoy was in a bar, and a drunken customer insisted that he prove he was the "real McCoy." After McCoy flattened the man, the drunk was willing to admit that the boxer must indeed be the genuine article.

Sources

Evans, Ivor H., ed. *Brewer's Dictionary of Phrase and Fable.* 14th ed. New York: Harper and Row, 1989.

Hendrickson, Robert. *The Dictionary of Eponyms: Names That Became Words.* New York: Stein and Day, 1985.

Rawson, Hugh. *Devious Derivations: Popular Misconceptions and More Than 1,000 True Origins of Commonplace Words and Phrases.* New York: Crown Publishers, 1994.

Red-letter day. ***A holiday, or a special day.***
Since the fifteenth century, saint's days have been marked in red ink in church almanacs and calendars. These occasions often meant a release from the daily drudgery of peasant life, making *red-letter days* something to look forward to and celebrate. Many calendars still designate holidays (literally, holy days) in this manner.

Using color to designate special days is not unique to Christians. The ancient Romans marked lucky days in the calendars in white chalk and used charcoal for days that were associated with bad omens. In medieval times religious festivals were indicated by purple ink, and cycles of the moon were marked in gold.

Sources

Lurie, Charles. *Everyday Sayings.* Detroit, MI: Gale Research, 1968.

Stimpson, George. *A Book about a Thousand Things.* New York: Harper and Brothers, 1946.

Wagner, Leopold. *Manners, Customs, and Observances: Their Origin and Signification.* London: William Heinemann, 1894.

Red tape. ***Excessive and annoying bureaucratic detail.***
Throughout the nineteenth century, official legal and government documents of the British Empire were typically tied with red ribbons. This excessive attention to formality was ridiculed by some as an antiquated and pointless tradition. In the 1850s, British essayist Thomas Carlyle coined the expression *red tape* in reference to a politician who was a master of administrative delay. As he wrote, the man was "little other than a red tape Talking machine, an unhappy Bag of Parliamentary Eloquence." The phrase was quickly

adopted as a description of the bureaucratic willingness to delay sensible policies by an excruciating attention to administrative detail and procedure. The expression *red tape* eventually became so infamous that lawyers and government officials quit using the red ribbons for their documents.

Sources

Derriman, James Parkyns. *Pageantry of the Law.* London: Eyre and Spottiswoode, 1955.
Safire, William. *Safire's Political Dictionary.* New York: Random House, 1978.
Stimpson, George. *A Book about a Thousand Things.* New York: Harper and Brothers, 1946.

Renaissance man. ***One who has interests and experience in a diverse range of areas.***
As generally defined, the Renaissance lasted from the mid-fourteenth century through the sixteenth century and was characterized by a desire to expand humankind's understanding of the world through the pursuit of science, art, and philosophy. Throughout most of the Middle Ages, access to higher learning was generally limited to those entering the clergy. Few in the upper classes knew more than the rudiments of reading and writing, and many never mastered that. However, the Renaissance extolled the virtues of a broad-based education, to include such disciplines as literature, art, science, theology, astronomy, and history. Beginning first in Italy, cities cultivated their best artists, architects, and poets. Among a host of talented individuals, one in particular stood out as the ultimate Renaissance man: Leonardo da Vinci, the illegitimate son of a Florentine notary. Da Vinci excelled in painting, sculpture, architecture, town planning, astronomy, military engineering, anatomy, mathematics, and botany. Believing that wide experience in a variety of fields was necessary to give depth to artistic expression, Leonardo said, "A painter is not admirable unless he is universal."

Some of the most admired figures in history have been called *Renaissance men,* as a tribute to their cultivation of knowledge in seemingly disparate fields. Benjamin Franklin, for example, began life as a printer's apprentice but became world famous for his scientific experiments with electricity, his satirical writings, and his diplomatic adventures. Others who have been awarded the title include Sir Walter Raleigh, Sir Thomas More, and Theodore Roosevelt.

Sources

Hale, J. R. *A Concise Encyclopedia of the Italian Renaissance.* New York: Oxford University Press, 1981.
Lorimer, Lawrence T. *The Encyclopedia Americana.* Danbury, CT: Grolier, 1989.

Renegade. ***Someone who rejects a cause, religion, or group for another.***
Between the eleventh and thirteenth centuries, thousands of Europeans set out for Jerusalem in an effort to reclaim the Holy Land from people they considered infidels. Although some of the Crusaders were driven by the spirit of adventure and profit, many were motivated, at least in part, by sincere religious convictions. Not surprisingly, those who remained at home were shocked to learn of Crusader conversions to Islam. Such converts were branded *renegades,* from the Spanish word for apostate.

For most Crusaders, conversion was the better alternative to decapitation. Captured Christian prisoners would be herded into an arena and forced to renounce Christianity. Those who refused were beheaded. The Muslim sultan Saladin (1137–1193) was skeptical of conversions made under duress and observed that he had never seen "a bad Christian become a good Saracen, nor a bad Saracen become a good Christian." Others converted because they found the lifestyle of the Arabic world appealing. As Fulcher of Chartes, a veteran of the First Crusade, described it, Jerusalem possessed a sophisticated and cosmopolitan culture. He observed that many of the French Crusaders adopted eastern fashions in food, dress, and other aspects of their daily lives. "We who had been occidentals have become orientals," he wrote in 1120. Crusaders who settled into life in Jerusalem were willing to form alliances with their Muslim counterparts.

They enjoyed cordial relations and even grew to respect the customs, traditions, and philosophy of the eastern world. From there, a few Europeans were susceptible to the ultimate heresy: renouncing the Christian faith and converting to Islam.

Sources

Finucane, Ronald C. *Soldiers of the Faith: Crusaders and Moslems at War.* New York: St. Martin's Press, 1983.

Simpson, J. A., and E. S. C. Weiner, eds. *The Oxford English Dictionary.* 2d ed. Oxford: Clarendon Press, 1989.

Rhodes scholar. ***A prestigious scholarship awarded for two years of study at Oxford University.***

Cecil Rhodes was best known during his life as an empire builder (see *Rhodesia*), but he left a lasting posthumous legacy in the form of the Rhodes scholarships. Rhodes was an Anglophile with a passion for the British Empire. He wanted to bring as much of Africa under the Crown as possible, and he even hoped that one day all of the English-speaking countries of the world (including the United States) might once again return to the fold of the empire. Rhodes believed that exposure to the best of British culture could help foster international unity, so in his will he established scholarships for men from the British colonies, the United States, and Germany to study at Oxford University, Rhodes's alma mater. Although high academic caliber was considered in selecting winners, Rhodes insisted that character, leadership, and athletic abilities also receive strong consideration. Disqualification on the grounds of race was forbidden. In 1976 the rules were modified to allow women into the competition for the awards.

Sources

Hendrickson, Robert. *Facts on File Encyclopedia of Word and Phrase Origins.* New York: Facts on File, 1987.

Palmer, Alan Warwick. *Dictionary of the British Empire and Commonwealth.* London: Murray, 1996.

Roberts, Brian. *Cecil Rhodes: Flawed Colossus.* New York: Norton, 1987.

Rhodesia. ***The former name for Zimbabwe, a country in southern Africa.***

Biographies of Cecil Rhodes (1853–1902) allude to his historical role in their titles, which describe him as "the colossus of southern Africa" and "empire maker." Rhodes was one of the eleven children born to an English vicar, and he was sent to Africa as a young man in the hope that it would improve his health. Shortly after he arrived at his brother's cotton farm in South Africa, both young men were lured to its diamond fields. He worked in the mines but also pursued his dream of attending Oxford University. For eight years, Rhodes divided his time between South Africa and Oxford until he was able to obtain his degree in 1881.

Rhodes was firmly convinced of the supremacy of the British Empire, and he entered politics in 1881 with the goal of bringing Africa under British rule. As one of the founders of the De Beers diamond company, Rhodes now had both wealth and power and was considered the most influential man in Africa. He succeeded in securing much of southern Africa for the British Crown and began to encourage white colonization. In 1890 the first white settlers began moving into the region that would eventually become the country of Rhodesia. Working for Rhodes's British South Africa Company, the colonists came in search of gold. They declined incorporation into South Africa and elected to become a self-governing colony. Rhodesia was formally recognized in 1895.

By 1963 African nationalism fueled the desire of black Africans to disassociate themselves from the British Empire. After years of strife and guerrilla warfare, Rhodesia was reborn as the independent state of Zimbabwe in 1980.

Sources

Hendrickson, Robert. *Dictionary of Eponyms: Names That Became Words.* New York: Stein and Day, 1985.

Palmer, Alan Warwick. *Dictionary of the British Empire and Commonwealth.* London: Murray, 1996.

Roberts, Brian. *Cecil Rhodes: Flawed Colossus.* New York: Norton, 1987.

Stephen, Leslie, and Sidney Lee, eds. *The Dictionary of National Biography.* London: Oxford University Press, 1921.

Rigmarole. ***A rambling, incoherent discourse.***

"Ragman's roll" is one of the few games we know of from the Middle Ages. Strings were attached to a series of verses bound together in a roll. Players drew a string at random, and the verse was read to the entire group. Most of the verses were highly unflattering or ridiculous and were supposed to describe the character of the person who drew the string. The supposed author of the verses was King Ragman, a figment of the medieval imagination.

In 1291 Scottish nobles were required to submit oaths of allegiance to Edward I of England. These documents were tied together with numerous seals, ribbons, and dangling pendants. When rolled up, they resembled the bound verses of the game, so they were also called a ragman's roll. The set is still preserved in the Tower of London.

By the sixteenth century the expression *ragman's roll* was a synonym for a list or catalog of items. Over time a new word emerged, which connoted a rambling, incoherent discourse and could be spelled variously. The word has yet to be standardized and is considered correct as either *rigmarole* or *rigamarole.*

Sources

Carver, Craig. *A History of English in Its Own Words.* New York: HarperCollins, 1991.

Mish, Frederick C. *The Merriam-Webster New Book of Word Histories.* Springfield, IL: Merriam-Webster, 1991.

Simpson, J. A., and E. S. C. Weiner, eds. *The Oxford English Dictionary.* 2d ed. Oxford: Clarendon Press, 1989.

Ring-around the roses. ***Popular childhood rhyme.***

Ring-around the roses,
A Pocket full of posies,
A-tishoo! a-tishoo!
We all fall down!

This children's verse was originally penned in reference to the bubonic plague, a disease transmitted to humans by the bite of a rat flea. The phrase *ring around the roses* refers to the small, round red rashes that first indicated the presence of the plague. *A pocket full of posies* represents the small bags of herbs that were held to the nose. This, it was mistakenly believed, would protect the user by warding off unhealthy air. *A-tishoo! A-tishoo! We all fall down!* tells the grim consequences of the disease: coughing, hacking, and sneezing, followed by death.

Sources

Kohn, George C., ed. *Encyclopedia of Plague and Pestilence.* New York: Facts on File, 1995.

McHenry, Robert, ed. *The New Encyclopedia Britannica.* 15th ed. Chicago: Encyclopedia Britannica, 1992.

Panati, Charles. *Panati's Extraordinary Endings of Practically Everything and Everybody.* New York: Perennial Library, 1989.

Riot Act, to read the Riot Act. ***To warn or sternly reprimand.***

In the eighteenth and early nineteenth centuries, Great Britain experienced serious rioting that was sparked by the Jacobite uprisings. The Jacobites were supporters of James II, whose reign had ended under controversial circumstances in 1688. Although laws against rioting had been enacted in the past, Parliament wanted a comprehensive and irrefutable response to the Jacobite agitation. As tensions increased during 1714–1715, the Riot Act was passed and was the first comprehensive law to suppress potentially riotous gatherings. The act stated that if 12 or more people had gathered unlawfully, a portion of the Riot Act ordering them to disperse would be read to them. If the assembled crowd had not dispersed within one hour, they would then be guilty of a felony, which could be punishable by death. The Riot Act was a milestone in the long struggle between governmental power and constitutional liberties in Great Britain, since it restricted freedom of assembly in the interest of civil order. The act was not officially repealed until 1973.

Reading the Riot Act was quickly adapted to more general situations, in reference to anyone who sternly rebukes a rebellious person or group of persons. The first recorded use of the expression in this context was in an 1819 letter: "She has just run out to read the Riot Act in the Nursery."

Sources

Evans, Ivor H., ed. *Brewer's Dictionary of Phrase and Fable.* 14th ed. New York: Harper and Row, 1989.
Hendrickson, Robert. *The Facts on File Encyclopedia of Word and Phrase Origins.* New York: Facts on File, 1987.
Stimpson, George. *A Book about a Thousand Things.* New York: Harper and Brothers, 1946.

Ritzy. ***Elegant, fancy.***

It is ironic that the man whose name became synonymous with exquisite luxury was the thirteenth child of a poor Swiss herdsman. When he was 16, César Ritz (1850–1918) left home and began working as a servant in restaurants. His ambition and willingness to learn every aspect of the business, from emptying slops to the proper techniques for decanting wine, resulted in his promotion to manager of a chic restaurant by the age of 19. Moving to Paris, he worked in a series of elegant establishments and developed an instinct for catering to the whims of the extremely wealthy.

Ritz's flair for creativity was demonstrated one blustery winter day when the heating plant broke down in the resort hotel at which he was employed. Knowing that a party of 40 wealthy Americans was about to arrive for lunch, Ritz ordered that the drawing room be prepared for the visitors, because that room's red velvet drapes gave it a warm appearance. He arranged for large copper pots to be filled with alcohol and set afire to heat the room, and each of the guests was given a warmed brick wrapped in flannel. Flaming crêpes suzette complemented the cozy atmosphere.

In 1892 Ritz was coaxed to London to work at the Hotel Savoy, where his attention to detail and elegance won him new admirers among the English upper class. When a quarrel with the director of the hotel resulted in Ritz's resignation, his patrons came to his defense, sending over 200 angry telegrams. The Prince of Wales, later to become Edward VII, wired that "where Ritz goes, we follow." With increasing confidence, financial resources, and a loyal clientele, Ritz established the first Ritz Hotel in 1898 by converting a Paris mansion. Over the next ten years, additional hotels sprang up in England and the United States. However, Ritz suffered a nervous collapse in 1902 and had to restrict his management activities to a few hotels within his international enterprise.

The rococo elegance of the Ritz Hotel in Paris inspired the use of the word *ritzy* as a synonym for something that is lavish or extravagant. Since what is elegant to one person may be ostentatious or vulgar to another, *ritzy* is used in both senses.

Sources

Mish, Frederick C. *The Merriam-Webster New Book of Word Histories.* Springfield, IL: Merriam-Webster, 1991.
Montgomery-Massingberd, Hugh, and David Watkin. *The London Ritz: A Social and Architectural History.* London: Aurum Press, 1980.
Ritz, Marie Louise. *Cesar Ritz: Host to the World.* Philadelphia: J. B. Lippincott Company, 1938.
Simpson, J. A., and E. S. C. Weiner, eds. *The Oxford English Dictionary.* 2d ed. Oxford: Clarendon Press, 1989.

River, to be sent up the river. ***To go to prison.***

In the criminal world of nineteenth-century New York, *to be sent up the river* meant serving time in the dreaded Sing Sing prison, located 33 miles north of New York City near the Hudson River. When it was constructed in 1825 under its infamous first warden, Captain Lynds, the institution was improbably named the Mount Pleasant prison. It was quickly dubbed Sing Sing, for the nearby town of Ossinging.

Captain Lynds was determined to make Sing Sing financially self-sufficient. Prisoners mined the stone used to build the prison walls, and after the facility was constructed, prisoners continued to perform hard labor mining stone and marble on the grounds. No nineteenth-century prison could be called comfortable, but conditions in Sing Sing were exceptionally bad. The prison was known as the "Bastille on the Hudson," and its damp and poorly ventilated cells were square boxes measuring 7 feet on a side. Corporal punishment was freely employed and included a number of torture devices that would not have been out of place in a medieval dungeon. Because of its proximity to New York City, conditions at Sing Sing were frequently "exposed" in the *New York Times,* which caused its desolate image to be cemented into national consciousness. Although being *sent up the river* originally referred only to Sing Sing, it eventually meant being sent to any prison.

Sources

Lawes, Lewis Edward. *Life and Death in Sing Sing.* Garden City, NY: Garden City Publishing Co., 1928.

McShane, Marilyn D. *Encyclopedia of American Prisons.* New York: Garland Publishing, 1996.

Sifakis, Carl. *The Encyclopedia of American Crime.* New York: Facts on File, 1982.

Sullivan, Florence James. *Sing Sing, Capital Punishment and "Honest Graft."* New York: Connolly Press, 1927.

Road to Damascus.
See Damascus, road to Damascus conversion.

Rob Peter to pay Paul. ***To take from one person in order to pay off a debt to another.***
The church of Saint Peter in Westminster was declared a cathedral in 1540, but ten years later the order was revoked and the church was absorbed into the diocese of London. The revenues that had previously gone to Saint Peter's were redirected to pay for massive repairs to Saint Paul's Cathedral, the more prominent church in the diocese. Although this is a tempting explanation for the expression, it is believed that the phrase may date back as far as the fourteenth century, so this is probably a false lead. The phrase is most likely a biblical allusion that became popular because of its alliteration.

Sources

Evans, Ivor H., ed. *Brewer's Dictionary of Phrase and Fable.* 14th ed. New York: Harper and Row, 1989.

Stimpson, George. *A Book about the Bible.* New York: Harper and Brothers, 1945.

Roland for an Oliver. ***To exchange tit for tat; repayment in kind.***
The historical Roland (d. 778) has been eclipsed by the legendary figure featured in the French epic poem, *The Song of Roland.* In the story Roland represents the flower of Frankish knighthood: strong, courageous, and loyal. He meets his match in another of Charlemagne's knights, Oliver. The two engage in a battle to determine who is the better warrior. Every blow Roland succeeds in landing, Oliver is able to return. After five days the exhausted warriors declare a draw, and the two become fast friends. A *Roland for an Oliver* means that one is resolved to respond to an attack with equal force. This refusal to let an opponent gain the upper hand eventually translated into an expression for an equitable exchange.

Sources

Hendrickson, Robert. *Facts on File Encyclopedia of Word and Phrase Origins.* New York: Facts on File, 1987.

Terry, Patricia, trans. *The Song of Roland.* Indianapolis: Bobbs-Merrill, 1965.

Roman holiday. ***A performance centered around extravagance, cruelty, and debauchery.***
Great spectacles involving chariot races, gladiators, and public executions became a normal part of city life in the late Roman Empire. These "games" had their origin in religious rites to honor the gods and funerary ceremonies for the aristocracy. The sacred component gradually became obscured, and the extravaganzas served as the primary form of entertainment for Roman citizens.

The spectacles, sponsored by the city, were free to the public. Special amphitheaters that could hold up to 60,000 people were built for huge productions. Aside from chariot races, gladiatorial combat was the most popular event. Gladiators usually fought to the death, although if the loser fought particularly well or displayed great courage, the crowd had the option of raising their hands in a collective demand for mercy. The gladiators were mostly slaves or prisoners trained for the arena, but eventually criminals and

Christians were forced to fight for sport. Other spectacles involved wild beasts, either pitted against each other or against an armed gladiator. Elephants, bears, and wildcats imported from other parts of the empire were used for this purpose.

The emperor Constantine I outlawed such spectacles in 325. His edict did not last, and the games continued until 405.

Sources

Adkins, Lesley, and Roy A. Adkins. *Handbook to Life in Ancient Rome.* New York: Facts on File, 1994.

Bunson, Matthew. *Encyclopedia of the Roman Empire.* New York: Facts on File, 1994.

Poliakoff, Michael. *Combat Sports in the Ancient World: Competition, Violence, and Culture.* New Haven, CT: Yale University Press, 1987.

Scullard, H. H. *Festivals and Ceremonies of the Roman Republic.* Ithaca, NY: Cornell University Press, 1981.

Rome. All roads lead to Rome. ***Said when all methods of doing something have the same result, so that there is no one correct way.***

Although ancient civilizations such as the Egyptians, Etruscans, and Carthaginians had constructed decent roads, the Romans were the first to build roads that could withstand the long-term effects of water damage. These consummate road builders began by digging out wide furrows until they reached rock or a firm foundation. The trench was then filled with small rocks or other materials that would assist with drainage. The surface of the road was paved with wide, flat stones that sloped slightly away from the center to the sides to encourage water runoff, and ditches were dug alongside the roads to carry the water away.

The Romans built more than 50,000 miles of roads using this labor-intensive method. The original purpose of this huge investment was to allow Roman troops to move quickly from one part of the empire to another. Another military function served by the road system was that it occupied the Roman army in between hostilities. Soldiers were vital to the maintenance of the vast network, and the work kept the troops from becoming restless and dangerous to the empire. The most important fringe benefit of the roads was economic expansion. Large-scale transportation of goods from one part of Europe to another became viable, and that in turn encouraged the development of markets and roadside inns.

The emperor Augustus erected a gilded pillar in the Roman forum that represented the center of the empire. From this point all roads radiated outward into the many lands controlled by Rome. Every road had milestones that clearly identified them in relation to Rome. During the height of the empire, then, the phrase *all roads lead to Rome* was literally true. After Rome's decline in the fourth and fifth centuries, road building almost ceased. However, some of the ancient roads were so well constructed that they are still in use after almost two thousand years. Historians have noted that Europeans living in the third century enjoyed better roads than subsequent generations did until the nineteenth century.

Sources

Adkins, Leslie, and Roy A. Adkins. *Handbook to Life in Ancient Rome.* New York: Facts on File, 1994.

Bunson, Matthew. *Encyclopedia of the Roman Empire.* New York: Facts on File, 1994.

Thompson, Logan. "Roman Roads." *History Today* 47, no. 2 (1997): 21–28.

Rome. When in Rome, do as the Romans do. ***A recommendation to behave in a manner consistent with one's companions or surroundings, regardless of one's personal values or tastes.***

In the early centuries of the Christian church, different communities celebrated particular rituals in various ways. Persecution had forced Christians to worship in secret, and thus individual enclaves observed their own traditions and sacred calendars. Over time each city developed characteristic Christian practices. After Christianity was legalized in 313, open worship exposed the disparate traditions, which prompted a series of church councils spanning several centuries to try to create ecclesiastical standards.

Inconsistent rules created an awkward situation for Saint Augustine, a recent convert to Christianity, when he was traveling from Milan to Rome during Lent. In Milan they observed fasts every day except Saturday and Sunday. Rome followed a different fasting schedule, and Augustine did not know which one he should observe. He wrote to his friend and mentor Saint Ambrose, who replied: "When I am in Milan, I do as they do in Milan. When I am in Rome, I do as the Romans do."

This phrase was thus coined as a guide for those with a meticulous regard for propriety, yet its modern implication is that morality can be altered depending on the circumstances and convenience of the individual.

Sources

Bunson, Matthew. *Encyclopedia of the Roman Empire.* New York: Facts on File, 1994.

Hendrickson, Robert. *Facts on File Encyclopedia of Word and Phrase Origins.* New York: Facts on File, 1987.

Paredi, Angelo. *Saint Ambrose: His Life and Times.* Notre Dame, IN: University of Notre Dame Press, 1964.

Roorback. ***A false story circulated to slander a political opponent.***

A book titled *Baron Roorback's Tour through the Western and Southern States* was published in the United States in 1844. Written in the style of a travel log, everything about this story was a hoax, beginning with the fictitious Baron Roorback. In one passage, the baron was traveling through a small southern town and witnessed a large encampment of black slaves being taken to a market for auction. The writer added that "forty of these unfortunate beings had been purchased, I was told, by the Hon. J. K. Polk, the present speaker of the House of Representatives; with the mark of the branding iron, with the initials of his name on their shoulders distinguishing them from the rest."

What made this passage especially shocking was that Polk was currently the Democratic candidate for the presidency of the United States. Slavery was a volatile political issue, and northern abolitionists were appalled at the suggestion that a presidential candidate might condone the branding of slaves. This bogus story was widely circulated in northern newspapers and was embarrassing to the southern-born Polk. Although he was a slaveholder, so was his opponent, Henry Clay. *Baron Roorback's Tour* was eventually exposed as a hoax, but not before thousands of people had heard the story and carried away a lingering suspicion of Polk. Even so, Polk won the election by a slim margin.

Responsibility for the fraud was later ascribed to an abolitionist named Linn from Ithaca, New York. He had lifted the passage about the slave encampment from *Excursions through the Southern States,* by English author George William Featherstonbaugh, and added the slur against Polk to stir up additional outrage against the practice of slavery.

Sources

Kohn, George C. *The Encyclopedia of American Scandal: From Abscam to the Zenger Case.* New York: Facts on File, 1989.

Safire, William. *Safire's Political Dictionary.* New York: Random House, 1978.

Stimpson, George. *A Book about American History.* Greenwich, CT: Fawcett Publications, 1960.

Rosie the Riveter. ***A woman who works in traditionally male, blue-collar occupations, such as construction or factory work.***

After the United States entered World War II in December 1941, 16 million men went overseas with the armed forces at precisely the same time that industries were stepping into high gear to meet war demands. Women were called upon to help fill the labor vacuum.

Although one-quarter of the work force in 1940 was female, women tended to be employed in secretarial or clerical jobs. Three years later women were needed in factories, munitions plants, and foundries. The government insisted that companies follow a policy of equal pay for equal work, and many women eagerly signed up for high-paying factory jobs. In 1943, the Four Vagabonds recorded a popular song called "Rosie the Riveter," and subsequently many of the women working in defense plants were known as Rosie. The image that persisted long after the war was of a pretty young woman wearing slacks and a bandanna knotted around her head as she welded airplane parts.

During the war a number of short, promotional films were made to help sell war bonds and bolster spirits on the home front. One movie company shooting film at the Willow Run Aircraft Factory in Ypsilanti, Michigan, found a real Rosie the Riveter. Rose Will Monroe was a young widow who so perfectly fit the profile of the popular song that she was subsequently featured in the films and on posters.

After the war, women workers confronted strong pressure to quit their jobs so that returning veterans could find employment. Most women returned home without protest, but Rose Will Monroe exemplified the many who could not afford to be jobless. Despite her factory skills, she subsequently worked as a taxicab driver, a seamstress, and a school bus driver. Monroe had always wanted to learn how to fly, and she finally obtained a pilot's license when she was in her fifties. She died in 1997 at the age of 77.

Sources

Panati, Charles. *Panati's Parade of Fads, Follies, and Manias: The Origins of Our Most Cherished Obsessions.* New York: HarperPerennial, 1991.

Sherrow, Victoria. *Women and the Military: An Encyclopedia.* Santa Barbara, CA: ABC-CLIO, 1996.

Weatherford, Doris. *American Women and World War II.* New York: Facts on File, 1990.

Wertheimer, Linda. "Rosie the Riveter: Obituary." *National Public Radio,* 2 June 1997.

Round robin. *A tournament in which every player or team plays one another in turn.*

The expression *round robin* is borrowed from sailor's jargon. Discipline has traditionally been extremely strict on oceangoing vessels, given the potential dangers of housing large numbers of men in close quarters for long stretches of time. Because of this, the ship's captain exercised almost unlimited power over the conditions on board his ship, and any who challenged him might face a court-martial. Consequently, it was difficult for seamen to voice complaints, even if their concerns were totally justified. In the seventeenth century French seamen developed a strategy called the *rond ruban,* or "round ribbon," to solve this problem. Complaints would be written out and signed by all petitioners. In order to disguise who had originated the potentially mutinous document, the signatures were written in a circle, thereby preventing any one person from being singled out as the ringleader. If the entire crew signed the document, it would be almost impossible for a captain to bring charges against all of them without badly damaging his own reputation. A 1612 diary entry from John Jourdain takes note of the *rond ruban* practice: "The Hectoures boat brought a petition to Sir Henrie Middelton, signed by most of them, in the manner of a circle, because itt should not bee knowne whoe was the principall of the mutiny."

In the nineteenth century the expression was adopted by American sports teams for tournaments in which all players would eventually play all the others.

Sources

Carver, Craig. *A History of English in Its Own Words.* New York: HarperCollins, 1991.

Lurie, Charles. *Everyday Sayings.* Detroit, MI: Gale Research, 1968.

Simpson, J. A., and E. S. C. Weiner, eds. *The Oxford English Dictionary.* 2d ed. Oxford: Clarendon Press, 1989.

Royal disease. *Hemophilia.*

Queen Victoria has been called the "grandmother of Europe" because of her remarkable fecundity and the favorable royal alliances made by her descendants. Her 9 children and 35 grandchildren married into the royal families of Germany, Russia, Spain, Greece, and Norway. Although these alliances were intended to solidify Britain's position as a world power, one of the unforeseeable consequences was that the deadly hemophilia gene was spread throughout Europe's royal and aristocratic families.

Queen Victoria was a remarkably healthy woman and would not submit to medical examinations. She was completely unaware that she was a carrier of the hemophilia gene until her own son and several of her grandchildren were diagnosed with the condition.

Hemophilia is a hereditary disorder manifested in the slow clotting of blood, which can lead to fatal hemorrhaging from the slightest of injuries. The gene is a recessive trait carried by women, although the harmful effects of the disease usually appear only in males. The most devastating effects of the hemophilia gene were felt by the Russian royal family. Alexandra of Hesse was Queen Victoria's granddaughter and a carrier of the gene. She married Czar Nicholas II and passed the disorder on to her only son and heir, Alexei. As a result of her son's suffering and her own distress, Alexandra came to rely on the dissolute monk Rasputin (see *Rasputin*), with devastating consequences.

Medical historians have speculated about how Queen Victoria came to be a carrier of hemophilia. None of her forerunners seem to have manifested the gene, but spontaneous mutation is improbable, estimated at a 1 in 50,000 chance. There is evidence that the queen's father, the duke of Kent, may have been sterile, which has generated rumors that Queen Victoria was illegitimate. Only DNA testing could answer the puzzle at this point, and it is unlikely her descendants would consent to exhumation.

Sources

Meacham, Jon. "Was Queen Victoria a Bastard?" *Newsweek* 126, no. 4 (1995): 56.

Potts, D. M. *Queen Victoria's Gene*. Gloucestershire: A. Sutton Publishers, 1995.

Rube Goldberg machine. ***An outlandishly complex and roundabout process for performing a simple function; a difficult way to achieve easy results.***

Rube Goldberg (1883–1970) earned a bachelor's degree in engineering from the University of California and got his first job designing pipes for the San Francisco Sewer Department. He became disenchanted with the life of a professional engineer very quickly and left his job within a year. After stints with a series of California newspapers, the *New York Evening Mail* recognized his talent and offered him a job as a cartoonist.

One of Goldberg's long-running comic strips featured Professor Lucifer Gorgonzola Butts, who was enraptured by technology and designed complex machines featuring gears, bathtubs, live animals, banana skins, pulleys, and bouncing balls to accomplish easy tasks such as licking a stamp or scratching one's back. One cartoon depicted a machine for closing the window. A frog jumps on a lever to release hot water onto a pile of yeast. The rising yeast triggers a spring that pushes a pet monkey off his ledge, whereupon he slips on a banana peel and falls on a pulley that closes the window.

Goldberg claimed that his cartoons were "symbols of man's capacity for exerting maximum effort to accomplish minimal results." Goldberg's cartoons struck a chord among people who were bewildered by the rapid mechanization of American life in the first half of the twentieth century. His satires of the machine age were not only popular but profitable. By 1928 his cartoons were nationally syndicated and earned him a staggering $125,000 a year. By the 1950s *Rube Goldberg* was included in most dictionaries to refer to ridiculously complicated procedures. It is often used in reference to government bureaucracy. Purdue University holds an annual Rube Goldberg Design Contest, in which engineering students compete to design a machine that takes at least 20 steps to perform a simple task. The team creating the most ludicrous and complicated process is the winner.

Sources

Goldberg, Rube. *The Best of Rube Goldberg*, comp. Charles Keller. Englewood Cliffs, NJ: Prentice-Hall, 1979.

Paneth, Donald. *The Encyclopedia of American Journalism*. New York: Facts on File, 1983.

McHenry, Robert, ed. *The New Encyclopedia Britannica*. 15th ed. Chicago: Encyclopedia Britannica, 1992.

Rubicon, cross the Rubicon. ***To take a decisive and irrevocable step.***
The Rubicon is a small river that served as a boundary marker between ancient Rome and Gallia Cisalpina. Its place in history was assured when Julius Caesar crossed it in direct contradiction to orders from the senate.

In 60 B.C., Julius Caesar, Pompey, and Marcus Licinius Crassus united to form the First Triumvirate, which ruled the Roman Republic. All three had been influential leaders in Rome, but sensing the senate's opposition to their power, they pledged mutual support for one another and thereby blocked any attempt to undermine their individual positions. The union was further cemented when Pompey married Caesar's daughter Julia. Caesar subsequently established himself as the most powerful commander in Rome by leading a number of successful campaigns in Gaul.

The First Triumvirate worked well for a few years, but after Crassus was killed in battle, tensions mounted between the two surviving members. When Julia died in childbirth, the estrangement between Caesar and Pompey was complete. Pompey and the senate sought to undercut Caesar by ordering him to disband his army in Gaul or be declared an enemy of the Republic. Caesar knew that his legions, a highly trained, experienced, and lethal fighting force, could crush any opposition mustered in Rome. He decided to seize power for himself. In 49 B.C. Caesar reached the bank of the Rubicon. By crossing the river at the head of an army, Caesar was taking an unheard-of step against the Roman Senate and was deliberately instigating civil war. In the war that followed, Caesar would set the standard for the meaning of the word *dictator.*

Sources

Bradford, Ernle D. *Julius Caesar: The Pursuit of Power.* New York: Morrow, 1984.

Fuller, J. F. C. *Julius Caesar: Man, Soldier, and Tyrant.* New Brunswick, NJ: Rutgers University Press, 1965.

Simpson, J. A., and E. S. C. Weiner, eds. *The Oxford English Dictionary.* 2d ed. Oxford: Clarendon Press, 1989.

Rule of thumb. ***A general guideline that is not formally defined but is understood.***
Standardized systems of measurement are fairly recent inventions. The metric system was first proposed by a French clergyman in 1670, and the International Bureau of Weights and Measures was established in 1876 to define universal measurement norms. Before the creation of such standards, measurements were highly subjective and were often based on the human body, such as the typical length of a man's foot or the weight a man could haul. This is probably how the expression *rule of thumb* originated.

A popular but inaccurate attribution for the expression *rule of thumb* relates to wife beating. Supposedly, in early English or American courts, a man had permission to beat his wife if the thickness of the rod was less than the width of the man's thumb. There may have been such a law on the books somewhere (although none has been discovered as yet), but it is certain that this is not the origin of the expression.

Sources

Hendrickson, Robert. *Facts on File Encyclopedia of Word and Phrase Origins.* New York: Facts on File, 1987.

McHenry, Robert, ed. *The New Encyclopedia Britannica.* 15th ed. Chicago: Encyclopedia Britannica, 1992.

Simpson, J. A., and E. S. C. Weiner, eds. *The Oxford English Dictionary.* 2d ed. Oxford: Clarendon Press, 1989.

S

Sabbatical. ***A leave of absence from a profession; offered especially by universities.***
The concept of a *sabbatical* is Hebrew in origin and probably developed as a method of soil conservation. The Book of Leviticus (25:3–4) reads: "Six years you shall sow your field, and six years you shall prune your vineyard, and gather in their yield; but on the seventh year there shall be a Sabbath of complete rest for the land, a Sabbath for the Lord. You shall not sow your field or prune your vineyard." Repayment of debts by people observing the sabbatical were suspended, for people could not be expected to repay a debt when their fields lay fallow. Sabbatical years were staggered, so that only one-seventh of the population was observing a sabbatical at any given time.

In the mid-nineteenth century universities began incorporating the concept of a sabbatical year for their professors. The purpose was to allow a professor who had been teaching for at least six years to have a year off in order to pursue specialized research or continuing education. The release time would revitalize faculty members, who would presumably be more productive as a result.

Private businesses have seen the benefits of sabbaticals as well. Individuals who have worked for a company for several years are a valuable resource, but boredom, stress, and overwork may cause them to seek employment elsewhere. Employees may be motivated by the prospect of earning a large block of time off to pursue their own interests. The potentially rejuvenating effect of sabbaticals serves the same function as leaving the soil fallow did in ancient Hebrew agriculture.

Sources

Bromiley, Geoffrey W., ed. *The International Standard Bible Encyclopedia.* Grand Rapids, MI: W. B. Eerdmans, 1988.

Roth, Cecil E., ed. *Encyclopedia Judaica.* New York: Macmillan, 1972.

Stimpson, George. *A Book about the Bible.* New York: Harper and Brothers, 1945.

Sabotage. ***To deliberately destroy property or obstruct normal operations.***
Sabot is a French word for wooden shoes. These shoes, carved from a single piece of wood, were uncomfortable and were worn only by the poor. In 1887 French laborers found another use for these shoes as part of their protest against the factory conditions to which they were subjected. The General Confederation of Labor recommended a policy of industrial warfare against employers, and tampering with expensive equipment captured the attention of factory owners in a way that protest rallies could not. The workers discovered that equipment could be easily damaged by dropping the small but sturdy *sabots* into a vital part of a machine. Thus the word *sabotage* was born. Other forms of sabotage adopted by the workers included pouring sand into machine bearings and allowing raw materials to spoil.

The word made its way into the English language when British journalists used it to describe the tactics of railway strikers in

France. Its current meaning is not tied to labor and describes any subversive activity designed to destroy property or impede smooth operations.

Sources

Lurie, Charles. *Everyday Sayings.* Detroit, MI: Gale Research, 1968.

Simpson, J. A., and E. S. C. Weiner, eds. *The Oxford English Dictionary.* 2d ed. Oxford: Clarendon Press, 1989.

Stimpson, George. *A Book about a Thousand Things.* New York: Harper and Brothers, 1946.

Sackcloth and ashes. ***A symbol of mourning or penitence.***

The sacrament of penance was designed to reconcile a person who had broken the laws of the church and now sought forgiveness. Smearing oneself with ashes and donning sackcloth (a coarse cloth made out of goat's hair) were often outward signs of penance. Pope Gregory (d. 604) defined three aspects of penance: conversion of the mind, confession with the mouth, and vindication of the sin. In other words, the sinner had to understand that he or she had committed a sin, had to be willing to acknowledge verbally the sin, and had to be willing to atone for the error. The contemporary association of *sackcloth and ashes* with public humiliation was not its original goal. Most sins, such as theft, adultery, violence, and bearing false witness, are in some way violations against the community. To regain the acceptance and trust of the community, it was believed that some sort of public acknowledgement of guilt and evidence of atonement was required, which was the object of wearing sackcloth.

By the twelfth century, public atonement had become very rare, and private confession between a priest and confessor had become the norm.

Sources

McDonald, William J., ed. *New Catholic Encyclopedia.* New York: McGraw-Hill, 1967.

Metford, J. C. J. *Dictionary of Christian Lore and Legend.* London: Thames and Hudson, 1983.

Stimpson, George. *A Book about the Bible.* New York: Harper and Brothers, 1945.

Sacred cow. ***Something that is exempt from criticism.***

Cows occupy a prominent place in the Hindu religion. Certain deities are believed to inhabit various parts of the cow, and the fertility of a cow is considered an indicator of future prosperity. In addition to their spiritual significance, cows serve a practical purpose for the people of India. Their milk, curds, and butter are staples of the diet, and dung is a crucial fuel source. As Mahatma Gandhi declared, "Mother cow is in many ways better than the mother who gave us birth. Our mother gives us milk for a couple of years and then expects us to serve her when we grow up. Mother cow expects nothing of us but grass and grain."

Given the spiritual and practical importance of the cow to Indian society, the killing of a cow is forbidden and, until the twentieth century, could be punished by death in certain parts of the country. Reverence for bovine animals does not extend to the male of the species, and there is no prohibition on the slaughter of bulls.

Sources

Eliade, Mircea. *The Encyclopedia of Religion.* New York: Macmillan, 1986.

Lall, H. K. *The Resurrection of Cow in India.* Hoshiarpur: Vedic Research Institute, 1973.

Walker, Benjamin. *The Hindu World: An Encyclopedic Survey of Hinduism.* New York: Praeger, 1968.

Sadie Hawkin's day. ***Dances or other social events at which it is socially acceptable for girls to ask boys for a date.***

The concept of *Sadie Hawkin's day* is derived from *L'il Abner,* Al Capp's legendary comic strip, which ran between 1934 and 1977. *L'il Abner* has been described as one of the few comic strips taken seriously by commentators on American culture. A satirical portrayal of small-town life, it had a wide range of exaggerated characters who made such everyday incidents as a lemonade sale into larger-than-life incidents. One of Capp's favorite plots was the annual Sadie Hawkin's day race, in which the women of the town had the opportunity to chase unmarried men about the town. If they caught one, they could marry him that same day. Not only did this invert traditional sex roles, but it reflected the popular conception that women are more aggressive than men in seeking out a partner, although they must generally do so in a covert fashion. Many people eagerly latched onto the concept of a Sadie Hawkin's day to allow girls to briefly escape their passive role in courtship. Beginning in the 1940s, some school districts declared certain dances to be Sadie Hawkin's dances. They are often held the first weekend of November.

Sources

Berger, Arthur Asa. *Li'l Abner: A Study in American Satire.* New York: Twayne, 1970.

Chase, William, and Harrison Chase. *Chase's Calendar of Events.* Chicago: Contemporary Books, 1994.

Sadist. ***A person who derives sexual satisfaction through the infliction of pain on others.***
Almost 200 years after his death, the Marquis de Sade (1740–1814) is still an enigmatic, controversial person who provokes wildly differing responses from his readers. To some, he was a brilliant philosopher who believed in the total liberation of humanity from the strictures of society. For others he was a selfish and perverted sociopath who devised elaborate justifications for the evil he inflicted.

Sade was born into a wealthy and aristocratic family. After serving in the military he married into a well-to-do bourgeois family and promptly began a series of affairs. In 1768, on Easter Sunday, Sade lured a prostitute to his home, locked her up, and sexually tortured her. After escaping, the woman spread the story of her treatment, which resulted in Sade's imprisonment. Sade spent most of the rest of his life in and out of prisons and insane asylums. Whenever he was released, he showed no inclination to reform, and he was usually arrested again within a few weeks or months. In prison he turned to writing as a means of relieving his boredom and anger. His plays and novels included graphic accounts of sexual torture and mutilation. The characters justified their actions by proclaiming that no restrictions should be placed on personal liberty and by insisting that nature should be the only guide to behavior. Most of Sade's works were censored during his lifetime, but he often directed performances of his plays while he was incarcerated, using the inmates as actors.

Copies of Sade's works circulated privately within wealthy and intellectual circles during the nineteenth century. The term *sadism* was coined by German neuropsychiatrist Richard von Krafft-Ebing.

Sources

Bullough, Vern L., and Bonnie Bullough, eds. *Human Sexuality: An Encyclopedia.* New York: Garland Publishing, 1994.

Cerrito, Joann, and Marie Lazzari, eds. *Nineteenth-Century Literature Criticism,* vol. 47. Detroit, MI: Gale Research, 1995.

Gear, Norman. *The Divine Demon: A Portrait of the Marquis de Sade.* London: F. Muller, 1963.

Hunt, Cecil. *Word Origins: The Romance of Language.* New York: Philosophical Library, 1962.

Salary. ***A fixed rate of compensation in exchange for employment.***
Salt was a precious commodity in the ancient world, so much so that it was routinely included in sacrificial offerings to the gods. Not only was its sodium essential to human dietary requirements, but salt served as a crucial preservative for meat. Its value was enhanced by the fact that it was often difficult to obtain and had to be transported over great distances. One of the oldest roads in Italy, the *Via Salaria* (Salt Route), was built to transport salt from the port city of Ostia to Rome and other parts of the empire. Along the coasts, seawater was captured in low walled enclosures and allowed to evaporate, producing salt in abundance. Roman soldiers who were stationed in such locations could easily afford to buy their own salt. For others who were stationed inland, a special allowance, called a *salarium,* was added to their regular pay for the purchase of salt. By the Middle Ages the word had lost its original association with salt and was used in a general sense for compensation.

Sources

Adshead, Samuel A. *Salt and Civilization.* New York: St. Martin's Press, 1992.

Hunt, Cecil. *Word Origins: The Romance of Language.* New York: Philosophical Library, 1962.

Mish, Frederick C. *The Merriam-Webster New Book of Word Histories.* Springfield, IL: Merriam-Webster, 1991.

Simpson, J. A., and E. S. C. Weiner, eds. *The Oxford English Dictionary.* 2d ed. Oxford: Clarendon Press, 1989.

Salt, below the salt. ***Having little status or position.***

Since ancient times, salt has been prized and sought after as a basic substance for seasoning and preserving food. Beginning in the Middle Ages, elaborate saltcellars were used for the storage of salt. These ornate devices were often made of silver and lavishly embellished. They could be shaped like ships, hourglasses, or animals and could stand several feet tall. Such works of art served as a centerpiece for the table. Placement of the saltcellar on the table also became a demarcation line for status. Individuals seated above the saltcellar were the high-ranking guests and family members, while servants, travelers, and distant relatives with little rank were placed below the saltcellar.

By the seventeenth century smaller containers for salt became more common and made the large, standing saltcellar obsolete.

Sources

McHenry, Robert, ed. *The New Encyclopedia Britannica.* 15th ed. Chicago: Encyclopedia Britannica, 1992.

Read, Herbert. *Encyclopedia of the Arts.* New York: Meredith Press, 1966.

Strayer, Joseph R., ed. *Dictionary of the Middle Ages.* New York: Scribner's, 1982.

Salt, not worth one's salt. ***Implies an individual is not a productive employee.***

See Salary.

Sandwich. ***Two pieces of bread with a filling such as meat or cheese.***

It is probably just as well that the earl of Sandwich is best remembered for creating this new snack, since most of his other exploits were embarrassing, scandalous, or both. John Montagu (1718–1792) became the fourth Earl of Sandwich when he was 11, and access to tremendous wealth and power at such a young age had unfortunate results. He became an avid gambler and joined the notorious Hell-Fire Club, a group of aristocratic rakes who toyed with black magic as an excuse to indulge in sexual orgies and drunkenness. On one such occasion, John Wilkes, a fellow member, played a nasty practical joke on Sandwich that made him the butt of jests. Wilkes had dressed a monkey in a bizarre outfit including a cape and horns, which he released just as Sandwich was evoking the Devil. Sandwich was so terrified he ran screaming from the building. Determined to get revenge, he tried a number of maneuvers to have Wilkes expelled from Parliament. The attacks backfired, and the outspoken and charismatic Wilkes was perceived as a champion of liberty, while his critics, including Sandwich, dropped in the public's esteem.

As lord of the Admiralty, Sandwich supported naval exploration, which prompted Captain Cook to name the Sandwich Islands (Hawaii) after him in 1778. However, his strategic decisions during the American Revolution were serious blunders. The earl was not particularly impressed with the fledgling American navy and preferred to keep his best ships close to home in case relations with France worsened. The few ships that were sent to the colonies were poorly supplied and manned, earning the description "floating wrecks." His administration was marked by a notoriously high amount of corruption, graft, and incompetence, and some historians have speculated that the American Revolution might have had a different outcome if not for Sandwich's mismanagement.

The earl's love of gambling frequently led to round-the-clock card games. According to the story, the bleary-eyed but hungry Sandwich was unwilling to leave the gaming table in order to get something to eat. He instructed his servant to bring him a slab of beef between two pieces of bread, and within a few years such a snack became known as a *sandwich.*

Sources

Boatner, Mark Mayo. *Encyclopedia of the American Revolution.* New York: D. McKay Co., 1966.
McHenry, Robert, ed. *The New Encyclopedia Britannica.* 15th ed. Chicago: Encyclopedia Britannica, 1992.
Stephen, Leslie, and Sidney Lee, eds. *The Dictionary of National Biography.* London: Oxford University Press, 1921.
Stimpson, George. *A Book about a Thousand Things.* New York: Harper and Brothers, 1946.

Sardanapalus. ***Effeminate and self-indulgent luxury.***

An account by the ancient writer Ctesias tells of the last king of Assyria, Sardanapalus, who lived in the seventh century B.C. As the story goes, he spent most of his time secluded behind palace walls. Delighting in an effeminate lifestyle, he wore women's garments and enjoyed spinning and making clothing. When his empire was threatened by the satrap of Media, he threw off this behavior and led three successful battles against the invaders. He finally met defeat when he was besieged at Nineveh. After withstanding the siege for two years, the king was convinced that victory was impossible. He set all his worldly goods, his concubines, and himself onto a funeral pyre and burned to death. The story was immortalized by Lord Byron in his poem "Sardanapalus" (1821) and in a painting by Delacroix (1827).

It is now believed that Sardanapalus was actually an amalgam of three ancient Assyrian kings: Ashurbanipal, his brother Shamash-shum-ukin, and Sin-shar-ishkun. Their reigns must have preceded the final conquest of the empire, which occurred before 605 B.C.

Sources

Evans, Ivor H., ed. *Brewer's Dictionary of Phrase and Fable.* 14th ed. New York: Harper and Row, 1989.
Hendrickson, Robert. *Facts on File Encyclopedia of Word and Phrase Origins.* New York: Facts on File, 1987.
McHenry, Robert, ed. *The New Encyclopedia Britannica.* 15th ed. Chicago: Encyclopedia Britannica, 1992.

Sardonic wit. ***A bitter, mocking sense of humor.***

There is a legend that a poisonous herb on the island of Sardinia can cause death by laughter. Although it is doubtful that anyone ever died from ingesting *herbs sardonia,* its taste is so acrid that it can produce involuntary convulsions in the facial muscles. These spasms can pull the face into an unnatural smile.

Sources

Evans, Ivor H., ed. *Brewer's Dictionary of Phrase and Fable.* 14th ed. New York: Harper and Row, 1989.
Hendrickson, Robert. *Facts on File Encyclopedia of Word and Phrase Origins.* New York: Facts on File, 1987.

Say it ain't so, Joe. ***Refers to the moment when a hero's integrity is in question.***

"Shoeless Joe" Jackson (1887–1951) earned his nickname because of his humble beginnings, when he was unable to afford even shoes. His natural athletic ability made him the star of the baseball team at the cotton mill where he had begun work at the age of 13. Eventually he was tapped by the Chicago White Sox and became popular with the fans.

Jackson's lack of sophistication and defensiveness about his poor background may have been a factor in his acquiescence in the scheme to throw the 1919 World Series to the Cincinnati Reds. Jackson was one of eight White Sox players who admitted involvement in the affair. Although he batted an impressive .375 during the series, he made some questionable defensive errors. Jackson was banished from baseball for life. According to legend, after the trial, a child pushed through the barrage of reporters on the steps of the Cook County courthouse, grabbed his hero's sleeve, and said, "Say it ain't so, Joe." The statement reflected the disillusionment many Americans felt as the apple-pie image of Jackson proved to be unfounded. The phrase *say it ain't so* is still commonly used when public officials or role models appear to have fallen from grace.

After his expulsion from baseball, "Shoeless

Joe" returned to his home in South Carolina. He invested his baseball earnings wisely and was able to enjoy a comfortable, if modest, lifestyle.

Sources

Hickok, Ralph. *The Encyclopedia of North American Sports History.* New York: Facts on File, 1992.

Kohn, George C. *The Encyclopedia of American Scandal: From Abscam to the Zenger Case.* New York: Facts on File, 1989.

Porter, David L. *Biographical Dictionary of American Sports: Baseball.* New York: Greenwood Press, 1987.

Scalawag. ***A rascal; a Southerner who collaborated with Reconstruction governments for private gain.***

This term has its origins in the Shetland Islands, where a *scalloway* was a filthy and uncombed sheep. The Scots-Irish brought the word with them to the United States, and it evolved into *scalawag,* meaning any sort of rascal or lowlife. After the Civil War, it assumed a political connotation when it was used as a disparaging term for white Southerners who cooperated with the Reconstruction programs.

Scalawags were perceived as being disloyal "white trash" who were willing to betray Southern interests, collaborate with the carpetbaggers, and thereby gain an unfair advantage in the reorganization of the South. Most scalawags were middle- to lower-class whites who had for generations resented the political and economic power wielded by elite slaveholders. These were the people courted by Northern carpetbaggers anxious to be elected to positions of power under the Military Reconstruction Acts. In most Southern states there simply were not enough carpetbaggers and newly enfranchised black voters to swing elections away from the Southern Democrats to the Republican party. By appealing to the longstanding hostility between the lower and upper classes of Southern whites, many carpetbaggers moved into important political offices. In the process, the stereotype of the treacherous scalawag was cemented in the minds of the defeated Southern aristocracy.

Sources

Faust, Patricia L. *Historical Times Illustrated Encyclopedia of the Civil War.* New York: Harper and Row, 1986.

Richter, William L. *The ABC-CLIO Companion to American Reconstruction, 1862–1877.* Santa Barbara, CA: ABC-CLIO, 1996.

Stimpson, George. *A Book about American History.* Greenwich, CT: Fawcett Publications, 1960.

Trefousse, Hans Louis. *Historical Dictionary of Reconstruction.* New York: Greenwood Press, 1991.

Scapegoat. ***Someone who is made to shoulder the guilt of others.***

As part of the Yom Kippur ritual, the ancient Hebrews selected a goat to placate Azazel, a wilderness demon. The goat symbolically carried all the sins of Israel with it, and when it was driven into the wilderness, the Hebrews would be purified. (In some accounts, the goat was killed by being pushed over the edge of a cliff.) The Bible reads (Leviticus 16:7):

> He shall take two goats and set them before the Lord at the entrance of the tent of meeting; and Aaron shall cast lots on the two goats, one for the Lord and the other lot for the scapegoat. Aaron shall present the goat on which the lot fell to the Lord, and offer it as a sin offering, but the scapegoat shall be presented live before the Lord to make atonement over it, that it may be sent away into the wilderness of Azazel.

The practice of endowing the collective sins of a people onto an animal or object is not unique to the ancient Hebrews. In parts of Scotland a dog was driven from town on New Year's Day, supposedly taking the residents' sins with it. The aborigines of Borneo set a canoe adrift, and Arab nomads drove off a camel.

Sources

Bromiley, Geoffrey W., ed. *The International Standard Bible Encyclopedia.* Grand Rapids, MI: W. B. Eerdmans, 1988.

Stimpson, George. *A Book about the Bible.* New York: Harper and Brothers, 1945.

Whittick, Arnold. *Symbols, Signs, and Their Meaning.* Newton, MA: C. T. Branford Co., 1960.

Scipio, continence of a Scipio. ***Someone whose integrity is above question.***

Scipio Africanus (236–183 B.C.) was a Roman general widely acclaimed for his skills as a leader and warrior. He conquered much of Spain and northern Africa and brought an end to the Second Punic War in 202 B.C. when he defeated Hannibal at Zama. Legend has it that during one of his campaigns, a beautiful princess was taken captive by Scipio's army. Scipio refused to see her, lest he be swayed by her and forget his principles. This is most likely an apocryphal tale.

Sources

Evans, Ivan H., ed. *Brewer's Dictionary of Phrase and Fable.* 14th ed. New York: Harper and Row, 1989.

Hornblower, Simon, and Antony Spawforth, eds. *The Oxford Classical Dictionary.* 3d ed. Oxford: Oxford University Press, 1996.

McHenry, Robert, ed. *The New Encyclopedia Britannica.* 15th ed. Chicago: Encyclopedia Britannica, 1992.

Scot-free. ***To escape payment.***

Many English words derived from the Scandinavian invaders of the Middle Ages. One such word was *skot,* meaning "contribution." The raiders often demanded *skots* in exchange for leaving the locals unmolested. The word made its way into English, and by the twelfth century it meant "tax." Medieval assessments were plentiful and included taxes collected by the church (church scot), taxes for burial (soul scot), annual donations to the papacy (Rome scot, or Peter's pence), and various scots owed to overlords, boroughs, and the monarch. There were also levies on plows, on animals killed during a hunt, and on the use of roads and bridges.

Taxes were not equitably distributed across the social spectrum. Although the poorest laborers were generally excused, the nobility paid far less in proportion to their wealth than did the wage laborers and merchants. Individuals who were exempt from taxes were called *scotfre.* After the word *scot* had dropped out of circulation, *scot-free* was still used to refer to a person who had escaped from an undesirable fate. One such example was the 1665 statement that "Oxford has escaped scotfre of the plague."

Sources

Carver, Craig. *A History of English in Its Own Words.* New York: HarperCollins, 1991.

Lurie, Charles. *Everyday Sayings.* Detroit, MI: Gale Research, 1968.

Mitchell, Sydney Knox. *Taxation in Medieval England.* Hamden, CT: Archon Books, 1971.

Simpson, J. A., and E. S. C. Weiner, eds. *The Oxford English Dictionary.* 2d ed. Oxford: Clarendon Press, 1989.

Strayer, Joseph P., ed. *The Dictionary of the Middle Ages.* New York: Charles Scribner's Sons, 1988.

Scottish play, the. ***Shakespeare's Macbeth.***

The theater has always been home to a number of superstitions. For example, an actor should never be told "good luck," but rather "break a leg." Accepting a gift of flowers before the play begins is said to result in a bad performance, and whistling in the dressing room is supposed to mean a short run. One of the oldest superstitions involves Shakespeare's *Macbeth,* and theater lore is replete with stories of ill-fated productions. A 1942 production featuring John Gielgud was hindered by the death of three members of the company. A 1954 production was plagued by a series of tragedies: an electrician was electrocuted, a visitor died from an accident with a stage spear, and the company manager suffered two broken legs.

Simply uttering the word *Macbeth* outside of a performance is supposedly enough to initiate an onslaught of misfortunes. For this reason many people in the theater will simply say *the Scottish play* in lieu of Macbeth. Other euphemisms are *that play* and *the unmentionable.* Actors who inadvertently say "Macbeth" in their dressing room are supposed to leave the room immediately, turn around three times, knock on the door, and ask permission to reenter the room.

A possible explanation for the rash of bad luck surrounding *Macbeth* was supplied by the famed actress Sybil Thorndike, who claimed that when stock companies were in dire financial straits, the companies resorted to the popular play in an attempt to reverse their flagging fortunes. Since this tactic often failed to solve financial problems, the play became associated with disappointment and disaster—and, by extension, with bad luck.

Sources

Law, Jonathan, ed. *Brewer's Theater: A Phrase and Fable Dictionary.* New York: HarperCollins, 1994.

Opie, Iona, and Moira Tatem, eds. *A Dictionary of Superstitions.* Oxford: Oxford University Press, 1989.

Scrap of paper. ***A contemptuous term for written agreements and treaties.***

After its revolution in 1830, Belgium was declared an independent nation. As a gateway between Great Britain and the European continent, Belgium's strategic position was too important to fall under the influence of a single power. All the major European nations signed a treaty in 1839 to guarantee the perpetual neutrality of Belgium.

In the war preparations of August 1914, German diplomats indicated that Germany would respect Belgian neutrality, but they insisted on the right to move their troops across Belgian land. Belgium, France, and England strenuously objected. British officials demanded that Germany reaffirm its commitment to the earlier treaty. When the British ambassador called on Chancellor Bethmann-Hollweg (1856–1921), he reportedly responded with this infamous statement: "Just for a word, neutrality, a word which in wartime has so often been disregarded. . . . Just for a scrap of paper, Great Britain is going to make war on a kindred nation who desires nothing better than to be friends with her."

German troops immediately commenced their invasion of Belgium, and there was international outrage at the action. The term *scrap of paper* was held out as a symbol of German contempt for law and peace. Although the expression will be forever linked with Bethmann-Hollweg, he did not coin it. In 1887 Kaiser Wilhelm of Germany announced to the Prussian Diet: "I will do my duty as I see it, without regard to scraps of paper called constitutions."

Sources

Pope, Stephen, and Elizabeth-Ann Wheal. *The Dictionary of the First World War.* New York: St. Martin's Press, 1995.

Stimpson, George. *A Book about a Thousand Things.* New York: Harper and Brothers, 1946.

Vizetelly, Frank H. *Desk-Book of Idioms and Idiomatic Phrases.* New York: Funk and Wagnalls, 1923.

Scratch, come up to scratch. ***To meet a standard, or prepare oneself for a challenge.***

The expression *come up to the scratch* was derived from the first set of rules governing the sport of boxing, written in 1743 by Jack Broughton (1704–1789). Pugilism in the seventeenth and eighteenth centuries was a bare-knuckled and brutal sport. Desperate men saw boxing as an opportunity to climb out of the gutter, provided they were willing to give spectators a good show of bravery, brawn, and blood. Broughton was a longshoreman by trade and discovered his aptitude for fighting while brawling with a fellow worker. He attracted the patronage of the duke of Cumberland, who encouraged Broughton's aggressive style. This led to tragedy in 1741, when one of Broughton's opponents died from his injuries. Broughton was badly shaken by the incident and decided that a set of rules would regulate the sport and lessen the likelihood of additional tragedies.

Broughton published his rules for the sport of boxing in 1743, and they remained in effect for over one hundred years. They barred the practices of hitting a man below the belt or when he was prostrate. Once a man was down, he was permitted 30 seconds to recover, after which he had to *come up to the scratch,* meaning the line drawn in the center of a ring at which the fighting commenced. If a fighter was unable to reach the line, the match was over. Broughton also introduced boxing gloves (first called "mufflers") in an attempt to make the sport more humane.

Although he was enormously popular and respected, Broughton's fighting days were numbered. In a 1750 fight his eyes became so badly swollen from his opponent's blows that he was temporarily blinded and lost the match. The duke of Cumberland had wagered £10,000 on the match. Outraged at the defeat, he dropped his patronage of Broughton, which brought a swift end to the pugilist's career. Broughton later taught boxing and operated a boxing arena in London. He had amassed a £7,000 fortune by the time of his death. Broughton is known as the "father of boxing" for his part in creating the sport's first set of formal rules.

Sources

Arlott, John, ed. *The Oxford Companion to World Sports and Games.* New York: Oxford University Press, 1975.

McHenry, Robert, ed. *The New Encyclopedia Britannica.* 15th ed. Chicago: Encyclopedia Britannica, 1992.

Stephen, Leslie, and Sidney Lee, eds. *The Dictionary of National Biography.* London: Oxford University Press, 1921.

Scratch a Russian and you'll find a Tatar. ***Despite a civilized veneer, a barbarian remains by nature a crude, unpolished brute who cannot be trusted.***

Modern Russia is a nation that shares both European and Asian characteristics. On the one hand, the linguistic and cultural traditions of the Rus civilization, which had emerged by the ninth century, derived from people of Indo-European descent inhabiting the area now known as Russia. However, beginning in the thirteenth century, Mongol armies, led by Genghis Khan, began sweeping through southern Russia. Called Tatars, these invaders were non-Christian nomads and were viewed with fear and contempt by Europeans. The Tatar period of Russian history, lasting from the thirteenth to the fifteenth centuries, has often been regarded as one of stultification, especially given the country's isolation from the West. By the time the Tatars were driven out of power, there had been a great deal of assimilation between the Russian and Mongol cultures.

In the nineteenth century many Europeans regarded all non-Europeans as little better than savages. Although the Russians were culturally closer to Europeans than Asians, the Russian-Tatar association was emphasized by those hostile to any political or military alliance with Russia. An American version of the proverb *scratch a Russian and you'll find a Tatar* is *scratch a Democrat and you'll find a Rebel,* used after the Civil War.

Sources

Brown, Archie. *The Cambridge Encyclopedia of Russia and the Former Soviet Union.* Cambridge: Cambridge University Press, 1994.

Davis, Paul K. *Encyclopedia of Invasions and Conquests: From Ancient Times to the Present.* Santa Barbara, CA: ABC-CLIO, 1996.

McHenry, Robert, ed. *The New Encyclopedia Britannica.* 15th ed. Chicago: Encyclopedia Britannica, 1992.

Titelman, Gregory. *Random House Dictionary of Proverbs and Sayings.* New York: Random House, 1996.

Scuttlebutt. ***Gossip.***

Scuttle was an eighteenth-century verb meaning to cut a hole in something. A scuttled ship, for example, was one that had been deliberately sunk. A scuttled-butt, or more commonly, *scuttlebutt,* was a large barrel with a hole cut in the top, from which the crew took its drinking water. The scuttlebutt was placed on deck so that seamen toiling in the hot sun could easily reach it. The forerunner of the office water cooler, it was a natural gathering place on ships. As sailors quenched their thirst, no doubt a good deal of chatting and rumor-mongering occurred. By the end of the nineteenth century, the word *scuttlebutt* had become synonymous with gossip.

Sources

Jeans, Peter D. *Ship to Shore: A Dictionary of Everyday Words and Phrases Derived from the Sea.* Santa Barbara, CA: ABC-CLIO, 1993.

Simpson, J. A., and E. S. C. Weiner, eds. *The Oxford English Dictionary.* 2d ed. Oxford: Clarendon Press, 1989.

Thrower, William R. *Life at Sea in the Age of Sail.* London: Phillimore, 1972.

Separate but equal. ***Something that pays lip service to equity but is inherently discriminatory.***

The infamous phrase *separate but equal* is shorthand for the doctrine that emerged from the Supreme Court's 1896 decision in

Plessy v. Ferguson. In 1890 the state of Louisiana approved the Separate Car Act, which mandated segregated seating on railroad passenger cars. Homer Plessy, who was seven-eighths Caucasian and one-eighth African, took a seat in a car reserved for whites and was forcibly removed by the conductor and a policeman. Plessy challenged the constitutionality of the segregation law by arguing that it violated the Fourteenth Amendment of the Constitution, which guaranteed equal protection of the law to all citizens. The case eventually made its way to the Supreme Court. The court sided with Louisiana and declared that it was not the intent of the Fourteenth Amendment to enforce social equality. Only Justice John M. Harlan dissented from the opinion, asserting that "our constitution is color-blind and neither knows or tolerates classes among its citizens."

Although *Plessy v. Ferguson* specifically addressed only railroad passenger cars, the doctrine of separate but equal was used to justify segregation for other public facilities, such as parks, drinking fountains, restaurants, and, perhaps most damaging, public schools. The school system in many southern states made a mockery of "separate but equal." While white children had textbooks and attended regular schools with plumbing, many black children met in dilapidated buildings lacking electricity or plumbing and had to scrounge for books. In 1951 a black clergyman named Oliver Brown attempted to enroll his daughter in an all-white public school but was denied permission. His case made its way to the Supreme Court in 1954, and in the landmark decision *Brown v. Board of Education,* the justices finally overturned the doctrine of separate but equal. Separate facilities were deemed "inherently unequal," and the decision affected the principle of segregation not only in schools but in all other public facilities.

Today the expression *separate but equal* calls attention to programs and policies that may subtly discriminate against a particular group.

Sources

Bessette, Joseph M., ed. *American Justice.* Pasadena, CA: Salem Press, 1996.

Lofgren, Charles A. *The Plessy Case: A Legal-Historical Interpretation.* New York: Oxford University Press, 1987.

Salzman, Jack, ed. *Encyclopedia of African-American Culture and History.* New York: Macmillan Library Reference, 1996.

Sequoia. ***A genus of conifer trees, which includes the largest species of tree in the world, the giant sequoia.***

Sequoyah (c.1760/1770–1843) was a giant among his people, the Cherokee Indians. As a result of a hunting accident in his youth, one of his legs was lame, and he was unable to support himself as a hunter. He became a craftsman, creating intricately worked silver ornaments that were highly valued among both the Indians and white traders. Sequoyah had had little contact with white people before he began trading in the 1790s, but when the War of 1812 broke out, he served as a volunteer under Andrew Jackson. Sequoyah became fascinated with the "talking leaves" he saw the soldiers using, and he was determined not only to learn to read but to develop a system of writing for his people.

In 1821 Sequoyah completed a syllabary that covered the 86 syllables of the Cherokee language. He taught his young daughter how to read the syllables, and she impressed the elders at the Cherokee National Council by reading aloud a message they had privately instructed Sequoyah to write down. The council sanctioned the teaching of Sequoyah's syllabary to the whole Cherokee nation, and eventually thousands of eastern Cherokees learned to read and write in their own language using Sequoyah's system.

Sequoyah served his people in many ways, lobbying for Cherokee rights in Washington and helping to resettle Indians who had been displaced by white expansion. In 1842 he set out on a quest to find traces of a legendary band of Cherokees who had supposedly migrated west of the Mississippi before the American Revolution. His search took him to Mexico, where he fell ill and died in 1843.

In 1847, as the Austrian botanist Stephan

Endlicher helped classify the thousands of new plant species found in North America, he named the giant trees of the Pacific Northwest in honor of the recently deceased Sequoyah.

Sources

Forman, Grant. *Sequoyah.* Norman: University of Oklahoma Press, 1938.

Hendrickson, Robert. *Dictionary of Eponyms: Names That Became Words.* New York: Stein and Day, 1985.

Hoxie, Frederick E., ed. *Encyclopedia of North American Indians.* Boston: Houghton Mifflin Company, 1996.

Markowitz, Harvey, ed. *American Indians.* Pasadena, CA: Salem Press, 1995.

Serendipity. ***Making beneficial discoveries purely by chance.***

English is a tremendously rich and varied language. Among the Indo-European languages, it has one of the largest number of words in common use (200,000 as compared to 184,000 in German and 100,000 in French). Within this enormous vocabulary many words have several shades of meaning. *The Oxford English Dictionary* lists 17 different definitions for the word "fine." One can have fine art, fine hair, a traffic fine, or do fine on a test, to name just a few of the variations.

It is therefore unusual to find a concept for which there is no English word. In 1754 the writer Horace Walpole recognized such a deficiency with regard to the phenomenon of making a fortunate discovery by chance. He deliberately created the word *serendipity,* which he derived from an old fairy tale, *The Three Princes of Serendip* (an ancient name for Sri Lanka). In this Persian story, three young princes have been sent out into the world by their wise old father, who believes that his children need to experience the world in order to be good rulers. In their travels the three princes seem to have astonishingly good luck. They always arrive just in time to rescue the damsel in distress, apprehend the thief, slay the dragons, and so forth. The young men were not looking for such adventures, but they possessed some unspecified quality that sparked happy coincidences. Walpole decided to call that phenomenon *serendipity.*

Sources

Bryson, Bill. *The Mother Tongue: English and How It Got That Way.* New York: Morrow, 1990.

Mish, Frederick C. *The Merriam-Webster New Book of Word Histories.* Springfield, IL: Merriam-Webster, 1991.

Simpson, J. A., and E. S. C. Weiner, eds. *The Oxford English Dictionary.* 2d ed. Oxford: Clarendon Press, 1989.

Seven deadly sins. ***Avarice, envy, gluttony, lust, pride, sloth, wrath.***

The seven deadly sins are so named because theologians claim that all other transgressions stem from these core sins. In his study of the nature of sin, Saint Thomas Aquinas drew the distinction between mortal sin (a deadly sin) and venial sin (a less serious sin). Venial sin weakens and twists the relationship between God and humanity. Deadly sin destroys the relationship between God and humanity. To Roman Catholics, if a person dies while in a state of mortal sin, the person is damned. Deadly sins require sacramental confession in order to be forgiven, while venial sins can be expiated by other means.

The seven deadly sins are offset by the seven virtues: faith, hope, charity, temperance, prudence, fortitude, and justice. In many religions, the number seven has special significance, and Christianity is no different. There were seven days of creation, seven sacraments, seven last words from the cross, seven gifts of the Holy Ghost, and seven corporal and spiritual works of mercy.

Sources

Matthews, Boris. *The Herder Symbol Dictionary: Symbols from Art, Archaeology, Mythology, Literature, and Religion.* Wilmette, IL: Chiron Publications, 1986.

McDonald, William J., ed. *New Catholic Encyclopedia.* New York: McGraw-Hill, 1967.

Panati, Charles. *Sacred Origins of Profound Things.* New York: Penguin Arcana, 1996.

Seward's folly. ***Alaska.***

After the Russians were humiliated in the Crimean War, they realized that they could not defend their colonial holdings on other continents. Russian leaders began looking for a way to rid themselves of their Alaskan territory. When Secretary of State William Seward (1801–1872) was approached, he was enthusiastic about the idea. Seward, an ardent expansionist, had been seeking to extend the nation's claims in Central America, the Pacific, and the Dutch East Indies, so the Alaskan apple was too tempting to resist. The Russians wanted $10 million for the 586,000 square miles of territory, but Seward was able to negotiate the price down to $7.2 million. The Senate was equally pleased with the deal. Alaska's strategic location in the Arctic Circle was a valuable asset, as was the potential profit from the region's fur, fishing, and mineral resources.

Most Americans were stunned when they heard the news of the proposed deal. Although a handful of sea captains testified to the value of the land, the average American viewed Alaska as a frozen and barren wasteland. Newspaper editorialists were generally opposed to the purchase and dubbed it "Seward's Folly" and "Seward's Icebox." Seward began a publicity campaign to win public support for the acquisition of Alaska, and there may have been payments to some newspapers and public officials to secure their backing. When the House of Representatives voted on the appropriations for the purchase of Alaska on 14 July 1868, the measure passed 113 to 43, with 44 abstaining. *Seward's folly* now belonged to the United States.

Despite the public's suspicion, Alaska eventually proved to be a sound investment for the United States government. In addition to other resources, oil was discovered in 1957, and since the completion of the trans-Alaska pipeline in 1977, Alaskan oil grosses up to $8 billion annually.

Sources

Johnson, Allen, and Dumas Malone, eds. *Dictionary of American Biography.* New York: Scribner's, 1964.

Magill, Frank N., ed. *Great Events from History: North American Series.* Pasadena, CA: Salem Press, 1997.

Stimpson, George. *A Book about American History.* Greenwich, CT: Fawcett Publications, 1960.

Shamrock. ***The national emblem of Ireland.***
Like many legends in Irish history, the story of the shamrock arose from an event in the life of Saint Patrick. In 433 a pagan Irish chieftain was preparing to celebrate a festival for a sun god. For the ceremony, all fires were to be extinguished and then rekindled at the appointed time. Saint Patrick refused to put out his fire, so the angry chieftain, accompanied by a group of druids, rode out to confront the missionary.

Patrick used this as an opportunity to proselytize, and he must have succeeded in capturing their attention, for he ventured into some of the finer points of Christian theology. However, it became obvious that his audience did not grasp the doctrine of the Trinity. Why did the Christians insist they had only one god? Are not God the Father, the Holy Spirit, and Jesus Christ three separate gods? The saint thereupon plucked a shamrock from the ground and used it to illustrate the concept. There are three separate leaves, he told his listeners, but they are joined to one stalk and are considered one plant. The legend does not say how his audience reacted to this analogy, but since Saint Patrick was one of the most successful missionaries in Christian history, they too may have yielded to his persuasion.

Sources

Panati, Charles. *Panati's Extraordinary Origins of Everyday Things.* New York: Harper and Row, 1987.

Stimpson, George. *A Book about a Thousand Things.* New York: Harper and Brothers, 1946.

Whittick, Arnold. *Symbols, Signs, and Their Meaning.* Newton, MA: C. T. Branford Co., 1960.

Shanghai. ***To abduct someone, especially for compulsory service on board a ship.***
To ensure that one's navy was adequately manned, the quasi-legal practice of impressing men into service had been common practice among European countries for centuries. The British monarchy, for example, reserved the right to "impress seamen on the ground of necessity for the preservation of the nation, just as the crown has the right to the services of every able-bodied man in cases of sudden invasion or insurrection." In

fact, the British propensity to impress seamen was a contributing factor to the War of 1812. The British had become accustomed to stopping American merchant vessels at sea and impressing any member of the crew believed to have been born in England, Scotland, or Ireland. Records indicate that between 1809 and 1810, 1,558 men from American vessels were impressed by the British.

The tactic of legally impressing men into service was not available to captains of merchant vessels, who resorted to outright kidnapping to obtain a full crew on their ships. Unsuspecting men and boys were drugged, beaten, and terrorized into service. A voyage to ports around the world might take months on a merchant vessel. With little means of communication, men who had been kidnapped could not contact their families or seek redress from authorities. There is no record of how many men were subjected to this sort of abduction, and it is likely that many died in service. Charitable societies, such as the Mission to Seamen in San Francisco and the Sailor's Home Society in London, were organized to try to combat crimping, but they had little influence.

When boys and men disappeared from port towns, it was often assumed that the unlucky individual had been pressed into service on a long-distance sea voyage. The far-off city of *Shanghai* evolved into a verb to describe what had happened to them.

Sources

Hutchinson, John Robert. *The Press-Gang Afloat and Ashore.* New York: E. P. Dutton, 1914.

Jeans, Peter D. *Ship to Shore: A Dictionary of Everyday Words and Phrases Derived from the Sea.* Santa Barbara, CA: ABC-CLIO, 1993.

Kindleberger, Charles Poor. *Mariners and Markets.* New York: New York University Press, 1992.

Zimmermann, James Fulton. *Impressment of American Seamen.* Port Washington, NY: Kennikat Press, 1966.

Sherman statement. ***An unequivocal refusal to stand for an office.***

Following the Civil War there was a natural impulse to nominate war heroes for important political positions, including the presidency. Ulysses S. Grant served two terms as president based largely on the admiration people had for his military leadership skills, despite his lack of political acumen.

After Grant retired, attention turned to William Tecumseh Sherman (1820–1891), the great Civil War general and architect of the Union victory in Georgia and the Carolinas. To say that Sherman had no interest in politics would be an understatement. At one point he said that if he were offered a term either in the White House or in a penitentiary, he would opt for prison. Sherman's flat rejection of politics was also his way of assisting his younger brother's political career. John Sherman had served as a governor, senator, and secretary of the Treasury and often contemplated a run for the presidency. When it became apparent in 1884 that interest in a William Tecumseh Sherman candidacy was gaining momentum, Sherman wired the following stark denial: "I will not accept if nominated, and will not serve if elected."

Sherman was determined to enjoy his retirement. In a letter to a friend Sherman detailed a few of the reasons he refused to consider a political career:

> Any senator can step from his chair at the capitol into the White House, and fulfill the office of the President with more skill and success than a Grant, a Sherman or a Sheridan, who were soldiers by education and nature, who filled well their office when the country was in danger, but were not schooled in the practices by which civil communities are, and should be governed. I have my personal affairs in a state of absolute safety and comfort . . . and would account myself a fool, a madman, an ass, to embark anew, at sixty-five years of age, in a career that may, at any moment, become a tempest-tossed by the perfidy, the defalcation, the dishonesty, or neglect of any one of a hundred thousand subordinates . . . not to say the

eternal worriment by a vast host of impecunious friends and old military subordinates.

Sherman never regretted his unequivocal refusal to run for office, although other politicians who uttered *Sherman statements* surely did. In his second term, Theodore Roosevelt had the highest approval rating of any president to date, but he declared that he would never seek another term. It proved to be a disastrous error. He was thereafter regarded as a lame duck and incurred all the problems associated with that weakened position. Roosevelt felt honor-bound to keep his word and left office in 1909. However, retirement did not sit well with Roosevelt, and he eventually launched an unsuccessful bid for president as leader of the Bull Moose party in 1912.

Sources

Johnson, Allen, and Dumas Malone, eds. *Dictionary of American Biography.* New York: Scribner's, 1964.
Merrill, James M. *William Tecumseh Sherman.* Chicago: Rand McNally, 1971.
Safire, William. *Safire's Political Dictionary.* New York: Random House, 1978.
Stimpson, George. *A Book about American History.* Greenwich, CT: Fawcett Publications, 1960.

Shibboleth. ***A slogan; a catchphrase that is characteristic of a political party or group.***
The origin of the word *shibboleth* ("grain" in Hebrew) comes from a biblical story told in the Book of Judges (12:1–4). Jephthah was the illegitimate son of a prostitute and lived among the tribe of Gilead. He was driven out of the community by his legitimate half-brothers who could not countenance his wild ways. Jephthah became a warrior and leader of a powerful band of nomads. When members of a heathen tribe attacked Gilead, the elders begged Jephthah to return and defend them. After a bit of justifiable stalling on Jephthah's part, he made peace with the people who had turned him out and began to avenge his tribe. His rapid success brought him new enemies, including the Israelite tribe of Ephraim. Some of the Ephraimites infiltrated Jephthah's forces and posed as allies. Jephthah was suspicious, so any man not personally known to the Gileadites was asked to say the word *shibboleth.* The Ephraimites were unable to pronounce the *sh* sound and said *sibboleth*—and were killed on the spot.

The wartime use of speech peculiarities has a long history. In the thirteenth century Sicilians rebelling against their French oppressors identified the French by their pronunciation of *ceci e ciceri* as *sesi e siseri.* During World War II Japanese agents posed as Chinese allies, but they could be unmasked by the ease with which they mastered words with *r* sounds—a difficult pronunciation for a native Chinese speaker but not for the Japanese.

By the seventeenth century *shibboleth* had come to mean a slogan that identified members of a group. An example of a contemporary shibboleth would be *no new taxes* as a Republican catchphrase.

Sources

Bromiley, Geoffrey, W., ed. *The International Standard Bible Encyclopedia.* Grand Rapids, MI: W. B. Eerdmans, 1988.
Buttrick, George Arthur, ed. *The Interpreter's Dictionary of the Bible.* Nashville, TN: Abingdon Press, 1962.
Mish, Frederick C. *The Merriam-Webster New Book of Word Histories.* Springfield, IL: Merriam-Webster, 1991.
Stimpson, George. *A Book about the Bible.* New York: Harper and Brothers, 1945.

Shivaree. ***An elaborate, noisy celebration; also, a mock serenade using horns, kettles, or other obnoxious noisemakers in honor of a newly married couple.***
Shivarees are usually associated with the French Cajun culture of Louisiana. The loud, boisterous celebrations are directly descended from the ancient French custom of the charivari, an obnoxious celebration that was held to harass newly married couples. The word *charivari* is believed to be derived from an old Latin word for headache.

The custom dates back to medieval times and varied in severity depending on the popularity of the couple. Typically, a charivari involved a mild, friendly hazing, but it could become cruelly malicious if sentiment ran against the couple: for example, when a widow remarried too quickly, or there was an unusually large disparity in the ages of the pair. The ritual consisted of a belligerent serenade on the wedding night, accompanied by the banging of kettles, ringing of cowbells, and blowing of horns. The vulgar display continued for several hours and could only be halted when the bridegroom had adequately "treated" the crowd. Giving alcohol to an unruly group could easily lead to worse behavior, and the charivari might last all night. However, if the bridegroom failed to treat the crowd, the couple's house was likely to be pelted with rotten vegetables, eggs, or dead animals.

In the early seventeenth century the Council of Tours forbade the practice of charivari, and the French Parliament periodically railed against the "tumults known as charivaris." Neither body was capable of calling a halt to the custom, and it continued into early modern times. When French immigrants brought the practice to the United States, it was considerably softened and the overly raucous elements were excluded. American shivarees are usually boisterous gatherings to celebrate weddings or other special events.

Sources

Mish, Frederick C. *The Merriam-Webster New Book of Word Histories.* Springfield, IL: Merriam-Webster, 1991.

Stimpson, George. *A Book about a Thousand Things.* New York: Harper and Brothers, 1946.

Walsh, William Shepard. *Curiosities of Popular Customs and of Rites, Ceremonies, Observances, and Miscellaneous Antiquities.* Philadelphia: Lippincott, 1897.

Short shrift. *Performing a task in a perfunctory manner.*

Immediately before an execution in the Renaissance, condemned prisoners were allowed the final rite of *shriving,* commonly known as *shrift.* During this ceremony a priest heard confession and granted absolution. Whether or not a prisoner died penitent was of great concern to members of the clergy, since unrepentant criminals could not be buried in sacred ground and were considered eternally damned.

During the Renaissance and early modern period, executions were performed in public, as it was believed that by witnessing them, observers would be deterred from criminal activities. However, the hordes of people who attended public executions generally regarded them as a macabre form of entertainment rather than a moral lesson. Most counties in England held public executions once or twice a year, and they typically drew crowds of 3,000 to 7,000 people. Penny broadsides known as "gallows literature" were sold to people anxious to learn the lurid details of the crime. Observing the condemned attest to remorse was an important part of the ritual, and a shriving ceremony was conducted in full view of the crowd. Pressure from an impatient and boisterous mob often made a mockery of the rite, and there was the potential for violence if the main event was delayed too long. Very brief shriving ceremonies, known as a *short shrift,* became customary on the scaffold.

Agitation from social reformers led to the abolition of public executions in England in 1868.

Sources

Cooper, David D. *The Lesson of the Scaffold: The Public Execution Controversy in Victorian England.* Athens: Ohio University Press, 1974.

Evans, Ivor H., ed. *Brewer's Dictionary of Phrase and Fable.* 14th ed. New York: Harper and Row, 1989.

Gatrell, V. A. C. *The Hanging Tree: Execution and the English People, 1770–1868.* New York: Oxford University Press, 1994.

McDonald, William J., ed. *New Catholic Encyclopedia.* New York: McGraw-Hill, 1967.

Simpson, J. A., and E. S. C. Weiner, eds. *The Oxford English Dictionary.* 2d ed. Oxford: Clarendon Press, 1989.

Show me, I'm from Missouri.

See Missouri.

Shrapnel. ***The metal fragments of an artillery shell designed to explode in the air above enemy troops.***

Henry Shrapnel (1761–1842) was a career officer in the British army. He was interested in designing artillery weapons that were superior to standard cannonballs and bullets. At his own expense he experimented with constructing hollow spheres filled with bullets and an explosive charge that could be ignited by a fuse. The fuses were timed so that they would explode shortly before impact, thus scattering a hail of high-velocity debris over the enemy. The weapon could inflict lethal damage on a large scale, and its military value was quickly recognized by the British. It was first used in 1803 in skirmishes between colonial Dutch and British forces in South America.

Shrapnel's new invention proved invaluable in the fight against Napoleon. The duke of Wellington asked that the weapon not be publicized, since the element of surprise would increase its devastating effect. Sir William Robe, who commanded British artillery during the peninsular campaigns, wrote to Shrapnel in August 1808 to praise his device: "It is admirable to the whole army and its effects dreadful. . . . I told the [Duke of Wellington] I meant to write to you. His answer was 'You may say anything you please; you cannot say too much.'" Variations on Shrapnel's invention continue to be used in modern warfare.

By keeping the weapon under close wraps, Shrapnel knew that he would forgo the fame he might have enjoyed, but Wellington requested that the inventor be well compensated. Having spent several thousand pounds of his own money in developing the weapon, Shrapnel appealed to the board of ordnance for restitution. The board replied that they had "no funds at their disposal for the reward of merit," although in 1814 Shrapnel was awarded an annual pension from the Treasury of £1,200.

Sources

Beeching, Cyril Leslie. *Dictionary of Eponyms.* London: Clive Bingley, 1979.

McHenry, Robert, ed. *The New Encyclopedia Britannica.* 15th ed. Chicago: Encyclopedia Britannica, 1992.

Mish, Frederick C. *The Merriam-Webster New Book of Word Histories.* Springfield, IL: Merriam-Webster, 1991.

Stephen, Leslie, and Sidney Lee, eds. *The Dictionary of National Biography.* London: Oxford University Press, 1921.

Siamese twins. ***Identical twins who are physically joined to each other, resulting from the incomplete division of a single fertilized ovum.***

Although Chang and Eng (1811–1874) were not the first pair of congenitally joined twins to survive birth, they became the most famous because of their tours of Europe and the United States as part of traveling circuses. Chang and Eng had been born in Siam (known as Thailand since 1939), where they were initially named simply "Left" and "Right." They were a curiosity in their village and even had an audience with the king of Siam. A British merchant convinced their mother that the boys could make a fortune in the West, and he paid her $500 in exchange for the right to exhibit the boys for two years. Although the merchant at times made $1,000 a month from Chang and Eng, the boys received a monthly allotment of only $50.

When Chang and Eng achieved legal autonomy at the age of 21, they took charge of their own tours and eventually accumulated a small fortune. They bought a farm in North Carolina, became American citizens, and adopted the surname Bunker. They returned to the sideshow circuit only when they were in need of funds. In 1843 the twins created a scandal when they announced their plans to marry two sisters, Addie and Sally Yates. The girl's parents initially forbade the match but relented when it became obvious that the foursome would otherwise elope. Separate households were established, with the twins alternating residence every three days. Chang and Addie had ten children, while Eng and Sally raised twelve.

Despite their remarkable physical similarity, the twins had distinctly different temperaments. Chang was the dominant twin and was often moody and drank to excess. Eng was quieter and had diverse intellectual interests. In the 1870s Chang's health began to fail, and he died from a stroke in 1874. Eng died a few hours later of unknown causes.

The term *Siamese twins* was coined by P. T. Barnum, with whom the twins occasionally traveled. The twins were initially known as the "Chinese Double-Boys" until Barnum coined the more exotic name for the pair. By the mid-nineteenth century the term was being used to describe any twins who were physically joined.

Sources

Collins, David R. *Eng and Chang: The Original Siamese Twins.* Toronto: Maxwell Macmillan Canada, 1994.

McHenry, Robert, ed. *The New Encyclopedia Britannica.* 15th ed. Chicago: Encyclopedia Britannica, 1992.

Wallace, Irving. *The Two.* New York: Simon and Schuster, 1978.

Sideburns. ***Whiskers on the sides of the face, with the chin clean shaven.***

Before they were called *sideburns,* whiskers on either side of a man's face were known by various and colorful names, including Piccadilly weepers and dundrearies. The word *sideburns* dates only from the late nineteenth century and comes from the American Civil War general Ambrose Burnside (1824–1881), whose impressive facial hair extended several inches down the sides of his face. This style was first called burnside whiskers, then merely burnsides, then sideburns—probably becoming associated more with their position on the face than with a Civil War general.

It may be a mercy that Burnside is remembered for his distinctive whiskers rather than his military maneuvers. He was a thoughtful, anxious person, and leading men into battle did not come easily to him. Over his own protests he was appointed to command the Army of the Potomac, but he was replaced in less than three months. A fellow commander once wrote, "Few men have risen so high on so slight a foundation as [Burnside]." In spite of his inadequacies as a military leader, after the war he served as governor of Rhode Island and two terms as a United States senator.

Sources

Hendrickson, Robert. *Dictionary of Eponyms: Names That Became Words.* New York: Stein and Day, 1985.

Johnson, Allen, and Dumas Malone, eds. *Dictionary of American Biography.* New York: Scribner's, 1964.

Panati, Charles. *Extraordinary Origins of Everyday Things.* New York: Perennial Library, 1987.

Sieg heil! ***An expression indicating blind, unquestioning obedience, now often used facetiously.***

Sieg heil means "Hail Victory" in German and was a common refrain in Nazi rallies during the Third Reich. The phrase is attributed to Ernst Hanfstaengl, a publicist and friend of Adolf Hitler's. Hanfstaengl had studied in the United States at Harvard University but returned to Germany in 1921 to join the Nazi ranks. His sociable demeanor and intuitive knack for handling propaganda made him useful to the party. In his autobiography Hanfstaengl recounts telling Hitler about the football games he attended at American universities. Hanfstaengl was enthralled by the marching music used to excite the crowds and was intrigued by how the cheerleaders led thousands of spectators in "the deliberate whipping up of hysterical enthusiasm." Chants such as "Harvard, Harvard, Harvard, rah, rah, rah!" seemed to have a hypnotic effect on the crowd. Hitler was very taken with the idea, and *sieg heil* was selected as the mantra to be chanted at the huge Nazi rallies. This expression is now so closely associated with the Nazi party that it is sometimes used to mock people whose behavior is reminiscent of fascist authoritarianism or mindless submission.

Sources

Comfort, N. A. *Brewer's Politics: A Phrase and Fable Dictionary.* London: Cassell, 1993.

Snyder, Louis L. *Encyclopedia of the Third Reich.* New York: McGraw-Hill, 1976.
Zentner, Christian, and Friedemann Budurftig, eds. *The Encyclopedia of the Third Reich.* New York: Macmillan, 1991.

Silhouette. *An outline drawing, usually black against a white background.*

Etienne de Silhouette (1709–1767) had the misfortune of offering a practical suggestion for national financial reform, for which he was soundly reviled. In 1759 Silhouette was appointed as France's minister of finance. The state was routinely spending far more than it earned, and over half of the nation's revenues went to military expenditures even in times of peace. There was an increasing demand for public works, yet the aristocracy paid no taxes and occupied itself in rounds of hunting, balls, and weekend parties.

Into this decadent playground stepped Silhouette, who was determined to bring spending in line with revenue. Pensions for the aristocracy were limited, and a luxury tax, sales tax, and income tax were proposed. Although gouging the poor was nothing new in France, Silhouette's reforms reached into the upper class, and this was fiercely resented. He was forced to resign just nine months after taking office, but in that brief time his name had become a synonym for cheap. Cheaply manufactured trinkets or clothing were said to be made *á la Silhouette,* "according to Silhouette." Pants without pockets were called silhouettes, for someone with no money had no need of pockets. Outline portraits, usually of faces, were very fashionable in eighteenth-century France, and they too were dubbed *silhouettes.* These inexpensive drawings had been a type of European folk art for centuries, produced by itinerant artists on street corners and in cafes. Although enjoyed by the wealthy, they were within the reach of the working class. Given that pedestrian association, they were known exclusively as *silhouettes* by the end of the eighteenth century.

Sources

Hendrickson, Robert. *Dictionary of Eponyms: Names That Became Words.* New York: Stein and Day, 1985.
McHenry, Robert, ed. *The New Encyclopedia Britannica.* 15th ed. Chicago: Encyclopedia Britannica, 1992.

Simony. *Buying or selling something spiritual in nature, usually used in the context of religious offices.*

A story from the Acts of the Apostles (8: 9) tells of Simon the magician, who traveled throughout Samaria and amazed crowds with his tricks and spells. When Simon heard the apostle Philip preach, he was so impressed that he quickly converted to Christianity. Later, the apostles Peter and John came to Samaria to help organize the Christian community there. Simon saw the wonders these two men performed, and he offered them money if they would give him the power to do the same. Peter chastised Simon for trying to buy the favor of God. The contrite Simon begged Peter's forgiveness, and it is said that he later founded a sect known as the Simoneans.

This incident was enough to link Simon's name with the sin of attempting to buy the church's blessing. Although considered a transgression since the founding of the church, simony was particularly associated with the Middle Ages and the Renaissance. Buying offices and indulgences (that is, paying a fee in exchange for absolution of sins) were the most common forms of simony, and their prevalence was part of the building discontent behind the Protestant Reformation.

Sources

Bromiley, Geoffrey W., ed. *The International Standard Bible Encyclopedia.* Grand Rapids, MI: W. B. Eerdmans, 1988.
Metford, J. C. J. *The Dictionary of Christian Lore and Legend.* London: Thames and Hudson, 1983.
Stimpson, George. *A Book about the Bible.* New York: Harper and Brothers, 1945.

Sinatra doctrine. *The willingness of the Soviet Union during its final years to allow the Eastern European countries to do things "their way."*

In 1968 the Soviet Union announced the Brezhnev Doctrine, which granted the

Soviets the right to intervene in any Warsaw Pact country in which a communist government was threatened. This doctrine was used to justify Soviet intervention in Czechoslovakia and to intimidate democratic movements in other nations within the Soviet orbit. In the late 1980s Mikhail Gorbachev, the secretary general of the Communist party, decided against the use of force to command allegiance to communist ideology. A cultural thaw within the Soviet Union ensued and led to growing restlessness among the satellite states to break ties with the Soviet Union. In 1989 Gennadi Garasimov, a spokesman for the Soviet foreign ministry, announced that the Brezhnev Doctrine was going to be replaced by the *Sinatra Doctrine,* which would permit the satellites to govern themselves as they saw fit. Paul Anka's song "My Way" had been immortalized by Frank Sinatra's rendition and was well known even in Eastern Europe. Its final lines extol an independent spirit: "The record shows I took the blows / And did it my way!"

The satellite states quickly seized the opportunity to determine their own path. In June 1989 Poland voted the democratic Solidarity party into power, and in the following year Romania, Czechoslovakia, and Yugoslavia made bids for democracy. By the early 1990s most of Eastern Europe had shaken off Communist governments, including the Soviet Union, which was officially dissolved in 1991.

Sources

Fuentes, Carlos. "Time Out for Sinatra Doctrine." *The Nation* 25, no. 6 (1990): 185–192.

Moritz, Charles, ed. *Current Biography Yearbook.* New York: H. W. Wilson, 1960.

Pickering, David, ed. *Brewer's Dictionary of Twentieth Century Phrase and Fable.* Boston: Houghton Mifflin Company, 1992.

Sinister. ***Suggesting an evil intent or occurrence.***

The 8 percent of the population that is left-handed may not welcome the news that the Latin word for left-handedness is *sinister.* This association stems from the ancient Greek and Roman belief in the process of divination. Messages from the gods came indirectly to people through oracles, signs in the stars, the behavior of animals, and rolls of the dice. By observing the sky, for example, it was possible to discern a divine message from patterns in the clouds, lightning flashes, or the flight of birds. If this activity occurred in the east, the omen was favorable, but signs in the western skies portended evil. Because Greek augurs faced north when looking for messages from the gods, the west was on their left side.

The Roman poets often alluded to the left when they wished to describe ominous, inauspicious circumstances. The word *sinister* slipped into the English language during the Renaissance because of the revival of interest in classical literature. It then lost its association with left-handedness and assumed its current meaning.

Sources

Mish, Frederick C. *The Merriam-Webster New Book of Word Histories.* Springfield, IL: Merriam-Webster, 1991.

Sacks, David. *Encyclopedia of the Ancient Greek World.* New York: Facts on File, 1995.

Simpson, J. A., and E. S. C. Weiner, eds. *The Oxford English Dictionary.* 2d ed. Oxford: Clarendon Press, 1989.

Sixty-four-dollar question (also $64,000 question). ***A difficult question that is crucial to an outcome.***

One of the first quiz shows to become a national fixation was *Take It or Leave It,* which made its debut on the radio in 1940. Contestants were asked up to six increasingly difficult questions on a particular topic. The first correct answer earned a $1 prize, and each subsequent correct answer doubled the prize, while a wrong answer meant losing everything. The final, and presumably most difficult question, was the $64 question. The term *$64 question* quickly slipped into the national vocabulary, especially after President Franklin Roosevelt used it to describe a perplexing problem. By 1950, $64 (about $390 in 1995 dollars) was no longer a sum that generated very much excitement and the program went off the air.

In 1955 CBS revised the idea for television and raised the stakes to $64,000. The show was a resounding success and usually captured over 80 percent of the viewing audience. Although the program had a good run, the television market was saturated by high-stakes game shows, and the public was disillusioned by the revelations of the "quiz show scandal." In 1958 *The $64,000 Question* was cancelled.

Sources

Brown, Les. *Les Brown's Encyclopedia of Television.* New York: New York Zoetrope, 1982.

Cole, Sylvia, and Abraham H. Lass. *Facts on File Dictionary of Twentieth-Century Allusions: From Abbott and Costello to Ziegfeld Girls.* New York: Facts on File, 1991.

DeLong, Thomas A. *Quiz Craze: America's Infatuation with Game Shows.* New York: Praeger, 1991.

Skeleton at the feast. ***A somber element in an otherwise festive atmosphere; also, a derogatory term for someone who does not appear to be enjoying a celebration.***

With at least 227 published works, the Greek historian Plutarch (46–120) was one of the most prolific writers of his day. He traveled widely throughout Greece and Egypt and compiled extensive observations of religious, political, and social customs. In his *Moralia* essays, Plutarch recounts a strange practice among the ancient Egyptians. During elaborate celebrations and feasts, a mummy would be placed at the table with the guests. The *skeleton at the feast* was supposed to remind the guests of their own mortality. The expression did not become popular in English until it was cited in Henry Wadsworth Longfellow's poem, "The Old Clock on the Stairs":

> In that mansion used to be
> Free-hearted Hospitality;
> His great fires up the chimney roared;
> The stranger feasted at his board;
> But like the skeleton at the feast,
> The warning timepiece never ceased,
> "Forever—never!
> Never—forever!"

Sources

Hendrickson, Robert. *Facts on File Encyclopedia of Word and Phrase Origins.* New York: Facts on File, 1987.

Simpson, J. A., and E. S. C. Weiner, eds. *The Oxford English Dictionary.* 2d ed. Oxford: Clarendon Press, 1989.

Slave. ***A person bound in servitude to another person or household.***

Slavery in the ancient and medieval world rarely involved the enslavement of people across racial lines. Most slaves came by their station through defeat in war. As a result, it was quite common for Italians to have slaves of Germanic descent, or for Russians to have Polish slaves. A large percentage of bondsmen were conquered Slavs, who were bought and sold throughout Europe and the Near East. These people referred to themselves as *sclavus,* and by the ninth century the word had become part of the Latin vocabulary in reference to any enslaved person. By the seventeenth century, *slave* was the English adaptation, although by that time most slaves were of African descent.

Sources

Mish, Frederick C. *The Merriam-Webster New Book of Word Histories.* Springfield, IL: Merriam-Webster, 1991.

Phillips, William D. *Slavery from Roman Times to the Early Transatlantic Trade.* Minneapolis: University of Minnesota Press, 1985.

Wiedemann, Thomas. *Greek and Roman Slavery.* Baltimore, MD: Johns Hopkins University Press, 1981.

Slush fund. ***A fund raised for undesignated purposes, usually used in the context of political corruption.***

This term originated in the days before refrigeration, when sailors depended on salted beef to carry them through long voyages. The meat had to be boiled before serving, which removed nearly all the fat. The rendered fat, known as *slush,* was skimmed off and stored in barrels. Slush was used to rub down the masts and rigging and was an excellent sealant against water rot when mixed with linseed oil and tallow soap. After setting some slush aside for this important shipboard function, there was plenty of boiled fat left over. This slush was sold in ports as a primary ingredient in the manufacture of soap and candles. The money obtained from the sale of slush went toward the purchase of a few indulgences for the crew.

In modern usage, the term is often associated with corruption, but it still retains the innocent connotation in references to money donated by individuals for general entertainment, such as office parties.

Sources

Hendrickson, Robert. *Facts on File Encyclopedia of Word and Phrase Origins.* New York: Facts on File, 1987.

Jeans, Peter D. *Ship to Shore: A Dictionary of Everyday Words and Phrases Derived from the Sea.* Santa Barbara, CA: ABC-CLIO, 1993.

Stimpson, George. *A Book about a Thousand Things.* New York: Harper and Brothers, 1946.

Smoke-filled room. ***A place where important decisions are engineered behind closed doors and presented to the public as a* fait accompli.**

This phrase was coined during the committee meetings for the Republican presidential nomination in 1920. Former newspaperman Warren G. Harding (1865–1923) was a dark-horse candidate and had served only one term in the U.S. Senate before making his bid for the presidency. A number of other candidates were far more qualified for the job, but Harding had an engaging personality, a fine speaking voice, few enemies, and an ambitious wife. Shortly before the convention, Harry Daugherty, Harding's campaign manager, made the following prediction: "The convention will be deadlocked, and after the other candidates have gone their limit, some 12 or 15 men, worn out and bleary-eyed for lack of sleep, will sit down about 2 o'clock in the morning in a smoke-filled room in some hotel and decide the nomination. When that time comes, Harding will be elected."

As the convention opened, there were three front-runners, and Harding's strategy was to let them deadlock. If Harding could be the second choice of a large percentage of delegates, he could succeed in capturing the nomination. After several ballots confirmed a hopeless stalemate, a group of influential senators and delegates met in a suite of the Blackstone Hotel in Chicago and apparently agreed to switch their votes to Harding to break the deadlock—thus bearing out Daugherty's prediction. One story, probably apocryphal, says that the power brokers summoned Harding to the suite and asked him to swear there were no skeletons in his closet. Harding excused himself for a few minutes to phone his mistresses and returned to verify that there would be no problems. He then emerged from the smoke-filled room assured of the Republican presidential nomination.

Sources

Levy, Leonard W., and Louis Fisher, eds. *Encyclopedia of the American Presidency.* New York: Simon and Schuster, 1994.

Safire, William. *Safire's Political Dictionary.* New York: Random House, 1978.

Stimpson, George. *A Book about American History.* Greenwich, CT: Fawcett Publications, 1960.

Sodom and Gomorrah. ***Symbols of corruption and sexual perversion.***

The biblical story of Sodom and Gomorrah, towns that were apparently so wicked that they were destroyed by a vengeful Lord, contains some passages that remain the subject of debate. Two angels were sent to Sodom to determine if the town was truly as wicked as rumor held. They took shelter with Lot, but the wicked townspeople of Sodom demanded that Lot "bring them out to us, so that we may know them." Lot replied,"I beg of you, my brothers, do not act so wickedly. Look, I have two daughters who have not known a man; let me bring them out to you, and do to them as you please; only do nothing to these men, for they have come under the shelter of my roof. (Genesis 19: 5–8). Commentators debate whether the passage actually suggests an intent to commit homosexual rape in the use of the verb "to know"; of the 942 occurrences of the term in the Old Testament, it implies carnal knowledge in only 10 instances. Regardless, *sodomite* became the term for a person engaging in noncoital copulation, especially with a member of the same sex.

In any event, the towns of Sodom and Gomorrah incurred the wrath of God, and "fire and sulphur" rained down on them. Their complete destruction has been taken to mean that the two ancient cities were punished for indulging in unbridled sexual license. A scientific explanation is suggested by the archaeological evidence. Apparently, a cataclysmic earthquake around the year 1900 B.C. devastated the once-fertile plain on which the cities of Sodom and Gomorrah were located. The images of "fire and sulphur" may have described the release of gases from shifts in the earth's crust.

Sources

Bromiley, Geoffrey W., ed. *The International Standard Bible Encyclopedia.* Grand Rapids, MI: W. B. Eerdmans, 1988.

Metzger, Bruce M., and Michael D. Coogan, eds. *The Oxford Companion to the Bible.* New York: Oxford University Press, 1993.

Neev, David. *The Destruction of Sodom, Gomorrah, and Jericho: Geological, Climatological, and Archaeological Background.* Oxford: Oxford University Press, 1995.

Panati, Charles. *Sacred Origins of Profound Things.* New York: Penguin Arcana, 1996.

Solecism. *Poor use of grammar, or other breaches of etiquette.*

Soli was an ancient city founded by Greek colonists around the eighth century B.C. Located in what is now south-central Turkey, Soli was on the edge of the Greek world, far removed from Athens, the cultural center of the empire. Over time the colonists at Soli developed their own dialect, which was ridiculed by the sophisticated Athenians. The Greek word *soloikismus* (solecism) was coined to refer to the bad grammar and the faux pas committed by the provincial settlers at Soli.

Inhabitants of colonial outposts have often been derided by elites from the motherland. American and Australian colonists were mocked by the English for their accents, as were Hispanic settlers in Latin America. These differences are known as *solecisms,* although the word is now used in a broader context in reference to any social flaw or shortcoming.

Sources

Grant, Michael. *A Guide to the Ancient World: A Dictionary of Classical Place Names.* New York: H. W. Wilson, 1986.

Hendrickson, Robert. *Dictionary of Eponyms: Names That Became Words.* New York: Stein and Day, 1985.

McHenry, Robert, ed. *The New Encyclopedia Britannica.* 15th ed. Chicago: Encyclopedia Britannica, 1992.

Simpson, J. A., and E. S. C. Weiner, eds. *The Oxford English Dictionary.* 2d ed. Oxford: Clarendon Press, 1989.

Sooner. *Someone from Oklahoma.*

In 1889 President Benjamin Harrison designated a large tract of land in the Oklahoma Territory for homesteaders, but only those who actually went to Oklahoma and intended to live there would be allowed to compete for the land. The settlers would line up at the edge of the territory on 22 April 1889, and at noon, a shot would be fired to start the race. Whoever was able to stake a claim first on a 160-acre plot of land would receive title. Estimates on the number who participated in the land rush range from 20,000 and 50,000.

According to the rules, no person attempting to occupy the land before the assigned day would be permitted into the competition. Some settlers were so anxious to ensure that they would obtain a desirable plot that they slipped into the territory under cover of darkness and hid until the race was under way. Such people were known as *sooners,* and although many were apprehended, there is no doubt that some of the people who claimed land in the great Oklahoma land rush had jumped the gun.

Sooner eventually lost its negative connotation and acquired a brash, adventuresome sense.

Sources

Adams, James Truslow, ed. *The Dictionary of American History.* New York: Scribner's, 1976.

Adler, Mortimer J., and Charles Van Doren. *The Annals of America.* Chicago: Encyclopedia Britannica, 1968.

Stimpson, George. *A Book about American History.* Greenwich, CT: Fawcett Publications, 1960.

Soup-can art. ***Art that depicts commonplace objects and appears to have no intrinsic aesthetic value.***

The son of Czechoslovakian immigrants, Andrew (Andy) Warhol (1928–1987) worked as a commercial illustrator for a decade before he began to exhibit his own distinctive paintings. In an era when abstract expressionism dominated the New York art market, Warhol exhibited simple, stark paintings of mundane objects. Focusing on the commonplace contents of his mother's kitchen, he painted such everyday items as Martinson's coffee cans, Coca-Cola bottles, and S&H green stamps. "I just paint things I always thought were beautiful, things you use every day and never think about," Warhol told an interviewer for *Time* magazine. His famous depiction of the Campbell's tomato soup can was succeeded by paintings of all 32 soup varieties. As Warhol commented, "Many an afternoon at lunchtime Mom would open a can of Campbell's for me, because that's all we could afford. I love it to this day."

The soup cans made their debut at a New York gallery in 1962 and received an avalanche of publicity. People were mystified by these small, pedestrian-looking paintings that were selling for $100 each. One art gallery up the road from Warhol's exhibit bought a few cans of Campbell's soup and placed them in the window with a sign: "Buy them cheaper here—60¢ for three cans." Warhol's paintings of everyday items sparked a wave of pop art that dominated the decade of the 1960s. Simple, realistic paintings of road signs, typewriters, hamburgers, and plumbing fixtures were suddenly selling for top prices. Critics decried this sort of art as a joke on the buyer, and Warhol's pictures were held up as examples of overpriced art that lacked imagination, beauty, or meaning. Despite the initial burst of excitement for pop art, it was never taken seriously by the general public.

Sources

Bockris, Victor. *Warhol.* London: Muller, 1989.

Turner, Jane, ed. *The Dictionary of Art.* New York: Grove's Dictionaries, 1996.

Sousaphone. ***A large brass instrument similar to the tuba, with a flaring bell and a wrap-around body that makes it ideal for marching bands.***

John Philip Sousa (1854–1932) was known as the "March King" and remains the most important figure in American band music. Sousa was a master at creating rousing, memorable tunes, typified by what he considered to be his best work, *Stars and Stripes Forever.* At the age of 25 he became director of the United States Marine Band, and he later toured the country with the Sousa Band.

Sousa was an excellent conductor, administrator, and showman and had an ear for tonal quality, which led him to experiment with the instruments in this band. In the mid-nineteenth century, Ignaz Stowasser of Vienna had perfected the helicon, a large contrabass tuba. Although the instrument provided a rich sound in band music, Sousa disliked it for concert performances because "the tone would shoot ahead and become too violent." He therefore modified the instrument so that the bell flared upward, allowing the music to be diffused throughout the concert hall. The new instrument was named a *sousaphone,* and no marching band was considered complete without one. Today, most sousaphones are built with their bells pointing forward rather than upward.

Sources

Beeching, Cyril Leslie. *Dictionary of Eponyms.* London: Clive Bingley, 1979.

Hitchcock, H. Wiley, ed. *The New Grove Dictionary of American Music.* London: Macmillan, 1986.

Sousa, John Philip. *Marching Along: Recollections of Men, Women, and Music.* Boston: Hale, Cushman and Flint, 1941.

Spartan. ***Sparse, uncomfortable, and consisting of only the barest necessities.***
Because it was the archrival of Athens, Sparta has acquired a reputation as the antithesis of Athenian culture as well. This characterization is fairly accurate. Although both cities demanded strong allegiance to the state, Athens valued artistic endeavors, great literature, and the stirring of a democratic impulse. In Sparta, however, service to the state far outweighed any other consideration. In the eighth century B.C. Sparta conquered and exploited the neighboring population of Messenia. While the Messenians produced necessities for Sparta, Spartan men devoted themselves to rigorous military training—a full-time occupation. Spartans had no personal property, and the state provided them with everything from food and shelter to an education. Only the warrior was valued in Sparta, and items or goods that were not useful in the training or support of that class were shunned. The term *Spartan simplicity* implies this lack of interest in luxury, comfort, or embellishment.

The militarism paid off. Between the seventh and the fourth centuries B.C. the Spartans had the best infantry in the Mediterranean and possibly in the entire world. However, the secretive, anti-intellectual Spartan traditions proved fatal, for they failed to adopt new battle techniques and became vulnerable to the impressive and innovative tactics of the Macedonian empire.

Sources
Hornblower, Simon, and Antony Spawforth, eds. *The Oxford Classical Dictionary.* 3d ed. Oxford: Oxford University Press, 1996.
McHenry, Robert, ed. *The New Encyclopedia Britannica.* 15th ed. Chicago: Encyclopedia Britannica, 1992.
Sacks, David. *Encyclopedia of the Ancient Greek World.* New York: Facts on File, 1995.

Spick and span. ***Clean and spotless.***
The puzzling term *spick and span* has its roots in the nautical world. A *spick* was a nail or spike. *Span* referred to a plank of new wood, unmarked and never before used. If a ship was *spick and span,* it meant that it was brand-new. Initially the phrase always appeared as *spick and span new.* Eventually the "new" was dropped, and the expression described something that was very tidy or had the appearance of being brand-new.

Sources
Jeans, Peter D. *Ship to Shore: A Dictionary of Everyday Words and Phrases Derived from the Sea.* Santa Barbara, CA: ABC-CLIO, 1993.
Stimpson, George. *A Book about a Thousand Things.* New York: Harper and Brothers, 1946.
Simpson, J. A., and E. S. C. Weiner, eds. *The Oxford English Dictionary.* 2d ed. Oxford: Clarendon Press, 1989.

Spider.
See Bruce and the spider.

Spoils system. ***Awarding government positions to the supporters of the winning candidate in an election.***
It was long considered customary for victorious armies to take the "spoils of war" by plundering the land and possessions of the defeated population. The word *spoils* found its way into the American political arena shortly after the development of the two-party system. It was considered fair game for a newly elected president to fill major government posts with his supporters. Thomas Jefferson was the first president to make heavy use of this practice, and his successors would follow his lead. In 1832 Senator William Learned Marcy of New York was quoted as saying that he could see "nothing wrong with the rule that to the victor goes the spoils." However, abuses of this system became so serious during the presidency of Ulysses S. Grant that efforts at reform gained momentum. In 1883 the Pendleton Civil Service Reform Act was passed by Congress. It established a merit system for government employees and protected them from job loss because of a change in political administrations.

Some of the highest political offices, such as ambassadorships and heads of departments, are exempt from this act, and still generally operate under the spoils system.

Sources

McHenry, Robert, ed. *The New Encyclopedia Britannica.* 15th ed. Chicago: Encyclopedia Britannica, 1992.

Safire, William. *Safire's Political Dictionary.* New York: Random House, 1978.

Stimpson, George. *A Book about American Politics.* New York: Harper, 1952.

Spoonerism. ***An unintentional transposition of initial sounds in the words of a phrase.***

The Reverend William Archibald Spooner (1844–1930) was no doubt very embarrassed when he referred to the "dear old Queen" as a "queer old Dean," but Spooner was renowned for such slips of the tongue. Spooner was a very well-educated man, but he had a number of odd characteristics. He was a tiny albino, with a large head, extremely poor eyesight, and a nervous disposition. Public speaking was always difficult for him, and as dean of New Oxford College his blunders received a wide audience. His congregation could hardly resist repeating such comical twists as "the Lord is a shoving leopard." Other well-remembered Spoonerisms included one spoken at a wedding ceremony: "It is kisstomary to cuss the bride." Attempting to speak of a "half-formed wish," Spooner instead stated, "We all know what it is to have a half-warmed fish inside us."

The technical name for Spooner's reversals is metathesis, in which letters, sounds, or syllables are inadvertently switched. The eponym *spoonerism* was in common use by 1900.

Spooner's strange reversals were not confined to his speech. The historian A. J. Toynbee recounted an incident while dining with Spooner. Some salt was spilled on the table, and Spooner proceeded to pour wine onto the salt. Pouring salt onto wine is a technique for preventing a wine stain.

Sources

Hunt, Cecil. *Word Origins: The Romance of Language.* New York: Philosophical Library, 1962.

McHenry, Robert, ed. *The New Encyclopedia Britannica.* 15th ed. Chicago: Encyclopedia Britannica, 1992.

Simpson, J. A., and E. S. C. Weiner, eds. *The Oxford English Dictionary.* 2d ed. Oxford: Clarendon Press, 1989.

Star Chamber justice. ***Proceedings that are handled in an unfair and arbitrary manner.***

The Court of the Star Chamber, which dates back to the time of Edward III, was intended to handle cases of interest to the king. It probably derived its name from the gilt stars that decorated the chamber's ceiling. The Star Chamber was not subject to common law and therefore had no jury. No appeals were permitted to the verdicts handed down by the king's counselors. Without the safeguards provided by common-law procedures, the court was free to use torture. The judge meted out punishments, which could be imprisonment, confiscation of property, or mutilation, although the Star Chamber was not permitted to sentence an individual to death.

The secretive and powerful nature of the Star Chamber made it a perfect tool for monarchs wishing to quash internal opposition. The chamber gained a notorious reputation for its arbitrary judgments and punishments and became a symbol of oppression during the Tudor and Stuart reigns. The gentry particularly hated the institution, and it was abolished by the Long Parliament in 1641.

Sources

Fritze, Ronald H., ed. *Historical Dictionary of Tudor England, 1485–1603.* New York: Greenwood Press, 1991.

Fritze, Ronald H., and William B. Robison, eds. *Historical Dictionary of Stuart England, 1603–1689.* Westport, CT: Greenwood Press, 1996.

Rachum, Ilan. *The Renaissance: An Illustrated Encyclopedia.* New York: Mayflower Books, 1979.

Steal someone's thunder. ***To take credit that belongs to another.***

Theaters of the eighteenth century designed innovative special effects to keep boisterous audiences entertained. There were water machines that simulated waterfalls and contraptions that allowed actors to fly across the stage. For the proper sounds, large casks filled with stones were shaken, pots were struck, and guns were fired off stage. One production of *Hamlet* managed to have real cannons fired. The sound of thunder had traditionally been produced by shaking sheets of metal, until playwright John Dennis invented a way to produce realistic thunder noises. In 1709 his play *Appius and Virginia* opened in London to miserable reviews. The only thing the critics liked was its thunder. Dennis used a wooden trough to roll large stones, which made a heavy, ominous sound. The play closed after a brief run. Shortly thereafter Dennis attended a production of *Macbeth*. In the opening scene, three witches appear in the midst of a thunderstorm. Dennis recognized the sound as coming from the apparatus he had designed. Although imitation is said to be the sincerest form of flattery, Dennis was outraged and complained bitterly about having his thunder stolen—literally.

Sources

Brockett, Oscar G. *History of the Theatre.* Boston: Allyn and Bacon, 1982.

Claiborne, Robert. *Loose Cannons and Red Herrings: A Book of Lost Metaphors.* New York: Norton, 1988.

Law, Jonathan, ed. *Brewer's Theater: A Phrase and Fable Dictionary.* New York: HarperCollins, 1994.

Stetson. *Distinctive, high-crowned western hats.*

John B. Stetson (1830–1906) was one of twelve children born into a New Jersey hatmaking family. As a young man he was diagnosed with consumption and was not expected to live. His family sent him westward, hoping that the wide-open spaces and dry air might improve his health. Stetson thrived in the West, and his health was restored. After a stint in the Colorado gold mines, he was ready to return to the East.

Setting up a one-man hat-making shop in Philadelphia, Stetson barely eked out a living. He sold his hats to local retailers and never had orders for more than a dozen hats at a time. Believing that his hats lacked a distinctive style, he began experimenting with different types of brims and crowns. His experience in the rugged outdoors inspired the design of a hat with a very large brim to serve as protection from sun and rain and with a high crown that would be cool. Calling his hat "the Boss of the Plains," Stetson hoped that the style would be popular among people who were entranced with the idea of the Wild West. Skeptics told him that Europe set the fashion for hats and that a Western style was not likely to be successful on the East Coast. In spite of the naysayers, the distinctive new hats quickly became popular, and by the end of his career Stetson's factory was producing more than 2 million hats a year. The association of the rugged cowboy with the Stetson hat has become an indelible part of American culture because of such movie legends as Gary Cooper and John Wayne. One cowboy paid tribute to the hat in verse:

> Used to decoy some rustler's lead,
> or as a pillow beneath my head;
> Coaxing a smoldering fire in the cold,
> panning dust in search of gold.
> Pushed up big and knocked down flat,
> has been the lot of my old Stetson hat.

Sources

Beeching, Cyril Leslie. *Dictionary of Eponyms.* London: Clive Bingley, 1979.

Bosquet, Patrick. "The Hat of the West: John B. and His Stetson." *Western Horseman* 58, no. 5 (1993): 18–20.

Johnson, Allen, and Dumas Malone, eds. *Dictionary of American Biography.* New York: Scribner's, 1964.

Stigma. *A mark of disfavor or disgrace.*

Slavery was a fundamental aspect of ancient Greek and Roman society. Slaves were usually taken from conquered populations and were either the property of a particular individual or owned by the state. There was little to distinguish slaves from other lowly citizens of a city, except an identifying slave collar or a particular kind of clothing. Although an escaping slave might try to blend in with the general population, fugitives who were apprehended were branded on the forehead to make any other bids for freedom more difficult. This brand was known as a *stigma*. Some cities also put a stigma on their slaves to prevent them from being stolen away into private enslavement. By the seventeenth century the word was no longer associated with a mark of slavery but was being used in a general context to refer to something that brought disgrace or shame on an individual.

Sources

Mish, Frederick C. *The Merriam-Webster New Book of Word Histories.* Springfield, IL: Merriam-Webster, 1991.

Phillips, William D. *Slavery from Roman Times to the Early Transatlantic Trade.* Minneapolis: University of Minnesota Press, 1985.

Wiedemann, Thomas. *Greek and Roman Slavery.* Baltimore, MD: Johns Hopkins University Press, 1981.

Stockholm syndrome. ***A psychological phenomenon that causes hostages to identify with their captors.***

During a 1973 bank robbery in Stockholm, four bank employees were held hostage for five days in the bank vault. During telephone conversations with journalists, the hostages began to relate how they distrusted the police but had faith in their kidnappers. At first it was assumed that the captives had been coerced into making such statements, but when they were freed, they insisted on walking side-by-side with their captors in order to ensure that the robbers would not be killed by police snipers. The hostages refused to testify against the kidnappers at their trial. One bank employee even claimed to be in love with one of her captors and obtained a divorce in order to marry him. Perhaps the best-known American case of the *Stockholm syndrome* is that of Patricia Hearst. Kidnapped in 1974 by the Symbionese Liberation Army, this American heiress became the willing dupe of these countercultural terrorists.

The Stockholm syndrome seems to be a coping mechanism for dealing with severe stress. Captives are placed in an infantile situation in which the ability to eat, speak, and move are at the mercy of the captor. The relationship assumes some characteristics of a child's feelings for a powerful parent. More recently the term *Stockholm syndrome* has been broadened to include the effect that long-term sequestration may have on a jury. With everything provided for them by the court, jurors may subconsciously identify with the prosecution as parent, to the detriment of the defendant.

Sources

Campbell, James F. *Hostage: Terror and Triumph.* Westport, CT: Greenwood Press, 1992.

Dershowitz, Alan. *The Abuse Excuse and Other Cop-Outs, Sob Stories, and Evasions of Responsibility.* Boston: Little, Brown, 1994.

Kuleshnyk, Irka. "The Stockholm Syndrome: Toward an Understanding." *Social Action and the Law* 10, no. 2 (1984): 37–42.

Stradivarius. ***The finest violins in the world; figuratively, something that stands above the rest.***

There are few craftsmen whose product is universally accepted as superior, but the violins of Antonio Stradivari (1644–1737) can claim this distinction. Stradivari was trained as a woodcarver and was later apprenticed to Nicolo Amati, a respected violin maker. By the time his tutor died in 1684, Stradivari's work was recognized as surpassing all his competitors, and his fame spread beyond Italy. Opening his own shop with the assistance of his two sons, Stradivari was one of those fortunate artisans whose greatness was recognized in his own lifetime. His name is still listed in the pantheon of world-class artists, and his work commands prices in the millions of dollars.

Stradivari's genius is attributed to the shape of the holes he carved and to the orange-brown varnish he developed, which has never been replicated. The influence of the varnish on a violin is crucial to the sound it will produce. If the varnish dries too hard, the violin will have a limited tonal range. If the consistency of the varnish is oily or thick, it suppresses the vibrations that give color to the sound. Stradivari created a varnish that dried to precisely the correct consistency. Some have duplicated the consistency of the master's varnish, but after a few months or a few years, when the varnish reaches its final state, it no longer resembles the Stradivarius finish. Despite all the tools of modern science, Stradivari's varnish recipe remains a mystery.

Sources

Hendrickson, Robert. *Dictionary of Eponyms: Names That Became Words.* New York: Stein and Day, 1985.

Hill, William Henry. *Antonio Stradivari: His Life and Work, 1644–1737.* New York: Dover Publications, 1963.

Sadie, Stanley, ed. *The New Grove Dictionary of Music and Musicians.* Washington, DC: Grove's Dictionaries of Music, 1980.

Strafe. ***To attack from above; usually a machine-gun attack on troops from low-flying aircraft.***

World War I aircraft were generally used for reconnaissance purposes, as pilots gathered information on the location and strength of enemy troops. However, the impulse to fire on vulnerable troops proved irresistible, and many pilots began bringing machine guns with them on their missions. The British were the first to make aggressive use of machine guns from the air, but the Germans were determined to return the assault in kind. Although most British planes were manned by a single individual, the Germans began using two-seater planes, allowing the passenger to devote himself to operating a rotating machine gun. *Gott strafe England* (God punish England) became the pilot's mantra. The phrase became so well known that the word *strafe* was one of the few German words to slip into common usage among the Allied powers during World War I.

Sources

Dickson, Paul. *War Slang: Fighting Words and Phrases of Americans from the Civil War to the Gulf War.* New York: Pocket Books, 1994.

Hallion, Richard. *Strike from the Sky: The History of Battlefield Air Attack, 1911–1945.* Washington, DC: Smithsonian Institution Press, 1989.

Simpson, J. A., and E. S. C. Weiner, eds. *The Oxford English Dictionary.* 2d ed. Oxford: Clarendon Press, 1989.

Sub rosa. ***Keeping information secret or in confidence.***

The ancient Romans had a passion for roses that was reflected in their religion, festivities, art work, and even cuisine. Garlands of roses were awarded to military and athletic heroes. The lovely scent of the rose was extracted into oils for daily bathing. Rose petals were used in the preparation of jellies, honey, and wine. A rose suspended over a council table indicated that all who were present were sworn to secrecy. To be *sub rosa,* or under the rose, was a custom as early as 477 B.C. and was depicted in Roman frescos. A bouquet of roses over a doorway was a gracious invitation to speak freely at a social gathering, without fear that the information would be repeated. The custom may derive from the legend of the god Eros, who bribed Harpocrates with roses to keep him from revealing indiscretions to Venus.

By the nineteenth century the expression *sub rosa* had taken on a legal connotation, in that information exchanged between lawyer and client must be confidential.

Sources

Leach, Maria. *Funk and Wagnalls Standard Dictionary of Folklore, Mythology, and Legend.* New York: Funk and Wagnalls, 1949.

Rose, Graham, and Peter King. *The Love of Roses: From Myth to Modern Culture.* London: Quiller Press, 1990.

Sword of Damocles. ***Something that warns of impending doom.***

Damocles was a courtier of Dionysius, the powerful tyrant of Syracuse from 405 to 367 B.C. According to a popular legend, one evening Damocles was speaking with excessive flattery about the wealth and splendor of the court, and he pronounced Dionysius the happiest of men. Dionysius persuaded Damocles to take his place so that he too might enjoy regal glory. After seating himself on the throne, Damocles noticed that there was a sword suspended above his head by a single horsehair. Thus Dionysius demonstrated that the splendor of royalty disguises the dangerous and unenviable aspects of the position. This is most likely an apocryphal tale.

Sources

Hunt, Cecil. *Word Origins: The Romance of Language.* New York: Philosophical Library, 1962.

McHenry, Robert, ed. *The New Encyclopedia Britannica.* 15th ed. Chicago: Encyclopedia Britannica, 1992.

Stimpson, George. *A Book about a Thousand Things.* New York: Harper and Brothers, 1946.

T

Tabloid. ***A newspaper with a small format, usually featuring short, sensational stories.***
The word *tabloid* was coined by the pharmaceutical firm of Burroughs, Wellcome and Company in 1884. Tabloids were specially formulated pills that were small, concentrated, and easily swallowed. Using refined ingredients and highly accurate machinery, Burroughs, Wellcome and Company was able to compress pills containing between one thousandth of a grain to sixty grains per dosage. The company won numerous awards for the excellence of its products.

Journalists latched onto the word to describe the format of a new type of newspaper. Alfred Harmsworth (1865–1922) was known for his skill in reorganizing and marketing troubled newspapers. On 1 January 1900 he launched an experimental edition of the *New York World*. The size of the newspaper was cut in half for easier handling, and the length of the articles was curtailed. Newspapers following the tabloid format were originally defined by the physical dimensions of the paper and the length of the stories. In 1903 Harmsworth again applied his remedy to the *Daily Mirror,* which had been considered a failure. By limiting the size, but also by including numerous pictures and gearing the content toward stories of popular interest, Harmsworth boosted the paper's circulation to over one million readers.

Burroughs, Wellcome and Company resented seeing their trademarked word being used in other media. They launched a number of lawsuits to protect their right to *tabloid,* but they ultimately lost. In 1903 a judge ruled that "the word tabloid has become so well-known in consequence of the use of it by the Plaintiff firm in connection with their compressed drugs that I think it has acquired a secondary sense in which it has been used and may legitimately be used so long as it does not interfere with their trade rights. I think the word has been applied generally with reference to the notion of a compressed form or dose of anything."

Sources

Carver, Craig. *A History of English in Its Own Words.* New York: HarperCollins, 1991.

Derdak, Thomas, ed. *International Directory of Company Histories.* Chicago: St. James Press, 1988.

McHenry, Robert, ed. *The New Encyclopedia Britannica.* 15th ed. Chicago: Encyclopedia Britannica, 1992.

Paneth, Donald. *The Encyclopedia of American Journalism.* New York: Facts on File, 1983.

Talk turkey. ***To get down to business, including all the unpleasant details.***
There is an old story about the source of this curious expression. In colonial days a white man and his Indian companion had gone out hunting and killed several crows and turkeys. When it came time to divide the spoils, the white man said, "I'll take this turkey, and this crow is for you." He continued separating the day's catch until he had all the turkeys. The Indian finally spoke up, saying "You talk all turkey for you. You never talk turkey for me." He insisted on receiving a fair share, and the spoils were then more evenly divided.

The first written version of this tale dates to 1830, and no better explanation for the expression has been discovered.

Sources

Holt, Alfred H. *Phrase and Word Origins.* New York: Dover Publications, 1961.

Lurie, Charles. *Everyday Sayings.* Detroit, MI: Gale Research, 1968.

Tar and feather. ***To subject to public indignity.***

The practice of pouring hot pitch on a naked person and rolling him or her in feathers was first specified in English law in 1189, to be applied to sailors found guilty of theft while at sea. In American history, tarring and feathering is almost always associated with mob violence. There were dozens of instances during the Revolutionary War, when it was a popular punishment for loyalists. In one case, British soldiers used the punishment on Thomas Ditson, a minuteman who was accused of trying to encourage British soldiers to desert. A group of New England women tarred and feathered Captain Floyd Ireson when he refused to go to the aid of seamen in distress. In the American West the punishment was considered proper vigilante justice for wifebeaters and card cheats. In the twentieth century, the Ku Klux Klan employed tar and feather to drive away "undesirables." Today the practice survives as a symbolic gesture of hostility, as when a few western ranchers tarred and feathered effigies of environmentalists whose policies seemed to threaten their way of life.

Sources

Sifakis, Carl. *The Encyclopedia of American Crime.* New York: Facts on File, 1982.

Stimpson, George. *A Book about American History.* Greenwich, CT: Fawcett Publications, 1960.

Wagner, Leopold. *Manners, Customs, and Observances: Their Origin and Signification.* London: William Heinemann, 1894.

Tar-heel. ***A resident of North Carolina.***

Tar was an important natural resource in colonial America, used in shipbuilding to waterproof the hulls. The thick pine forests of the Carolinas were rich in the resin that could be boiled down into tar and pitch. Great Britain, whose empire depended largely on naval strength, was a large consumer of tar, and in 1705 the British Parliament began offering bounties to companies that could fill the huge orders for the sticky by-product of pine trees. The Carolinas were eager to take advantage of the offer and began shipping enormous amounts of tar to Great Britain. Charleston alone exported 60,000 barrels of tar and pitch a year during the 1720s. When Parliament reduced the monetary reward for tar, South Carolinians lost interest and turned to the more profitable venture of rice cultivation. North Carolina continued to produce tar.

One well-known, though probably apocryphal, tale claims that during the Carolina campaign of 1781, some resourceful North Carolinians poured tar into a stream and impeded the retreat of British troops. Residents of the state were called both tar-boilers and tar-heels, an allusion to people who were so poor they walked about barefoot and picked up tar on their feet. These terms were initially derogatory appellations, but by the late nineteenth century, North Carolinians had taken to calling themselves *tar-heel* with pride.

Sources

Cooke, Jacob Ernest, ed. *Encyclopedia of the North American Colonies.* New York: Scribner's Sons, 1993.

Stimpson, George. *A Book about American History.* Greenwich, CT: Fawcett Publications, 1960.

Tasmania. ***An island state of Australia, located off its southeastern coast.***

The first European to catch sight of this island was the self-educated Dutch navigator Abel Tasman (1603–1659), who was commissioned by the Dutch East India Company in 1642 to explore the South Pacific. After sailing for months through huge expanses of ocean, Tasman at last came upon a large island to the south of Australia. He named it Van Diemen's Land after the governor-general of the company, who had given Tasman the appointment for the expedition. On this trip Tasman also discovered New Zealand and charted much of the unexplored shorelines of New Guinea and Australia.

Despite this monumental voyage through perilous seas, Tasman's sponsors in the Dutch East India Company were unhappy with his accomplishments, since he had not discovered "one rich silver or gold mine for the solace of the stockholders." He retired from the sea in 1651and never achieved the fame accorded to other major explorers.

In 1825 Van Diemen's Land became a colony of the British Empire. To develop the distant land, convict labor was used, meaning that criminals from Great Britain were forced into virtual slavery for a period of no less than seven years. Van Diemen's Land was known as a violent and brutal society in which a large percentage of the inhabitants lived under oppressive conditions. By the 1840s the Anti-Transportation League, which opposed the convict labor system, began heavy campaigning against the transport of convicts to the island. The practice was outlawed in 1853, and to commemorate the end of that chapter of its history, the island was renamed Tasmania in honor of its discoverer, 200 years after his historic voyage.

Sources

Allen, Oliver E. *The Pacific Navigators.* Alexandria, VA: Time-Life Books, 1980.

McHenry, Robert, ed. *The New Encyclopedia Britannica.* 15th ed. Chicago: Encyclopedia Britannica, 1992.

Robson, L. L. *A Short History of Tasmania.* New York: Oxford University Press, 1985.

Tawdry. ***Cheap and vulgar ornamentation.*** Etheldreda (630–679) was a saintly Anglo-Saxon queen who devoted herself to God from an early age. As a child she had been married to Tonbert, prince of the Gyrwe, but he died before Etheldreda was of an age to consummate the union. The young widow was endowed with the Isle of Ely from her husband's estate. Etheldreda wanted to follow a religious vocation and retreated to the Isle of Ely for about five years. Her father, who had other plans for her, proceeded to arrange another politically advantageous marriage. In 660 she was married against her will to Egfrith, king of Northumbria. The famous medieval historian, the Venerable Bede, wrote that "although she lived with him for twelve years, she preserved the glory of perpetual virginity." Egfrith, in need of an heir, did everything he could to persuade his wife to assume normal wifely duties. After much negotiation and consultation with church authorities, it became apparent that Etheldreda would not be shaken from her vow of chastity, and a separation was arranged. Etheldreda retreated once again to the Isle of Ely, where she founded a monastery and presided over it for the rest of her life.

The saintly Etheldreda confessed to one major sin in her youth—the sin of vanity. She loved to adorn herself with golden chains and necklaces. When she began to suffer from a cancer of the throat, she considered it a punishment for her youthful infatuation with jewelry. As she reported to her confessor, "Once I used to wear vain necklaces around my neck, and now, instead of gold and pearls, God in his goodness has weighted it down with this red, burning swelling." Although the tumor on her neck was opened and drained, she died in 679 from complications of the disease. She was canonized shortly after her death.

In Norman times Etheldreda's name was rendered as Audrey. It was customary to hold a fair on the Isle of Ely on her feast day, October 17. Cheap necklaces and scarves, known as Saint Audrey's laces, were sold at this fair. Over time the thick accent of the islanders condensed the expression to *Sin-t audrey lace* and finally simply to "tawdry lace." This is an example of aphesis, the loss of the first, unstressed syllable of a word. By the seventeenth century the word *tawdry* was being used to describe any sort of cheap, showy goods.

Sources

Mish, Frederick C. *The Merriam-Webster New Book of Word Histories.* Springfield, IL: Merriam-Webster, 1991.

Stephen, Leslie, and Sidney Lee, eds. *The Dictionary of National Biography.* London: Oxford University Press, 1921.

Walsh, Michael, ed. *Butler's Lives of the Saints.* San Francisco: Harper and Row, 1985.

Teddy bears. ***A plush-covered stuffed animal in the shape of a bear.***

In the late nineteenth century stuffed bear toys were very popular in Germany. In 1902 George Bergreldt and Company began importing these bears to the United States, and they were again all the rage. That same year President Theodore Roosevelt had gone to Mississippi on one of his many recreational hunting trips. His entourage captured a small bear and brought it to the camp for the president to shoot. Roosevelt, who prided himself on his athletic skills and hunting abilities, was not interested in shooting a helpless young bear tied to a tree and insisted that the animal be set free.

Roosevelt was already an extremely popular president, and the public loved this story. Clifford Berryman of *The Washington Star* drew a cartoon of the incident in which the president is shown turning his back on an adorable bear cub that is being dragged forward by a rope. Titled "Drawing the Line in Mississippi," the cartoon was reproduced and circulated throughout the country. Morris Michtom, a toy-store owner in Brooklyn, saw the picture and noted the similarity to the stuffed bears that were already favorites with children. He decided to market his own version of the bear, with movable arms and legs. The bear was displayed in the window of Michtom's store with a copy of Berryman's cartoon and a sign saying "Teddy's bear." Such bears were shortly being called *Teddy bears.*

Michtom wrote a letter to Roosevelt asking permission to use his name. Surprisingly, he received a handwritten note from the president saying that he doubted his name would help sell toys, but that Michtom was welcome to try. Within a few years there was an all-out bear craze in the United States. In Roosevelt's 1904 reelection campaign he had small teddy bears created and attached by a ribbon to some of his campaign buttons.

Bears continue to be a popular toy, and in the 1980s, the Teddy bear concept was updated. A new series was produced, with resemblance to such famous namesakes as Scarlett O'Beara, Humphrey Beargart, and Kareem Abdul-Jabbear.

Sources

Cantine, Marguerite. "Haunting Bears." *Antiques and Collecting Magazine* 99, no. 4 (1994): 15–17.

McClintock, Inez Bertail. *Toys in America.* Washington: Public Affairs Press, 1961.

Panati, Charles. *Extraordinary Origins of Everyday Things.* New York: Perennial Library, 1987.

Stimpson, George. *Information Roundup.* New York: Harper, 1948.

Teetotaler. ***One who abstains from all alcoholic beverages.***

In colonial America the consumption of alcoholic beverages, especially beer and ale, was very high and occurred in all segments of society and at all ages. By the early nineteenth century the spirit of reform was in the air, and alcohol was blamed for a number of social ills such as poverty, immorality, laziness, and insanity. The American Temperance Society was founded in 1826 with the objective of educating Americans about the value of sobriety. Some of the early members of the movement favored moderation and defined a sober lifestyle as consuming beer and wine but abstaining from hard liquor. Others were opposed to any and all alcoholic consumption. The latter group referred to themselves as "total abstainers" in order to distinguish themselves from the more "permissive" branch of the movement. The word *teetotaler* came about when one of the stringent reformers proclaimed that temperance movements should advocate "capital T-total abstinence." The total abstainers were thereafter known as teetotalers.

Sources

Carver, Craig M. *A History of English in Its Own Words.* New York: HarperCollins Publishers, 1991.

Jaffe, Jerome H., ed. *Encyclopedia of Drugs and Alcohol.* New York: Macmillan Library Reference, 1995.

Simpson, J. A., and E. S. C. Weiner, eds. *The Oxford English Dictionary.* 2d ed. Oxford: Clarendon Press, 1989.

Termagant. ***A quarrelsome, shrewish woman.***
The Crusades exposed Europeans to stories, goods, and new ideas from the Near East, and soldiers returning to their homes were a conduit for this cultural exchange. Previously unknown were foods such as oranges, lemons, cinnamon, and nutmeg and fabrics such as silk and taffeta. Perhaps the most significant import was Arabic knowledge in the form of texts on mathematics, astronomy, chemistry, and medicine.

Along with these beneficial by-products came some misconceptions about the East and about Islam in particular. Many stories circulated among the Crusaders regarding strange, twisted, or unnatural habits of the Muslims, one of which was the belief that they worshipped a violent, turbulent deity known as the *termagant*. This fierce god was portrayed in long, flowing robes, which led people to believe it was female. The termagant was incorporated into medieval morality plays that were popular among all classes in Europe. By the fourteenth century, the word *termagant* was being used in a general sense to denote a violent and overbearing woman.

Sources

Erbstosser, Martin. *The Crusades.* Leipzig: Edition Leipzig, 1978.
Jobes, Gertrude. *Dictionary of Mythology, Folklore, and Symbols.* New York: Scarecrow Press, 1962.
Simpson, J. A., and E. S. C. Weiner, eds. *The Oxford English Dictionary.* 2d ed. Oxford: Clarendon Press, 1989.

Thermopylae. ***A critical and decisive moment, resulting in either triumph or utter defeat.***
Thermopylae, a pass in east-central Greece between Mount Oeta and the Malic Gulf, was the site of a historic battle during the Greco-Persian Wars (492–449 B.C.). The Persians had launched a series of offensive attacks against the Greek city-states, the most serious of which was the Battle of Marathon (490 B.C.) at which the Persians were defeated. Ten years later they returned under the leadership of Xerxes and faced a Greek army under the command of the Spartan king Leonidas. At Thermopylae pass a two-day battle ended in a standoff. On the evening of the second night, a Greek traitor guided the Persians to an advantageous site behind the Greek army. Leonidas ordered most of his troops to retreat, while he and 300 of his best soldiers fought to the last man. Although this was a terrible loss for the Greeks, the fierce bravery of Leonidas became an icon of Greek heroism and reinforced the idea that Spartans never surrendered. As a result of the battle of Thermopylae, the Persians succeeded in capturing a huge portion of east-central Greece, although within a year the Greeks had regained the territory following the battle of Salamis.

Sources

Margiotta, Franklin D. *Brassey's Encyclopedia of Military History and Biography.* Washington, DC: Brassey's, 1994.
McHenry, Robert, ed. *The New Encyclopedia Britannica.* 15th ed. Chicago: Encyclopedia Britannica, 1992.
Sacks, David. *Encyclopedia of the Ancient Greek World.* New York: Facts on File, 1995.

Thin blue line. ***The American police force.***
The British have historically honored their army by referring to them as the "thin red line" that protects civilization from the wilder elements (see *Thin red line*). Since the 1960s, when Americans were suddenly confronted with masses of protesting students and civil rights marches, the police have been referred to as the *thin blue line.* The allusion to the much better known thin red line was not widely used until 1988, when a feature-length documentary gained national attention. Errol Morris's *The Thin Blue Line* was about the unsolved murder of a Dallas police officer in 1976.

Thin red line. ***The British army.***
One of the attitudes that propelled British colonial expansion was the belief that the British presence would serve as a civilizing influence on colonized lands. Smartly dressed British officers imported the customs

of Victorian England into the wilds of India, Africa, and the Middle East. As the families of soldiers and government officials moved to colonial outposts, they were equally intent on maintaining their standards, even in improbable surroundings. Photographs from the era reveal properly dressed English matrons serving high tea on the Serengeti Plains, while wild animals graze in the background.

The preservation of these British enclaves depended on the military might of the British army. Dressed in their characteristic red uniforms, the army was described as a *thin red line* that separated the civilized few from the uncivilized masses. The phrase originated at the Battle of Balaclava in 1854, when the 93rd Highlanders had to spread themselves along a line because they did not have time to assemble in the traditional square formation. An 1899 poem by Frederick William Ward, titled "God Defend the Right," celebrated "the thin red line/That girdles round the globe" as the mainstay of the British Empire.

The British army did not always wear red uniforms, and early prints show English soldiers in white, blue, gold, and multicolored uniforms. However, soldiers often wore a scarlet cross on their uniforms, a symbol of England's patron saint, Saint George. In the mid-sixteenth century, scarlet coats became the established uniform for British soldiers.

Sources

Carman, W.Y. *British Military Uniforms from Contemporary Pictures: Henry VII to the Present Day.* New York: Arco, 1968.

Evans, Ivor H., ed. *Brewer's Dictionary of Phrase and Fable,* 14th ed. New York: Harper and Row, 1989.

Messenger, Charles. *History of the British Army.* Novato, CA: Presidio, 1986.

Third degree. *To subject someone to rigorous questioning or rough treatment.*

The expression *third degree* is most likely of Masonic origin. Freemasonry evolved out of the guilds of stonemasons and cathedral builders during the Middle Ages. Over time, as cathedral construction declined, the character of the societies changed. Nonmasons were accepted as honorary members, and the purpose of the order shifted to emphasize brotherhood, companionship, moral development, and philanthropy. Medieval masonry still serves as an allegory for moral development, and the gavel, the compass, the rule, the level, and so on all retain symbolic meanings.

The Freemasons have used the expression *third degree* at least since the 1770s, to describe the highest honor in Freemasonry. The three degrees of Freemasons are: the entered apprentice, the fellow craft, and the master mason. Not surprisingly, the third degree is the most difficult to attain, and a mason must pass difficult proficiency tests and service requirements before he qualifies for this honor. Master Mason Albert G. Mackey's account of the third degree ceremony indicates the reverence masons have for the rite:

> Master Mason: The third degree in all the different rites. In this, which is the perfection of symbolic or ancient craft masonry, the purest of truths are unveiled amid the most awful ceremonies. None but he who has visited the holy of holies, and traveled the road of peril, can have any conception of the mysteries unfolded in this degree.

In 1866 the expression *third degree* was used in reference to the most serious type of burn injury. At about the same time it became codified into U.S. law in reference to the severity of a crime, but the order is inverted—that is, in a legal sense, third degree is the least serious grade of a crime, with first degree being the worst.

Sources

Hendrickson, Robert. *Facts on File Encyclopedia of Word and Phrase Origins.* New York: Facts on File, 1987.

Mackey, Albert G. *Lexicon of Freemasonry: Containing a Definition of All Its Communicable Terms, Notices of Its History, Traditions, and Antiquities and an Account of All the Rites and Mysteries of the Ancient World.* Philadelphia: Moss, 1867.

McHenry, Robert, ed. *The New Encyclopedia Britannica.* 15th ed. Chicago: Encyclopedia Britannica, 1992.

Thirteen. ***An unlucky number.***
Numbers often carry symbolic meanings for particular cultures and religions. For example, the number seven was regarded as holy among many ancient cultures because each phase of the moon lasts seven days. The ancients also believed that there were seven planets, further endowing the number with luck. By contrast, the number 13 has negative connotations across many cultures. Babylonians believed 13 was the number of the underworld and was the destroyer of perfection. Ancient Hebrews believed there were 13 evil spirits. Since there were 13 guests at the Last Supper (the 12 disciples and Jesus), many Christians consider the number ominous. Thirteen was also unfavorable because it lacked the harmony of 12, often considered the luckiest of numbers.

Superstitions about 13 linger, despite skepticism about the mystical significance of numbers in general. Many hotels omit a thirteenth floor, and Friday the thirteenth is considered doubly bad luck because it falls on the day Jesus was crucified. It is said that when Princess Margaret of England was born in 1930 the registration of her birth was delayed so that she would not be the thirteenth baby registered. Psychologists have coined the word *triskaidekaphobia* to refer to the fear of the number 13.

Sources
Matthews, Boris. *The Herder Symbol Dictionary: Symbols from Art, Archaeology, Mythology, Literature, and Religion*. Wilmette, IL: Chiron Publications, 1986.
McHenry, Robert, ed. *The New Encyclopedia Britannica*. 15th ed. Chicago: Encyclopedia Britannica, 1992.
Panati, Charles. *Panati's Extraordinary Origins of Everyday Things*. New York: Harper and Row, 1987.

Thirty pieces of silver. ***The price of a betrayal.***
According to the New Testament, Judas betrayed Jesus to the Jewish elders in exchange for 30 pieces of silver. There is no way to determine the contemporary value of this amount, since the term *piece of silver* was used to describe a variety of coins. However, based on the most common silver coins that circulated during Jesus' lifetime, 30 pieces was a rather paltry sum. Little is known about the character of Judas. He served as the treasurer for the band of disciples and appears to have been responsible for purchasing food for the group. There are indications that he was parsimonious and possibly a thief. The book of John (12.5–6) reports that Judas was offended by the waste of expensive perfume at an anointing ceremony. "'Why was the perfume not sold for three hundred denarii and the money given to the poor?' He said this not because he cared about the poor, but because he was a thief; he kept the common purse and used to steal what was put into it." Of course, the opinions of contemporaries would have been slanted by the later fact of Jesus' betrayal. According to one tradition Judas regretted his action and returned the money to the Jewish leaders before hanging himself. The money was then used to buy a field where the poor could be buried (see *Potter's Field*).

Sources
McDonald, William J., ed. *New Catholic Encyclopedia*. New York: McGraw-Hill, 1967.
McHenry, Robert, ed. *The New Encyclopedia Britannica*. 15th ed. Chicago: Encyclopedia Britannica, 1992.
Stimpson, George. *A Book about the Bible*. New York: Harper and Brothers, 1945.

Thistle. ***The national emblem of Scotland.***
Countries that have national emblems have traditionally selected something that represents great valor or dignity. Great Britain uses the rampant lion, the United States has its eagle, Japan has the rising sun. Scotland's thistle, a common and rather unattractive plant, is therefore unique among national emblems. The explanation comes from an ancient story so shrouded in folklore that it is difficult to determine if it actually occurred.

In the tenth century Scotland was reeling from the assaults of Viking raiders who descended on small communities with ruthless ferocity in their quest for loot. After the first spate of attacks there was an ominous new development. The Vikings began to take a liking to the British Isles, where the climate was congenial and land was more plentiful than in the densely populated coastal regions of Norway. The Vikings decided to make themselves at home, and they began to select more desirable but better defended targets for their raids. According to legend, sometime during the reign of Malcolm I (943–954) the Vikings planned a surprise nighttime assault on Staines Castle. In the darkness, they removed their shoes in order to wade through the moat and found that the dry moat was instead filled with thistles. The outraged yells and curses roused the castle and betrayed the presence of the invaders, who were soundly defeated. The thistle has since become a symbol of Scottish independence.

The Scottish Order of the Thistle was founded by James VII of Scotland in 1687. It originally consisted of the sovereign and 8 knights, but in 1827 the number was increased to 16. Next to the Knights of the Garter, it is the oldest and most prestigious order in Britain.

Sources

Isaacs, Alan, and Jennifer Monk, eds. *The Cambridge Illustrated Dictionary of British Heritage.* Cambridge: Cambridge University Press, 1986.

Keay, John, and Julia Keay, eds. *Collins Encyclopedia of Scotland.* New York: HarperCollins, 1994.

Whittick, Arnold. *Symbols, Signs, and Their Meaning.* Newton, MA: C. T. Branford Co., 1960.

Throw to the lions. *To abandon to an unpleasant fate.*

In the Roman Empire execution by wild animals was considered a shameful death and was initially reserved for foreign deserters of the Roman army. The punishment was eventually extended to common criminals and to Christians. There were a number of reasons for Roman hostility to Christians. Christians refused to worship pagan gods or idols and therefore would not participate in the Roman tradition of paying respect to statues of the emperors. The fact that most early Christians were drawn from the lowest classes of society made them easy targets of suspicion. Christian customs such as meeting in secret and celebrating the Eucharist were easily misunderstood, and rumors that the Christians practiced infanticide and cannibalism were rife.

The fire of Rome in A.D. 64 was the catalyst that turned suspicion of Christianity into hatred and persecution (see *Fiddle while Rome burns*). The emperor Nero successfully made the Christians into scapegoats, and a flood of mock trials followed. Many Christians were *thrown to the lions* to satisfy public anger. Execution of Christians ceased in 313 with the Edict of Toleration, and public executions of other criminals declined during Emperor Constantine's reign. He officially outlawed such spectacles in 325, but not until the fifth century, under Emperor Honorius (393–423), were public executions finally abolished.

Sources

Bunson, Matthew. *Encyclopedia of the Roman Empire.* New York: Facts on File, 1994.

Ferguson, Everett, ed. *Encyclopedia of Early Christianity.* New York: Garland Publishing, 1997.

Plass, Paul. *The Game of Death in Ancient Rome: Arena Sport and Political Suicide.* Madison: University of Wisconsin Press, 1995.

Wiedemann, Thomas E. *Emperors and Gladiators.* New York: Routledge, 1995.

Thug. *A brutish, violent criminal.*

The Thugs were a secret Hindu society that worshipped Kali, the Hindu goddess of destruction. The word *thug* is derived from the Sanskrit word *sthag,* meaning "conceal." These violent cult members preyed on wealthy travelers by insinuating themselves into the confidence of the victim, sometimes traveling with the person for days. Luring the wayfarer to a secluded place, the Thugs would always approach the victim from behind, wrap a noose around his neck, and strangle him. Because the goddess did not wish to see blood spilled, strangulation was the preferred method of murder, although drowning, burning, and poisoning were sometimes employed. Women were not acceptable victims for the goddess, and some Thugs speculated that their downfall in the nineteenth century occurred because women were improperly offered as sacrifices.

The secret society of Thugs was first mentioned in the twelfth century, although accounts of bandits who made a practice of strangling their victims goes back at least to seventh-century India. The Thugs tended to be particularly active whenever a festival or fair attracted travelers. Many Thugs held responsible positions in their communities and were able to identify likely victims to their fellow members. Gangs were careful to select wealthy sacrifices whenever possible in order to take advantage of the opportunity for robbery.

When the British began to colonize India, they soon launched a crusade to rid the countryside of the Thugs. After the British solicited the cooperation of the local people, over 3,000 Thugs were arrested between 1833 and 1837. Approximately 500 were persuaded to give evidence for the state, 412 were hanged, and the rest were either transported or imprisoned for life. Stray bands of Thugs continued to operate for a few decades, and the last-known Thug was executed in 1882.

Sources

Bruce, George Ludgate. *The Stranglers: The Cult of Thuggee and Its Overthrow in British India.* New York: Harcourt, Brace and World, 1969.

Hutton, James. *Thugs and Dacoits of India.* Delhi: Gian Publications, 1981.

McHenry, Robert, ed. *The New Encyclopedia Britannica.* 15th ed. Chicago: Encyclopedia Britannica, 1992.

Simpson, J. A., and E. S. C. Weiner, eds. *The Oxford English Dictionary.* 2d ed. Oxford: Clarendon Press, 1989.

Walker, Benjamin. *The Hindu World: An Encyclopedic Survey of Hinduism.* New York: Praeger, 1968.

Thumbs down. ***A simple, definitive indication of disapproval.***

Among the varied forms of bloodthirsty public spectacles enjoyed by the ancient Romans, none were more popular than the gladiator contests. It is believed that this practice had its roots in Etruscan funeral services for men of great status. Because the deceased was thought to need armed attendants in the next world, servants of the dead man fought in gladiatorial combats at the funeral, with those killed being "chosen" as attendants.

Gladiatorial combats for public consumption began in the third century B.C., when pairs of men were matched in a sword battle that was not over until one of the contestants had been mortally wounded. Combats became more exotic over time, with hundreds of pairs of men competing using swords, knives, tridents, and hot irons. Some gladiators were on horseback while others used nets to try to entangle their opponents. When one of the gladiators was on the verge of defeat, he would appeal to the crowd for mercy. If the majority turned their *thumbs down,* the losing gladiator was condemned to death and quickly dispatched by his opponent. On rare occasions the crowd would be impressed by the skill and bravery of the gladiator and would wave handkerchiefs to indicate that his life should be spared.

Most gladiators were either slaves or criminals, and they attended special schools where they were trained in military arts. By the first century A.D., the state began to fear that the schools might be used to create private armies, so four state-sponsored gladiator schools were established. The training camps were capable of producing 10,000 gladiators on demand and were huge enterprises that employed physicians, tailors, masseurs, and armorers. Although the outlook for most gladiators was bleak, a successful fighter could become famous, wealthy, and in some cases politically powerful. If a gladiator survived a number of notable combats, he might even be discharged from further service.

Sources

Bunson, Matthew. *Encyclopedia of the Roman Empire.* New York: Facts on File, 1994.

Plass, Paul. *The Game of Death in Ancient Rome: Arena Sport and Political Suicide.* Madison: University of Wisconsin Press, 1995.

Poliakoff, Michael. *Combat Sports in the Ancient World: Competition, Violence, and Culture.* New Haven, CT: Yale University Press, 1987.

Stimpson, George. *A Book about a Thousand Things.* New York: Harper and Brothers, 1946.

Wiedemann, Thomas E. *Emperors and Gladiators.* New York: Routledge, 1995.

Tin Pan Alley. ***The popular music industry or the publishers and composers of such music.***

Tin Pan Alley refers to the area between 48th and 57th streets on Seventh Avenue in New York City. Beginning in the 1890s a number of composers and music publishers congregated in this district. The nickname may have come from the tinny sound of cheap pianos used by the people hired to promote sheet music.

Tin Pan Alley revolutionized the way music was marketed. Throughout most of the nineteenth century sheet music was sold as a commodity, in the same way that books and newspapers were hawked. The music itself tended to be bland, sentimental tunes inspired by English and American folk melodies. In the late 1880s a new group of composers, inspired by Jewish and Eastern European musical traditions, pumped fresh life into the industry. In 1892 a song by Charles K. Harris, "After the Ball," stunned the industry when it sold over 5 million copies. Suddenly publishers realized that with the proper promotion, sheet music could be lucrative. Tin Pan Alley became noted for aggressive and creative marketing of songs, such as paying singers to perform the songs at street corners, department stores, and cafés, investing in musical reviews and vaudeville performances, and, by the 1920s, sponsoring recordings for radio. George M. Cohan, Irving Berlin, Cole Porter, and Jerome Kern all benefited from the energetic promotional techniques of Tin Pan Alley.

The influence of these New York music publishers sharply declined in the 1960s when they proved incapable of competing with new styles of music, namely rock and roll and country music. The name *Tin Pan Alley* remains associated with a certain style of music popular on Broadway at the turn of the century and in the golden days of radio.

Sources

Ewen, David. *The Life and Death of Tin Pan Alley: The Golden Age of American Popular Music.* New York: Funk and Wagnalls Co., 1964.

Hendrickson, Robert. *Facts on File Encyclopedia of Word and Phrase Origins.* New York: Facts on File, 1987.

Hitchcock, H. Wiley, and Stanley Sadie, eds. *The New Grove Dictionary of American Music.* New York: Grove's Dictionaries of Music, 1986.

Jackson, Kenneth T., ed. *The Encyclopedia of New York City.* New Haven, CT: Yale University Press, 1995.

Tinker's dam. ***A worthless object regarded with contempt.***

Tinkers traveled from town to town mending household utensils, particularly repairing cracks or holes in cooking implements. Soldering worked well, but the tinker had to keep the hot liquid from running out the back of the hole. A dam made out of clay was shaped to hold the solder in place until it set. Once the hole was mended, the dam was tossed out. If something is not worth a *tinker's dam,* then it no longer has any conceivable purpose.

Sources

Mish, Frederick C. *The Merriam-Webster New Book of Word Histories.* Springfield, IL: Merriam-Webster, 1991.

Stimpson, George. *A Book about a Thousand Things.* New York: Harper and Brothers, 1946.

Titanic. ***A huge undertaking that is slated for disaster.***

According to *The Oxford English Dictionary,* when the word *titanic* originated in the eighteenth century, it referred to the Titans, an ancient mythological race of gods. It was a synonym for anything monumental, enormous, or colossal. The meaning of the word would be forever changed after the events of 14 April 1912.

The *Titanic* was billed as the biggest man-made object that ever moved. It was the largest and most luxurious ship in the world, and the White Star Line was eager to publicize its maiden voyage. Thousands of promotional postcards were circulated, and companies whose products were used on the ship, such as the elegant scented soap of the Vinolia Toilet Soap Company, took out full-page advertisements in magazines. The *Titanic,* heralded as unsinkable, had a double-bottomed hull that was divided into 16 watertight compartments. The ship could remain afloat with up to 4 of these compartments flooded. However, when the ship ran against an iceberg, 6 of the compartments were flooded. Within three hours the ship had sunk, with a loss of over 1,500 lives. The ship had been well supplied with every amenity, except adequate lifeboats.

Among the casualties of the *Titanic* shipwreck was Captain Edward Smith, who was later blamed for allowing the ship to proceed at a dangerously high speed through a known ice field. Also lost was President Taft's aide, Major Archibald Butt, who reportedly vowed to shoot any man who tried to reach a lifeboat before all the women and children were safely aboard. Among the survivors was Joseph Bruce Ismay, president of the White Star Line, which owned the *Titanic.* Ismay was criticized for not going down with the ship beside Captain Smith. As a result of the tragedy, improved safety measures were instituted, including better radio contact between vessels, mandatory provision of sufficient lifeboats, and the formation of the International Ice Patrol.

After 1912 the word *titanic* assumed a new meaning that permanently associated it with a colossal disaster. The expression *rearranging deck chairs on the Titanic* alludes to situations in which superficial, cosmetic solutions are proposed as a remedy for major problems.

Sources

Eaton, John P. *Titanic, Triumph and Tragedy.* New York: Norton, 1995.

McHenry, Robert, ed. *The New Encyclopedia Britannica.* 15th ed. Chicago: Encyclopedia Britannica, 1992.

Ritchie, David. *Shipwrecks: An Encyclopedia of the World's Worst Disasters at Sea.* New York: Facts on File, 1996.

Tommy Atkins. ***A British soldier.***

In 1815 the British War Office issued the *Soldiers Account Book,* in which soldiers were to document their service record, duties, battles, and injuries. Each book also had a place for the soldier to write his name, address, and age. A model form displaying how data should be recorded was included, and the hypothetical name "Thomas Atkins" was used in all the books given to privates. It was therefore most familiar to the common soldier and soon became a nickname for enlisted men in the British army. The 1892 poem "Tommy" by Rudyard Kipling helped to popularize the term outside the army:

> I went into a theatre as sober as could be,
> They gave a drunk civilian room, but 'adn't none for me;
> They sent me to the gallery or round the music 'alls,
> But when it comes to fightin', Lord! they'll shove me in the stalls!
> For it's Tommy this, an' Tommy that, an' "Tommy, wait outside";
> But it's "Special train for Atkins" when the trooper's on the tide.
> The troopship's on the tide, my boys, the troopship's on the tide,
> O it's "Special train for Atkins" when the trooper's on the tide.

Sources

Hendrickson, Robert. *Facts on File Encyclopedia of Word and Phrase Origins.* New York: Facts on File, 1987.

Simpson, J. A., and E. S. C. Weiner, eds. *The Oxford English Dictionary.* 2d ed. Oxford: Clarendon Press, 1989.

Stimpson, George. *Information Roundup.* New York: Harper, 1948.

Tontine. ***A form of investment in which dividends are divided among all the original subscribers. As subscribers die, the dividends to the surviving members increase, until the final survivor receives all the dividends.***

The *tontine* was an investment scheme devised by Italian banker Lorenzo Tonti (1635–1690). In 1653 Cardinal Mazarin was given the task of replenishing the depleted coffers of Louis XIV of France. He turned to Tonti, who put his own distinctive spin on some old investment ideas. The plan was designed to allow the state to float a loan based on the anticipated return of the principal of many modest investments. Meanwhile, regular dividends would attract investors into the plan. In Tonti's scheme, participants contributed to the investment principal and earned small dividends. This was intended to be a life-long commitment, because as each member died, that share of the dividends was split among the surviving members. In essence, the subscribers were betting on surviving one another. As the tontine neared the end of its existence, the few remaining members earned very large dividends, with the final survivor taking it all. After the last survivor died, the original investment reverted to the state.

Cardinal Mazarin was impressed with the tontine concept, but the French Parliament was suspicious of any plan that essentially gambled on people dying. However, in the 1680s, when France was engaged in major wars and facing a financial crisis, the legislature granted permission to initiate a tontine. The plan established in 1689 required that each investor pay 300 livres, or $1,500 in today's currency. After a 40-year run, the tontine ultimately paid its final survivor $367,500. Because the state was entitled to keep all of the principal, the plan became a lucrative means of raising funds, although it was a long time before the state collected its prize. The success of the tontines encouraged other countries (including England, Ireland, and the United States) to adopt them. The benefits of government-sponsored tontines inspired private tontines, but they were especially subject to fraud and were less stable. After some widely publicized failures and the suspicious deaths of subscribers, tontine schemes were banned in the United States.

Sources

Cooper, Robert W. *An Historical Analysis of the Tontine Principle: With Emphasis on Tontine and Semi-Tontine Life Insurance Policies.* Philadelphia: S. S. Huebner Foundation for Insurance Education, 1972

Hendrickson, Robert. *Dictionary of Eponyms: Names That Became Words.* New York: Stein and Day, 1985.

Mish, Frederick C. *The Merriam-Webster New Book of Word Histories.* Springfield, IL: Merriam-Webster, 1991.

Tony awards. ***The annual awards for the New York theater season, considered the most respected awards in American theater.***

Antoinette Perry (1888–1946) was a well-liked and respected actress, director, and producer in the golden years of Broadway. When she unexpectedly died in 1946, her loss was so deeply felt within the Broadway community that there was an immediate campaign to create a lasting memorial to her. From the age of 6, Perry had declared her wish to become an actress. Her well-to-do parents deemed that profession unacceptable for their daughter, but she steadfastly pursued her dream and made her acting debut at age 16. Perry's acting ability was complemented by her startling, fragile beauty, and within a year she was traveling throughout the country to appear in acclaimed productions.

At the age of 21 Perry abruptly decided to leave the theater when she married Frank Wheatcroft Frueauff, the president of Denver Gas and Electric Company. The former actress now rubbed elbows with some of the wealthiest people in the country, but she continued to be active in the New York theater world. When her husband died in 1922, Antoinette was left with an estate valued at over $13 million, but she had little sense of purpose. At the age of 36 she returned to the stage as an actress, then turned to producing and directing plays, most notably the 1944 hit *Harvey.* During the war years Perry became active in war relief charities. She helped to initiate the Stage Door Canteens, which were places any man in a uniform could come for free entertainment and nonalcoholic drinks. Celebrities mingled with servicemen, and a soldier might have his drink served by Dorothy Lamour and coat checked by Hume Cronyn while he was entertained by Al Jolson and Marlene Dietrich. These fabled gatherings provided the inspiration for the movie *Stage Door Canteen* in 1942.

When Perry, overworked and overextended, died of a heart attack in 1946, there was a huge outpouring of grief from the Broadway community. Several memorials were proposed, including naming an acting school for her and erecting a statue of her in Times Square. It was finally decided to name an annual theater award in her honor. Hollywood had been granting the Oscars to acknowledge cinematic talent for 18 years, and it was believed that American theater deserved a similar type of recognition. The first Tony Awards were presented on 6 April 1947 in New York City's Waldorf-Astoria Hotel and have now become the country's most prestigious theatrical award. The medallion given to winners bears the masks of comedy and tragedy on one side and a likeness of Antoinette Perry on the other.

Sources

Bordman, Gerald Martin. *The Oxford Companion to the American Theatre.* New York: Oxford University Press, 1992.

Gustaitis, Joseph. "The Woman behind the Tony." *American History* 32, no.1 (1997): 16–21.

James, Edward T., ed. *Notable American Women, 1607–1950: A Biographical Dictionary.* Cambridge, MA: Belknap Press, 1971.

Totem pole, low man on the totem pole. *Lacking in seniority.*

Among many American Indian tribes, a totem was an animal spirit that protected an individual or family. The most common spirits were the beaver, eagle, and bear. The killing of a totemic animal was strictly forbidden. Indians of the Pacific Northwest often expressed this tradition in the use of totem poles. Usually carved from a single log of a tree, some totem poles reached up to 80 feet. A series of familial totems would be carved into the log, making it a kind of family crest. A particular historical event might be depicted on the pole, or a reference to a mythic story with which the family wished to be associated.

The expression *low man on the totem pole* implies that an individual lacks status or seniority. This is a misunderstanding of the manner in which totem poles are read. Since the totem poles usually tell a story, the location of a figure on a pole has no hierarchical implications. The carving of totem poles was especially prevalent during the early half of the nineteenth century, but scarcely 50 years later the practice had all but died out. Pressure from missionaries and the government to ban native ceremonial practices undermined the training of wood carvers. The potlatch, a ceremonial feast that occurred during the erection of totem poles, was officially outlawed by the Canadian government in 1884, and the carving of new poles dropped off as a result. A resurgence of ethnic pride in the mid-twentieth century has led to a revival of the art.

Sources

Markowitz, Harvey, ed. *American Indians.* Pasadena, CA: Salem Press, 1995.

McHenry, Robert, ed. *The New Encyclopedia Britannica.* 15th ed. Chicago: Encyclopedia Britannica, 1992.

Stewart, Hillary. *Totem Poles.* Seattle: University of Washington Press, 1990.

Trial by fire. *An arduous and difficult test of one's abilities.*

This term derives from the medieval practice of ordeals, which were judicial processes used to learn the judgment of God. Ordeals were resorted to when there was not enough evidence to determine the outcome of a case. Ordeals could involve trials by water, poison, or hot irons, but the most common was trial by fire. The accused was asked to handle fire, and after a set period of time the wounds would be examined for signs of infection. Any indication of damage was taken as a sign of God's disfavor, and the accused would be presumed guilty.

The practice may be traced to an event related in the Book of Daniel 3:19–30. King Nebuchadnezzar was furious with three of Daniel's followers, Shadrash, Meshach, and Abednego, because they would not worship pagan gods. He ordered the trio thrown into the blazing fire of his furnace. The fire was so hot that the soldiers overseeing the execution were consumed, but the Hebrews were untouched by the flames surrounding them. The ability of the three men to withstand the trial of fire was taken to be a sign of divine providence, and they were freed.

Trials by fire were sanctioned by the

Catholic church, which required preliminary preparations of fasting, prayer, and blessing of all the items needed for the ordeal. The accused was sometimes asked to put a hand into a fire, to dash through a large pyre, or to walk on hot coals. It was not always the accused who had to undergo the ordeal. If a nobleman refused to comply, the *accuser* might have to submit to the trial in order to prove the legitimacy of his charge. One famous example involved the eleventh-century bishop of Florence, who had been accused of selling ecclesiastical offices and other crimes. Citizens of Florence asked that he be made to undergo trial by fire to prove his innocence. The bishop refused. In 1068 a monk at a nearby monastery offered to submit himself to the trial on behalf of the accusers. In front of an audience of 3,000 enthralled Florentines, the monk slowly walked barefoot on two inches of burning coals for the space of six feet. He appeared to emerge from the trial unscathed, which validated the charges against the bishop and led to his deposition. The monk was henceforth known as Peter Igneous. Trials by fire and other physical ordeals were outlawed by the Fourth Lateran Council in 1215, although isolated communities occasionally revived the practice.

Sources

Broughton, Bradford B. *Dictionary of Medieval Knighthood and Chivalry.* New York: Greenwood Press, 1986.

McDonald, William J., ed. *New Catholic Encyclopedia.* New York: McGraw-Hill, 1967.

Strayer, Joseph R. *The Dictionary of the Middle Ages.* New York: Scribner's, 1982.

Triangle trade. *A morally questionable but profitable business arrangement.*

The original *triangle trade* referred to a pattern of commerce practiced by New Englanders in the eighteenth century. Although the southern colonies had abundant tobacco, cotton, and lumber to export, the New England colonies had no such staples to trade for manufactured goods. Because of colonial trade regulations, New Englanders could not export their natural bounty, fish and grain, to Great Britain. In order to obtain cloth, building materials, guns, and other goods from Europe, the New England colonies devised an elaborate trading arrangement known as the triangle trade.

The three corners of the triangle were New England, the African Gold Coast, and the West Indies. Ships leaving New England carried rum, flour, and tar to Africa. These goods were traded for slaves. Traveling to the West Indies, usually Jamaica, the slaves were sold in exchange for sugar, molasses, and cash. This arrangement provided New Englanders with cash and a staple crop, sugar, which could be exported to England in exchange for the manufactured goods so desperately needed. The triangle trade officially ended in the early nineteenth century, when Great Britain passed laws abolishing trade in slaves anywhere in the British Empire, closing off the West Indies to the slave trade.

The term is still occasionally used to describe other business ventures that exploit human misery for monetary gain—for example, the use of cheap Third World labor by modern multinational corporations.

Sources

Adams, J. T. *Dictionary of American History.* New York: Scribner's, 1976.

Cooke, Jacob E., ed. *Encyclopedia of North American Colonies.* New York: Scribner's Sons, 1993.

Inikori, Josepah E., and Engerman, Stanley L., eds. *The Atlantic Slave Trade: Effects on Economies, Societies and Peoples in Africa, the Americas, and Europe.* Durham: Duke University Press, 1992.

Tuxedo. *A type of formal evening wear for men.*

Tuxedos are now considered to be formal attire in menswear, but when they were introduced in the 1880s they were actually regarded as a casual alternative to the formal white tie, tails, and top hat that was required evening wear for well-dressed Victorian gentlemen. The tuxedo has no tails and probably would have been dismissed as a scandalous breach of etiquette had it not been introduced by one of the wealthiest and most socially prominent families in New York.

The Lorillard family, heirs to a tobacco fortune, were the owners of Tuxedo Park, a 13,000-acre tract of land in New York State. They turned the area into a fashionable summer resort where the wealthy could escape the pressures of New York City.

In 1886 the Tuxedo Club, which was devoted to the propagation and managed hunting of wildlife, was established there. The patriarch of the family, Pierre Lorillard, wished to have something less formal to wear to his club. He commissioned a number of tailless black jackets, reminiscent of the English riding jackets popular with hunters. After the coats were made, Pierre lost his nerve and decided against wearing them in public. However, his son Griswold and several of his friends wore the coats, and a new fashion was born for the well-to-do.

The addition of the cummerbund, the colorful sash worn around the waist, soon became a standard accessory for the tuxedo. The fashion originated among British colonials living in India, who took the idea from the sash worn by Indian men for formal occasions. This was called the *kamarband,* or "loin sash." The name was eventually anglicized to *cummerbund.*

Sources

Mish, Frederick C. *The Merriam-Webster New Book of Word Histories.* Springfield, IL: Merriam-Webster, 1991.

Panati, Charles. *Extraordinary Origins of Everyday Things.* New York: Perennial Library, 1987.

Stimpson, George. *A Book about a Thousand Things.* New York: Harper and Brothers, 1946.

Twinkie defense. ***A legal strategy in which personal responsibility for a criminal act is downplayed in light of a questionable psychological disorder.***

In San Francisco, on 27 November 1978, former city supervisor Dan White (1946–1985) shot and killed San Francisco mayor George Moscone and supervisor Harvey Milk. These assassinations raised a firestorm of controversy, since it was believed that White's homophobia had been the driving force behind his murder of the openly gay Harvey Milk. White's defense attorney claimed that the consumption of a high-sugar diet had caused White's depression to spin out of control. Journalists latched onto this peculiar defense and dubbed it the *Twinkie defense.* The jury was apparently impressed with this strategy, as they decided to convict White of manslaughter rather than murder. White was sentenced to seven years and eight months in prison, but he committed suicide less than a year after his release.

Subsequent trials have expanded on the Twinkie defense to include such other excuses for criminal behavior as premenstrual syndrome, sleep disorders, and migraine headaches.

Sources

Dershowitz, Alan. *The Abuse Excuse and Other Cop-Outs, Sob Stories, and Evasions of Responsibility.* Boston, Little, Brown, 1994.

Salter, Kenneth W. *The Trial of Dan White.* El Cerrito, CA: Market and Systems Interface, 1991.

Sifakis, Carl. *The Encyclopedia of American Crime.* New York: Facts on File, 1982.

Weiss, Mike. *Double Play: The San Francisco City Hall Killings.* Reading, PA: Addison-Wesley Publishing Co., 1984.

Twisting the lion's tail. ***Political actions or statements that are designed to attack Great Britain.***

Despite the strong bond between the United States and Great Britain, there are occasions when it has been politically useful to make inflammatory statements against the British. Beginning in the nineteenth century, Americans of Irish descent comprised as much as one-fifth of the voting public. Statements that whipped up anti-British sentiment were practically guaranteed to appeal to this large bloc of voters, while not seriously alienating any other segment of the population.

The shield of England contains a glorious lion rearing up on its hind legs, which has become a symbol of the British monarchy. *Twisting the lion's tail* implies an action that is annoying the lion but not inflicting any major harm.

Sources

Evans, Ivor H., ed. *Brewer's Dictionary of Phrase and Fable.* 14th ed. New York: Harper and Row, 1989.

Safire, William. *Safire's Political Dictionary.* New York: Random House, 1978.
Stimpson, George. *A Book about American Politics.* New York: Harper, 1954.

Typhoid Mary. ***A person who is a catalyst for undesirable or dangerous developments.*** Mary Mallon (1870?–1938) worked as a cook for a series of wealthy New York City families. Although she was immune to the disease, she was a carrier of the typhoid bacillus, which is easily transmitted to others through food preparation. Families Mary worked for often contracted the disease, sometimes only days after her she began her employment. During these outbreaks Mary assisted the families with the difficult task of nursing the stricken, earning their gratitude and often a healthy bonus. She almost always left her job soon after the onset of the disease, only to resurface as a cook for a family in another part of the city. By 1907 the New York City Department of Health had made the connection between several typhoid outbreaks and Mary's employment. She refused to cooperate with authorities, denied that she was the cause of any illness, and stated that she seldom washed her hands before cooking and saw no need to. She was committed to an isolation center and remained there for three years.

After Mary promised to abstain from any employment involving the handling of food, the health authorities allowed her release in 1910. She changed her name and promptly began cooking again. Sanitation workers were again able to follow a trail of typhoid outbreaks to Mary's kitchen, and in 1915 she was apprehended once more. She spent the last twenty-three years of her life confined in an isolation center on North Brother Island. At least fifty-one cases of typhoid and three deaths are directly attributed to Mary Mallon.

Sources

Kohn, George C. *The Encyclopedia of American Scandal: From Abscam to the Zenger Case.* New York: Facts on File, 1989.
Leavitt, Judith Walzer. *Typhoid Mary: Captive to the Public's Health.* Boston: Beacon Press, 1996.
McHenry, Robert, ed. *The New Encyclopedia Britannica.* 15th ed. Chicago: Encyclopedia Britannica, 1992.
Panati, Charles. *Panati's Extraordinary Endings of Practically Everything and Everybody.* New York: Perennial Library, 1989.

U

Ugandan affairs. *Illicit sex.*

This British euphemism for illicit sex was the direct result of a smear campaign initiated by Idi Amin, the president of Uganda from 1971 to 1979. Uganda actually comprises four traditional kingdoms, and many members of royal families from these traditional kingdoms assumed positions of power within the Ugandan Republic. One such person was Princess Elizabeth Bagaaya (1936–), the sister of the king of Toro, a Ugandan principality. Bagaaya graduated from Cambridge University and in 1964 became the first black African woman to practice law in Britain. She later served as minister of foreign affairs for Uganda, and in 1974 she chaired the Uganda delegation to the United Nations. A woman of remarkable beauty, she occasionally worked as a model, and photographs of her appeared in *Vogue, Harper's Bazaar,* and other major fashion magazines.

This combination of beauty and intelligence caught the eye of Ugandan dictator Idi Amin. After a brief acquaintance, Amin asked Bagaaya to be one of his wives (he had two at the time). Thinking the proposal was a joke, Bagaaya turned him down. Amin was enraged and began an international campaign to smear her reputation. He claimed that the princess had been discovered having sex with a white man in a public toilet at the Orly Airport in Paris. He also produced a number of nude photographs of a woman he identified as Bagaaya. Ever eager for scandals involving the rich and famous, British tabloids seized onto the salacious story. Bagaaya immediately returned to England and began a series of lawsuits against the tabloids. She eventually won her case with 15 of the papers, but by then the expression *Ugandan affairs* as a euphemism for illicit sex was well established.

Sources

Brockman, Norbert C. *An African Biographical Dictionary.* Denver: ABC-CLIO, 1994.

Elizabeth, Princess of Toro. *Elizabeth of Toro: Odyssey of an African Princess.* New York: Simon and Schuster, 1989.

Gamarekian, Barbara. "Actress, Lawyer, Model, Diplomat." *New York Times,* 21 December 1986, B14.

Simpson, J. A., and E. S. C. Weiner, eds. *The Oxford English Dictionary.* 2d ed. Oxford: Clarendon Press, 1989.

Uncle Sam. *A personification of the United States, depicted as a dapper man wearing a top hat.*

The widely accepted belief is that source for *Uncle Sam* was Samuel Wilson, a prosperous New York merchant. During the War of 1812, Wilson had a contract to supply beef and pork to the military. To distinguish the crates of meat that were destined for government use, he put "US" on the outside of the crates, an abbreviation for the United States. During a routine inspection of the warehouse, an official asked a worker what the designation meant. The worker did not know and jokingly replied that perhaps it referred to his employer, Uncle Sam. This reference became popularized as soldiers referred to their rations as coming from "Uncle Sam."

One of the earliest personifications of the American spirit was Brother Jonathan (see *Brother Jonathan*). Between the 1830s and 1860s both characters were equally popular with cartoonists and the American public, although Brother Jonathan eventually became obsolete. When cartoonists first began portraying Uncle Sam, he was a clean-shaven gentleman in solid black clothes. The beard was added during the Lincoln presidency, and the colorful clothing, borrowed from the American flag, was adopted in the late nineteenth century. The enormously popular cartoons of Thomas Nast (1840–1902) finally crystallized the image of Uncle Sam.

Although Uncle Sam's association with Samuel Wilson can never be definitively proven, in 1961 Congress passed a resolution acknowledging him as the namesake for the character.

Sources

McHenry, Robert, ed. *The New Encyclopedia Britannica.* 15th ed. Chicago: Encyclopedia Britannica, 1992.

Mish, Frederick C. *The Merriam-Webster New Book of Word Histories.* Springfield, IL: Merriam-Webster, 1991.

Panati, Charles. *Extraordinary Origins of Everyday Things.* New York: Perennial Library, 1987.

Unsafe at any speed. ***An informal charge leveled at products that are believed to be unsafe or otherwise defective.***

In 1965 consumer safety advocate Ralph Nader (1934–) published his best-selling book *Unsafe at Any Speed: The Designed-In Dangers of the American Automobile.* It was a scathing attack on the Detroit automobile industry for what Nader claimed was their emphasis on profits and styling over the safety of the passengers. The Chevrolet Corvair came under particular attack, condemned as "one of the nastiest cars ever built." Nader heightened public awareness over the lack of automobile regulations, and federal legislation was drafted to address the concerns. In 1966 the National Traffic and Motor Vehicle Safety Act was passed, largely because of the efforts of Ralph Nader.

Nader continued to represent consumer interests in his challenges to corporate lobbyists, advertising claims, liability laws, and unsafe products. When corporations test products, from diet cookies to children's pajamas, they speak of creating something that is *safe at any speed* in order to avoid the negative publicity that can be engendered by angry consumers and their advocates.

Sources

Moritz, Charles, ed. *Current Biography Yearbook.* New York: H. W. Wilson, 1968.

Nader, Ralph. *Unsafe at Any Speed: The Designed-In Dangers of the American Automobile.* New York: Grossman, 1965.

Utopia. ***A perfect, idealized society.***

Sir Thomas More (1478–1535) devoted much of his life to improving the social and political situation of sixteenth-century England. He eventually became a martyr to this cause, when his convictions became inconvenient to Henry VIII. More was an idealist who believed that society could be reformed through hard work, good will, and democratic principles. In 1516 he published *Utopia,* a treatise that explored what a society would be like if human beings could create an earthly paradise.

More tells of meeting an enigmatic figure named Raphael Hythloday, who had supposedly accompanied Amerigo Vespucci on his voyages of exploration. On one such journey, they came upon an island paradise named Utopia located somewhere in the oceans of the Western Hemisphere. According to Hythloday, the island was divided into 54 counties, each with its own village. No village was more than a day's walking journey from its neighbors. An elective body, the island council, met every three days to discuss matters of concern to the islanders. Perhaps even more novel than the idea of a democratic government were the social and economic arrangements on the fabled island of Utopia. Every able-bodied person was required to work a six-hour day. Because everyone worked, there was plenty of food as well as other necessities. Each person was required to labor on a farm for two years, so that he or she would know what it meant to raise food from the soil. All goods were owned by the community, preventing any single individual to gain economic control. Jewelry and other luxuries were given to children as toys, and villagers associated such trinkets with childishness. The vices of gambling and idleness were unknown, and people spent their free time engaged in productive activities such as gardening, improving their homes, or attending musical recitals. Most of the people were Christians, but other forms of worship were practiced and welcomed.

To the sixteenth-century reader, shackled under the weight of authoritarian governments, grinding poverty, and senseless warfare, More's *Utopia* was a ray of hope for a better world. In the centuries to come, his book inspired a series of Utopian experiments in the United States, such as Ephrata (1732), New Harmony (1825), Brook Farm (1841), and the Oneida community (1848). Few of these communities lasted more than a generation, but they had an important influence on American intellectual history. In the twentieth century, the kibbutz movement in Israel is an attempt at the utopian ideal that parallels many features of More's vision.

Sources

Cayton, Mary Kupiec, ed., *Encyclopedia of American Social History.* New York: Maxwell Macmillan International, 1993.

Logan, George M. *The Meaning of Utopia.* Princeton, NJ: Princeton University Press, 1983.

Mish, Frederick C. *The Merriam-Webster New Book of Word Histories.* Springfield, IL: Merriam-Webster, 1991.

V

Valentine's day. ***February 14, a day on which sentimental expressions of love and friendship are encouraged.***

Little is known about the origin of the custom of Saint Valentine's day. There were two early Christian martyrs named Valentine, although neither one seems to have had any association with romantic longings. The earliest Saint Valentine was a pagan physician who converted to Christianity and became a priest. He was imprisoned in Rome during the Christian persecutions and restored sight to the daughter of his jailer. On 14 February 269 he was clubbed to death and subsequently beheaded. A purely apocryphal story about this saint claims that the Roman army was desperately short of men, so the emperor forbade young men to marry in hopes of driving them into the service. Young lovers turned to the priest Valentine, who was willing to perform marriage ceremonies in secret. The other Saint Valentine was the bishop of Umbria, and he was martyred sometime in the 270s.

Most likely, the romantic traditions of Saint Valentine's day derive from pagan customs. A festival honoring the goddess Juno occurred in mid-February. Young men selected the names of the eligible women by lot, and the pair kept company for the duration of the festival. A similar custom, also set in the early spring, developed in medieval England. Rather than attempting to obliterate all pagan customs, early church leaders often grafted a Christian saint or a celebration onto an existing pagan ceremony. Such was probably the case with Saint Valentine's day.

Sources

Knowlson, T. Sharper. *The Origins of Popular Superstitions and Customs.* London: C. W. Laurie, 1910.

Panati, Charles. *Extraordinary Origins of Everyday Things.* New York: Perennial Library, 1987.

Walsh, William Shepard. *Curiosities of Popular Customs and of Rites, Ceremonies, Observances, and Miscellaneous Antiquities.* Philadelphia: Lippincott, 1897.

Van Buren jinx. ***Refers to the odds against a vice-president making a successful bid for the presidency.***

In 1988 George Bush broke the *Van Buren jinx* when he became the first sitting vice-president to be elected to the presidency since Martin Van Buren a century and a half earlier. Nine vice-presidents inherited the presidency because of death or resignation:

- John Tyler, 1841 (succeeded William Henry Harrison)
- Millard Fillmore, 1850 (succeeded Zachary Taylor)
- Andrew Johnson, 1865 (succeeded Abraham Lincoln)
- Chester Arthur, 1881 (succeeded James Garfield)
- Theodore Roosevelt, 1901 (succeeded William McKinley)
- Calvin Coolidge, 1923 (succeeded Warren G. Harding)
- Harry Truman, 1945 (succeeded Franklin Roosevelt)
- Lyndon Johnson, 1963 (succeeded John Kennedy)
- Gerald Ford, 1974 (succeeded Richard Nixon).

Richard Nixon, Hubert Humphrey, and Walter Mondale all ran for the presidency immediately after their vice-presidential term but lost. Richard Nixon succeeded when he reentered politics eight years later.

The vice-presidency is a curious political position. With few formal responsibilities, an ambitious politician suddenly cast in a supporting role can permanently fade into the background. In 1848 Daniel Webster declined a vice-presidential place on the Whig ticket by declaring, "I do not propose to be buried until I am dead." Some analysts speculate that more vice-presidents will move directly into the Oval Office in the future, given the two-term limitation on presidents and the vice-president's growing function as party builder and public spokesman.

Sources

Angel, Jerome, and Walter Glanze. *Cleopatra's Nose, the Twinkie Defense, and 1500 Other Verbal Shortcuts in Popular Parlance.* New York: Prentice-Hall Press, 1990.

Nelson, Michael. *Guide to the Presidency.* Washington, DC: Congressional Quarterly, 1996.

Vandal. ***One who knowingly and maliciously destroys the property of another.***

The Vandals were originally of Scandinavian descent but migrated to the Baltic region some two thousand years ago. A seminomadic and warlike people, the Vandals frequently raided and were raided by the Visigoths. Under pressure by the Huns by the fifth century, the Vandals began encroaching on the Roman provinces, but soon they stopped sacking communities and became Roman citizens and protectors of the empire. The worst of the barbarian invasions was yet to come. The Goths, the Huns, and the Visigoths were more numerous and more destructive than the Vandals. However, it was the Vandals who were forever associated with wanton destruction, perhaps because they were the first "barbarians" to shake the stability of the Roman Empire.

Sources

Davis, Paul K. *Encyclopedia of Invasions and Conquests from Ancient Times to the Present.* Santa Barbara, CA: ABC-CLIO, 1996.

McHenry, Robert, ed. *The New Encyclopedia Britannica.* 15th ed. Chicago: Encyclopedia Britannica, 1992.

Simpson, J. A., and E. S. C. Weiner, eds. *The Oxford English Dictionary.* 2d ed. Oxford: Clarendon Press, 1989.

Veni, vidi, vici. ***I came, I saw, I conquered; a laconic statement that something has been quickly and efficiently accomplished.***

Victorious Roman generals had become accustomed to following their military conquests with a grand procession known as a *triumph.* The general met with the senate outside the city, and if the victory was deemed worthy of a triumph, a date was set for the procession. The winding road that the general would take into the city was strewn with flowers. The senators led the procession, followed by trumpeters and wagons containing the spoils of war and any important prisoners such as commanders or kings. Then came the general in a magnificent chariot and wearing the robes of Jupiter. In his hand he carried an ivory scepter, and an olive wreath adorned his head. A slave standing behind him held a golden crown above his head and whispered in his ear, "Remember, thou art only a mortal." The troops followed behind, and sometimes there were models of the captured cities or maps of the campaign exhibited on wagons.

Julius Caesar (100–44 B.C.) had enjoyed his fair share of triumphal processions, but the celebrations he authorized after his victory in the civil wars were generally considered in poor taste. Triumphs were usually observed after battles with foreign enemies, not after a demoralizing civil conflict whose outcome was as yet unclear. Consequently, Caesar showed uncharacteristic modesty after his victory at the Battle of Zela in 47 B.C. He had been embroiled in a siege in Egypt when Pharnaces II of Pontus took the opportunity to expand his own empire into some Roman provinces in Turkey. As soon as the Egyptian campaign had been won, Caesar hastened to Zela and soundly defeated the upstart king. Returning to

Rome, Caesar declined the traditional triumph and gave a simple report of his activities: *Veni, vidi; vici.*

Sources

Bradford, Ernle D. *Julius Caesar: The Pursuit of Power.* New York: Morrow, 1984.
Fuller, J. F. C. *Julius Caesar: Man, Soldier, and Tyrant.* New Brunswick, NJ: Rutgers University Press, 1965.

Vicar of Bray. ***A person who holds on to a position despite changing administrations, usually accomplished by agreeing with whoever is in power.***

The vicar of Bray, in Berkshire, England, began his service under Henry VIII as a Catholic. Over the course of the next 40 years he switched between Protestantism and Catholicism, depending on who was in power. When Henry's son Edward VI became king (1547–1553), it was convenient to be a Protestant. An urgent conversion to Catholicism was necessary under the reign of Bloody Mary (1553–1558), and then back to Protestantism during the reign of Queen Elizabeth (1558–1603).

The vicar dismissed reproaches of his religious versatility, and when accused of being a traitor, he replied: "Not so neither, for if I changed my religion, I am sure I kept true to my principle, which is to live and die the Vicar of Bray!"

Sources

Rachum, Ilan. *The Renaissance: An Illustrated Encyclopedia.* New York: Mayflower Books, 1979.
Uden, Grant. *Anecdotes from History.* New York: Barnes and Noble, 1968.

Victorian. ***Refers to styles or values reminiscent of the moral conservatism of the nineteenth century.***

Queen Victoria's reign was longer than that of any other king or queen of Britain, lasting more than 63 years. From 1837 to 1901 Victoria left her stamp on Great Britain and, through her progeny, on the rest of Europe as well. By the end of her long reign the queen had become a national icon, and her image was emblazoned on coins, stamps, statues, paintings, and buildings throughout the world.

The term *Victorian* refers not only to the values promoted by the queen but to the morally conservative tone that dominated much of the nineteenth century. Victoria herself was not a cheerless prude. She enjoyed a passionate marriage with her husband Prince Albert and was known to have a sense of humor that was often hidden from the public because of her shyness. Certainly she was fiercely devoted to the concepts of duty, obligation, the traditional family, and a Protestant work ethic. Victoria was convinced that hard work, cleanliness, sobriety, and virtue were the keys to a more enlightened era. These values coincided with the sentiments of a growing middle class and became diffused throughout English society and beyond. Later generations branded the Victorian era with repressive stereotypes, but there has recently been a renewed nostalgia for Victorian values.

Sources

Hendrickson, Robert. *Dictionary of Eponyms: Names That Became Words.* New York: Stein and Day, 1985.
Himmelfarb, Gertrude. *The De-Moralization of Society: From Victorian Virtues to Modern Values.* New York: A. A. Knopf, 1995.
Marsden, Gordon, ed. *Victorian Values: Personalities and Perspectives in Nineteenth-Century Society.* New York: Longman, 1990.

Virginia. Yes, Virginia, there is a Santa Claus. ***Said when one wishes to emphasize a point to a skeptical audience.***

In 1897 eight-year-old Virginia O'Hanlon Douglas wrote a letter to the editor of the New York *Sun* and received a memorable answer written

> Dear Editor,
> I am 8 years old. Some of my little friends say that there is no Santa Claus. Papa says "If you see it in the *Sun,* it is so." Please tell me the truth, is there a Santa Claus?

Replied Francis P. Church,

Virginia,

Your little friends are wrong. They have been affected by the skepticism of a skeptical age. They do not believe except what they see. They think that nothing can be which is not comprehensible by their little minds.

All minds, Virginia, whether they be men's or children's, are little. In this great universe of ours, man is a mere insect, an ant, in his intellect, as compared with the boundless world about him, as measured by the intelligence capable of grasping the whole of truth and knowledge.

Yes, Virginia, there is a Santa Claus. He exists as certainly as love and generosity and devotion exist, and you know that they abound and give to our life its highest beauty and joy.

Alas! How dreary would be the world if there was no Santa Claus! It would be as dreary as if there were no Virginias. There would be no childlike faith then, no poetry, no romance to make tolerable this existence. We should have no enjoyment, except in sense and sight. The eternal light with which childhood fills the world would be extinguished.

Not believe in Santa Claus? You might as well not believe in fairies! You might get your Papa to hire men to watch all the chimneys on Christmas Eve to catch Santa Claus, but even if they did not see Santa Claus coming down, what would that prove?

Nobody sees Santa Claus, but that is no sign there is no Santa Claus. The most real things in the world are those that neither children nor men can see.

Did you ever see fairies dancing on the lawn? Of course not, but that's no proof they are not there. Nobody can conceive or imagine all the wonders that are unseen and unseeable in the world.

You tear the baby's rattle and see what makes the noise inside, but there is a veil covering the unseen world which not the strongest man, or even the united strength of all the strongest men that ever lived, could tear apart. Only faith, fancy, poetry, love, romance, can push aside that curtain and view and picture the supernatural beauty and glory beyond.

Is it all real? Ah, Virginia, in all this world there is nothing else as real and binding.

No Santa Claus? Thank God he lives and he lives forever. A thousand years from now, maybe 10 times 10,000 years from now, he will continue to make glad the hearts of children.

Source

Church, Francis P. *Is There a Santa Claus?* New York: Grosset and Dunlap, 1934.

W

Walk the plank. ***A legendary form of execution inflicted by pirates in which the condemned was forced to walk off the end of a plank extending from the side of the ship to out over the ocean.***

Tales of pirates forcing people to walk the plank to their deaths are probably an embellishment on the pirate mystique. During the seventeenth and eighteenth centuries, pirates regularly tossed victims overboard, but this is less appealing to the popular sense of drama than the image of a condemned person teetering on the end of a plank before falling into the churning sea below. There is only one authenticated report, and that came from a British seaman. In 1769, as he was about to be hanged for mutiny, George Wood confessed to the chaplain at Newgate prison that some loyal crew members who had refused to participate in the mutiny had been forced to walk the plank. Nearly all other infamous tales that include this practice derive from adventure stories.

Sources

Botting, Douglas. *The Pirates.* Alexandria, VA: Time-Life Books, 1978.

Cordingly, David. *Under the Black Flag: The Romance and Reality of Life among the Pirates.* New York: Random House, 1996.

Lurie, Charles. *Everyday Sayings.* Detroit, MI: Gale Research, 1968.

Wall Street. ***The seven-block street in Manhattan in which key financial institutions of the United States are located.***

The name *Wall Street* is a vestige of the early Dutch settlement on the island of Manhattan. In 1614 a handful of Dutch immigrants formed the colony of New Netherlands, with the island of Manhattan quickly becoming the main settlement of the colony because of its strategic location. By the 1650s English immigrants, who viewed the Dutch as an impediment to their expansion, had already established communities to the north and south of Manhattan. Fearing English encroachment, in 1653 the Dutch built a wall between the Hudson and East rivers along the northern edge of their settlement. They called it *da Waal.* No English incursion materialized, but the wall stayed in place as protection against possible attacks by Indians or other New Englanders. In 1664, the English Crown decided to incorporate the colony and sent four warships to seize it from the Dutch. Convinced by the show of force, the settlers surrendered to the English without a shot being fired. The street that ran alongside *da Waal* was named Wall Street by the English settlers. The actual wall was demolished in 1699.

Over the course of the next three centuries Wall Street became closely associated with banking and finance. A number of important banks were located there, and the New York Stock Exchange took up residence on the street in 1903. Throughout most of the eighteenth and nineteenth centuries, Wall Street's influence was primarily regional, since other stock exchanges and banks located in Boston, Philadelphia, and Chicago were equally important to the nation's financial health. By the turn of the twentieth century Wall Street banks were the only institutions in the United States capable of providing the massive amounts of capital required to finance major industrial developments. Leadership gradually shifted to New York, and by the end of World War I, Wall Street institutions had acquired an international reputation as authorities in high finance.

Sources

Jackson, Kenneth T., ed. *The Encyclopedia of New York City.* New Haven, CT: Yale University Press, 1995.

McHenry, Robert, ed. *The New Encyclopedia Britannica.* 15th ed. Chicago: Encyclopedia Britannica, 1992.

Porter, Glenn. *Encyclopedia of American Economic History: Studies of the Principal Movements and Ideas.* New York: Scribner's, 1980.

War of Jenkins' Ear. ***A war between England and Spain from 1739 to 1744.***

Very little is known about the life of Robert Jenkins (fl. 1731–1738) other than the famous incident that helped spark a full-fledged war between England and Spain. In 1731 Jenkins was captain of a merchant vessel, the *Rebecca,* which sailed between Jamaica and England. On April 9 the ship was waylaid and boarded by a Spanish privateer, Captain Fandino, who was widely known to have a reputation for cruelty and ruthlessness. After robbing the *Rebecca* of all of her valuables, Captain Fandino sliced off one of Jenkins' ears and went on his way. When the *Rebecca* returned to her London port, Jenkins reported his case to the king and the governor of the West Indies. However, there was at that time a temporary lull in the centuries-long hostility between England and Spain, and not wanting to upset the delicate balance, the British government disregarded the incident.

In 1738 Anglo-Spanish tension once again began to boil over in the face of British violations of trading restrictions in Spanish America and bullying on the part of Spanish privateers. Parliament clamored for a renewed war against Spain, and the seven-year-old incident of Jenkins' ear was revived for the occasion. Jenkins was summoned before the House of Commons to recount his tale, and he even produced a scrap of dried flesh that he claimed was his severed ear. When asked to describe his feelings during the attack, Jenkins claimed, "I committed my soul to God, and my cause to my country." Jenkins' ordeal was now widely publicized, and the public was outraged. Within a year war had been declared, and the story of Jenkins' ear was recited repeatedly to rouse volunteers to rid the oceans of Spanish privateers. The War of Jenkins' Ear consisted mostly of privateering with occasional minor raiding on the Georgia-Florida colonial frontiers. After four years of fighting, with no significant gain on either side, the war merged into the broader European conflict known as the War of the Austrian Succession (1744–1748).

Sources

Adams, J. T. *Dictionary of American History.* New York: Scribner's, 1976.

Cooke, Jacob E., ed. *Encyclopedia of North American Colonies.* New York: Scribner's Sons, 1993.

Kohn, George C. *Dictionary of Wars.* New York: Facts on File, 1986.

Watergate.

See -gate.

Waterloo, to meet one's Waterloo. ***To be defeated in a final and decisive contest.***

At the Battle of Waterloo, Napoleon Bonaparte met his final defeat after 23 years of warfare between France and the other European powers. In pursuit of his ambitious goals, Napoleon had seized Spain and Portugal and waged war on Britain, Austria, and Russia. His disastrous Russian campaign in the winter of 1812 decimated his army and spelled the beginning of the end of his imperialistic adventures. Within two years Napoleon had been driven into exile on the island of Elba. The nations of Europe heaved a collective sigh of relief and believed that they were finally rid of the Corsican general. They were wrong.

From Elba Napoleon was keeping close watch on European affairs, and less than a year after his banishment, he sensed the time was right for him to reclaim France. As he marched toward Paris, his old troops joined the ranks, and he was welcomed back into the city with wild applause. After reestablishing himself at the head of the French army, Napoleon launched a campaign toward Belgium and succeeded in forcing the duke of Wellington's troops into a defensive position just outside of Waterloo. On 18 June 1815 Napoleon made a huge tactical error when he delayed his attack until the afternoon in order to allow the ground to dry out. This delay gave Wellington's Prussian allies time to reach Waterloo and join the British. The tide turned quickly once the Prussians arrived, and Napoleon had lost his final battle.

The Europeans would not tolerate a renewed threat from France, and having learned a lesson by granting Napoleon too many liberties on Elba, the former emperor was sent to the tiny island of St. Helena in the South Atlantic, where he lived until his death six years later. The word *Waterloo* in reference to an utter defeat was in use within a year of the battle.

Sources

Connelly, Owen. *Historical Dictionary of Napoleonic France, 1799–1815.* Westport, CT: Greenwood Press, 1984.

Schom, Alan. *One Hundred Days: Napoleon's Road to Waterloo.* New York: Atheneum, 1992.

Simpson, J. A., and E. S. C. Weiner, eds. *The Oxford English Dictionary.* 2d ed. Oxford: Clarendon Press, 1989.

Waving the bloody shirt.
See Bloody shirt.

"We are not amused." ***Used tongue-in-cheek to indicate that something lacks dignity.***

A good deal of ink has been spilled in the debate over whether or not Queen Victoria (1819–1901) made this statement. One story claims that a personal attendant in the royal household had told a scandalous tale during a dinner at Windsor Castle, prompting the famous put-down from the queen. Another story claims that the reprimand was delivered to Admiral Maxse, a man who did a well-known imitation of the queen. When the queen asked to see this impersonation, the admiral obliged, putting a handkerchief on his head and blowing out his cheeks. At that point the queen presumably delivered the immortal snub. Queen Victoria denied ever uttering the phrase; she possessed a keen sense of humor that makes it unlikely.

Part of the jest may lie in the fact that Queen Victoria did frequently refer to herself as *we,* as when she said, "We are rather short for a queen." The "royal we," in which a monarch refers to himself or herself in the plural, has been in common use for centuries. It may have originated in the late Roman Empire, when there were two emperors who ruled from different cities but issued joint proclamations. *The Oxford English Dictionary* provides examples of the "royal we" dating from the Middle Ages to the twentieth century. In the early modern period, the custom may have been associated with a monarch's desire to appear to be speaking on behalf of the people.

Sources

Corey, Melinda, and George Ochoa, eds. *The Encyclopedia of the Victorian World.* New York: Henry Holt, 1996.

Rees, Nigel. *Sayings of the Century.* London: Allen and Unwin, 1984.

Simpson, J. A., and E. S. C. Weiner, eds. *The Oxford English Dictionary.* 2d ed. Oxford: Clarendon Press, 1989.

Wedgwood blue. ***A pale blue with a light gray undertone.***

Josiah Wedgwood (1730–1795), who came from a long line of English potters, revealed an early talent at the potter's wheel. As a young man he had to have a leg amputated, and during his extended convalescence, he read and experimented with innovative ceramic techniques. By the time he was ready to found his own business, Wedgwood was creating unique, tasteful, and affordable ceramics that were eagerly bought by a burgeoning middle class.

In 1775 Wedgwood introduced jasperware, an unglazed stoneware that has become most closely associated with the Wedgwood name. Wedgwood vases were usually decorated with classical reliefs carved on a top layer of white glass. Neoclassical artwork and architecture was enjoying sensational success in Europe, and Wedgwood's tasteful pottery was popular among the aristocratic set who had been to Rome as part of the obligatory continental tour. The vases came in a variety of colors, such as green, lilac, yellow, black, and maroon. By far the most popular was the soft, muted blue that was created by staining the pottery with metallic oxides after the high firing of the paste.

Josiah Wedgwood died an enormously wealthy man. His factory was managed by his descendants for generations, and many of his techniques have not changed substantially over the intervening two hundred years. *Wedgwood blue* is still the most popular color of jasperware.

Sources

Beeching, Cyril L. *A Dictionary of Eponyms*. London: Clive Bingley, 1979.

McHenry, Robert, ed. *The New Encyclopedia Britannica*. 15th ed. Chicago: Encyclopedia Britannica, 1992.

Stephen, Leslie, and Sidney Lee, eds. *The Dictionary of National Biography*. London: Oxford University Press, 1921.

Turner, Jane. *The Dictionary of Art*. New York: Grove's Dictionaries, 1996.

Where's the beef? *A no-nonsense demand to see more substance.*

In 1984 the Wendy's fast-food restaurant chain began an advertising campaign built around the query, "Where's the beef?" Other chain restaurants were featuring double- and triple-layer hamburgers with names like Big Mac and Whopper, while Wendy's was relying on old-fashioned hamburgers. Their angle was to publicize the fact that their single hamburgers had as much beef as the "big name" burgers. Four television commercials featuring feisty octogenarian Clara Peller showed her skeptically examining shrunken hamburgers overwhelmed by huge buns and demanding, "Where's the beef?" The ads were an immediate success. Market surveys reveal that the *where's the beef?* slogan has the highest recall of any television commercial in history.

The phrase was subsequently picked up by politicians and journalists to call attention to lack of substance. In one of the televised debates of the 1984 presidential race, Democratic hopeful Walter Mondale challenged Gary Hart about his "new ideas" by demanding, "Where's the beef?" It proved to be the most memorable line of the campaign.

Sources

Home, Scott. "Joe's Beef: The Hard Sell." *Advertising Age* 59, no. 48 (1988): 44–46.

Wendy's Library (1997), from the Wendy's International Company Homepage [Online]. Available http://www.wendys.com [August 1997].

Whipping boy. *One who is forced to accept the blame for others.*

In many parts of the world it was once believed that the royal family was chosen by God. Royal children were therefore semi-sacred beings who could not receive corporal punishment. The use of whipping boys is an old custom, in which royal children were raised and educated side by side with someone of lesser birth. When punishment was warranted, it was administered to the commoner while the prince was forced to watch. The theory was that by observing his friend and companion receive the whipping he deserved, the young princeling would scramble to amend his ways. Unfortunately, it may have instead reinforced the sense of privilege and superiority that often comes with believing one is anointed by God for leadership.

By the Renaissance this practice was becoming obsolete, but it is known that Edward VI (1537–1553) of England had a whipping boy. Edward was sickly his entire life, and perhaps his frail condition was the reason for the renewal of the custom. Barnaby Fitzpatrick was the stalwart young man who was caned for Edward's enlightenment.

Sources

Evans, Ivor H., ed. *Brewer's Dictionary of Phrase and Fable.* 14th ed. New York: Harper and Row, 1989.

Hendrickson, Robert. *Facts on File Encyclopedia of Word and Phrase Origins.* New York: Facts on File, 1987.

Weir, Alison. *The Children of Henry VIII.* New York: Ballantine Books, 1996.

Whirling dervish. ***Something that spins in a seemingly uncontrolled fashion.***

Dervishes are members of an Islamic mystic fraternity, first organized in the thirteenth century by the Persian mystic Jalad ad-Din ar Rumi. The men who belong to the dervishes practice strict self-discipline, poverty, and a mendicant lifestyle. The main rituals of the fraternity involve inducing hypnotic trances and ecstatic experience through recitation and dance.

Whirling is done in groups of about twelve. Participants wear tall, brown conical hats, short-waisted jackets, and pants with voluminous legs. They rise in unison and slowly begin to whirl, using the left heel as an axis. The eyes are closed, and the head drops to the left shoulder. The palm of the right hand is raised above the head, with the left hand held down, a sign of giving and taking. As the rhythm of the dance gains momentum, their pants balloon out in a circle around their waists. The dervishes do not whirl in unison, but rather at the speed at which each individual is best able to achieve a meditative trance. Most dervishes whirl at a rate of 30 to 60 revolutions per minute. Whirling usually lasts around ten minutes, when a leader signals them to stop.

Although dervish communities played an active role in the religious and social life of Islam during the Middle Ages, orthodox Muslims no longer regard them as having an important theological role. Whirling is still popular in Konya, Turkey, where the tomb of the dervish founder is located.

Sources

Eliade, Mircea, ed. *The Encyclopedia of Religion.* New York: Macmillan, 1986.

McHenry, Robert, ed. *The New Encyclopedia Britannica.* 15th ed. Chicago: Encyclopedia Britannica, 1992.

Seabrook, William. *Adventures in Arabia among the Bedouins, Druses, Whirling Dervishes, and Yezidee Devil Worshippers.* New York: Harcourt, Brace and Company, 1927.

White Elephant. ***A useless and burdensome gift.***

According to Hindu mythology, in ancient times all elephants had wings, were snowy white, and resembled clouds as they floated through the sky. One day a group of elephants alighted on a tree in order to hear the teachings of a famous sage as he lectured his students. The tree broke under the weight of the elephants, and some of the students were killed. The angry sage cursed the elephants, after which they lost their wings and their snowy color.

In reality, white elephants are genetic rarities, but they are prized by the Hindus for the cloudlike symbolism they evoke. It is forbidden to put a white elephant to work, and it must be well fed and cared for. A *white elephant* is therefore a dubious gift, one that has little practical value and is difficult to maintain. There is a story that the fabulously wealthy king of Siam kept a menagerie of white elephants, and when he wished to bring ruin upon one of his subjects, he simply gave a gift of a burdensome white elephant.

Sources

Hendrickson, Robert. *Facts on File Encyclopedia of Word and Phrase Origins.* New York: Facts on File, 1987.

Stimpson, George. *A Book about a Thousand Things.* New York: Harper and Brothers, 1946.

Walker, Benjamin. *The Hindu World: An Encyclopedic Survey of Hinduism.* New York: Praeger, 1968.

White feather, to show the white feather. ***To act in a cowardly manner.***

This expression derives from the sport of cockfighting, which was popular in ancient India, China, Greece, and Persia. Although opposed by Christian teachings, it eventually spread into Europe and became a prevalent form of entertainment in the Renaissance. The natural belligerence of the cocks was made lethal by attaching two-inch metal spurs to the feet of the birds. Several pairs of birds would be released into the cockfighting pit at once, and the contest was allowed to continue until all birds except one were either killed or badly wounded. Most countries passed laws against cockfighting in the nineteenth century, although it is still practiced surreptitiously in many areas of the world.

The most aggressive fighting birds were those descended from the Indian red jungle fowl. Pure-bred gamecocks had no white feathers, and the presence of such a feather indicated crossbreeding, meaning that the bird would not fight as aggressively. Among the English, white feathers became a symbol of cowardice. Soldiers accused of such behavior might find a white feather placed in their quarters. During World War I, after huge losses on the Western Front resulted in dwindling numbers of volunteers, young men who were seen out of uniform were sometimes presented with white feathers by strangers on the street. Boxers who lacked pugnacity were said to fight with more white feathers than red.

Sources

Pope, Stephen, and Elizabeth Ann Wheal. *The Dictionary of the First World War.* New York: St. Martin's Press, 1995.

Simpson, J. A., and E. S. C. Weiner, eds. *The Oxford English Dictionary.* 2d ed. Oxford: Clarendon Press, 1989.

Stimpson, George. *A Book about a Thousand Things.* New York: Harper and Brothers, 1946.

White man's burden. ***An imperialistic attitude that justified European and American domination of the Third World because of the civilizing influence they supposedly had on those regions.***

Rudyard Kipling's (1865–1936) poem "The White Man's Burden" appeared in *McClure's Magazine* in February 1899. The publication of the poem coincided with the Spanish-American War, which had sparked lively debates about the wisdom of imperialism. Many of the war's supporters believed that Americans should intervene in order to bring democracy and opportunity to the Cubans. Great Britain had long used such arguments to justify expansion into Africa, India, and Asia. As the argument ran, the British certainly benefited from exploitation of the raw natural resources, but the natives benefited from the introduction of Christianity, medical advances, public works, and wise British administration.

Rudyard Kipling was a passionate advocate of British imperialism. Most of his stories and novels celebrate the adventures of British colonialists who bring civilization to the "savages" in exotic foreign lands. "The White Man's Burden" was purportedly told from the point of view of a seasoned but weary colonialist advising the United States about its responsibility for the moral and physical welfare of the darker races. The first stanza contains the following sober advice for the ambitious imperialist:

> Take up the White Man's burden—
> Send forth the best ye breed—
> Go, bind your sons to exile
> To serve your captives' need;
> To wait, in heavy harness,
> On fluttered folk and wild—
> Your new-caught sullen peoples,
> Half devil and half child.

The poem, while firing the imagination of some, raised a storm of controversy, satire, and criticism. In 1901 Mark Twain replied, "The White Man's Burden has been sung. Who will sing the brown man's?"

Sources

Lurie, Charles. *Everyday Sayings: Their Meanings Explained, Their Origins Given.* Detroit, MI: Gale Research, 1968.

Palmer, Alan Warwick. *Dictionary of the British Empire and Commonwealth.* London: Murray, 1996.

Shanks, Edward. *Rudyard Kipling: A Study in Literature and Political Ideas.* London: Macmillan and Co., 1940.

Stimpson, George. *A Book about a Thousand Things.* New York: Harper and Brothers, 1946.

Widow's peak. ***A V-shaped front hairline.***

Almost all cultures have designated special colors or clothing styles to be worn by people in mourning. The ancient Greeks and Romans wore white, as it was believed to represent purity and sanctity. By the Middle Ages the basic color of mourning in Europe was black, to represent the grief of the soul. Medieval women who were in mourning were also required to cover their hair, and a bonnetlike headdress that came to a *V*-point in the front was traditionally used by widows. The headdress could be covered by a piece of black silk that would conceal the woman's face or be folded back to create a veil covering the hair and shoulders. In either case the distinctive *V*-shape of the headdress showed through and became associated with widows.

Long after ornate headdresses were no longer worn, the term *widow's peak* was used to describe hairlines that came to a point on the forehead. Folklore has it that women who are born with such a hairline are the most beautiful but are also destined to be widowed at a young age.

Sources

Cunnington, C. Willett, and Phillis Cunnington. *Handbook of English Medieval Costume.* Boston: Plays, 1969.

Evans, Ivor H., ed. *Brewer's Dictionary of Phrase and Fable.* 14th ed. New York: Harper and Row, 1989.

Witch hunt. ***An investigation characterized by irrational hysteria and wild accusations.*** In the late seventeenth century, Salem, Massachusetts, was a small town that suffered from a number of tensions and hostilities common to insular communities, including land disputes and resentment over appointments to church and town offices. In 1692 several teenage girls began to act in an irrational and rebellious manner, blamed their behavior on witches, and started naming names. As in England, colonial courts admitted spectral evidence, that is, testimony by a person who claimed to have seen a devil or been tormented by a witch, even though others could not see the specters. As the witchcraft trials got under way, fear and suspicion were so rife that the flimsiest allegations were sufficient to ostracize the accused. Observers who objected to the arbitrary nature of the proceedings were likely to be accused themselves, making it dangerous to voice opposition to the trials. Given the rivalries among the townsfolk, it is no coincidence that many of the accusers brought charges against members of families who were viewed as social and economic competitors. Nineteen people were eventually executed and hundreds of others arrested. When a number of highly respected individuals, including the governor's wife, were accused, it became obvious that hysteria rather than witchcraft had taken Salem by storm.

The expression *witch hunt* was given wide circulation in the 1950s when Senator Joseph McCarthy launched his investigation to uncover communist sympathizers (see *McCarthyism*). The fear of communism, the willingness to condemn people based on rumor, and the reluctance to confront the accusers for fear of being targeted were all reminiscent of Salem. The analogy was highlighted when Arthur Miller wrote his award-winning play *The Crucible* in 1953, a dramatization of the Salem witch trials that was a thinly veiled condemnation of the McCarthy hearings.

Sources

Boyer, Paul. *Salem Possessed: The Social Origins of Witchcraft.* Cambridge, MA: Harvard University Press, 1974.

Klingamann, William. *Encyclopedia of the McCarthy Era.* New York: Facts on File, 1996.

Kohn, George C. *The Encyclopedia of American Scandal: From Abscam to the Zenger Case.* New York: Facts on File, 1989.

Rosenthal, Bernard. *Salem Story: Reading the Witch Trials of 1692.* Cambridge: Cambridge University Press, 1995.

Y

Yen. ***A yearning for something.***

The current connotation of the word *yen* implies a mild desire for something. However, when the word was coined in the late nineteenth century, it referred to the uncontrollable cravings suffered by Chinese immigrants who were addicted to opium.

Opium is the milky juice produced from the seeds of the poppy plant. Poppies grow wild in the Middle East and reached Asia by way of Arab traders in the thirteenth century. By the seventeenth century, the Chinese had devised a way to smoke opium, and two centuries later, it was estimated that 25 percent of the Chinese population indulged in the habit. British colonial trading practices encouraged the use of the drug, because they deliberately flooded the Chinese market with cheap opium in an effort to balance the deficit caused by the export of Chinese tea.

In the 1850s large numbers of Chinese immigrants came to the United States, bringing with them the practice of smoking opium. Meanwhile, the American medical community had begun investigating the negative effects and addictive qualities of opium. Possible complications from opium use include breathing difficulties, hallucinations, convulsions, restlessness, weakness, chills, cramping, nausea, and loss of appetite. Concern over the misuse of opium prompted the U.S. Congress to pass a series of laws in the 1880s to reduce the importation of the drug into the country. The new laws forced recreational opium consumption to go underground. Opium dens continued to exist, but the drug became more expensive, and Chinese immigrants who were accustomed to daily opium began to experience withdrawal. The Chinese expression *in-yān*, "craving for opium," was used to refer to these painful symptoms. Over time this expression was altered to *yen-yen*, and then simply *yen*. The terrible craving for opium was cited in Donald Lowrie's 1912 memoir, *My Life in Prison:* "I even saw two or three guys eat chloride of lime to stop their yen."

Sources

Jaffe, Jerome H., ed. *Encyclopedia of Drugs and Alcohol.* New York: Macmillan Library Reference, 1995.

Mish, Frederick C. *The Merriam-Webster New Book of Word Histories.* Springfield, IL: Merriam-Webster, 1991.

Simpson, J. A., and E. S. C. Weiner, eds. *The Oxford English Dictionary.* 2d ed. Oxford: Clarendon Press, 1989.

Yes, Virginia, there is a Santa Claus.

See Virginia.

Young turk. ***A radical insurgent who seeks to take command of an organization.***

The Ottoman Empire was founded by Prince Osman in the thirteenth century and greatly expanded over the next two hundred years through war, alliances, and the purchase of territory. Controlling access to the Middle and Far East, the Ottoman Empire was unrivaled in its strategic and economic power. Beginning in the sixteenth century poor leadership and the decline of Ottoman-controlled trading routes led to the gradual decay of the once-mighty empire. By the late nineteenth century the empire was known as "the sick man of Europe."

In 1889 there emerged a group of radicals known as the *Young Turks,* who wished to shake off the authoritarian regime of the Ottoman sultan Abdulhamid II. These initial attempts to overthrow the Ottoman government were unsuccessful, but uprisings of Young Turks occurred again in 1908 and after World War I. They finally forced the abdication of the sultan in 1922. Though middle-aged by then, the Young Turks had at long last brought about a republican government.

The term *young turk* is now used to describe insurgents, usually liberals, who wish to eradicate oppressive traditionalism associated with the establishment.

Sources

McHenry, Robert, ed. *The New Encyclopedia Britannica.* 15th ed. Chicago: Encyclopedia Britannica, 1992.

Ramsaur, Ernest Edmondson. *The Young Turks: Prelude to the Revolution of 1908.* New York: Russell and Russell, 1970.

Safire, William. *Safire's Political Dictionary.* New York: Random House, 1978.

Z

Zealot. ***A person whose commitment to a cause has become fanatical.***

The Zealots were a Jewish sect that flourished in first-century Judea. Deriving their name from the Hebrew word *"zeal,"* meaning indignation, the Zealots believed they were duty bound to combat any transgressions of God's law. Their intense opposition to Roman administration of Judea led them to condone acts of violence against not only Romans but also Jews who collaborated with the Romans. One of the early leaders of the Zealots was a Galilean named Judah. The first-century historian Josephus writes: "Judah incited his countrymen to revolt, upbraiding them as cowards for consenting to pay tribute to the Romans and tolerating mortal masters, after having God as their Lord." Josephus had no sympathy for the Zealots because he blamed them for provoking the retaliation of the Romans that ultimately led to the destruction of the Temple. In his classic work *The Jewish War,* Josephus implied that the sect was more of a terrorist organization than a religious group.

It is believed that Judah died around A.D. 6 when a Jewish revolt was suppressed by the Romans. The Zealots fled to the desert and continued their opposition to the Romans. Sixty years later the Romans crushed even that token resistance to their administration. Surviving Zealots captured the fortress of Masada and withstood a lengthy siege until defeat seemed inevitable. They then chose to commit mass suicide rather than submit to the Romans (see *Masada complex*).

The first recorded use of the word *zealot* to refer to someone with fanatical enthusiasm was in 1638.

Sources

Hengel, Martin. *The Zealots: Investigations into the Jewish Freedom Movement in the Period from Herod I until 70 A.D.* Edinburgh: T and T Clark, 1989.

Metzger, Bruce M., and Michael D. Coogan. *The Oxford Companion to the Bible.* New York: Oxford University Press, 1993.

Roth, Cecil E., ed. *Encyclopedia Judaica.* New York: Macmillan, 1971.

Zoroastrianism. ***One of the world's oldest living religions, based on the teachings of the prophet Zoroaster.***

Zoroaster lived during the sixth century B.C. in the area that is now Iran. His teachings converted the king Vishtaspa, after which his influence spread throughout south-central Asia. Zoroaster was one of the first prophets to proclaim monotheism. Another central tenet of his teaching was the belief in an evil spirit, which was in constant rivalry with the True God for the souls of human beings. Zoroaster believed that individuals had the freedom to decide between the forces of good and evil, which thus influenced how they would be treated in the afterlife. Modern historians of religion believe that these teachings may have laid the foundations for Judaism and Christianity in subsequent centuries.

Zoroastrianism lost most of its followers to Islam, but it still survives in India and isolated pockets in Iran.

Zoroastrianism

Sources

Eliade, Mircea, ed. *The Encyclopedia of Religion*. New York: Macmillan, 1986.

Glasse, Cyril. *The Concise Encyclopedia of Islam*. London: Stacey International, 1989.

Herzfeld, Ernst. *Zoroaster and His World*. Princeton, NJ: Princeton University Press, 1947.

SUBJECT INDEX